SNAKES

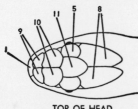

SIDE OF HEAD
(Harmless snake)

Upper labials
Lower labials

HEAD SCALES

1. Rostral
2. Nasals
3. Loreal
4. Preoculars
5. Supraoculars
6. Postoculars
7. Temporals
8. Parietals
9. Internasals
10. Prefrontals
11. Frontal
12. Mental
13. Chin shields

14. Ventrals

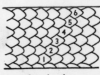

TOP OF HEAD

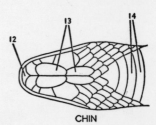

CHIN

SECTIONS OF BODIES

Counting scale rows

Keeled scales

Smooth scales

Scale pits present

No scale pits

UNDERSIDES OF TAILS

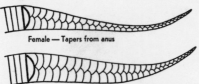

Female — Tapers from anus

Male — Stout at base

Single anal plate

Divided anal plate

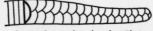

Stump-tail — part lost through accident

S0-CAA-758

A Field Guide
to Reptiles and Amphibians

THE PETERSON FIELD GUIDE SERIES

EDITED BY ROGER TORY PETERSON

THE PETERSON FIELD GUIDE SERIES

A Field Guide to Reptiles and Amphibians

of the United States and Canada
East of the 100th Meridian

BY ROGER CONANT

Illustrated by

ISABELLE HUNT CONANT

HOUGHTON MIFFLIN COMPANY, BOSTON

COPYRIGHT © 1958 BY ROGER CONANT

ALL RIGHTS RESERVED INCLUDING THE RIGHT TO REPRODUCE
THIS BOOK OR PARTS THEREOF IN ANY FORM

LIBRARY OF CONGRESS CATALOG CARD NUMBER: 58-6416

ISBN: 0–395–07567–x

NINTH PRINTING   W

PRINTED IN THE U.S.A.

TO

THE YOUNGER HERPETOLOGISTS

OF AMERICA

whose high standards of professional ethics
and spirit of mutual cooperation
assure them a brilliant future
in their chosen field.
Without their enthusiastic aid
this book would have been
another five years in the making.

Editor's Note

THE AMATEUR NATURALIST who is interested in herpetology, the science of reptiles and amphibians, has a distinct advantage over his fellows. Unlike the bird watcher, he can catch and handle his animals, and, unlike most botanists and entomologists, who must dry and mount their specimens in order to preserve them, the herpetologist can keep his captives alive, often for long periods of time. He can study them and enjoy them as pets. The keeping of live reptiles and amphibians has become an important adjunct of the biology classroom and of the summer camp.

Roger Conant, keenly aware of these facts because of the thousands of questions he has received on the subject, has included a section in this book on how to house and feed reptiles and amphibians, and sprinkled through his text are numerous other hints on the subject. Hence this *Field Guide* serves a double purpose — it enables the reader to identify his specimen and then tells him how to care for it if he wants to keep it.

Mr. Conant has served as Curator of Reptiles at the Philadelphia Zoological Garden for more than two decades, and he was formerly associated with the Toledo Zoological Park in a similar capacity. His *Reptiles of Ohio*, now in its second edition, has been called by Karl P. Schmidt and other leading authorities a model state herpetology. His *Reptiles and Amphibians of the Northeastern States* has been used as a text in natural history courses at Cornell University, Rutgers University, and in courses for amateur naturalists at many museums. His interest in herpetology was first kindled as a lad in Boy Scout camp, and his long association with Scouting resulted in his being invited to prepare the merit badge pamphlet on reptile study.

Isabelle Hunt Conant, the illustrator, who is Mrs. Roger Conant, was official photographer at the Philadelphia Zoo for nearly a decade. She has accompanied her husband on many collecting expeditions to various parts of the United States and Mexico. Some of these trips were made expressly to obtain specimens with which to illustrate this book.

The magnitude of the problem of securing live specimens of virtually every species and subspecies of reptile and amphibian east of the 100th meridian and then keeping them alive and healthy, sometimes for months, almost staggers the imagination. Four years and the assistance of scores of friends and colleagues were required to complete this part of the project. During all this time Roger Conant continued in his full-time capacity at the Zoo. Even had he been able to devote *all* his time to the task, it probably would have taken three years to get the complete list of animals, for collecting many herps is a seasonal matter.

Standardization of vernacular names of North American birds was begun in 1886 (and is only now reaching stabilization), but the herpetological names have remained in a state of confusion. Some species have labored under several common names while other names have been bestowed on more than one species. Mr. Conant recently served as Chairman of the Committee on Herpetological Common Names for the American Society of Ichthyologists and Herpetologists. This Committee has prepared a list that it is hoped will aid in standardizing the names of our reptiles and amphibians. The common names in the Committee's list have been followed throughout this book.

Roger and Isabelle Conant have produced a *Field Guide* that we are very proud to add to the Series. Do not leave it on the library shelf when you travel about the countryside. Put it in the glove compartment of your car, in your knapsack, or in the pocket of your jacket.

ROGER TORY PETERSON

Acknowledgments

LIMITATIONS of space present a distinct handicap to every *Field Guide* author, for there isn't room enough to express one's gratitude in proper fashion to all those who have helped. My dilemma is compounded by the fact that a small army of herpetologists — professional and amateur and some of them total strangers — scoured the plains and forests, descended into caves, risked pneumonia by wading in swamps on early spring nights, drove hundreds of miles, and in general displayed incredible enthusiasm in ferreting out rare specimens just to contribute to the cause. There is scarcely space to list them all by name, let alone thank them in full. Actually an account of their activities plus our own adventures afield on behalf of this book would make entertaining reading. Collectively we amassed close to 3000 live reptiles and amphibians, and some 600 of them are illustrated herein, a considerable number in color for the first time.

Several close friends and colleagues played major roles in helping bring this book to its completion. Albert Schwartz, one of the most vigorous and enthusiastic field men I have ever met, provided many rarities, made his wealth of data on South Carolina available to me, read my manuscript in its entirety, checked our plates and drawings for accuracy, and probably contributed more man-hours to this book than any other person save the author and illustrator. Sherman A. Minton, Jr., and Philip W. Smith, in conducting their herpetological surveys of Indiana and Illinois, respectively, were in constant and close communication with me for more than four years. They supplied numerous specimens and were extremely helpful during the development of my distribution maps. Ralph W. Axtell did much to clarify distributions in southern Texas and in several of the lizard genera, notably *Holbrookia*. He too supplied many rarities, and, although only a student while this book was in progress, he showed a perspicacity for detecting discrepancies in manuscript that would put many of his elders to shame. Coleman J. Goin, in conjunction with his Florida handbook (co-authored with Archie Carr), provided more *different* species than anyone else, and he supplied unpublished data on the genus *Siren*. Fred R. Cagle placed the facilities of his department at Tulane University at my disposal on several occasions, helped in clarifying many turtle-distribution problems, and contributed

ix

his unique knowledge of the genus *Graptemys* by drawing the distribution maps for that perplexing group of turtles. Donald W. Tinkle laboriously checked hundreds of records in the Tulane collection, helped many times with field work, and contributed much data on the genus *Sternothaerus*. John W. Crenshaw, Jr., prepared the maps for the *floridana-concinna* complex of the genus *Pseudemys* and made available his scholarly doctoral thesis on the group. William E. Duellman's contributions of specimens and data are gratefully acknowledged, and his enthusiasm and prompt response to numerous queries were morale builders on numerous occasions. Wilfred T. Neill helped with the maps and many portions of the text, and gave me many important specimens, even on two occasions transporting them a thousand miles to assure their live arrival instead of trusting them to a common carrier.

Charles M. Bogert, W. Frank Blair, and the late Karl P. Schmidt repeatedly went out of their way to render prompt professional help, and they served as a voluntary "committee" to which I referred problem after problem. Bogert and Schmidt made special trips to our home at Taunton Lakes to check our plates for us, and so did M. Graham Netting and Neil D. Richmond. Netting in a sense is the godfather of this *Field Guide*, for he had contracted to write it but resigned in my favor when pressure of duties forced him to abandon the project. He and Grace L. Orton, who was to have been his co-author, very courteously gave me the preliminary notes they had made on ranges, etc.

Edmond V. Malnate made unique contributions: as a professional artist he aided Mrs. Conant with her illustrations on innumerable occasions; as a herpetologist he assisted repeatedly with the drudgery of research, recording, and reading manuscript; and as my neighbor he drove me to work every day in stony silence while I concentrated upon writing or editing as we rode along. Mary Mowry, of the Beck Engraving Company in Philadelphia, tutored Mrs. Conant in the techniques of coloring photographic prints with water-color dyes. Freeman M. Shelly, Director of the Philadelphia Zoo, showed a lively interest in the progress of this book and several times permitted me to readjust my work schedule at the Zoo in order to take care of details or to meet deadlines as they developed.

James A. Oliver carefully checked all the average and record sizes listed for the various species and subspecies, and he graciously supplemented my information with many data of his own.

The accuracy and completeness of this book, and of the distribution maps especially, have been enormously increased by a wealth of unpublished information made available to me by professional colleagues. Their invaluable contributions fall into three categories:

1. Those who loaned or specially prepared complete sets of range maps for whole states or provinces based upon their own

collecting and research. They are Paul Anderson (Missouri), Reeve M. Bailey (Iowa), Arthur A. Davis and Albert A. Barden, Jr. (Maine), Sherman Bleakney (eastern Canada), Arthur N. Bragg (Oklahoma amphibians), Ralph L. Chermock (Alabama), Sherman A. Minton, Jr. (Indiana), M. Graham Netting and Neil D. Richmond (Pennsylvania), Robert G. Webb (Oklahoma reptiles), Edgar M. Reilly, Jr. (New York snakes), Albert Schwartz (South Carolina), and Philip W. Smith (Illinois).

2. Those who also supplied maps and distributional data but in a different manner or on a somewhat lesser scale were: Roger W. Barbour and William M. Clay (Kentucky), L. Neil Bell (southern Florida), W. J. Breckenridge (Minnesota), Bryce C. Brown (Texas), Herndon G. Dowling (Arkansas), James A. Fowler and Charles J. Stine, Jr. (Maryland), Richard L. Hoffman (Virginia), Richard M. Johnson and Glenn Gentry (Tennessee), E. B. Shelley Logier (Canada), Richard B. Loomis (Nebraska), Bernard S. Martof (Georgia), Hobart M. Smith (Mexico), and George C. Wheeler (North Dakota).

3. Those (in addition to persons specifically mentioned above) who loaned me manuscripts or galley proofs in advance of publication were: Max Hecht (genus *Necturus*), Richard Highton (*Plethodon*), John S. Mecham (*Eumeces*), and Wilmer W. Tanner and Richard B. Loomis (*Lampropeltis*).

Each section of the manuscript and each group of maps were checked by two or more herpetologists, usually the experts on the species in question. Many of the persons named above had a part in so doing. Others were: Walter Auffenberg, Archie F. Carr, Harold A. Dundee, Richard A. Edgren, Jr., Richard E. Etheridge, Howard K. Gloyd, Arnold B. Grobman, Francis Harper, Norman E. Hartweg, Carl F. Kauffeld, Laurence M. Klauber, John M. Legler, Joseph Curtis Moore, James A. Oliver, Clifford H. Pope, Ottys Sanders, Charles F. Walker, Aaron O. Wasserman, and Richard G. Zweifel.

For the gift or loan of live specimens, for locality data or other information, for assistance rendered to me and Mrs. Conant in the field, or for help in other ways I am also indebted to most of the persons enumerated above, plus the following: Sylvan J. T. Adams, Ross Allen, William B. Allen, Jr., Anton F. Baarslag, Jr., Lewis H. Babbitt, Joseph R. Bailey, Clinton L. Baker, Richard J. Baldauf, A. James Barton, Phil J. Baur, Dan Beard, Ted Beimler, Kenneth Bergstrom, Irving H. Black, Albert P. Blair, Donald Boyer, Bayard H. Brattstrom, William E. Brode, Laura Brodie, Harold J. Brodrick, Elmer E. Brown, Richard Bruder, Royal Bruce Brunson, R. W. Buck, W. Leslie Burger, Bartley J. Burns, Charles E. Burt, Joseph M. Cadbury, David Caldwell, Kenneth D. Carlander, Charles C. Carpenter, Allan H. Chaney, Pete S. Chrapliwy, Roland C. Clement, Jack B. Clinch, Doris M. Cochran, J. T. Colwick, Harold A. Conant, Roger K. Conant, Paul Connor,

Fannye A. Cook, Gerald P. Cooper, John E. Cooper, M. L. Crimmins, Raymond J. Cummins, Sarah Cunius, Lawrence Curtis, Edmund Cuthbert, Anna May Davis, William K. Davis, Edward Dawkins, William G. Degenhardt, Willard E. Dilley, Alfred Dinkins, Richard F. Dooley, Robert Dooley, E. R. Dunn, Ralph Dury, James C. Eggert, Lon Ellis, Edward T. Endy, Ruth G. Endy, Edward Fernandez, Henry S. Fitch, Alvin Flury, John W. Forsyth, M. J. Fouquette, Jr., Maurice Fox, Harry W. Freeman, Charles M. Fugler, Samuel E. Fulton, John B. Funderburg, Jr., Michael Geison, George H. Gifford, Luther C. Goldman, Robert E. Gordon, Kenneth L. Gosner, Werner H. Gottsch, Robert R. Grant, Jr., N. Bayard Green, Walter J. Greer, William Haast, Charles P. Hackenbrock, Nelson G. Hairston, William J. Hamilton, Jr., Julian R. Harrison, III, Philip Harter, William G. Hassler, Mr. and Mrs. J. C. Haver, Robert E. Hellman, Max Hensley, Carl Herrmann, Gabrielle L. Hildebrand, Clark Hubbs, George E. Hudson, Robert G. Hudson, Robert L. Humphries, Victor H. Hutchinson, Robert F. Inger, Pauline James, David L. Jameson, Harvey Janson, Clifford Johnson, James Johnson, James E. Keeler, James H. Kenefick, J. P. Kennedy, Thomas Kennerly, James Kezer, John D. Kilby, William A. King, Jr., James C. Knepton, Jr., William J. Koster, William H. Kroll, D. A. Langebartel, James Lazell, Jr., Kenneth C. Lehman, Moody J. R. Lentz, Harry R. Lindaman, Hague L. Lindsay, Jr., Ernest A. Liner, Arthur Loveridge, Charles H. Lowe, Jr., George H. Lowery, Jr., James A. MacMahon, Paul S. Martin, T. Paul Maslin, Karl H. Maslowski, Wayne McAlister, Edwin H. McConkey, Edward McCrady, George P. Meade, Pat Menichini, Robert R. Miller, William W. Milstead, J. E. Moore, Daniel H. Moreno, James E. Mosimann, James M. Moulton, Robert Cushman Murphy, John G. New, Arthur E. Newkirk, Hudson M. Nichols, John T. Nichols, Dennis R. Paulson, James A. Peters, David Pettus, Walker Powell, William F. Pyburn, George B. Rabb, Roger Rageot, Louis W. Ramsey, Edward C. Raney, Robert Reese, William J. Riemer, Jones Robertson, William B. Robertson, Hugo G. Rodeck, Bernard Roseman, Douglas A. Rossman, F. William Rugg, Jay M. Savage, Don Sellers, Mrs. F. E. Simmons, Robert S. Simmons, George H. Smith, Robert M. Stabler, Robert C. Stebbins, William H. Stickel, Walter Stone, Kirk Strawn, Arthur Stupka, Paul L. Swanson, J. H. Tabony, Jr., James R. Tamsitt, Edward H. Taylor, Samuel R. Telford, Jr., Theo Telotte, Edward S. Thomas, Wilmot Thornton, Gordon R. Thurow, F. W. Trautman, Milton B. Trautman, Charles A. Triplehorn, Frederick A. Ulmer, Jr., Thomas M. Uzzell, Jr., Barry D. Valentine, Percy Viosca, Jr., E. Peter Volpe, Harold J. Walter, Carl H. Watson, John E. Werler, Ralph M. Wetzel, George C. Wheeler, Duke Wilder, E. A. Wood, John T. Wood, William H. Woodin, Robert E. Woodruff, John C. Wottring, A. H. Wright,

Phillip M. Youngman, Robert Zeller, William E. Ziebach, and Louise D. Zillig.

Sherman A. Minton, Jr., M.D., Frederick A. Shannon, M.D., and Louis Spitz, M.D., offered several helpful suggestions on first-aid treatment for snake bite and they also checked the text and illustrations on this subject. Edmond V. and Georgette A. Malnate posed for the photographs reproduced on Plate 3.

Roger Tory Peterson has been ever helpful, and we are also greatly indebted to Paul Brooks, Lovell Thompson, Morton H. Baker, Austin Olney, David Harris, and Helen Phillips, all of the staff of the Houghton Mifflin Company, for their patience and counseling.

Prime credit also must be given to the contributors to herpetological literature and upon whose works I have drawn heavily. If this were a scientific treatise their names would be scattered through the pages of the text with references to their specific contributions. Many of their papers are listed in the Bibliography.

By Way of Definition

UNTIL about a century ago it was customary to classify all the animals listed in this book simply as "reptiles," and some people still think of them in that way. Actually they form two natural groups, the Classes Reptilia and Amphibia among the vertebrates (backboned animals), and they are placed below the birds and mammals and above the fishes. They are cold-blooded, deriving heat from outside sources and controlling their body temperatures by moving to cooler or warmer environments as necessary.

The following definitions will apply to all the species found in eastern North America:

REPTILES are clad in scales, shields, or plates, and their toes bear claws. (The clawless Leatherback sea turtle is an exception. Softshell Turtles have only a few scales on their limbs.) Young reptiles are miniature replicas of their parents — in general appearance, if not always in coloration and pattern. To this Class belong the crocodilians, turtles, lizards, and snakes. Extralimital is the only surviving member of a fifth group, the tuatara, now confined to tiny islets off the coast of New Zealand.

AMPHIBIANS have moist, glandular skins and their toes are devoid of claws. Their young pass through a larval, usually aquatic stage (tadpoles among the frogs) before they metamorphose into the adult form. The word "amphibious" is based upon Greek words and means "living a double life." Belonging to the Class Amphibia are the salamanders (including newts) and the frogs and toads. A third group occurs in the tropics, consisting of the burrowing, or aquatic, snake-shaped caecilians.

Map of eastern North America showing the area covered by this *Field Guide*. All reptiles and amphibians known to occur in the *unshaded* portions of the United States and Canada are included. Since these animals lack the mobility of birds and rarely leave their normal habitats, geography can be of considerable importance in making accurate identifications. Maps showing the ranges of all the species (and subspecies) are grouped together at the back of the book (pp. 313 to 352, inclusive).

Contents

A Field Guide
to Reptiles and Amphibia

I

Introduction

INTEREST in reptiles and amphibians has increased vastly in recent years, and even the lowly serpent, long a symbol of evil, now has its champions. Time was when the only "good" snake was a dead one. Nowadays serpents, although still maligned by many people of older generations, are far more tolerated than they used to be. Most young persons, having been exposed to reptiles in summer camps or science classrooms, have discovered that the snake is a useful creature and, in most varieties, utterly harmless. And with this new approach much of the antipathy toward lizards and frogs and other scaly or slimy creatures is vanishing also.

The sharpened interest in these animals has not been confined to the layman or amateur naturalist alone. Herpetologists have also been active, and the accumulation of new study material has resulted in a flood of papers and monographs on various species and groups. These I have attempted to condense and interpret for the lay reader, but I have done so with mixed emotions — with satisfaction on the one hand that so much new knowledge is available, but with a realization on the other that there is still so much to be learned. Herpetology has not yet achieved the stability enjoyed by North American ornithology, in which field no new species have been described for many years. Field work, plus careful evaluation of material already available in our museums, has led to numerous shifts in scientific names and to the description of many new subspecies — and even a few new species — while this book was in preparation, and the end is not yet in sight. It is fully anticipated that additional species and subspecies will eventually be discovered, especially of cave-dwelling salamanders. Most of the basic facts are available, however, and the amateur naturalist now has an excellent chance of identifying any reptile or adult amphibian that may come to hand. Although much research has been done on tadpoles and larval salamanders, large gaps in our knowledge of these sub-adult forms still remain. This, coupled with the lack of popular interest in them, has resulted in their being omitted.

Using This Book: Anyone familiar with Roger Tory Peterson's *Field Guide to the Birds* will have no trouble consulting this book, for the approach is the same. But nine times out of ten (or perhaps even ninety-nine times out of a hundred), the reader will have his

1

specimen at hand before he attempts identification. The Boy Scout with his lizard, the biology student with her frog or salamander, or the sportsman with his freshly killed snake will bring book and animal together for comparison. Except for the basking turtle and an occasional other specimen, the techniques employed in bird watching will have little application. The vast majority of reptiles and amphibians are hiders, seldom to be seen at all by day unless one goes hunting for them. Even those that prowl are apt to be mere streaks in the grass. Accurate identification, for the most part, depends upon a careful, close-range check.

Quite naturally, you will turn to the pictures first, and many times your specimen may match one of them exactly. If it doesn't, then pick out the illustration it most closely resembles and consult the text for that species — page references appear directly opposite each plate. Read about the key characters, the points of difference that are diagnostic of each separate kind, and also check the section headed "Similar species" to eliminate others that may resemble the one in hand. Details of anatomy and pattern are shown in the line drawings to which you will find references in the text. Time spent studying the illustrations inside the endpaper covers of this book will be well invested, for it will help you to understand the things for which to look.

In trying to make identifications remember that animals are not cut out by die-stamping machines or patterned by a trip through a printing press. Variation is a normal part of nature, and some species may show bewildering modifications of coloration and pattern. Bear in mind, also, that frogs and lizards may change colors; a brown one, for example, may turn to green a minute later. I have tried to include the major variations by mentioning them in the text, especially in the cases of those species which are illustrated in black-and-white instead of color. Aberrant specimens or hybrids between species may be found occasionally, and they may even confound the experts. If you have real trouble in trying to make sure what you have caught, take it to the nearest natural history museum, zoo, or college supporting a zoology department and ask for help.

Only a few of the snakes are dangerous, and all such found within our area are portrayed upon Plates 29 and 30. Learn to recognize them on sight and resolve to let them strictly alone unless you are of age and have been given professional coaching on how to handle them. Also be cautious about picking up most turtles and large harmless snakes; they can and will bite in self-defense. Suggestions on how to catch and handle them are portrayed on Plates 1 and 2.

The word "herptiles," recently coined and now coming into frequent use, appears occasionally in this book. It is simply a short way of saying "reptiles and amphibians." Professional herpetologists, many of whom are not above using slang when talking among themselves, go even farther — they may use just plain "herps" in referring to reptiles and amphibians, or to other herpetologists!

Area: The area embraced by this book includes all of the United States and Canada east of the 100th meridian. This is an artificial boundary, but it approximates the eastern edge of the Great Plains, a region where many species reach the limits of their ranges. Relatively few eastern herptiles penetrate farther westward, although some, like the Leopard Frog and certain turtles, follow rivers to the Rocky Mountains or even beyond. Conversely, many reptiles and a few amphibians of the western arid lands spill over to the eastward, this being especially true in Texas. As a consequence, a fair number of western genera are represented in this book.

Range: Knowing where a specimen was collected can be of great importance in making identification. Reptiles and amphibians lack the mobility of birds and seldom wander far from their natural habitats. An Arkansas Kingbird may occasionally appear in some such faraway place as New England, setting bird watchers agog and scurrying to add it to their life lists. But an Ozarkian salamander may be expected to stay at home. If the salamander emulated the Arkansas Traveler, it would have to leave its cave or mountain stream, and it would then literally dry up and blow away. So check the origin, and be not ashamed. If you take your specimen to a professional herpetologist and ask his help, his first question quite probably will be "Where did it come from?"

The ranges are stated in brief at the end of each species or subspecies discussion, but they are shown in detail on the maps at the back of the book. Since geography is such an important crutch to lean upon, references to the maps are given in two places — opposite the plates and in the text.

Maps: The general range of each species and subspecies is shown by a pattern of dots, cross hatching, etc., on the maps grouped at the back of this book, but don't expect to find your reptile or amphibian evenly distributed throughout the area indicated. A Water Snake, for example, seldom wanders far from stream or pond or brook, and, toward the west, where rivers are far apart, many miles may separate localities in which to look for specimens. Obviously, on maps small enough to fit into a *Field Guide* it would be impossible to show all details.

It is possible that you may find a specimen outside the known range of its species. There are several reasons why this may happen. For example:

1. People have a well-meaning but misguided habit of turning loose any pets that become a burden. Turtles and "horned toads" fall into this category and so do the little green "chameleons" sold at the circus. Most die quickly, but sometimes the waifs establish themselves in their new locations, at least for a time. The Redeared Turtle has done so in Michigan, the Western Diamondback Rattlesnake in Wisconsin, and the Texas Horned Lizard in Florida

and elsewhere. A number of tropical species have been introduced, most of them accidently, into Florida or (rarely) other southern states, and some kinds have developed temporary colonies only to die out after periods of frost or other adverse conditions. The exotic species that seem now to be well established are included in this book.

2. You may chance upon a bona-fide range extension. Many herptiles are so secretive that they are readily overlooked, and, although herpetology has acquired a legion of new adherents in recent years, there are still many areas that have not been collected at all, or only sketchily. If your outlander seems to be in a proper habitat and especially if it occurs in colonies, you may have something worth reporting.

3. On rare occasions you may find a specimen that tends to look like a distant subspecies instead of matching exactly the race you would expect in your immediate vicinity. This phenomenon is an expression of relationship. Related subspecies theoretically have had common ancestors, and it is not surprising to find the inherited characteristics of one race appearing occasionally in populations of another race. Actually this type of phenomenon may be commonplace within areas of intergradation — where two subspecies of the same species share a common boundary. There may be a nearly perfect blending of the two races with some individual specimens showing characteristics of *both* subspecies. Care must be taken in trying to identify such specimens, and it is perfectly correct to refer to them as "intergrades" or "intermediates." The areas of intergradation vary greatly in size; they are usually narrow in regions of sharp physiographic changes, such as along an escarpment, where grasslands give way to forests, etc. But they may be very wide where changes in the environment are less pronounced. Only a few of the broader areas of intergradation are shown on the distribution maps and these are indicated by the overlapping of patterns (spotting, hatching, etc.). Bear in mind that intergradation may take place for varying distances on both sides of any common boundary between subspecies. In some cases subspecies that once were probably connected through intergrades now occupy completely separate ranges, but they still retain sufficient similarity to be considered as races rather than as distinct species.

At this point, some comment might be made about hybrids. Crosses between species occur occasionally in nature, but such mismatings are almost always between animals of closely related species, and they may take place at various localities within their common ranges. The products of hybridization are frequently infertile or incapable of transmitting all their own characteristics to offspring. Intergrades, on the other hand, are members of freely breeding populations, and are restricted to geographical regions where the ranges of two or more subspecies come together.

An attempt has been made to present maps that are as complete and accurate as possible, and toward that end they were submitted to many specialists for checking and criticizing. I make no claim to perfection, however, for it would take several lifetimes to run down every possible locality reference and to check the vast numbers of specimens preserved in the museums. Some states have been much more thoroughly collected than others or the data about their herptiles is much better organized or more readily accessible. As soon as this book is published, however, there will be a rash of range extensions called to my attention or reported in the scientific literature. This smoking-out process is a healthy sign of interest, and is the usual by-product whenever a large collection of range maps appears in print.

The maps may be used to prepare a personal check list; just tabulate or check off the species occurring in your own state or region. They also may be used for a life list by placing a check mark after the name of each species or subspecies that you encounter.

Illustrations: We have illustrated this book the difficult way. Not being artists, we have depended upon photography, an art in which Mrs. Conant is singularly skilled. She has made all the pictures, done all the darkroom work, and then, having prepared a print to scale, has colored it by hand, using the living animal as a model. This has been a time-consuming task, but it has enabled us to record the colors with great accuracy, something not yet consistently achievable with the color films now on the market and the commercial processing of them that is available.

My part in the job has been to pose the animals, inventing tricks to render them motionless for a few seconds, and then keeping them alive and healthy until the print was colored or retouched (for the black-and-white plates). At one time we had in excess of 200 snakes, lizards, turtles, frogs, toads, and salamanders in our house. (Not all were of different species!)

This book is the first of the *Field Guides* concerned with zoology to be illustrated directly from life. There is only one dead animal portrayed in the entire lot of photographs: it is a Leatherback Turtle, a rare marine species that few herpetologists have ever seen alive. For the picture of this species we are indebted to The American Museum of Natural History. We have borrowed one other picture — that of the Tennessee Cave Salamander, from Dr. Edward McCrady — because our live specimen of this rare subterranean amphibian, loaned by Dr. Arnold B. Grobman, had only a stumpy, partially regenerated tail. Some of the Rattlesnake pictures were made through the close cooperation of Carl F. Kauffeld.

Obtaining the animals alive has given me the extraordinary opportunity of getting acquainted with them firsthand, and I have not had to depend in such large measure upon faded, stained, or distorted pickled specimens for data as might otherwise have been the case.

The photographs for the black-and-white plates have been prepared with as much care as those for the color plates. Again, the live animals were used as models for such retouching as was needed to restore pattern details that were obscured by highlights on shiny amphibians, turtle shells, etc.

A black line across a color or black-and-white plate indicates a change in scale.

The plates are supplemented by a large collection of line drawings showing for the most part key characters that are useful in distinguishing between genera or between species or subspecies. These also were executed by Mrs. Conant. Many are completely original, but others have been adapted from figures appearing in numerous scientific publications.

Subspecies: The problem of what to do about subspecies had to be resolved early in the planning stages of this book.

Roger Tory Peterson, in his *Field Guide to the Birds,* wisely relegated subspecies to an appendix. Through binoculars the detection of minor details is difficult, especially since many avian subspecies are based upon differences that require examination in the laboratory rather than in the field. The situation with reptiles and amphibians is quite another matter, for, with the specimen at hand, accurate identification to subspecies is normally quite possible.

A black salamander with red cheeks, another with red legs, another with metallic frosting plus white dots, and still another that is black all over — each looks very different (Plate 32). Indeed, all were considered distinct species until recent studies showed them to be subspecifically related. To illustrate just one and bury the others in the text would be unfair — both to the amateur naturalist and to these distinctively marked animals.

There are many other examples. A uniformly black snake, a yellow one with dark stripes, and others with bold patterns of dark blotches, all are races of the same species (Plate 22). One of the harmless Milk Snakes is almost a perfect mimic of the venomous Coral Snake, yet it is very different from its northern relatives.

So subspecies are in — and the problems that go with them. Some subspecies are separated from their closest relatives by minutiae that will bore the field man, but the data are briefly summarized for those who wish to know. We have tried to include, upon the plates or among the pen-and-ink drawings, illustrations of the species *and subspecies* that are visually different and can be told apart without recourse to the microscope, complicated scale counts, or checks upon internal anatomy.

If a subspecies is visually distinct enough to warrant inclusion upon the plates, it also rates a separate heading in the text. Less easily defined subspecies (and a few rare ones) are included with those they most closely resemble. My methods of presenting or listing subspecies are variable and unorthodox, but all races are included. It should be borne strongly in mind that most persons will refer to the illustrations first and the text afterward. Hence, the text has been made to fit the pictures and *not* vice versa.

Taxonomists (zoologists who classify animals) are far from agreement as to what constitutes a subspecies. It is the general practice to recognize those races (subspecies) that have been defined as such by the author of a review or monograph of a genus or species. In less well studied groups, opinions tend to differ. It is a well-known fact that most animal populations are subject to clinal variations. A cline is a geographical trend in which a certain structural, color, or pattern characteristic shows a gradual change from one part of the range to another. For example, Wood Frogs have long hind legs in the northeastern states, but very short ones in northern Canada and Alaska. The populations at opposite ends of the range are so different they easily could be classified as different subspecies or even distinct species — if it were not for the gradually changing populations in between them. Often two or more clines are involved, and these may manifest themselves in different directions, one cline progressing from south to north, while another *in the same species* progresses from east to west. Many of the disputes concerning subspecies result from differences of opinion in the interpretation of clines. One taxonomist might consider all Wood Frogs to belong to a single full species devoid of subspecies; whereas a less conservative one might divide them into two or three or even more subspecies.

Suffice it to say, without becoming deeply involved in this controversial subject, that no two books or lists that include subspecies are apt to be quite in agreement. More stability will undoubtedly be achieved as study material accumulates from critical localities and becomes available to the research worker. In preparing this *Field Guide* I have endeavored to bear the layman's problems in mind, and have stressed the subspecies that *look* different to him. This means that from the taxonomic point of view I have been quite conservative in many instances but distinctly radical in others. In the main I have followed *A Check List of North American Amphibians and Reptiles* (Sixth Edition, 1953), by Karl P. Schmidt. This, incidentally, is an important book for anyone who wishes to study herpetology further. I have used the classification for higher groups (orders, families, and subfamilies) of reptiles as outlined by Alfred S. Romer in his *Osteology of the Reptiles*.

For those readers of the *Field Guide* who are being exposed to subspecies for the first time, the following should be borne in mind: the scientific name is the clue. If there are three parts to the name (a trinomial), then there are one or more additional related subspecies, each of which bears the same first two names. For example, *Lampropeltis getulus niger* (Black Kingsnake), *Lampropeltis getulus holbrooki* (Speckled Kingsnake), and *Lampropeltis getulus getulus* (Eastern Kingsnake) are all subspecies of the same species. The repetition of *getulus* in the name for the Eastern Kingsnake shows that it was the first member of the group to receive scientific description. In this book the words "subspecies" and "race" are considered to be synonyms and are used interchangeably. If there are only two parts to a scientific name (a binomial), then no subspecies are known or recognized. The term "form" is used to designate any population of reptiles or amphibians that bears a scientific name and regardless of whether a species or subspecies is involved.

Size: Herptiles may continue to grow as long as they live, rapidly at first but more slowly after maturity. Hence, giant specimens *may* be encountered on very rare occasions. The greatest length that I believe to be *authentic* is given for each animal included in this book. Longer measurements will be called to my attention, no doubt, and some of these may be accurate. Evaluating claims is not easy, for some snake hunters are as notorious as certain anglers. Serpents, like fish, shrink remarkably in size when stretched along a rule or measuring tape. Hearsay "evidence" about big snakes is not difficult to find. The longest serpent native to the United States is the Indigo Snake, with a maximum known length of 103½ inches, or slightly less than 9 feet.

Reptiles and amphibians thus do not attain "standard" lengths. In most instances three measurements are given under the subheading "Identification" — for example, "4–7; record 8¼." This means that average adults of the species in question vary from 4 to 7 inches in total length, and that the largest one measured 8¼ inches. In the cases of lizards, which so frequently lose their tails and then grow new but *shorter* ones, the approximate maximum head–body lengths also are given. In some species, notably among the Map and Softshell Turtles, females not only grow much bigger than males but they also look different; in such cases there are separate measurements for the two sexes. Sizes of young reptiles at the time of hatching or birth are also given in most instances. Sizes at transformation of amphibians from the larval to the adult form are not included for two reasons: there is a dearth of such information for many species, and variation in size is considerable and subject to environmental conditions. (If a pond dries up, to mention an example, tadpoles may transform into toadlets or froglets at a much smaller size than if the pond remained filled with water.)

All measurements are given in inches save in the case of the crocodilians, for which total lengths are expressed in feet and inches. The proper methods of making measurements are illustrated on the back endpapers.

Voice: Frogs and toads are quite vociferous, at least in season, but only a few other herptiles of our area produce vocal sounds

The crocodilians grunt, roar, and bellow, and the Mediterranean Gecko makes a faint mouselike squeak. Kissing, squeaking, popping, and yelping noises have been reported occasionally in salamanders, but the sounds in this last group are usually produced mechanically, as when air is suddenly exhaled through the lips.

Each kind of frog or toad has its own distinctive call, and nearly all may be readily identified by ear after a little practice. The calls normally are associated with the breeding season when males of most species assemble in or near shallow water and start singing lustily for their mates. Some choruses are enormous and may be composed of several kinds all singing at the same time. Local weather conditions are of paramount importance in stimulating frogs into calling and breeding, and even human activities may start them off, such as when areas are flooded during irrigation and temporary ponds or puddles are formed. Choruses, usually weak, without the enthusiasm of mating time, and composed largely or wholly of young frogs, may sometimes be heard out of season. A few southern species may be vocal at almost any time of year, and treefrogs may call intermittently throughout the summer months. The onset and duration of the breeding season may vary greatly, depending upon locality, latitude, and weather conditions. The times mentioned in the text are only approximations. Certain migratory birds arrive in any given locality on almost the same day every year, but frogs and toads, being cold-blooded animals and at the mercy of the weather, are highly irregular.

Describing the calls of animals of any kind presents many obstacles, but I have been greatly aided by a large number of recordings made in the field and given to me by W. Frank Blair, Charles M. Bogert, John C. Wottring, and Richard G. Zweifel.

Conservation: Even herptiles have a place in the balance of nature. They are an important source of food for other animals — herons eat frogs, for example. Lizards and amphibians are largely insectivorous, and the value of snakes in destroying rodents has long been recognized. Their secretive natures and nocturnal habits help to protect many of them from human enemies, but a small and ignorant segment of our population still thinks it necessary to slaughter every one on sight, snakes especially. Naturalists have long since learned to let the reptiles and amphibians alone or to take only such specimens as may be necessary for identification, study, or educational purposes.

If you chance upon a colony, don't collect more than you need. Remember that it takes time, effort, and money to care for a large collection of herptiles; only zoos or other large institutions are equipped for handling great numbers. So select only one or two specimens, and turn the others loose where you found them. Transporting home more than you need places you in the same category as the game hog who stuffs his hunting coat with birds or mammals far beyond the legal limit.

Also, be kind to habitats. Some species, such as certain salamanders, occur only in restricted areas. By ripping up all the
rocks and other shelters, you might do such irreparable damage as
to decimate severely or even exterminate the colony. Replace
rocks, logs, and boards after you overturn them. Mind your
outdoor manners, and leave the countryside in the same or better
condition than you find it.

For the Serious Student: If you have a deep interest in herptiles
you may wish to read further on the subject or even join one of
the organizations devoted to their study. Several general references are listed in the bibliography (p. 308). If there is a report
available on any or all of the reptiles and amphibians of your
own state or region, get a copy and keep it handy for ready reference. Reptile clubs have been established in many cities, and
information about them can be obtained by inquiring at your
local zoo or natural history museum. There are two national
organizations; you can get in touch with them as follows:

Herpetologists League (publishers of the journal *Herpetologica*)
— write to Major Chapman Grant, Route 1, Box 80, Escondido,
California, or to Dr. Hobart M. Smith, Department of Zoology,
University of Illinois, Urbana, Illinois.

American Society of Ichthyologists and Herpetologists (publishers of the journal *Copeia*) — write to Roger Conant, Philadelphia Zoological Garden, Philadelphia 4, Pennsylvania.

II

Making and Transporting the Catch

YOUR OWN two hands are the best tools for catching reptiles and amphibians. Most kinds can just be grabbed, but you had better be quick about it, for they are adept at slipping away. But *never try to catch a poisonous snake without proper tools*. Learn to recognize the dangerous species instantly.

Large harmless snakes can be caught without equipment after a little practice. One method is to immobilize the snake by stepping on it gently while you reach for the nearest stick with which to pin down its head. Or you can use your other foot instead of a stick — if you are good at balancing yourself. Once the head is under control, you can pick up the serpent by using the same technique illustrated for the Rattlesnake on Plate 1 (p. 14). Another method requires more skill and nerve. This consists of seizing the snake by tail or body and slinging it quickly between your legs, meantime clamping your legs together to hold the reptile as in a vise. By pulling the snake slowly forward — tail first, of course — you will eventually come to the head and can grasp it just behind the jaws. Wear bluejeans or clothe yourself in some other tough fabric before you try this, however. Some nonvenomous snakes can bite hard, and you will be exposed to attack from the rear.

A slapping-down technique can be used for those lizards and frogs that freeze in place instead of dashing away. This consists of slapping your flattened hand over them, pinning them down while you grasp a leg (or legs) with your other hand. Don't slap too hard, or there will be casualties. You will have best success in stalking your quarry if you *don't look directly at it*. Move in at an angle, watching it out of the corner of your eye.

Numerous other tricks are used to catch herptiles by hand, and you may invent some of your own. Tools are essential for some purposes, though, and particularly since considerable field work consists of overturning rocks and other objects beneath which reptiles and amphibians may have taken shelter. Each herpetologist has his own opinion about what implements are best. Here are some of the important tools and their uses.

Snake Stick (or Snake Hook): This is an L-shaped instrument with the long arm serving as a handle; the short arm consists of a piece of metal flattened at the bottom and suitable for pinning a snake to the ground (Fig. 1, p. 12). A golf putter that has been

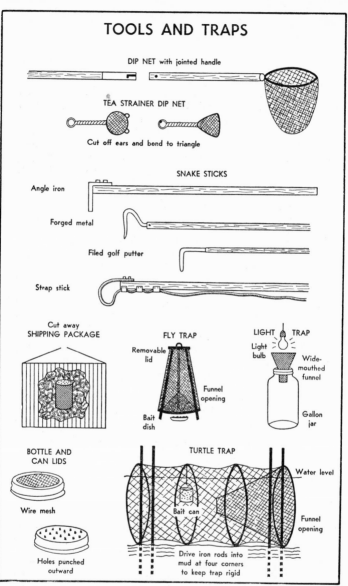

TOOLS AND TRAPS

DIP NET with jointed handle

TEA STRAINER DIP NET

Cut off ears and bend to triangle

SNAKE STICKS

Angle iron

Forged metal

Filed golf putter

Strap stick

Cut away
SHIPPING PACKAGE

FLY TRAP

Removable lid

Funnel opening

Bait dish

LIGHT TRAP

Light bulb

Wide-mouthed funnel

Gallon jar

BOTTLE AND CAN LIDS

Wire mesh

Holes punched outward

TURTLE TRAP

Water level

Bait can

Funnel opening

Drive iron rods into mud at four corners to keep trap rigid

Fig. 1. Tools used in catching and transporting reptiles and amphibians. (Also see pp. 11, 14, and 15.) Fly and light traps are useful for gathering live insects to feed captive lizards, toads, treefrogs, etc.

filed down makes a good snake stick. So also does a forged and tempered metal hook securely fastened to a wooden handle. A more simple and easily constructed type consists of an angle iron screwed to the end of a square stick, but it may break or bend if you use it for turning rocks. You will want to experiment, especially in deciding what handle length is best suited to your own stature and techniques. The traditional forked stick is of little value. If the fork is too large, small snakes will slip right through it; if too small, it may severely injure the neck of a large snake.

Snake Tongs: A mechanical device 3 or 4 feet long that depends upon spring action. By pressing a hand grip, rubber-padded jaws can be made to grasp the body of a snake. Releasing the grip frees the snake. Such tongs are available commercially.

Strap Stick: A wooden pole, square or rectangular in cross section, and equipped with a leather strap set in metal guides. This is more suited for use with captive snakes than as a field implement. Unless the leather is very stiff or reinforced by a piece of wire, it is difficult to release the reptile once it is caught, and the snake may tear or break its neck in its efforts to escape. The advantage of this tool lies in being able to keep the serpent well away from you.

Potato Rake and Stevedore Hook: See Plate 2 (p. 15) for use of these tools.

Collecting Bags: Save flour, salt, and sugar sacks. Launder them carefully and stitch the edges on a sewing machine. The original stitching is usually so coarse that small snakes or lizards can readily force their way through it. Loop one or two large bags through your belt to have them handy, and carry small ones in your pocket. If you catch amphibians, wet the bottoms of the bags and throw in a handful of moss, wet leaves, or other damp vegetation. Putting these animals in plain bags will dry them out, and they will die of desiccation. Even reptiles will survive better if their environment is moist. Remove all livestock from bags as soon as possible; otherwise they may develop sore noses and feet from trying to escape. Wash bags thoro   before using them again.

Plastic bags are favored by some field men — the type you use in a refrigerator, but bags fashioned from   vy, sturdy plastic. These are translucent (even almost t   nt) so you can see your catch, and lizards cannot climb   as they frequently do in cloth bags. Canvas bags are t   v and too closely woven for most purposes. Burlap is use   almost all herptiles; the weave is so open and loose they   t through it with little effort.

Bottles and Cans: Punch holes in lids with   ints *aimed outward*. A tidier job can be done by soldering s   wire to the inner side of a screw-top lid, the kind that is on   in the center and is little more than a rim. Both bottles and cans have advan-

HANDLING THE CATCH (1)

Holding a lively, struggling animal so that it won't bite or scratch you, hurt itself, or get away requires a knowledge of the captive's anatomy and abilities. Here are illustrated several grips that have proved efficient. These are only for brief, temporary transportation; specimens should be placed in bags, bottles, etc., as quickly as possible.

1. A BULLFROG, like other amphibians, is slippery. Encircle its waist with your fingers so that it cannot kick itself free. Any large or medium-sized frogs may be held in the same way, but small frogs are best grasped by the legs.

2. A SNAPPER'S TAIL makes a good handle, but keep the head aimed away from your leg.

3. LARGE SALAMANDERS should be held firmly but gently with the entire hand. Let the head protrude. Small salamanders can be caged briefly within your clenched fist.

4. LIZARDS are best immobilized by holding their feet, but the body should also be gripped, to prevent sudden lunges. Make it a practice *never* to grab or hold a lizard by the tail, for it may break right off in your hands.

5. SOFTSHELL TURTLES are difficult to hold. Pressing against the neck with your fingers will help keep the head from protruding far enough to turn around and bite at you. Also watch out for flailing legs with their sharp claws. Large Snappers should be carried in this same fashion.

6. PINNING DOWN a Rattlesnake with a snake stick. Press down firmly but not hard enough to cause injury.

7. CLOSE-UP, showing finger grip.

8. THE SERPENT IN HAND. Grasp the body firmly to prevent the snake from jerking loose and imbedding a fang in your finger in the process.

9. THE "SNAKE PULLMAN," equipped with an inner screened lid, is an excellent container for shipping or carrying dangerous snakes. Captive Rattlers, Copperheads, and Cottonmouths will balance themselves on a snake stick while being transferred from one cage or container to another.

CAUTION: Don't attempt to catch or handle venomous snakes unless you have received professional coaching and are prepared to suffer the serious consequences of a snake-bite accident.

Plate 2   15

HANDLING THE CATCH (2)

Before going afield the herpetologist should equip himself with a few simple tools and containers. Here are some and how to use them. Additional equipment is described on pp. 11 to 17 and illustrated in Fig. 1, p. 12.

1. BAGGING A SNAKE. This is most easily accomplished if you have a companion to hold it open for you.

2. TYING THE KNOT. A simple overhand knot works best. The use of string is not recommended — it is something extra to carry with you, it might come loose, and small snakes, in struggling to get out, have been known to push string right off the neck of a bag.

3. CARRYING THE BAG. With your hand well above the knot and the bag held away from your leg, a venomous snake may be safely transported. In the case of a harmless species, the knot and the empty part of the bag may be thrust upward under your belt, letting the snake dangle there until you return to your car or base. This leaves both hands free to catch something else.

4. BOTTLES are safest for bringing home small fragile specimens. They will retain moisture better, and they may save your catch from injury. More than one collector has sat or stepped upon a collecting bag with fatal consequences to the inmates thereof.

5. TURTLE TRAPS must always be set with their uppermost parts above the water, otherwise the turtles will drown.

6. A POTATO RAKE or similar tool is useful for overturning rocks. The long handle enables you to stand erect and keeps you well away if by chance you should uncover a poisonous snake.

7. A STEVEDORE'S HOOK works well on logs, boards, and smaller rocks, but it requires stooping over and more caution about the dangerous snakes. An advantage is that it can be thrust under your belt when not in use.

tages and disadvantages. Bottles can be broken, but you can see their contents. Cans will stand being dropped, but they will rust, and you cannot tell in advance whether an animal is ready to leap out the moment you remove the lid.

Dip Net: An ordinary crabbing net will do as a starter, but a deeper, finer-mesh bag will be necessary for holding baby turtles. Cut the handle in half and provide it with a ferrule and locking device for quick assembling or dismounting. The original handle will be too long to fit comfortably into the average automobile.

Tea Strainer Dip Net: An ordinary tea strainer, bent to triangular shape and with its ears lopped off or folded out of the way, makes a handy gadget for catching salamanders. These slippery and elusive amphibians, which normally hide or scurry away when rocks are overturned along tumbling brooks, can often be worked into a tea strainer dip net. When one gets in clap your hand over top and you've made your capture.

Turtle Trap: There are several different ways to trap turtles, but a simple, efficient device can be made from three sturdy wire hoops and a supply of stout corded fisherman's netting with a 1-inch mesh or slightly smaller. Make the hoops 30 inches in diameter, give or take a little. (Measure the trunk of your car or your storage closet to see what size will fit conveniently.) Tie netting to the hoops to form a collapsible barrel-shaped trap about 4 or 5 feet long. At one end fashion a narrow slitlike throat extending into the trap and through which a turtle can enter readily (Fig. 1, p. 12). The other end of the "barrel" can be netted over solidly or another throat can be installed. For the bait, select a tin can with a tight-fitting lid and about the same size as an ordinary drinking tumbler. Punch numerous holes through the can, through lid, sides, and bottom. Fill the can with freshly chopped raw fish or chicken entrails and hang it from the top of the trap so that the bait is completely submerged. The trap can be kept rigidly in place by driving iron bars or rods (the rods used for reinforcing concrete are ideal) down through the ends of the trap and into the mud (Plate 2, p. 15). As an alternate the trap can be made to float by attaching it to two logs or two pieces of timber, one along each side.

Headlamps: Amphibians, especially frogs and toads in chorus, are easily found after dark with the aid of a flashlight. So are Water Snakes, salamanders, and certain other herptiles. For many purposes a headlamp, strapped around your forehead and powered by batteries fastened to your belt, is superior, particularly since it leaves both hands free for grabbing. Headlamps can be purchased from sporting goods stores or camp outfitters.

Lizard Catchers: Slingshots or rubber-band guns can be employed to stun lizards, but some risk is involved; a few may be killed or permanently injured instead of just being rendered temporarily immobile. Noosing lizards is safer. Attach a small noose of horsehair or fine thread or wire to the end of a pole measuring a few feet in length. Slip the noose over the lizard's head and let it come to rest around the neck. Jerk the pole quickly upward and the lizard is yours! This method requires practice, but is quite efficient when mastered.

Shipping Containers: It occasionally may be necessary to send specimens to a friend or an institution like a zoo or museum. Large snakes or turtles should be bagged and then placed inside a strong wooden box such as the "snake Pullman" shown on Plate 1 (p. 14). These can be sent by express. Smaller herptiles require special packing. Use a can or bottle prepared as described above, nearly fill it with slightly damp paper towels (moister for amphibians, less so for reptiles), and place the animals inside. The towels not only will prevent desiccation but will keep the animals from getting shaken up too much. Nest the can or bottle in the center of a cardboard box filled with excelsior, shredded paper, or even plain crumpled newspapers. Allow at least 3 inches of packing on *all* sides of the can or bottle. This material will serve as insulation against heat or cold, and the space between its components becomes a reservoir of air during shipping. The package may be sealed on the outside if desired. Mark it "Perishable" and use air service if the recipient is some distance away. Small harmless animals, such as baby alligators, baby turtles, etc., may be shipped via parcel post. Snakes of all kinds are barred from the mails. They must be sent by express.

Before attempting any extensive collecting, check into your state or provincial game and fish laws. Closed seasons may be stipulated for turtles and frogs in some states, turtle traps (because they also catch fish) may be prohibited or restricted in others, the catching of frogs through the use of lights at night may be forbidden in still others. You may have to apply for a collecting permit. Herptiles enjoy far more protection than they used to get. Arizona, of course, is completely out of our territory, but it furnishes an example of the increasing interest in reptiles. In that state "horned toads" and the venomous Gila Monster may not be collected at all.

Be sure to keep a record of the source of your specimens. If you should find something rare and wish to tell a professional herpetologist about it, he will need certain basic information — the exact locality in which it was found, the date, collector's name, a description of the habitat, notes on the animal's behavior, and any other pertinent data.

III

Care in Captivity

AFTER YOU CATCH a snake or frog or turtle, what do you do with it? If you are the average outdoor enthusiast you will hold it briefly, check its identity, admire its coloration and pattern, and then turn it loose where you found it. But maybe you would like to keep it for a time. Most reptiles and amphibians are relatively easy to maintain in captivity. They are fun to watch, and the surest way to learn something about them is to keep them close at hand.

Housing the Catch: The most versatile of all "cages" for herptiles is a home aquarium. Perhaps there is one left over from a former interest in mollies, guppies, or other "tropical" fishes. If not, aquariums are inexpensive to buy. Get a roomy one — 15 inches or more in length and at least 8 to 10 inches in both width and depth. Then make a heavy or tight-fitting lid of screen wire tacked onto a wooden frame; this is very important, for reptiles and amphibians can crawl, leap, or push their way out with startling agility. Even salamanders, because of the natural adhesion of their wet bodies against the glass, can readily walk up and out. If you are planning to keep lizards or treefrogs, build two hinged doors into the lid so that you can get your hand down inside to service half of their [quarters at a time (Fig. 2, p. 19). Don't try to catch these little animals and remove them every time their cage needs cleaning. And that brings up an important rule: Don't handle your specimens more than is necessary. Most of them will settle down and thrive best when they are undisturbed.

Once it is equipped with a lid, your aquarium is ready to serve as a terrarium, a cage, or as a true aquarium for aquatic species.

Preparing a Terrarium: Attractively planted terrariums make excellent homes for many herptiles. Fill the bottom of an aquarium with small clean pebbles to a depth of an inch to provide drainage. Cover them with a ¼-inch layer of charcoal chips to help keep the soil sweet. Then add about an inch of loamy or sandy soil. Small plants can be rooted in this, but it is easier and much more practical simply to put the plants in a flower pot, and place the pot (or pots) in the terrarium with its base resting on the charcoal or pebble layer. When you clean up, you lift out the pot instead of having to uproot the plants each time. Frogs and lizards of some kinds like to cling to the sides of the pot. Typical hot-house plants should be selected and ones that will stand watering every

Pool and beach for turtles and frogs

Locked cage for snakes

Terrarium for lizards and treefrogs

Temporary quarters in gallon jar

Fig. 2. Living quarters for the smaller herptiles are easily made **from** old aquariums, wooden boxes, and gallon pickle or mayonnaise jars.

day. When they are sprinkled the lizards will lap up the **drops.** (Many lizards will *not* drink from a water dish.) Other **terrarium** residents, such as frogs and toads, need a shallow water **container** made of glass, plastic, or nonrusting or noncorroding metal. **Small** branches may be placed in the cage for those specimens that **like** to climb.

For lizards from arid habitats the terrarium should be **floored** with plain, clean, dry sand (no pebbles or charcoal), and **cactus** plants may be used as an appropriate decoration. Such **plants** cannot stand a daily sprinkling, but water for the lizards **can be** provided by filling a shallow container to the brim and letting **a** little of the water spill over to provide a circle of damp **sand** around the dish.

Snakes normally do not make good terrarium animals, for **they** may burrow down out of sight and root up plants, pebbles, **and** charcoal. Many toads and turtles may do likewise. Such **speci**mens, if they are to be seen at all, are best kept on bare **pebbles,** but potted plants and shelters may, of course, be added.

Hiding places are a necessity. A piece of bark with its **concave** side down makes a good shelter under which the residents **may** secrete themselves; natural cork bark, procurable from most **first**class florist shops, is ideal. Small flat stones may be piled up **to** make a miniature cave, but they must be stacked carefully so they will not fall upon the animals. Small flattish cardboard boxes, with their lids in place and with holes cut through their sides, may also be used, but in the damp environment of a terrarium they may disintegrate; they are better suited for dry cages.

The Semi-aquatic Terrarium: Water-loving turtles, newts, and the more aquatic types of frogs often do best if they have a choice of wet and dry environments. This can be accomplished by inserting a partition across the center of the aquarium and piling pebbles on one side of it. The partition can be of stone or slate, or, if these are not at hand, a piece of wood may be used with its ends held firm by inserting small wooden wedges between them and the glass. The pebbles provide a beach on which a potted plant and a shelter may be placed; the other half of the aquarium may be left in open water. Baby turtles may need a ramp, perhaps a small rough stone or piece of bark, on which to climb ashore. Young caimans and alligators require similar but much larger accommodations. Their pens should be big enough so that they can stretch out straight either in or out of the water.

The True Aquarium: Only a few kinds of reptiles and amphibians can live in water in straight-sided aquariums with no place to crawl out. These include Mud, Musk, and Softshell Turtles, Rainbow, Mud, and Swamp Snakes, aquatic Newts, Sirens, Amphiumas, Mudpuppies, Waterdogs, and Hellbenders. All of these should have a stone cave at the bottom of the aquarium to serve as a retreat. Aquatic vegetation may be used with most of them, and, in fact, some plant growth to furnish resting and hiding places is almost an essential for the smaller species mentioned above.

The Cage: The simplest type of cage is, once again, the home aquarium. For snakes, fold or cut sheets of newspaper (about six to eight pages in thickness) to fit the bottom of the aquarium exactly. These will serve to absorb excess moisture, and when they become soiled they are easily discarded and replaced. More substantial cages are not difficult to construct. The one illustrated in Fig. 2 (p. 19) has wooden sides, back, and bottom, a glass front, and a screened top. The top is hinged to open at the back and is provided with hasp and staple for a lock. No air holes are necessary at the sides if the top is completely screened; in fact, snakes will rub their noses sore on any rough objects, such as wire tacked over air holes, at cage-floor level.

Install a water dish large enough for the snake to submerge itself completely but heavy enough so that it cannot be tipped over. Also provide a hiding place. Bark or stones will do, but here is where the cardboard box with a hole in its side serves to perfection. With the snake inside the box it is a simple matter to lift out the serpent and its house while the cage is cleaned. Most snakes thrive best if their quarters are kept completely dry save for the contents of the water dish.

Temporary Quarters: A gallon wide-mouthed glass jar can serve as a temporary home for almost any small or medium-sized reptile or amphibian. This can be equipped with stones, sticks, etc., but plain crumpled paper towels are more practical. These can be dampened slightly (for lizards and snakes) or wet thoroughly (for amphibians and turtles). Not only do the towels supply moisture but they also serve as hiding places. The jar should be cleaned at least every other day, and before replacing the towels a small amount of cool (not cold) water should be poured in to give the animals a chance to get a drink. In general, temporary quarters should not be used much more than a week or so. Transfer their inmates to permanent cages or terrariums as quickly as you can.

Outdoor Turtle Pens: Large turtles are scarcely household pets, but they are easily accommodated if you have a spacious back-yard wherein you can construct a turtle pen. Surround an area measuring 5 feet by 8 feet (or larger) with a wire fence or a masonry wall, making sure that the wire or the foundations descend into the ground for about a foot to discourage burrowing. This distance is adequate for most turtles, but if you keep such efficient diggers as Gopher Tortoises you will need a floor in your pen covered by a foot or more of well-packed soil. The sides of the enclosure should rise about 30 inches; the exact height can be determined by testing just how high a wall you can step over comfortably, for stepping over eliminates any need for a door. The outer walls *must* bend well inward or have a substantial overhang, for otherwise the more agile turtles, Stinkpots and Snappers especially, will climb up and out. A shallow pool of stone or concrete and built so that water will not leak out of it should cover not more than half the pen. This must have gently sloping sides so that even a Box Turtle can climb out at any point, and it should not be more than 12 or 15 inches deep. If at all possible, install a drain at the lowest spot and connect this with a sewer or tile line. (In summertime you may need to clean your pool almost daily, and baling it out with a bucket soon becomes a burdensome chore.) Shelters, in the form of logs or stumps should be provided, both in the water and out, for those reptiles that wish to hide, but keep all such objects away from the outer walls or they will serve as ladders for would-be escapees.

Don't try to keep large Snappers with other turtles, or babies of any aquatic kinds with adults of their own or other species. During the excitement of feeding time the smaller specimens may be seriously injured or even decapitated by their more voracious elders.

The turtle pen also serves as an excellent place in which to let turtles hibernate over winter. After nightly temperatures begin to drop regularly into the low fifties scrub the pool thoroughly and fill it with fresh water. Then fill the pen to the brim with wet leaves, tossing them over land and water alike and atop the turtles. If the weather stays cool the turtles will remain quiescent under their blanket, but if it turns warm some of them will burrow to the surface to bask briefly before their winter sleep. Occasionally they may be active enough to walk out of their enclosure; to be sure they don't, string wire mesh a foot or more in width around the perimeter of the pen, or roof it in completely if it is small. If the leaves tend to dry out, they should be sprinkled to keep the hibernaters from dying from desiccation.

If summer camps, wherein large and elaborate turtle pens make interesting adjuncts to the nature department, it is best to liberate any native turtles at the end of the season, especially since most camps close long before the reptiles are ready to retire for the winter. Exotic turtles or those not occurring locally should be given to a zoo or museum. Don't turn them loose in a strange environment.

Temperatures: Reptiles and amphibians are cold-blooded animals whose temperatures closely approximate the temperatures of the room or cages in which you keep them. When they are cold, body functions slow down and appetites are poor or nonexistent. When they are too warm they suffer distress; too much heat will kill them. Temperatures of 75 degrees to 85 degrees are best for the majority of reptiles; amphibians will thrive under somewhat cooler conditions.

In summertime, herptiles may be kept in any comparatively cool place, such as a well-ventilated camp building or in the basement of your home. Some sunshine is usually essential for lizards and turtles; snakes can get along without it if they eat well and are given good food. In any event, provision must be made so that the animals can bask or retreat to the shade in accordance with their own desires. Hence, outdoor cages should be roomy and supplied with hiding places. Never set a cage wholly in the sunshine or in a spot where the sun may strike it later in the day and roast your pets.

In wintertime, normal room temperatures (without too much nightly chilling) are suitable for most amphibians. Reptiles, if they are to be active, need to be kept warmer. Therefore, during the cooler months your herpetological menagerie should be installed in a warm part of the house, and the best location can be determined by running a few tests with a thermometer for a day or two. Check for the ideal temperatures mentioned above. Avoid too much drop at night; for example, don't place cages in a bedroom where the window normally would be opened at night.

Supplementary heat may be needed, especially for lizards, and this can be supplied by placing an electric lamp (with reflector) atop the cage in such a way as to direct the heat downward. If the cage is large, the lamp should be mounted at an end or side so the reptiles may retreat to a cooler spot if they wish. If the cage is small, then the lamp should be left on only for limited periods of time. Basking places for lizards, in the form of twigs or small branches, should be provided. Feed the lizards when they are well warmed up.

Don't expect any of your pets to eat with the same avidity in the wintertime as they do in warm weather, even when they are well supplied with heat. Some of them, turtles, caimans, and alligators in particular, will go off feed for weeks or months at a time. When hunger strikes are long continued, it is often best to transfer the fasters to cooler quarters (to temperatures in the fifties) until spring, but they must be kept moist.

Food: The very large majority of reptiles and amphibians are carnivorous or insectivorous. A few eat vegetable matter.

A good basic food for alligators, caimans, aquatic salamanders, and virtually all kinds of turtles is canned dog food. Be sure the brand you buy has been fortified with vitamins and minerals. You can make your own mixture, if you like, by adding a drop or two of a liquid vitamin concentrate and a pinch of bone meal or oyster-shell flour to raw lean hamburger and then stirring thoroughly. Mold the mixture (or dog food) into small rounded pellets and place them not in the water but at its edge. The animals will then take a piece at a time into the water. (Of course, if your pets are in straight-sided aquariums you will have to drop the food right in with them, but do it sparingly and with due regard for their appetites. There is no point in fouling the water unnecessarily.) Most of these animals will also eat chopped fish (be sure to include the entrails) and any natural food such as insects, worms, or freshly killed tadpoles or crayfish (crack the shells thoroughly) that may come your way.

Turtles of almost all kinds will also eat some vegetable matter. A piece of lettuce or other leafy vegetable should be given at least once each week. Lawn cuttings are savored by some. Tortoises and Box Turtles should have greens as well as a variety of soft fruits and berries. Even though they may show a preference for vegetable matter (Tortoises especially) they should be given a chance to eat meat occasionally.

Some kinds of reptiles and amphibians require live insects or other invertebrates. Frogs and toads and most lizards are in this category, and the motion of their prey serves as a triggering mechanism for springing into action. Some of these animals will starve to death even if surrounded by platoons of dead insects. Drop in a live one and it is seized at once.

Supplying live insects is not difficult during the warmer months. Examine window screens at night for beetles and moths attracted by the lights inside. The simplest device for collecting them consists of a jelly glass and a card. Place the glass over the insect, and then slide the card between its rim and the screen. The same apparatus may be used for imprisoning the spiders that you will find in basements, under eaves, or other lurking places. A light trap is an efficient way of getting nocturnal insects in quantity. Get a gallon glass jar and solder a wide-mouthed kitchen funnel to a large hole cut through its lid. Screw on the lid, place the jar on the ground outdoors at night, and set an electric light bulb an inch or two above the mouth of the funnel (Fig. 1, p. 12). Insects will fly to the light and then tumble into the jar. A fly trap, for use in daytime, can be made on the same general pattern, but upside down and of wire (also see Fig. 1). This is set an inch or so above a dish of meat or fish. The flies are attracted to the bait, but in leaving it they fly upward. They strike the wire funnel, walk up it, pass through its neck, and then enter the wire cage above.

Obtaining insects in wintertime is another matter, at least if you live in Canada or the northern states. If you are plagued with roaches, consider it a blessing in disguise, for here is a ready-made food for many kinds of herptiles. Live crickets may be purchased from bait supply houses. If you intend keeping lizards and frogs in any quantity you will have to raise flies and meal worms or other insects, and you will have to start weeks or months ahead of time. Consult your local pet store or your government department of entomology for instructions.

Small salamanders and frogs will eat tubifex worms, which you can buy at most tropical fish dealers. Larger amphibians eat earthworms, which you can probably dig up for yourself except in the coldest weather. Snakes have specialized feeding habits, and their food is mentioned in the text for each group or species.

A Suggestion: Keeping reptile and amphibian pets is an inter-esting pastime, but it does take time and effort. In many instances you will find it practical to hold specimens for only a few days or weeks, studying them until you grow quite familiar with them and then liberating them where you caught them. Do not turn them loose in a strange environment. In any event do not keep them after it is obvious that they are deteriorating for lack of food or for some other reason.

Pet-store Turtles: The inane practice of painting the shells of baby turtles with enamel promotes sales (so say the vendors), but it does these reptiles no good. Flake off the enamel at once with a knife or a razor blade — do not use paint remover. A tur-tle's shell is living tissue and it grows just as the rest of the animal does; enamel, by sticking to the shell, causes deformities and arrested growth. If you buy a pet-store turtle pick out a lively one and one that has some weight. Sometimes they are kept so long and improperly that they are virtually starved or desiccated before they are sold at retail. The commercial, so-called "turtle food," consisting largely of dried ant "eggs" (really pupae), is not recommended. Turtles with soft shells or whose eyes are closed or show evidences of a cheesy exudate, are usually suffering from a dietary deficiency.

Words of Caution: Remember that many persons dislike reptiles, snakes especially. Your neighbors may resent your keeping herptiles unless you can assure them that your pets are under strict control at all times. Lock all snake cages to forestall escapes and to prevent the younger members of your family from getting into mischief. *Under no circumstances should venomous snakes be kept in a private home or apartment.*

IV

What About the
Snake-bite Problem?

THE BEST ANSWER is not to get bitten. Most bites result from the careless handling of venomous snakes by amateurs or by failure to follow proper precautions in the field.

Don't keep venomous snakes in captivity unless you have had experience and use escape-proof cages. It is well to let all poisonous snakes alone. Even in trying to kill them people have been bitten and have died. Snake bite can be an extremely serious thing. If complications develop you may be hospitalized for weeks and the experience may cost you a thousand dollars or more.

In the field wear protective clothing in those districts where poisonous snakes are known to occur. Rubber or knee-high leather boots are of some help. Wear high leather shoes for hiking or climbing, not canvas shoes or oxfords. Watch where you put your hands when you climb. Don't thrust hands or feet under rock ledges, logs, or stumps that might harbor serpents. Use tools to overturn rocks or logs. Stay on paths or trails and watch where you walk. Never go off alone, and always remain within call of your companions.

Fortunately, snake bite is rather rare, and with proper, energetic treatment probably 98 per cent of the victims recover. Your chances of being killed by a snake are considerably fewer than being struck by lightning.

Snake venom is a liquid, usually yellowish in color, secreted by glands on the sides of the head and injected into a victim through hollow fangs (Fig. 3, p. 27). Venoms vary from species to species. In some they attack the blood stream, destroying corpuscles and preventing clotting. Conversely, others promote clotting. Some digest away the tissues. Still other kinds attack the nervous system. Most venoms combine two or more effects. The venoms of the Rattlesnakes, Copperheads, and Cottonmouths are similar enough so the same treatment can be used for all. The accepted procedure consists of: (1) use of a tourniquet; (2) incision and suction; and (3) injection of serum. (See Plate 3, p. 30, for detailed first-aid instructions.)

Serum (antivenin) should be injected by a doctor, but it is well to stock it at your summer home or other locality if there is danger of snake bite. It is not always procurable in a hurry. The use of ice in treating snake bite (cryotherapy), which has received wide

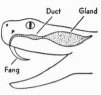

Fig. 3. VENOM MECHANISM OF A PIT VIPER

Duct   Gland

Fang

| Diagram showing location of venom gland, duct, and fang | Bony structure of the head in striking position | Position of mouth and fangs just before impact |

publicity, is still in the experimental stage and is not recommended as a first-aid measure.

Symptoms of snake bite consist of *discoloration* at the site of the bite, marked *swelling*, and great *pain*. The puncture marks from the fangs may not always clearly show. The bites of harmless snakes usually draw far more blood than do bites from venomous ones, and there may be a whole series of scratches or tooth marks. Be sure that a poisonous snake is involved before you start wielding knife or razor blade. Check for the symptoms mentioned above. Most people can identify a Rattlesnake, but in the case of the other dangerous species the culprit is not always seen clearly and the descriptions of eyewitnesses, under pressure of excitement, may be erroneous and misleading. Don't waste time trying to kill the snake, but, if there is another member of your party who can dispatch it, an examination of the carcass will let you know for certain whether or not a venomous species is involved. Compare it carefully with the illustrations and text in this book. Handle the dead snake with extreme care. Reflex action may last a long time, and supposedly dead Copperheads and Rattlesnakes have been known to bite! A quick way to be certain is to study the illustrations on Plates 29 and 30 as soon as you acquire this *Field Guide*, so that you can recognize all the dangerously poisonous species on sight.

A word of caution about bites on fingers or toes: making cuts on digits can cause severe damage if it is not done with great care and skill. In such cases, it is often best not to cut fingers or toes at all, but rather to apply the tourniquet halfway up the forearm or lower leg (or ahead of the swelling), make linear incisions a few inches below it, and apply suction in this region.

The doctor upon his arrival can test the victim for serum sensitivity, he will have proper drugs and stimulants, and he can arrange for transfusions, if necessary, and the use of antibiotics. If you are certain that a poisonous snake is concerned, waste no time in summoning medical help and getting the patient to a hospital.

The bite of a Coral Snake — fortunately extremely rare — presents special difficulties. The venom attacks the nervous system, especially that portion which controls respiration, and the patient may die from suffocation. Ordinary first-aid treatment is largely ineffective, and more reliance must be placed upon serum and medical aid.

Prepare for snake bite in advance by studying the directions that come with your suction kit. Review them and practice with the kit at least once a year.

The B-D Asepto Snake Bite Outfit, manufactured by Becton, Dickinson & Co., Rutherford, N.J., is one of the best kits on the market. Antivenin is a product of Wyeth Laboratories, Philadelphia, Pa. Both may be obtained through any first-class drugstore.

V

Crocodilians

FAMILY CROCODYLIDAE

HUGE lizard-like reptiles occurring in many of the warmer parts of the world. Only two, the American Alligator and the American Crocodile, are found in the United States.

Crocodile: Subfamily Crocodylinae

AMERICAN CROCODILE *Crocodylus acutus* p. 31
Identification: 7½'–12'; record 15' (in U. S.) to 23' (in So. Amer.). The long tapering snout is the hallmark of the American Crocodile. General over-all coloration gray or tannish gray with dusky markings. A large tooth (4th) in lower jaw shows prominently when mouth is closed (Fig., p. 31). This is visible only at close range and is not well developed in young individuals. *Young:* Gray or greenish gray with narrow black crossbands or rows of spots; about 8" or 9" when hatched.

This Crocodile, now rare in the United States, is confined chiefly to the Everglades National Park, Biscayne Bay, and the Florida Keys. Any crocodilian seen in salt or brackish water from Miami southward and along the Keys will *probably* be this species. The Alligator rather rarely leaves fresh water, but is known to occur on Big Pine and other Keys. Although neither of these big reptiles normally attacks human beings, large adults should not be approached. Wounded ones are very dangerous, especially Crocodiles, which are vicious fighters when aroused or captured. Eggs are buried in sand, which may be scooped into low mounds; nests normally are left unguarded, although the female may return to them occasionally.
Similar species: Alligator has broadly rounded snout and no boldly conspicuous tooth in lower jaw. Spectacled Caiman has curved bony ridge in front of eyes.
Voice: *Male:* A low rumble or growl, less intense than and without penetrating power of the Alligator's roar. *Young:* A high-pitched grunt.
Range: Extr. s. Florida and the Keys; Greater Antilles; s. Mexico to Colombia and Ecuador. Map 1

FIRST AID FOR SNAKE BITE

What to do for snake bite should be part of the mental equipment of everyone who spends much time out of doors. If you work,
live, or play where venomous snakes are prevalent, buy yourself a
snake-bite suction kit. Keep it handy, and practice using it at
least once a year.

In case of a bite, keep calm. Assure the victim he has an excellent
chance of recovery. Make him sit or lie still. Remove rings or
bracelets at once if bite is on hand, wrist, or arm. Send someone to
summon a doctor. Follow the steps shown on the opposite page.

1. APPLY TOURNIQUET a few inches above the bite. It must
   impede circulation but not shut it off completely.

2. TEST ITS TIGHTNESS by forcing a finger under it. Loosen
   tourniquet for 30 to 60 seconds every 15 minutes.

3. STERILIZE razor blade or sharp knife, using flame or anti-
   septic. If neither is available, omit sterilization rather than
   incision.

4. MAKE A CUT not more than $\frac{1}{4}''$ deep and $\frac{1}{2}''$ long through
   each fang puncture and parallel to the long axis of the limb.

5. APPLY SUCTION CUP over wound, squeezing air from bulb
   and moistening rim of cup. (Use your mouth for suction if no
   kit is available.) Apply for 3 to 5 minutes, then remove cup,
   squeeze it out, and reapply again in 5 minutes.

6. MOVE TOURNIQUET UPWARD as swelling advances.
   Make additional cuts and apply suction to them.

7. USE TWO SUCTION CUPS (or more) if they are available. If
   not, then rotate cup from one incision to another.

8. APPLY WET COMPRESS over wound. Suction should be
   continued en route to the hospital.

Use a necktie, belt, etc., if no regular tourniquet is at hand.
Avoid use of alcoholic beverages. Antivenin (snake-bite serum) is
best administered by a doctor. Arrange for transportation of the
patient to a hospital.

Be sure that a poisonous snake was involved before starting first aid.
Additional information on the snake-bite problem will be found
on p. 26.

1. Apply Tourniquet

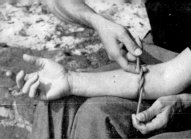

2. Test Its Tightness

3. Sterilize

4. Make a Cut

5. Apply Suction Cup

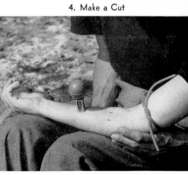

6. Move Tourniquet Upward

7. Use Two Suction Cups

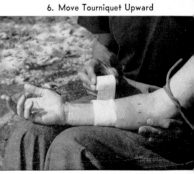

8. Apply Wet Compress

YOUNG

ALLIGATOR

CAIMAN

CROCODILE

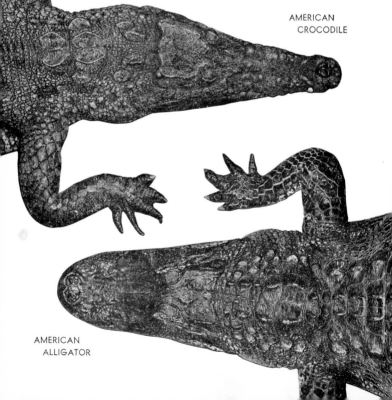

AMERICAN
CROCODILE

AMERICAN
ALLIGATOR

Plate 4   31

CROCODILIANS

YOUNG

	Map	Text
AMERICAN ALLIGATOR	1	32

Black with yellowish lines. Head smooth in front of eyes
(as in photograph of adult Alligator).

| **SPECTACLED CAIMAN** | | 32 |

Gray with dark brown crossbands. A curved, bony, crosswise ridge in front of eyes.

| **AMERICAN CROCODILE** | 1 | 29 |

Gray or greenish gray with black crossbands or rows of
spots. Head tapering toward snout (as in photograph of
adult Crocodile).

ADULTS

| **AMERICAN CROCODILE** | 1 | 29 |

Tapering head; 4th tooth of lower jaw fitting into a groove
in upper jaw and remaining visible when mouth is closed.

| **AMERICAN ALLIGATOR** | 1 | 32 |

Broadly rounded snout.

Note: All the animals depicted on any one plate are shown in scale
with one another. *But* a black line across a plate denotes a change
in scale, as in the case of the young crocodilians on the opposite
page, which are proportionately larger than the adults.

Side of head:

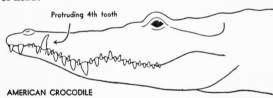

Protruding 4th tooth

AMERICAN CROCODILE

Top of head:

Curved bony ridge

SPECTACLED
CAIMAN
(Young)

Alligator and Caiman: Subfamily Alligatorinae

AMERICAN ALLIGATOR   *Alligator mississipiensis*   p. 31
  Identification: 6′–12′; record 19′ 2″. The broadly rounded snout
  will distinguish this big reptile from the American Crocodile, the
  only species with which an adult Alligator could possibly be
  confused in the field. General coloration black, but light
  markings of young may persist (not too conspicuously) into
  adulthood. *Young:* Bold yellowish crossbands on black ground
  color; about 9″ at hatching.
  The Alligator is a characteristic resident of the great river
  swamps, lakes, bayous, and marshes of Florida and the Gulf and
  Lower Atlantic Coastal Plains. All sizes bask, smaller ones most
  frequently. Watch for eyes, heads, or snouts protruding from
  water surface of 'gator holes along wilder waterways of the
  South. Nests, mounds of vegetable debris 4 to 7 feet in diameter,
  2 or 3 feet high, and in which the eggs are buried, should be approached with caution from spring to early autumn, when there
  may be a guarding female in attendance nearby.
  Similar species: American Crocodile has tapering snout and,
  except in small individuals, a lower jaw tooth protrudes conspicuously outside upper jaw near snout (Fig., p. 31). Spectacled Caiman has curved, bony, crosswise ridge in front of eyes
  (Fig., p. 31).
  Voice: *Adult male:* A throaty, bellowing roar with great carrying
  power. *Young:* A moaning grunt, like saying *umph — umph —
  umph* with mouth closed and in a fairly high key. All sizes hiss;
  the female grunts like a pig in calling her young, which she
  may actively protect from other predators. They may remain
  with her until the spring after they hatch.
  Range: North Carolina to the Florida Keys and west to cent.
  Texas. Extermination over large areas, plus the finding of
  escaped pet specimens in numerous localities, makes the preparation of a range map difficult. When given protection, the Alligator prospers and soon reoccupies areas where it has long been
  absent.   Map 1

SPECTACLED CAIMAN   *Caiman sclerops*   p. 31
  Identification: 3½′–6′; record 8′ 8″. *Not native,* and included
  here only because great numbers of juveniles are sold in the pet
  trade as "baby alligators." Escaped or liberated specimens may
  occasionally be met in the field, even in northern states (at least
  in summer). Ground color greenish-, yellowish-, or brownish-
  gray with dark brown crossbands. Bony ridge in front of eyes
  (Fig., p. 31) may be broken or irregular, but it is by far the best
  means of identification. *Young:* About 8″ at hatching.

Similar species: Young Alligators are *black* with yellowish crossbands. Other small crocodilians are imported for the pet trade. If in doubt, consult the nearest zoo or natural history museum.

Range: S. Mexico to ne. Brazil.

VI

Turtles

FAMILY CHELYDRIDAE

Snapping Turtles: Subfamily Chelydrinae

LARGE fresh-water turtles with short tempers and long tails; of economic value and ranging collectively from Canada to South America. This subfamily and the one containing the Musk and Mud Turtles (p. 35) are subdivisions of the Family Chelydridae.

SNAPPING TURTLE *Chelydra serpentina* pp. 47, 79
  Identification: 8–12, record 18½; 10 to 35 lbs., but to 86 lbs. for fattened captive ones. Ugly both in appearance and disposition, this fresh-water "loggerhead" is easily recognized by its large head, small plastron, and long tail, which is saw-toothed along the upper side. Carapace in adults varies from almost black to light "horn" brown. *Young:* (Plate 6) Blackish or dark brown, a light spot at edge of each marginal scute. Carapace very rough and with 3 fairly well defined longitudinal keels. (The rugose condition becomes less prominent as turtle grows older; adults tend to become smooth, but usually retain traces of the keels.) Tail as long as carapace or longer. Carapace about 1" to 1¼" at hatching.
  Any permanent body of fresh water, large or small, is a potential home for a Snapper; it even enters brackish water. Snappers *rarely bask* as most other turtles do. Under water they are usually inoffensive, pulling in their heads when stepped upon. They often bury themselves in mud in shallow water with only eyes showing. On land they may strike repeatedly; a favorite maneuver is to stand with hind quarters elevated and jaws agape and then lunge forward. Small and medium-sized specimens may be carried by their tails (Plate 1, p. 14). Keep plastron side toward your leg. Omnivorous — food includes various small aquatic invertebrates, fishes, reptiles, birds, mammals, carrion, and a surprisingly large amount of vegetation. Economically very important: large numbers are caught for making soups and stews.
  Similar species: Alligator Snapper has an extra row of scutes between marginals and costals. Mud and Musk Turtles have short tails and (adults) smooth shells.
  Range: S. Canada to Gulf of Mexico; Atlantic Ocean to Rocky Mountains, and introduced farther west.

Subspecies: COMMON SNAPPING TURTLE, *Chelydra serpentina serpentina* (illustrated on Plates 6 and 10). As described above and with range as stated. FLORIDA SNAPPING TURTLE, *Chelydra serpentina osceola*. Similar, but with the knobs on the keels more toward the centers of the large scutes; 3 rows of large "teeth" on tail instead of one. *Young:* Chestnut-brown; keels and ridges very prominent. Cent. and s. Florida.

Map 3

ALLIGATOR SNAPPING TURTLE
Macroclemys temmincki   pp. 47, 79

Identification: 15–26+; 35–150 lbs., record 219 lbs. The huge head with its strongly hooked beak, the prominent dorsal keels, and the *extra row of scutes* on each side of the carapace set the Alligator Snapper aside from all others. Likely to be confused only with Common Snapper. *Young:* (Plate 6) Brown, shell exceedingly rough; tail very long.

This gigantic fresh-water turtle, our largest and one of largest in the world, often lies at bottom of lake or river with mouth wide open. A curious pink process on floor of mouth resembles a worm, wriggles like one, and serves as a lure for fishes.

Similar species: Common Snapper has a saw-toothed tail, a smaller head, and also lacks the extra row of scutes between costals and marginals.

Range: S. Georgia and n. Florida to cent. Texas; north in Mississippi Valley to Kansas, Illinois, and sw. Indiana.   Map 2

Musk and Mud Turtles:
Subfamily Kinosterninae

THESE ARE the "stinkpots," the "skillpots," and the "stinking-jims" that often take the fisherman's hook. Such inelegant names derive from a musky secretion exuded at the time of capture from two glandular openings on each side of the body. These are situated where the skin meets the underside of the carapace.

"Bottom crawlers" would be a good way to describe these reptiles. They are aquatic, the Musk Turtles especially, and rarely leave the water except during rains or in the nesting season. They bask in the open occasionally, but are more likely to "take the sun" in shallow water with only part of the shell exposed above the surface. Try to catch them if you can, for identification is difficult without flipping them over for a look at the plastron. Use a net or hold the shell far back — their jaws are strong, necks long, and many are very short-tempered.

The Musk Turtles (*Sternothaerus*) have relatively small plastrons that offer little protection for the legs. The anterior lobe is movable on a transverse hinge situated between the 2d and 3d *pairs* of plastral scutes (Fig. 4, below), but the hinge usually is not apparent to the eye. It may be demonstrated, however, by moving the front tip of the plastron up and down. The pectoral scutes are squarish. This genus ranges from southern Ontario southward to and through the Gulf States.

The Mud Turtles (*Kinosternon*) have much larger plastrons equipped with *two readily discernible* transverse hinges (Fig. 4, below). (The hinges are not developed in the young of either genus.) The pectoral scutes are triangular in shape. *Kinosternon* ranges from New England to northern South America.

The two genera share the following characteristics: there are barbels (downward fleshy projections) on the chin and/or neck. The marginal scutes, including the nuchal, are almost always 23 in number. Most other turtles have 25. At hatching the young vary from about ¾″ to 1″ in carapace length.

These turtles are often mistaken for young Snappers, but the Snapping Turtle has a long tail with saw-toothed projections on top. Musk and Mud Turtles have short tails, but these are useful in distinguishing sexes. Males have longer, stouter tails; in females the tails may be little more than nubbins. Males also have 2 rough patches of skin on the hind leg; the patches touch each other when the knee is flexed.

Fig. 4. PLASTRONS OF MUD AND MUSK TURTLES

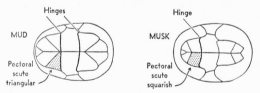

STINKPOT *Sternothaerus odoratus*   pp. 47, 78
  Identification: 3¼–4½; record 5⅜. The only Musk Turtle occurring north of "Dixie." Three characteristics distinguish it from all other Musk Turtles: (1) 2 light stripes on head; (2) barbels on chin *and throat*; and (3) scutes of carapace usually do not overlap (except in very young). Dark pigment may at least partly obscure the head stripes, and in extreme cases the head may be uniformly black. Smooth carapace varies from light olive-brown to almost black and may be irregularly streaked or spotted with dark pigment. Plastron *small* and with *single* hinge. *Male:* Broad areas of skin showing between scutes of plastron; tail thick and terminating in a blunt, horny nail. *Female:* Only small areas of skin showing between plastral scutes; tail very small and with or without a sharp horny nail. *Young:* Carapace black, rough in texture, and with prominent middorsal keel that

gradually disappears with age; traces of a smaller keel on each side; head stripes prominent; light spot on each marginal (see Plate 6).

Extraordinarily abundant in many bodies of water, but not often observed except in shallow, clear-water lakes, ponds, and rivers. In these it may be seen leisurely patrolling the bottom in search of food, its shell looking like a rounded stone, and the illusion being heightened by the green algae that grow on many specimens. Still waters are preferred.

If a turtle ever falls on your head or drops into your canoe, it probably will be this one. Slanting boles of relatively slender trees are occasionally ascended by several species of turtles in wooded swamps, along watercourses, or at edges of marshes, where horizontal basking places are at a premium. Because of small size of plastron and consequent greater mobility of legs, the Stinkpot climbs the highest, sometimes 6 or more feet above surface of water. Sleepy ones may not drop off until your boat passes below them.

Similar species: All other Musk Turtles share the following: (1) heads with *dark* spots, stripes, or streaks on light ground color; (2) barbels on chin *only*; and (3) each large scute of carapace slightly overlapping its neighbor to the rear. Mud Turtles have *large* plastrons with *two* hinges. Snappers have long stout tails.

Range: New England and s. Ontario to s. Florida; west to Wisconsin and Texas. The Stinkpot occurs in many of the larger, more sluggish streams that penetrate the mountains, but it is lacking at the higher elevations.   Map 7

RAZOR-BACKED MUSK TURTLE
Sternothaerus carinatus   p. 78

Identification: 4–5; record 5⅞. The upper shell reminds one of the legendary razor-backed hog. A keel is present in *all* turtles of this species, from newest hatchling to oldest adult, and sides of carapace slope down like a tent (Fig. 5, p. 38). Head with dark spots on light ground color. Carapace with dark spots, streaks, or blotches; old adults may lose their patterns and become almost plain horn-colored; scutes slightly overlapping. Plastron *small*; a *single* hinge; *no* gular scute. Barbels on *chin only*.

A turtle of the streams and great river swamps of the mid-South. Carapace often shows signs of disease in that margins of shell are irregular where bone and overlying tissue have crumbled away. Basks much more frequently than other Musk Turtles.

Similar species: Stinkpot normally has 2 light lines on head; also has barbels on *throat* as well as chin. All Mud Turtles have *large* plastrons with *two* hinges.

Range: Se. Mississippi to cent. Texas; north to Arkansas and se. Oklahoma.   Map 8

Fig. 5. TRANSVERSE CROSS SECTIONS OF YOUNG MUSK TURTLES

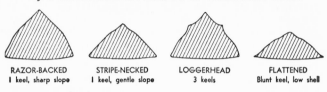

| RAZOR-BACKED | STRIPE-NECKED | LOGGERHEAD | FLATTENED |
| 1 keel, sharp slope | 1 keel, gentle slope | 3 keels | Blunt keel, low shell |

LOGGERHEAD MUSK TURTLE

Sternothaerus minor minor   pp. 47, 78

Identification: 3½–4½; record 5. The only Musk Turtle with *3 distinct keels* (Fig. 5, above). Distinguishing this reptile would be easy if one could stop right there. But, alas, the keels vanish in old adults. Check the following things first and then allow for sex and age: scutes of carapace overlapping; plastron *small* with *one* hinge and 1 gular scute; barbels on *chin only*; head normally marked with dark spots on a light ground color. *Old male:* Head enormously enlarged. *Female:* Carapace streaked, spotted, or blotched. *Young:* 3 keels that may persist into adulthood; carapace strongly streaked with dark rays; hatchling with *pink* plastron (see Plate 6).

A common turtle of the large clear Florida springs. Like the Stinkpot, it may climb up snags or cypress knees a considerable distance above the water.

Similar species: Stinkpot has carapace scutes that do *not* overlap, barbels on chin *and neck*, and normally 2 light lines on each side of head. Stripe-necked Musk Turtle has only 1 keel. Mud Turtles have *large* plastrons with *two* hinges.

Range: Cent. Georgia to se. Alabama and n. Florida.   Map 9

STRIPE-NECKED MUSK TURTLE

Sternothaerus minor peltifer   p. 78

Identification: 3–4; record 4½. Dark stripes on sides of head and neck. A single middorsal keel, prominent in young (Fig. 5, above) but disappearing in older specimens. Carapace gray or brown with dark streaks or spots; large scutes slightly overlapping. Plastron *small*, with *one* hinge; single gular scute. Barbels on *chin only*. *Young:* Traces of an additional keel may be evident on each side of carapace.

At home in many streams and rivers of the mid-South. Ascends clear, shallow creeks to elevation of approximately 1000 feet at the edges of the mountains.

Similar species: (See Fig. 5, above, for shapes of shells.) Sides of head in both Razor-backed and Loggerhead Musk Turtles are marked with dark spots on a light ground color; also, Razor-back has *no* gular scute. Stinkpot has 2 light lines on head and barbels on chin *and* throat Mud Turtles have *large* plastrons with *two* hinges.

Range: E. Tennessee to the Pearl River, Mississippi.   Map 9

FLATTENED MUSK TURTLE *Sternothaerus depressus*   p. 78
Identification: 3–4; record 4 3/16. An extraordinary little turtle that looks almost as though a man with a heavy foot had trod upon it. In comparison with other Musk Turtles the carapace is quite flattened, even in old adults. In the young there is a blunted dorsal keel and the carapace flares out at sides (Fig. 5, p. 38); older specimens have flat shells rounded at edges. Head and neck with network of dark lines on light ground color. Scutes of carapace slightly overlapping. Plastron *small*, a gular scute present. Barbels on *chin only*.

Range: Black Warrior River system of nw. Alabama.   Map 8

STRIPED MUD TURTLE *Kinosternon bauri*   p. 78
Identification: 3–4; record 4¾. The 3 light stripes on the shell (one down center and another at each side) may be obscure, par-ticularly in older turtles. If in doubt, also check the head for 2 light stripes on each side. In some specimens scutes of carapace are so nearly transparent that vague outlines of underlying bony structure may be seen through them. *Young:* A narrow mid-dorsal keel; carapace rough; a light spot on each marginal.

Less aquatic than other Mud Turtles, often prowling on land, even in daytime. Habitats include wet meadows, ditches, and other small, shallow bodies of water; also found in deep drainage canals.

Similar species: Musk Turtles have *small* plastrons with only *one* hinge.

Range: Okefenokee Swamp, Georgia, to Florida Keys.

Subspecies: STRIPED MUD TURTLE, *Kinosternon bauri palmarum* (illustrated on Plate 9). As described above and with lower beak heavily streaked with dark pigment. All of range ex-cept lower Florida Keys. KEY MUD TURTLE, *Kinosternon bauri bauri.* Similar but darker; both head and shell stripes may be obscured or almost obliterated by dark pigment; lower jaw not streaked or only slightly so. Lower Florida Keys, from Big Pine Key to Key West.   Map 11

YELLOW MUD TURTLE *Kinosternon flavescens*   p. 78
Identification: 4–5; record 5¾. The yellowish chin and throat, that sometimes may be seen from a distance when the turtle is prowling in shallow water or basking at the surface, is a good field character (at least for the western subspecies). But the 9th marginal scute makes identification positive. This scale is

distinctly higher than the 8th marginal (10th marginal is also high). Carapace, usually flat or even depressed on top, is olive-brown to olive-green in coloration. Head and neck olive above. *Young:* 9th and 10th marginals as low as 8th (or even lower); 9th and 10th begin to enlarge when shell reaches a length of about 2½".

A common turtle throughout much of the range, occurring in a wide variety of bodies of water, but usually those with muddy bottoms. Toward the west it also utilizes such artificial habitats as cattle tanks, irrigation ditches, cisterns, and sewer drains. May appear on land during rains, while migrating when pools are drying up, or when merely foraging.

Similar species: In all our other Mud Turtles, 9th marginal scute is same size or only slightly larger than 8th. Musk Turtles have *small* plastrons with only *one* hinge.

Range: Illinois to n. Mexico.

Subspecies: YELLOW MUD TURTLE, *Kinosternon flavescens flavescens* (illustrated on Plate 9). As described above. S. Nebraska to se. Arizona and Coahuila. Mexican subspecies. ILLINOIS MUD TURTLE, *Kinosternon flavescens spooneri.* Similar but with soft parts black or dark gray, carapace dark brown, and yellow pigment restricted to barbels and front half of lower jaw. Sand prairies of cent. and nw. Illinois; adj. Iowa and Missouri.   Map 10

EASTERN MUD TURTLE
Kinosternon subrubrum subrubrum   pp. 47, 78

Identification: 3–4; record 4⅞. Adults have no distinctive field marks, but throughout most of its range this is the only Mud Turtle. Carapace smooth and some shade of brown, varying from olive "horn" color to almost black. The large double-hinged plastron may be plain yellowish brown or slightly to heavily marked with black or dark brown. A broad bridge between the shells. Head spotted, mottled, or irregularly streaked with yellow. *Young:* (Plate 6) Carapace rough, black or very dark brown, and with a middorsal keel; an imperfect additional keel on each side. Plastron usually black in center and along the sutures (sometimes virtually solid black); lighter parts yellow, orange, or reddish; a bright spot on each marginal.

Essentially an aquatic reptile, but wandering away from water more often than the Stinkpot. Shallow water preferred — ditches, wet meadows, small ponds, marshes, etc. This Mud Turtle has a strong tolerance for brackish water, and is often abundant at inner edges of tidal marshes and on many offshore islands.

Similar species: Striped Mud Turtle has striped head and carapace. Yellow Mud Turtle has 9th marginal scute much higher than 8th. Musk Turtles have *small* plastrons with only a *single* hinge.

Range: Sw. Connecticut and Indiana to Gulf Coast. Map 12

MISSISSIPPI MUD TURTLE
Kinosternon subrubrum hippocrepis p. 78

Identification: 3–4¾. The distinctive characters of two very different turtles are combined in this Mud Turtle. It has the large double-hinged plastron of its genus, but also sports 2 light head stripes like the Stinkpot's. Otherwise, similar to Eastern Mud Turtle, with which it intergrades chiefly east of Mississippi River.

A common turtle of bayous, lagoons, and great swamps of lower Mississippi Valley.

Similar species: In Yellow Mud Turtle the 9th marginal scute is much higher than 8th.

Range: Missouri to Louisiana and e. cent. Texas. Map 12

FLORIDA MUD TURTLE
Kinosternon subrubrum steindachneri p. 78

Identification: 3–4; record 4¾. Like the Eastern Mud Turtle, but with two main differences: (1) movable hind lobe of plastron is short, often shorter than front lobe; and (2) bridge connecting plastron to carapace is quite narrow. Hence, plastron is smaller, proportionately, than in any other Mud Turtle, and in size it approaches the less extensive plastron of a Musk Turtle. Another point of similarity: many adult males have greatly enlarged heads, rivaling those of big male Loggerhead Musk Turtles.

Drainage ditches, marshes, sloughs, ponds, and other small bodies of water. More aquatic than Eastern Mud Turtle, with which it intergrades in northern Florida.

Similar species: Striped Mud Turtle has light stripes on head and carapace. Musk Turtles have only *one* plastral hinge.

Range: Peninsular Florida. Map 12

FAMILY TESTUDINIDAE

Box and Water Turtles: Subfamily Emydinae

A LARGE GROUP with representatives in all the continents except Australia, and with many kinds in eastern North America (genera *Clemmys*, p. 42, to *Emydoidea*, p. 65, inclusive). This subfamily and the one containing the Gopher Tortoises (p. 65) are subdivisions of the Family Testudinidae.

Spotted, Bog, and Wood Turtles:
Genus *Clemmys*

THESE ARE residents chiefly of the Northeast; other members of the genus occur in Europe, Asia, and North Africa, and one lives in our Pacific states. Most of these turtles live well in captivity, but they need a "land" area of some size, over which to wander and exercise, plus shelters, both in and out of the water, where they can hide whenever they wish.

SPOTTED TURTLE   *Clemmys guttata*   pp. 47, 62
    Identification: 3½–4½; record 5. The "polka-dot turtle." The yellow spots are extremely variable in number. Hatchlings usually have 1 spot in each large scute, but older turtles may be well sprinkled, their spots totaling 100 or more. Conversely, spots may be few or (rarely) lacking entirely. In such cases, examine head and neck for several yellow or orange spots. *Young:* (Plate 6) About 1⅛" at hatching.
    At home in marshy meadows, bogs, swamps, small ponds, ditches, or other shallow bodies of water. Seldom in a hurry. Basking specimens usually enter the water rather leisurely when disturbed, hiding themselves nearby in mud or debris at bottom. *Much* more frequently seen in spring than at other seasons.
    Similar species: Bog Turtle has a large orange head patch. Blanding's Turtle has great numbers of yellow spots and a *hinged plastron*.
    Range: S. Maine to extr. e. Illinois; south in the East to Georgia.   Map 6

BOG TURTLE   *Clemmys muhlenbergi*   p. 62
    Identification: 3–3½; record 4¼. Formerly called "Muhlenberg's turtle." The head patch sometimes is yellow or split into 2 parts. Large scutes of carapace may have yellowish or reddish centers. *Young:* About 1" at hatching.
    Although the Bog Turtle still occurs in certain areas, it is rare or completely absent in many regions where it once was fairly abundant. Sphagnum bogs, swamps, and clear, slow-moving meadow streams with muddy bottoms are preferred. Man's propensity for draining and "reclaiming" such habitats has contributed to its disappearance.
    Similar species: Spotted Turtles, a rare few of which completely lack yellow dots on their shells, have many separate yellow or orange spots on their heads and necks.
    Range: New York to w. North Carolina in disjunct colonies; from near sea level in the North to 4000 feet in the southern mountains.   Map 4

WOOD TURTLE *Clemmys insculpta* pp. 47, 62
   Identification: 5½–7½; record 9. The "sculptured turtle."
   Shell very rough; each large scute in the form of an irregular
   pyramid rising upward in series of concentric grooves and ridges.
   Orange on neck and limbs led to vernacular name of "redleg"
   back in the days when this was an important market turtle.
   Young: (Plate 6) Shell broad and low, brown or grayish brown;
   no orange on neck or legs; tail almost as long as carapace; 1 ³⁄₁₆″
   to 1 ⅝″ at hatching.
   Next to Gopher Tortoises and Box Turtles, this is our most
   terrestrial turtle. Although quite at home in water and hibernating there, it frequently wanders far afield through woods and
   meadows, across farmlands, and — often with fatal results —
   on roads and highways. As a pet it is unexcelled among reptiles,
   usually showing far more responsiveness than one might expect
   from a turtle.
   Similar species: Both other "land turtles" occurring within the
   range of Wood Turtle (Blanding's and Eastern Box) have
   strongly *hinged* plastrons. Adult Diamondbacks are also sculptured, but are restricted to maritime marshes and their environs
   along the coast; baby Diamondbacks are strongly patterned
   (Plate 5).
   Range: Nova Scotia to e. Minnesota; south in uplands to
   Virginia. Map 5

Box Turtles: Genus *Terrapene*

THESE ARE the "dry-land turtles" that close their shells tightly
when danger threatens. Their hallmark is a broad hinge across
the plastron, providing movable lobes both fore and aft (Fig.,
p. 62); these fit so neatly against the upper shell that in many
individuals not even a knife blade may be inserted. With such
close-fitting armor, Box Turtles are well adapted for a terrestrial
life, even though they are much more closely related to some of
the water turtles than to the Gopher Tortoises they superficially
resemble. The upper jaw ends in a down-turned beak. In hatchlings (average 1⅛″ to 1¼″) the hinge is not functional. The
young have a median dorsal ridge, evidences of which may persist
in adults. Box Turtles, strictly North American, range widely
over the eastern and central United States and through Mexico.
   As adults, Box Turtles are kept more frequently as pets than
any other turtles. Most adapt themselves readily to captivity,
requiring only a back yard or a box of dirt for digging and a shallow
pan of water for an occasional soaking. They are omnivorous, and
are fond of fruits, berries, and raw hamburger. Many people feed
them table scraps. Ages of 30 and 40 years are common, and a
very few may reach the century mark.

EASTERN BOX TURTLE

Terrapene carolina carolina pp. 47, 62

Identification: 4½–6; record 6½. A "land turtle" with a high, domelike shell and an extremely variable coloration and pattern. Both upper and lower shells may be yellow, orange, or olive on black or brown; either dark or light colors may predominate. *Male:* Rear lobe of plastron with central concave area; eyes sometimes red. *Female:* Plastron flat or slightly convex; eyes normally brown. *Young:* (Plate 6) Shell much flatter; mostly plain grayish brown, but with spot of yellow on each large scute.

Although essentially terrestrial, these turtles sometimes soak themselves by the hour (or day) in mud or water. During hot, dry weather they burrow beneath logs or rotting vegetation, but sharp summer showers usually bring them out of hiding, often in numbers.

Similar species: Top of carapace is flattened in Ornate Box Turtle. Gopher Tortoises have no plastral hinges. Blanding's Turtle has flatter shell, profusion of light dots, and plastral lobes that don't shut tight. Obese Box Turtles also cannot close tight (thus leaving themselves vulnerable to enemies); but, by pushing down one lobe at a time with the fingers, you can check on whether the closure in the turtle's younger and slimmer days would have been complete.

Range: S. Maine to Georgia, west to Michigan, Illinois, and Tennessee. Intergrades with all three other races.

Subspecies: GULF COAST BOX TURTLE, *Terrapene carolina major*. Attains larger size (in excess of 7") and has rear margin of carapace flaring outward instead of extending almost straight downward as in Eastern Box Turtle. Tendency for light markings to be obscured by black or horn color in adults. Gulf Coast, Florida panhandle to e. Texas. Map 28

FLORIDA BOX TURTLE *Terrapene carolina bauri* pp. 47, 62

Identification: 5–6½; record 6¾. The light radiating lines may be broken or irregular, at least on some scutes. Also the 2 head lines may be interrupted or incomplete. Usually 3 but sometimes 4 toes on each hind foot. *Young:* Yellowish middorsal stripe, involving keel; pattern mottled, yellowish or greenish on dark brown (see Plate 6).

Range: Peninsular Florida and lower Keys. Map 28

THREE-TOED BOX TURTLE

Terrapene carolina triunguis p. 62

Identification: 4½–5; record 6½. Don't depend entirely on the toes — it sometimes has 4! The Florida Box Turtle also usually has only 3 toes on each hind foot, and so do some specimens of all other subspecies. A marked tendency for pattern to be replaced (sometimes completely) by plain olive- or horn-colored areas;

plastron often plain yellow or horn-colored. Orange or yellow spots usually conspicuous on both head and forelimbs.

Similar species: In Ornate Box Turtle carapace is flattened on top and the pattern of "rayed" yellow lines is quite constant. Habitat will often separate the two. Ornate most often occurs in open, treeless areas; Three-toed, like its related subspecies, in woodlands, thickets, etc.

Range: Missouri to Texas and Alabama.   Map 28

ORNATE BOX TURTLE   *Terrapene ornata ornata*   p. 62
  Identification: 4–5; record 5¾. Well ornamented above and below and showing far less variation than other Box Turtles. Light lines radiate downward from 3 centers on each side of carapace. The strong plastral pattern is quite characteristic. Other features: carapace flat on top, sometimes dished-in, and almost never with any traces of a keel; plastron large, usually as long as, or longer than, carapace.

  A species of the plains and prairies, often found in sandy areas and able to tolerate more arid conditions than its eastern relatives. Burrows to escape heat; rainstorms sometimes result in the appearance of incredible numbers.

  Similar species: Three-toed and Eastern Box Turtles, aside from their different patterns, also have high, arched shells and usually retain evidences of a dorsal keel.

  Range: Indiana to se. Wyoming, south through Texas; range discontinuous toward northeast. Western subspecies. Map 26

Diamondback Terrapins:
Genus *Malaclemys*

MOST CELEBRATED of American turtles. Their succulent flesh, when properly (and laboriously) prepared, rates high upon the gourmet's list. During the heyday of the "terrapin" fad, market hunting seriously reduced them in numbers, but their popularity has waned and they have made a strong comeback in many areas. Terrapins are reptiles of the coastal marshes, rarely straying from salt or brackish water. Their food includes fish, crustaceans, mollusks, and insects. Seven races are recognized, all of a single species, and ranging, collectively, from Massachusetts at least to s. Texas.

Concentric grooves and ridges or concentric dark and light markings on each of the large scutes of the carapace are characteristic. So are the flecked or spotted heads and legs. The carapace has a central keel, low and inconspicuous in the Atlantic Coast races, but prominent and often knobbed in the subspecies along the Gulf of Mexico. Individual variation is great, and some forms are confusingly alike; therefore it is well to lean heavily on geography (the

YOUNG TURTLES (1)

	Map	*Text*
WESTERN PAINTED TURTLE	21	55

Pale wormlike markings. *Plastron:* Dark area large and
with outward extensions.

MIDLAND PAINTED TURTLE   21   54

No bold markings. *Plastron:* Dark central blotch.

SOUTHERN PAINTED TURTLE   21   55

Broad red, orange, or yellow stripe.

EASTERN PAINTED TURTLE   21   54

The large scutes have light borders. *Plastron:* Usually unmarked.

NORTHERN DIAMONDBACK TERRAPIN   19   48

Dark lines parallel edges of scutes (both shells).

RED-EARED TURTLE   24   57

Red patch behind eye. *Plastron:* Circular markings large
and involving all parts of shell.

YELLOW-BELLIED TURTLE   24   57

Large yellow patch behind eye. *Plastron:* Circular markings on forepart of shell.

PENINSULA COOTER   23   60

Curved lines on shell. *Plastron:* Unmarked. Dark spots
on anterior marginals.

SLIDER   22   59

Markings circular, especially on marginals. *Plastron:*
Markings chiefly along seams.

CHICKEN TURTLE   30   64

Network of light lines; has striped "pants" (Fig., p. 110).

FLORIDA SOFTSHELL   34   73

Head striped; large round spots. *Plastron:* Dark.

EASTERN SPINY SOFTSHELL   35   70

Small circular spots. *Plastron:* Light and nearly matching
underside of carapace.

SMOOTH SOFTSHELL   33   70

Indistinct dots and dashes. *Plastron:* Light. (Underside
of carapace brown.)

WESTERN PAINTED

SOUTHERN PAINTED

MIDLAND PAINTED

EASTERN PAINTED

NORTHERN
DIAMONDBACK

RED-EARED

YELLOW-BELLIED

PENINSULA COOTER

SLIDER

CHICKEN

FLORIDA
SOFTSHELL

EASTERN SPINY SOFTSHELL

SMOOTH SOFTSHELL

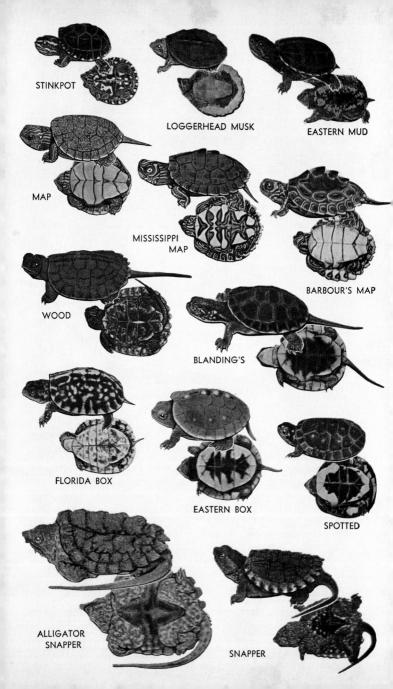

STINKPOT

LOGGERHEAD MUSK

EASTERN MUD

MAP

MISSISSIPPI MAP

BARBOUR'S MAP

WOOD

BLANDING'S

FLORIDA BOX

EASTERN BOX

SPOTTED

ALLIGATOR SNAPPER

SNAPPER

Plate 6   47

YOUNG TURTLES (2)

	Map	Text

STINKPOT   7   36
Light head lines. Edge of shell with light spots.

LOGGERHEAD MUSK TURTLE   9   38
3 keels along top of shell. *Plastron:* Pink.

EASTERN MUD TURTLE   12   40
No lines on head. *Plastron:* Orange to pale yellow; dark
at center.

MAP TURTLE   14   49
Yellow spot behind eye; maplike lines on shell. *Plastron:*
Dark lines along seams.

MISSISSIPPI MAP TURTLE   18   51
Yellowish crescent behind eye. *Plastron:* Broad dark
markings with open centers.

BARBOUR'S MAP TURTLE   16   50
Saw-backed; broad light area behind eye and another
across chin.

WOOD TURTLE   5   43
Shell rough; head dark, unmarked; long tail.

BLANDING'S TURTLE   29   65
Light marks on head; chin yellow; long tail.

FLORIDA BOX TURTLE   28   44
Yellow middorsal stripe; irregular pattern.

EASTERN BOX TURTLE   28   44
Light spot in each large scute. *Plastron:* Dark pigment
concentrated toward center.

SPOTTED TURTLE   6   42
Light spot in each large scute *and spots on head.* *Plastron:*
Dark pigment toward center.

ALLIGATOR SNAPPING TURTLE   2   35
Shell extremely rough; beaks strongly hooked; long tail.

SNAPPING TURTLE   3   34
Shell rough, edged with light spots; long tail.

place where the turtle is seen or collected) in making identifications.

Females grow considerably larger than males. The sizes given in the text are the standard full lengths of the carapace (see back endpaper). Terrapin marketers use a different system — the length of the *plastron* from its front end to the bottom of the notch at the rear.

NORTHERN DIAMONDBACK TERRAPIN

Malaclemys terrapin terrapin   pp. 46, 62

Identification: Adult females 6–8¾; males 4–5½. The salt-marsh or brackish-water habitat is a good field character. Concentric rings or ridges and spotted head and limbs clinch identification when turtle is at hand. Coloration extremely variable: some specimens have carapace boldly patterned with dark rings on a ground of light gray or light brown, others have shell uniform black or dark brown; plastron orange or yellowish- to greenish-gray, and with or without bold dark markings. In this race the carapace is wedge-shaped when viewed from above, with widest part in rear half; plastron has nearly parallel sides. *Young:* (Plate 5) More brightly patterned than most adults; about 1⅛″ to 1¼″ at hatching.

Coastal marshes, tide flats, coves, estuaries, inner edges of barrier beaches — in general, any sheltered and unpolluted body of salt or brackish water.

Similar species: The rough-shelled Wood Turtle has orange on head and limbs, and it avoids salt water. Snappers and Mud Turtles frequently enter brackish water — Snapper has a long saw-toothed tail, Mud Turtles have hinged plastrons.

Range: Coastal strip, Cape Cod to Cape Hatteras.

Subspecies: CAROLINA DIAMONDBACK TERRAPIN, *Malaclemys terrapin centrata.* Very similar, but with sides of carapace more nearly parallel, and sides of plastron tending to curve inward toward rear. Coastal strip, Cape Hatteras to n. Florida. FLORIDA EAST COAST TERRAPIN, *Malaclemys terrapin tequesta.* Carapace dark or horn-colored and without a pattern of concentric circles; centers of large scutes only a little lighter than areas surrounding them. E. coast of Florida. MANGROVE TERRAPIN, *Malaclemys terrapin rhizophorarum.* Dark spots on neck fused together, producing boldly streaked appearance; bulbous bumps on dorsal keel; has striped "pants." The Florida Keys, chiefly among mangroves.   Map 19

ORNATE DIAMONDBACK TERRAPIN

Malaclemys terrapin macrospilota   p. 62

Identification: Adult females 6–8; males 4–5½. The orange or yellow centers of the large scutes distinguish this Diamondback from all other races. Bulbous bumps or tubercles on middorsal keel are evident in many specimens, juveniles and males especially. *Young:* Entire shell light horn color, except that dorsal scutes are narrowly bordered with black; tubercles also black.

At home in coastal streams and passes, especially those bordered by mangroves. Also may wander offshore or take refuge in the tall stiff grasses that characterize many Gulf beaches.

Range: Florida w. coast, Florida Bay to the panhandle.

Subspecies: MISSISSIPPI DIAMONDBACK TERRAPIN, *Malaclemys terrapin pileata.* A dark turtle; carapace usually uniform black or brown; skin very dark; plastron yellow, often clouded with a dusky shade; a strongly tuberculate central keel; edges of shell orange or yellow and turned upward; most males and some females with a black "mustache" on upper jaw. Averages larger, the record size (an enormous female) 9⅜". Marshes and estuaries of Gulf Coast from Florida panhandle to w. Louisiana. TEXAS DIAMONDBACK TERRAPIN, *Malaclemys terrapin littoralis.* Similar to Mississippi Diamondback, but with a deeper shell that has its highest point toward rear of carapace; skin greenish gray, heavily marked with black spots; plastron nearly white; "mustache" usually missing. Coast of Texas and probably well south along the Mexican littoral. Map 19

Map Turtles and Sawbacks:
Genus *Graptemys*

THESE ARE lake and river turtles. They are shy, quick to plunge from their basking places, and usually difficult to capture. Among them are some of our most beautifully marked and grotesquely adorned turtles. There are nine species, all found in the eastern United States, but several are confined to single river systems emptying into the Gulf of Mexico. All have dorsal keels; in several there are projections upward from the keel (hence the name Sawbacks). Hatching size varies from 1⅛" to 1½". In the young, the patterns are brightest and the spines best developed; males tend to retain most of the juvenile characteristics; females lose many of them and are often smudged with dark pigment. The heads of adults are quite broad in four species (Map, Mississippi, Alabama, and Barbour's); adult females of the last two have enormously enlarged heads that are efficient machines for crushing the shells of snails and fresh-water clams.

MAP TURTLE *Graptemys geographica* pp. 47, 63
Identification: Adult females 7–10¾; males 4–6¼. A young or well-marked specimen carries a map on its back, the light markings resembling an intricate system of canals or waterways laid out on a chart. Shell moderately low; keel may have mere

suggestions of knobs on it. A more or less longitudinal yellow spot behind eye, variable in size and shape, but usually largest in specimens from southern part of range. *Female:* Head considerably enlarged; pattern obscure. *Young:* Dorsal keel pronounced; plastral pattern consisting of dark lines bordering seams between the scutes (see Plate 6). Adults have virtually plain plastrons.

The Map Turtle prefers large bodies of water — rivers rather than creeks and lakes rather than ponds. A confirmed but wary basker; slow to retreat into hibernation. In northern lakes it may sometimes be seen walking about under ice (at slow-motion speed) after early cold snaps. Snails and crayfish are the chief foods. **Similar Species:** In False Map Turtle traces of upward projections are usually evident along keel, and head is relatively small. Mississippi Map Turtle has yellow crescent behind eye. Painted Turtles have *un*keeled shells. In Sliders and Cooters the crushing surface in roof of mouth is ridged (smooth in Map Turtle). Tap turtle gently on snout to make it open mouth. Use a stick, *not* your fingers!
Range: Lakes George and Champlain, westward through St. Lawrence and Great Lakes drainage to Wisconsin; Mississippi drainage from s. Minnesota south to Arkansas and n. Alabama; Susquehanna drainage, New York to Maryland.   Map 14

BARBOUR'S MAP TURTLE *Graptemys barbouri*   pp. 47, 63
Identification: Adult females 7–10½; males 3½–5. The male is a dwarf compared with his mate. Females attain really imposing dimensions, and their heads are enormously enlarged. Adult males retain most markings of young, but big females become smudged and blotched with dark pigment that effectively hides their patterns. *Young:* Strong sawteeth on back; small longitudinal keel on each costal plate; *broad* olive area between and behind eyes. Light markings on marginals, if present, are *narrow*; all the light curved markings on carapace of juvenile illustrated on Plate 6 are reduced or completely absent in many specimens. Light bar *across* or paralleling curve of chin (Fig. 6, p. 51). Half-grown individuals have *deep* plastrons (viewed in profile). Plastral spines present.

Many of these turtles have been caught in the clear waters of the Chipola River (Florida) by swimmers equipped with water goggles. There the turtles are often found resting on the bottom or on submerged snags or logs. Beneath the surface they lose their shyness and are easily approached. Here is a clue for getting a bashful turtle to stick out its neck. Put your specimen in an aquarium or large jar full of water and sit quietly; usually the head and neck will soon be extended, so that you can check on their markings. Named for Thomas Barbour, herpetologist and long director of Harvard's Museum of Comparative Zoology.

Similar species: Alabama Map Turtle has *longitudinal* light bar running back from point of chin (Fig. 6, below), *broad* light markings on marginals, and no plastral spines. Mississippi Map Turtle has narrow light crescent behind eye.

Range: Streams flowing into Gulf of Mexico — from the Escambia River to the Apalachicola system (Florida panhandle and adj. Georgia and Alabama).   Map 16

Fig. 6

CHINS OF
MAP TURTLES

Longitudinal
light bar

Curved
light bar

ALABAMA   BARBOUR'S

ALABAMA MAP TURTLE *Graptemys pulchra*   p. 63
Identification: Adult females 7–8½; males 3½–5. Big females have grotesquely enlarged heads and strongly resemble females of Barbour's Map Turtle, even to being smudged and blotched with dark pigment. Adult males retain most markings of juveniles. *Young:* A middorsal black line involving the spines; a *broad* olive area between and behind eyes. Light markings on marginals *wide and prominent.* A *longitudinal* light bar running back from point of chin (Fig. 6, above). Half-grown specimens have *shallow* plastrons (viewed in profile).

This and other Map Turtles feed to a large extent upon snails and other mollusks, the shells of which are crushed by the broad surfaces of the jaws. Aquatic insects also figure largely in the diet, especially of males, which do not have such powerful shell crackers as females.

Similar species: Barbour's Map Turtle has a light bar *across* or following curve of chin (Fig. 6, above), and the light markings on marginals are narrow or obscure. Mississippi Map Turtle has narrow light crescent behind eye.

Range: Streams flowing into Gulf of Mexico — from the Pearl River system to the Escambia River system (e. Louisiana to extr. w. Florida).   Map 15

MISSISSIPPI MAP TURTLE *Graptemys kohni*   pp. 47, 63
Identification: Adult females 6–9¾; males 3½–5. The crescent behind the eye is the best feature. This sometimes is broken into 2 or 3 parts, but fragmented or whole it cuts off the narrow yellow head stripes from the eye. The eye, on gross inspection, is a wide white ring with black center. Toenails on forefeet of large males are elongated. *Young:* These and young of the False Map Turtle, although they have brownish carapaces, are the "graybacks" of the pet trade. Babies are saw-backed, the rear margin of the carapace is "toothed," and there is an intricate design of double dark lines on the plastron (see Plate 6).

Similar species: In races of the False Map Turtle one or more light neck stripes reach eye. In Texas Map Turtle the light postorbital stripe extends *backward*.

Range: Mississippi Valley, from Missouri and Illinois southward and chiefly west of the River; Mobile, Alabama.   Map 18

FALSE MAP TURTLE   *Graptemys pseudogeographica*   p. 63

Identification: Adult females 5–9; males 3½–4½. Variable, but usually with this combination of characters — carapace brown, middorsal keel with suggestions of knobs, light spot or line behind eye. Some of the light neck stripes *reach eye*. Head relatively small. *Males:* Greatly elongated toenails on forelegs. *Young:* Saw-backed, spines black; rear of shell "toothed"; a well-developed plastral pattern. Adults retain indications of the spines, but the "teeth" of the shell and the plastral pattern become much reduced as turtles grow older.

These reptiles and their close relatives often choose basking spots shunned by other turtles, assaying seemingly impossible climbs up slippery snags that rise at steep angles from the surface of the water.

Similar species: A light crescent prevents neck stripes from reaching the eye in Mississippi Map Turtle. In the Map Turtle the keel is lower, and knobs are weak or lacking; head broader and plastral pattern much reduced or absent.

Range: Mississippi Valley from Nebraska, Minnesota, and West Virginia to Louisiana; Sabine River drainage, Texas and Louisiana.

Subspecies: OUACHITA MAP TURTLE, *Graptemys pseudogeographica ouachitensis* (illustrated on Plate 8). A prominent squarish or rectangular light spot behind eye; 1 to 3 light neck lines reach eye; a pair of light spots on jaws, one under the eye and another similar one on chin (Fig. 7, below). Occupies most of the range of the species. SABINE MAP TURTLE, *Graptemys pseudogeographica sabinensis*. Similar, but with postorbital light spot oval or elongate; 5 to 9 light neck stripes reach eye; transverse bands under chin; plastron (in juveniles) with more and finer lines. Sabine River drainage. FALSE MAP TURTLE, *Graptemys pseudogeographica pseudogeographica*. Yellow postorbital line narrow; no enlarged spots on mandibles; fewer lines on legs. Attains maximum size of the species; the other races average considerably smaller. Existing as a pure population only at extreme northern edge of range of species; intergrades with Ouachita Map Turtle throughout a very large area.   Map 13

OUACHITA
MAP TURTLE
Light spot behind the
eye and 2 below it

Fig. 7

BIG BEND TURTLE
A large light spot on
side of head, small
one behind eye

TEXAS MAP TURTLE *Graptemys versa* p. 63
Identification: Adult females 4–5; males 2¾–3½. Smallest of the Map Turtles. A light yellow or orange line (often J-shaped) extending *backward* from eye. Plates of carapace have a quilted effect (at least more anterior ones do); they are high and rounded at their centers, the sutures forming rather deep grooves between them.
Similar species: Texas Slider has broad light stripes, spots, or vertical bars on its head.
Range: Colorado River system, Texas. Map 20

RINGED SAWBACK *Graptemys oculifera* p. 63
Identification: Adult females 5–8½; males 3–4. *Broad* light rings on costal plates of carapace. Head has a "clownish" appearance, as though smeared with grease paint — light mandibles, large postorbital yellow spot, and 2 broad light neck stripes entering eye. This and next two species are the spiniest of our turtles. Dorsal spines very conspicuous in the young and adult males, somewhat less so in large females. Also in big females, the light rings may be partially obscured by dark pigment. In juveniles the rear corners of the marginals project outward to give shell a saw-toothed appearance.
  The jaws, scissor-like in action, are useful in dismembering insects, which, with mollusks, constitute the principal food of all three Sawbacks.
Similar species: Head markings similar in Black-knobbed and Yellow-blotched Sawbacks; but their names describe those two. In Black-knob, spines are widened and flattened, and rings on carapace are narrow. In Yellowblotch, light shell markings are of solid colors or are invaded by ground color of shell; they do not form a series of broad, symmetrical rings.
Range: Pearl River system, s. Mississippi and adj. Louisiana.
Map 17

YELLOW-BLOTCHED SAWBACK
Graptemys flavimaculata p. 63
Identification: Adult females 4–6; males 3–4. *Solid* areas of yellow or orange in each of the large scutes of the carapace. These may be invaded by or surround areas of the dark ground color, but they do not form a series of symmetrical rings. Head markings and gross anatomy are similar to those of Ringed Sawback.
Range: Pascagoula River system, Mississippi. Map 17

BLACK-KNOBBED SAWBACK *Graptemys nigrinoda* p. 63
Identification: Adult females 4–5; males 3–4. The spines are broadly knobbed at their tips, like metal spikes struck by a heavy hammer. Light rings on carapace are *narrow*.
  This turtle and the other two Sawbacks are most common in

streams with moderate current, a bottom of sand or clay, and an abundance of brush, logs, and flood-stranded debris.

Range: Alabama-Tombigbee-Black Warrior River system, Alabama. Map 17

Painted Turtles:
Genus *Chrysemys*

THESE ARE readily identified by their *smooth, unkeeled shells* and attractive patterns of *red, yellow*, and *black* (or olive). In many parts of the North they are the most conspicuous of turtles, basking by the hour on logs, stumps, or rocks. They live chiefly where the water is shallow, the aquatic vegetation profuse, and the bottom soft and muddy — in ponds, marshes, ditches, edges of lakes, backwaters of streams, and (westward) in prairie sloughs, cattle tanks, and river pools. Their food in nature consists largely of aquatic vegetation, insects, crayfish, and small mollusks.

The shells often become encrusted with a red or brownish deposit (easily scraped away by thumbnail or knife) that may hide the true coloration. Females average larger than their mates. Fully adult males have very long nails on their forefeet. Hatchlings are usually an inch or less in shell length; *their* carapaces are keeled.

There is only one species, but four distinct subspecies. Where the ranges of these approach one another there are broad areas of overlap in which individual turtles may *combine* the characteristics of different subspecies.

EASTERN PAINTED TURTLE *Chrysemys picta picta* pp. 46, 110
 Identification: 4½–6; record 7⅛. A unique turtle, our only one in which the large scutes of the carapace are in *straight rows across* the back. In other turtles all the plates down the center alternate with those of the 2 outer rows. The olive front edges of the large scutes collectively form light bands across carapace — a good field mark easily seen through binoculars when the turtle floats at surface in clear water. Look also for bright yellow spots on head (2 on each side). For basking specimens, red and black margins of shell are also good checks. Plastron is plain yellow or with a small dark spot or two. (See Plate 5 for young.)
 Range: Nova Scotia to Alabama. Map 21

MIDLAND PAINTED TURTLE
Chrysemys picta marginata pp. 46, 110
 Identification: 4½–5½, record 7⅜. Very similar to Eastern Painted Turtle, but with large scutes of back alternating instead of running straight across. There is also a dark plastral blotch that is variable in size, shape, and intensity from one turtle to

the next. Typically it is oval, involves all, or nearly all, of the scutes, is half (or less) than width of plastron, and does not normally send out extensions along the seams. (See Plate 5 for young.)

Range: S. Quebec and s. Ontario to Tennessee. Map 21

SOUTHERN PAINTED TURTLE

Chrysemys picta dorsalis pp. 46, 110

Identification: 4–5; record 6. A *broad* red stripe down the back and a plain yellow plastron. Stripe is sometimes yellow; plastron may show 1 or 2 small black spots. Juveniles are widely sold in the pet trade. (See Plate 5 for young.)

Range: Extr. s. Illinois to nw. Alabama and the Gulf; extr. se. Oklahoma. Map 21

WESTERN PAINTED TURTLE

Chrysemys picta belli pp. 46, 110

Identification: 5–7; record 9⅞. Largest of the Painted Turtles and the one with the most intricate pattern. Not much red on marginals; light, irregular lines appear on carapace, these sometimes so extensive as to form a netlike pattern. Most of plastron occupied by a large dark figure that sends branches out along seams of scutes. (See Plate 5 for young.)

Range: W. Ontario and Missouri to Vancouver Island; disjunct colonies in the Southwest. Map 21

Cooters and Sliders: Genus *Pseudemys*

THESE INCLUDE most of the big basking turtles, an abundant group in ponds and streams of the Southeast, where people call them Cooters,* and the Mississippi Valley, where they are known as Sliders. They are brown or olive in general appearance with streaks, whorls, or circles of brown or black on a lighter ground color. The carapace of adults is usually wrinkled with numerous, chiefly longitudinal furrows, and its rear margin is saw-toothed. The head stripes are usually yellowish. Only a few have field marks recognizable at a distance (through binoculars). Even in hand they are difficult to identify, particularly since hybridization between species is of rather frequent occurrence. There are four groups, whose chief characteristics are as follows:

1. POND SLIDERS (*scripta*). Usually a prominent patch (or patches) of red or yellow on side of head. Lower jaw rounded (flat in all other groups — see Fig. 8, p. 56). Includes Yellow-bellied, Red-eared, Cumberland, and Big Bend Turtles.

*Derived from *kuta*, a word for turtle in several African dialects and brought to America during early slave days.

Fig. 8. JAWS OF COOTERS AND SLIDERS

POND SLIDERS
Rounded lower jaw

ALL OTHERS
Flattened lower jaw

2. RIVER COOTERS AND SLIDERS (*concinna*). A light C-shaped figure on 2d costal scute (Fig. 9, below). Under surfaces with numerous dark markings — on plastron, bridge, and marginals. Includes River, Suwannee, and Mobile Cooters and the Slider and Texas Slider.

3. COASTAL PLAIN COOTERS AND SLIDERS (*floridana*). Light vertical line (or lines) on 2d costal scute (Fig., p. 95). Plastron unmarked or only lightly patterned; dark markings on bridge and marginals fewer and less conspicuous than in the River species. Includes Florida and Peninsula Cooters and Missouri Slider.

4. RED-BELLIED TURTLES (*rubriventris* group). Plastron usually red, orange, or coral, at least around edges. Light arrow (Fig., p. 95) at front of head (also shared by the Pond Sliders). Sharp notch at tip of upper jaw bordered on each side by a pronounced cusp (Fig., p. 95). Cutting edges of jaws saw-toothed. Includes Red-bellied, Florida Red-bellied, and Alabama Red-bellied Turtles.

Adult males have greatly elongated nails on their forelimbs, and their shells are rather flat compared with the well-arched shells of females. Males, especially of Pond Sliders and Red-bellied Turtles, also tend to become dark and to lose their patterns at a smaller size than their mates. Females grow the larger. Hatchlings have a carapace length ranging from slightly over 1″ to 1¾″; the babies are strongly and colorfully marked, and are popular in the pet trade.

All of these turtles are largely vegetarian. Captives should be

Fig. 9

Second costal scute (arrow). Turtles of the River Cooter group have a light "C" on this scute; those of the Coastal Plain Cooter group lack it.

COASTAL PLAIN
(floridana group)

RIVER
(concinna group)

provided with natural aquatic plants or, in their absence, with lettuce, carrot tops, or other greens. Most of them will eat raw meat, fish, shellfish, worms, insects, etc.

The genus *Pseudemys* ranges from the United States to Argentina. It is advisable to rely heavily on geography, eliminating those species and subspecies not known from your own region (see Maps 22 to 25 and 27).

YELLOW-BELLIED TURTLE
Pseudemys scripta scripta   pp. 46, 110
  Identification: 5–8; record 10¾. The yellow blotch behind the eye is the most conspicuous field mark, but this is strongly evident only in the young and many females. Vertical yellow bands on carapace show best when shell is wet. Yellow underside of both shells marked with round dusky smudges, one toward rear of each marginal and others on forward part of plastron. These markings may be reduced or obscure in older individuals, especially in adult males, which may completely lose their original patterns, becoming dark and mottled like old male Red-eared Turtles. Vertical stripes on "seat of the pants," and *narrow* yellow stripes along front surface of forelegs (Fig., p. 110). *Young:* (Plate 5) Smudges or eyelike spots on marginals, bridge, and forepart of plastron. Such markings may appear all over the plastron, but in that case the anterior ones are darker and better formed.

  One of the most ubiquitous turtles of the Southeast. Utilizes a wide variety of habitats, including rivers, ditches, sloughs, lakes, and ponds.
  Similar species: Chicken Turtle also has striped "pants," but yellow stripe on each foreleg is *broad*, and carapace is long and narrow. Also see introductory section on Cooters and Sliders (p. 55).
  Range: Dismal Swamp region, Virginia, to n. Florida. Intergrades with Red-eared Turtle in the Gulf region.   Map 24

RED-EARED TURTLE *Pseudemys scripta elegans*   pp. 46, 110
  Identification: 5–8; record 11. The broad *reddish stripe* behind the eye is unique among North American turtles, but not all Red-ears have it. Rarely, the red is replaced by yellow. Most trouble will result in trying to identify adult specimens in which development of dark pigment (melanism) is advanced. This is a phenomenon in which black appears on both shells in form of bars, spots, or blotches. These spread and run together, obliterating details of original pattern, and in extreme cases producing a nearly uniform black or very dark turtle. Even limbs, head, and tail become dark. Change may start at any age from young adulthood onward, but males are more susceptible to melanism than females. *Young:* Carapace green and with a low keel; plastron profusely marked with dark eyelike spots (see Plate 5).

Baby Red-ears, commonest of all pet turtles, are sold in enormous numbers. This is a thoroughly aquatic species preferring quiet water with a muddy bottom and a profusion of vegetation. Basks on logs or other projections above water or in masses of floating plants, but seldom hauls out on bank.

Similar species: See introductory section on Cooters and Sliders (p. 55).

Range: Ohio and Iowa to New Mexico. Introduced into other areas through escape or intentional liberation of captive specimens.

Subspecies: CUMBERLAND TURTLE, *Pseudemys scripta troosti*. Similar but with a narrower *yellow* stripe behind eye, fewer and much wider stripes on legs, neck, and head; dark spots under marginals smaller in diameter than light spaces between them. Upper portions of the Cumberland and Tennessee river valleys from e. Kentucky to ne. Alabama. BIG BEND TURTLE, *Pseudemys scripta gaigeae*. A large, round, black-bordered yellow spot on side of head, and a smaller but similar spot right behind eye (Fig. 7, p. 52). Big Bend region, Texas, and adj. Mexico, but intergrading with Red-eared Turtle in s. Texas. Map 24

RIVER COOTER *Pseudemys concinna concinna* p. 95
Identification: 9–12; record 12¾. The light *C* rarely can be picked out through binoculars, especially if the turtle has basked long enough for its shell to dry. Hence, the quarry must be in hand for accurate checking. Concentric circles are usually well developed in association with the *C* and on other scutes. Dark plastral pattern tends to follow seams between large scutes. All (or almost all) marginals have dark spots usually in form of 2 dark concentric circles, and some of these touch the dark markings on the bridge between the two shells.

Indigenous to streams of the Piedmont and following such streams to Atlantic Coast. Hybridization between this species and Florida Cooter is of such frequent occurrence within the Coastal Plain that many specimens show some of the characters of both. Because of this and the great difficulty of capturing such wary turtles in the turbid silt-laden rivers of the region, it is usually practical to list sight records merely as "Cooters."

Similar species: See Florida Cooter.
Range: Cent. Virginia to e. Alabama. Map 22

SUWANNEE COOTER
Pseudemys concinna suwanniensis p. 95
Identification: 9–13; record 16⅜. Darkest and largest of the Cooters. Out of water, upper shell may look virtually plain black. Ground color of legs and head also very dark, but head stripes are whitish- to greenish-yellow. Characteristic ventral markings of the river group are strongly evident, with marginal dark spots in contact with dark markings on bridge. Ground

color of plastron usually yellow, but brightly tinged with orange in some parts of range.

This is the "suwannee chicken" esteemed by epicures and said to be even more toothsome than the other members of the group. Abundant and conspicuous in clear spring runs of Florida's upper west coast, and frequently wandering into the big springs themselves. Also occurs in Gulf of Mexico in the turtle-grass flats off mouths of streams, and occasionally appears far out in the Gulf, its shell encrusted with barnacles.

Similar species: Peninsula Cooter has light "hairpins" on head (Fig., p. 95) and lacks a *C*; also, its ventral markings are greatly reduced. Red-bellied Turtles also lack *C*; there is an arrow on their heads, and their upper jaws have a notch and cusps (Fig,. p. 95). Also see Pond Sliders (p. 55).

Range: W. Florida, Apalachicola River region to Tampa Bay.

Subspecies: MOBILE COOTER, *Pseudemys concinna mobilensis*. Similar but somewhat smaller and with the ground color of carapace, head, and legs much lighter; head stripes orange-yellow or reddish. Gulf Coast streams, Florida panhandle to extr. se. Texas. Map 22

SLIDER *Pseudemys concinna hieroglyphica* pp. 46, 95
Identification: 9–13; record 14¾. The Mississippi Valley representative of the river group of Cooters and Sliders. A light *C* (Fig. 9, p. 56) and a strong plastral pattern are in evidence. Many individuals have shell "pinched in" anterior to hind legs.

Like other basking turtles, this one slides into water at least sign of danger. Hybridization with Missouri Slider occurs frequently; the baby Slider depicted on Plate 5 is somewhat intermediate between the two species.

Similar species: Missouri Sliders lack the *C* and their plastrons are only slightly patterned, if at all. Red-eared Turtles have an oval reddish patch on side of head; old darkened Red-ears may be distinguished by rounded shape of lower jaw (flat in Sliders — see Fig. 8, p. 56). Map Turtles and Sawbacks have strong keels or projections down their backs. In Painted Turtles rear margin of carapace is smooth (not notched or saw-toothed).

Range: S. Illinois and se. Kansas to cent. Alabama, n. Louisiana, and adj. Texas. Map 22

TEXAS SLIDER *Pseudemys concinna texana* p. 95
Identification: 7–10; record 10¾. Head markings exceedingly variable, but broad yellowish stripes, spots, or vertical bars are always present, either joined together or separated by dark pigment. The ventral pattern is typical of the river group, but is represented by narrow lines that become dim as the turtle grows and may disappear altogether in old adults. Upper jaw has a notch flanked by a cusp at each side, as in Florida Red-bellied Turtle (Fig., p. 95). *Old male:* Shell, head, and limbs rather

uniformly mottled, completely obscuring original pattern. (Some females approach this mottled condition.) Pair of swollen ridges extending downward from nostrils and terminating in the cusps.

Rivers constitute the chief habitat, but this turtle is also found in ditches and cattle tanks.

Similar species: Red-eared and Big Bend Turtles have rounded lower jaws (flat in Sliders — see Fig. 8, p. 56). Texas Map Turtle has keel down back and carapace has a quilted effect.

Range: Cent. and s. Texas and adj. Mexico.   Map 22

FLORIDA COOTER *Pseudemys floridana floridana*   p. 95
  Identification: 9–13; record 15⅝. The unmarked plastron and dark "doughnuts" or thick hollow ovals on underside of the marginals are characteristic. Numerous stripes on head, but they normally do not join to form "hairpins" except in regions where intergradation takes place with Peninsula Cooter. One or more vertical light stripes on 2d costal scute (Fig., p. 95).

  A turtle of the Coastal Plain, a resident of permanent bodies of water — ponds, lakes, big swamps or marshes, *and* rivers. Except in times of flood, Coastal Plain streams are quiet and sluggish and similar to lakes in many respects. This turtle will frequently be seen basking, but its extreme wariness results in its seldom being caught.

  Similar species: River Cooter and its subspecies have heavy ventral markings (Plate 12) and a *C* on the 2d costal scute (Fig. 9, p. 56). Yellow-bellied Turtle has striped "pants" (Fig., p. 110), and there may be a large yellow patch on side of head. Chicken Turtle also has striped "pants" but its carapace is marked with network of light lines. Red-eared Turtle has a reddish oval on each side of head. In Painted Turtles the rear margin of carapace is smooth (not notched or saw-toothed).

  Range: Coastal Plain from Maryland to Alabama, but excluding peninsular Florida.

  Subspecies: MISSOURI SLIDER, *Pseudemys floridana hoyi.* Similar but smaller (maximum about 12″); shell relatively short and broad; head stripes numerous and often broken or twisted. S. Illinois and se. Kansas to the Gulf.   Map 23

PENINSULA COOTER
Pseudemys floridana peninsularis   pp. 46, 95
  Identification: 9–13; record 15⅞. The only Cooter with a pair of light "hairpins" atop the head (Fig., p. 95). One or both of these may be broken or incomplete. (Submerge turtle in water to make its head come out.) Plastron usually completely unmarked, but marginal spots may be stronger and more numerous than shown on Plate 12. *Young:* (Plate 5) Plastron yellow or with slight tinge of orange; never strongly orange or reddish.

A turtle of lakes, sloughs, wet prairies, canals, and Florida's great springs and spring runs; also lives in the Everglades north of Tamiami Trail. Although extremely wary at or above water's surface, it can be closely approached when it is submerged. Divers equipped with face masks usually find this and other turtles easy to capture under banks of clear streams and springs. **Similar species:** Suwannee Cooter has all the characteristics of River Cooters and Sliders — a light *C* on 2d costal (Fig. 9, p. 56) and heavy dark ventral markings. Florida Cooter has dark "doughnuts" on the marginals. Plastron of Florida Red-bellied Turtle is reddish, orange, or coral and almost always marked with at least some dark pigment. Peninsula Cooter occasionally hybridizes with both Suwannee Cooter and Florida Red-belly, and it intergrades with Florida Cooter where their respective ranges meet.
Range: Florida peninsula, but excluding s. tip.   Map 23

RED-BELLIED TURTLE *Pseudemys rubriventris*   p. 110
Identification: 10–12½; record 15¾. The only big *basking* turtle throughout most of its range. Much larger than Painted Turtles, with which it often suns on logs or snags. A notch in upper jaw is flanked by a cusp at each side as in Florida Redbelly (Fig., p. 95). Adult females with vertical reddish line on each of first 3 costal scutes. Old males mottled with reddish brown. Coloration and pattern highly variable, and melanism is almost universal among large adults in some areas, notably in southern New Jersey. Among the virtually black specimens, the reddish markings usually persist, but they may be quite vague. (You may have to wet the shell to see them.) Ground color of plastron is yellow, marked with large gray smudges and bordered by a wash of pink or orange-red. Plastrons of old males often mottled with pink and light charcoal-gray. *Young:* Carapace with slight keel and patterned (with yellow or olive on green) in same basic design as in adult female illustrated. Plastron with large dark pattern on coral-red ground color (Fig. 10, below).
A turtle of ponds, rivers, and, in general, relatively large bodies of fresh water.
Similar species: In both River Cooter and Florida Cooter, upper jaw is rounded, lacking both notch and cusps. In Painted Turtles there are 2 bright yellow spots on each side of head.
Range: S. New Jersey and e. West Virginia to ne. North Carolina; Plymouth County, Massachusetts.   Map 25

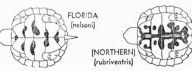

Fig. 10

PLASTRAL PATTERNS
OF BABY RED-BELLIED
TURTLES

FLORIDA
(nelsoni)

(NORTHERN)
(rubriventris)

BOX, WOOD, AND SPOTTED TURTLES; DIAMONDBACKS

	Map	*Text*

ORNATE BOX TURTLE   26   45
Carapace: Flattened or depressed on top; radiating light
lines. *Plastron:* Transverse hinge; bold light lines.

EASTERN BOX TURTLE   28   44
Carapace: High, domelike; yellow, orange, or olive mark-
ings on dark brown or black. *Plastron:* Transverse hinge.
Pattern variable.

FLORIDA BOX TURTLE   28   44
Shell arched, highest toward rear, and with radiating light
lines; 2 yellow stripes on head.

THREE-TOED BOX TURTLE   28   44
Orange on head; 3 toes on *hind* foot; shell pattern much
reduced or absent.

BOG TURTLE (MUHLENBERG'S)   4   42
Orange head patch; small size.

SPOTTED TURTLE   6   42
Scattered yellow spots; orange or yellow spots on head.

BLANDING'S TURTLE   29   65
Carapace: Profuse light spots. *Plastron:* Transverse hinge.
Bright yellow throat.

WOOD TURTLE   5   43
Orange on head and legs; shell rough, sculptured.

ORNATE DIAMONDBACK TERRAPIN   19   48
Orange or yellow in center of each large scute. Salt and
brackish water only.

NORTHERN DIAMONDBACK TERRAPIN   19   48
Concentric rings on each large scute. Salt and brackish
water only.

Blanding's and all the Box Turtles
have a hinge across the plastron.

ORNATE BOX

EASTERN BOX

Plastron

Plastron

FLORIDA BOX

THREE-TOED BOX

BOG

BLANDING'S

SPOTTED

Plastron

WOOD

NORTHERN DIAMONDBACK

ORNATE DIAMONDBACK

TEXAS MAP ♂

BLACK-KNOBBED SAWBACK ♂

RINGED SAWBACK ♂

ALABAMA MAP ♂

YELLOW-BLOTCHED SAWBACK ♂

BARBOUR'S MAP ♂

♀

MISSISSIPPI MAP ♂

FALSE MAP ♂ ♀

MAP ♂ ♀

Plate 8   63

MAP TURTLES AND SAWBACKS

(Females of all species grow larger than males.)

	Map	*Text*

TEXAS MAP TURTLE   20   53
Horizontal or J-shaped line behind eye; scutes of carapace
distinctly convex (examine closely).

BLACK-KNOBBED SAWBACK   17   53
Rounded black knobs; narrow light rings.

RINGED SAWBACK   17   53
Broad light rings.

YELLOW-BLOTCHED SAWBACK   17   53
Solid orange or yellow spots.

ALABAMA MAP TURTLE   15   51
Broad light bars on marginals; *longitudinal* light bar under
chin (Fig. 6, p. 51); female large and big-headed like
Barbour's Map Turtle.

BARBOUR'S MAP TURTLE   16   50
Narrow light markings on marginals; a *curved* or transverse
bar under chin (Fig. 6, p. 51). *Mature female:* Very
large; head enormous; pattern obscure.

MISSISSIPPI MAP TURTLE   18   51
Yellow crescent, cutting off neck stripes from eye.

FALSE MAP TURTLE   13   52
Yellow spot behind eye; neck stripes reach eye; middorsal
spines conspicuous.

MAP TURTLE   14   49
Yellowish spot behind eye; maplike pattern; middorsal
spines not prominent.

♂ means male, ♀ female.

FLORIDA RED-BELLIED TURTLE *Pseudemys nelsoni* p. 95
  Identification: 8–12; record 13⅜. Many of these turtles have
  a distinctly reddish appearance (quite noticeable when submerged in clear water) that contrasts with the darker Peninsula
  and Suwannee Cooters. Other specimens may be darker and
  more somber, but plastron is almost always strongly tinted with
  orange, red, or coral, at least around margins. Light vertical band
  on the 2d costal is variable in width; it may be relatively narrow
  or quite wide. The light head stripes are few in number, but
  they include a *slender arrow* with its shaft between the eyes and
  its point at the turtle's snout; also the notch in upper jaw is
  flanked by a strong cusp on each side (Fig., p. 95). *Young:*
  Plastron orange to scarlet-orange (rarely yellow); dark plastral
  markings tend to be in form of solid semicircles with flat sides
  along seams between scutes (Fig. 10, p. 61).
    A turtle of streams, ponds, lakes, ditches, sloughs, marshes,
  and mangrove-bordered creeks.
  Similar species: Peninsula and Suwannee Cooters *lack:* (1) notch
  and cusps; and (2) arrow on head.
  Range: Florida peninsula.
  Related species: ALABAMA RED-BELLIED TURTLE, *Pseudemys alabamensis.* Similar, but with numerous head stripes,
  including the "arrow." Gulf Coast from vicinity of Apalachee
  Bay, Florida, to vicinity of Mobile Bay, Alabama; possibly
  also e. Texas.   Map 27

CHICKEN TURTLE *Deirochelys reticularia* pp. 46, 110
  Identification: 4–6; record 10. The light netlike pattern on the
  carapace and the extra-long, strongly striped neck are good
  characters, but they may be invisible if the shell is coated with
  mud or algae or the turtle refuses to stick out its neck. In the
  case of timid specimens, look at the "seat of the pants." The
  hind legs are *vertically striped* (Fig., p. 110). Also look at the
  forelegs; each one has a *broad* yellow stripe along its front surface.
  Many specimens have a longitudinal dark bar, spot, or spots on
  bridge. Carapace is sculptured with small linelike ridges, is
  much longer than wide, and is widest over the hind legs. *Young:*
  (Plate 5) Carapace with a slight keel; about 1⅛" at hatching.
    An inhabitant of still water — ponds, marshes, sloughs, and
  ditches. Frequently walks about on land. Chicken Turtles
  used to be sold in numbers in fish markets in the South, and
  their flesh is still esteemed as food.
  Similar species: Yellow-bellied Turtle also has striped "pants,"
  but yellow lines on forelegs are *narrow* and carapace is much
  rounder.
  Range: Coastal Plain from se. North Carolina to e. Texas.
  Subspecies: FLORIDA CHICKEN TURTLE, *Deirochelys
  reticularia chrysea* (illustrated on Plate 13). Netlike pattern
  orange or yellow, bold and broad in younger specimens, but less

conspicuous in old ones; rim of carapace boldly edged with orange; plastron orange or bright yellow, unpatterned. Florida peninsula. EASTERN CHICKEN TURTLE, *Deirochelys reticularia reticularia* (young illustrated on Plate 5). Similar but with the netlike lines greenish or brownish and much narrower; entire turtle less brightly colored. North Carolina to Mississippi River. WESTERN CHICKEN TURTLE, *Deirochelys reticularia miaria*. This race has a rather flat appearance; netlike lines broad, but only a little lighter than the ground color between them; plastron with dark markings along seams; *underside* of neck unpatterned in adults. Louisiana and e. Texas northward to extr. se. Missouri and se. Oklahoma. **Map 30**

BLANDING'S TURTLE *Emydoidea blandingi* pp. 47, 62
Identification: 5–7½; record 10¼. The "semi-box turtle." Hinge across plastron permits the movable lobes to be pulled well upward toward carapace, but closure is far less complete than in Box Turtles. Light spots often tend to run together, forming bars or streaks. *Bright yellow on chin and throat* is a good field character, being easily seen through binoculars when turtle basks or floats at water's surface. *Young:* (Plate 6) Carapace virtually plain gray or grayish brown; plastron blackish with an edging of yellow; tail much longer proportionately than in adults. About 1⅛″ to 1¼″ at hatching.
Essentially aquatic, but often wanders about on land, although seldom far from marshes, bogs, lakes, or small streams. Usually hisses sharply when picked up in the field. Named for Dr. William Blanding, an early Philadelphia naturalist.
Similar species: Spotted Turtle has few and well separated spots and *no plastral hinge*. Box Turtles can close up tightly, and they have hooklike beaks.
Range: Nova Scotia to Nebraska; range discontinuous and spotty east of Ohio and Ontario. **Map 29**

Gopher Tortoises:
Subfamily Testudininae

THE ONLY tortoises native to the United States. The feet are stumpy, the hind ones elephant-like. The heavily scaled forelimbs, which fold against the opening of the shell, provide good protection for the head and neck. Carapace high and rounded, each scute with or without a light center. In males the plastron is usually deeply concave toward the rear. Captives eat grass, lettuce, and a variety of other vegetables and fruit; some show interest in meat. There are only three species, two in our territory and another in the far Southwest and adjacent Mexico. The subfamily is represented in all the continents save Australia.

GOPHER TORTOISE *Gopherus polyphemus*   p. 78
   Identification: 6–9½; record 14½. This is the "gopher" of
southern epicures. The stumpy feet, completely without webs,
and the rigid, unhinged plastron make identification easy. Carapace brown or tan; plastron yellowish; soft parts grayish brown.
Old adults are virtually smooth, but younger ones have conspicuous growth "rings." In comparison with Texas Tortoise,
the Gopher Tortoise's carapace is longer in proportion to its
width and its feet are smaller. *Young:* Considerable orange or
yellow on soft parts, plastron, and marginals; each large carapace scute yellowish but bordered by brown; about 1⅝" at
hatching.

   An accomplished burrower, its tunnels sloping downward from
surface and then usually leveling off underground. Excavations
vary from 10 to 35 feet long, and have a "bedroom" large enough
to turn around in at the terminus. Many other animals seek
shelter or live permanently in "gopher" burrows, these running
the gamut from insects to burrowing owls, raccoons, and opos-
sums. The Gopher Frogs, Indigo Snake, and Diamondback
Rattler are frequent guests — a good point to remember before
you start probing into a tunnel.

   The Tortoises emerge in good weather — usually in the morn-
ing before the heat is too great — to forage upon grass, leaves,
and such wild fruits as they can find.
Similar species: Box Turtles have a hinge across plastron.
Range: Sandy regions of Gulf Coastal Plain from s. South
Carolina to extr. e. Louisiana and most of Florida.   Map 32

TEXAS TORTOISE *Gopherus berlandieri*   p. 78
   Identification: 5½–8; record 8⅝. The rounded carapace is
nearly as broad as long, and its coloration varies from tan to
dark brown. Specimens showing growth rings have a finely
sculptured appearance. Feet stumpy; plastron rigid. Gular
scutes of plastron may be greatly elongated, forked, and curved
upward, especially in adult males, which are thus equipped with
a weapon useful in overturning masculine opponents during
breeding activities. *Young:* Each large scute of carapace with a
yellow center, and each marginal edged with same color; about
1⅝" (both across and lengthwise) at hatching.

   An arid-land counterpart of the Gopher Tortoise. Long burrows may be constructed in sandy soil, but where digging is
difficult Texas Tortoises excavate barely enough to hide themselves, or they may take shelter beneath rocks, stumps, or debris.
They prowl actively in hot weather, but usually in early morning
or late afternoon. Food includes fruits (tunas) of prickly pear,
young shoots, flowers, and other vegetation.
Similar species: Box Turtles have a hinge across plastron.
Range: S. Texas and ne. Mexico.   Map 31

SEA TURTLES: FAMILIES CHELONIIDAE AND DERMOCHELYIDAE

LARGE TURTLES of tropical seas. They turn up frequently and some of them even nest along the shores of the Gulf and the Atlantic Ocean in our southern states. Many are lured northward by the warm waters of the Gulf Stream to appear later, lost and chilled, along beaches and in estuaries as far north as New England, Nova Scotia, or Newfoundland. Rarely, they even follow the Stream to northern Europe. Their limbs are modified into flippers. All five kinds have relatives in the Pacific Ocean.

Measurements and weights for larger specimens are usually unreliable because of (1) the difficulty of lifting and maneuvering such huge animals, (2) varying techniques of measuring, and (3) estimates which, although sheer guesswork when made, get mellowed by time and repetition and are finally accepted as truth. The sizes given for each species are approximations. Measurements may be taken along the *curve* of the shell. (Making accurate straight-line carapace measurements is almost impossible without a gigantic pair of calipers or other cumbersome tools.) Adult sea turtles often are battered or encrusted with barnacles, making identification more difficult. If in doubt, be sure to check the scute and headplate diagrams. Be careful in handling or approaching large sea turtles: they bite and their flippers can deliver punishing blows.

ATLANTIC GREEN TURTLE *Chelonia mydas mydas* p. 79

Identification: 30–42; record 60+; usual weight 120–200 lbs.; record 850 lbs. General coloration brown. (This turtle's name derives from the greenish fat of the body.) Carapace light or dark brown, sometimes shaded with olive; often with radiating mottled or wavy dark markings or large dark brown blotches. Only 4 costal plates, the 1st *not* touching the nuchal. *One* pair of prefrontal plates between eyes (Fig. 11, p. 68). Large scutes of carapace do not overlap. *Young:* Dorsum dark brown; venter white except ends of flippers, which are black but edged with white; a keel down center of back and a pair of keels down plastron; about 2″ at hatching.

A turtle of considerable importance, since its flesh is much esteemed. Overhunting has seriously reduced its numbers.

Similar species: Hawksbill has *2 pairs* of prefrontals and large scutes on carapace may overlap. In both Loggerhead and Ridley the 1st costal touches the nuchal.

Range: Warmer parts of Atlantic, chiefly in shallow waters along the continental shelf; straggling north to Massachusetts and south to n. Argentina.

Fig. 11. HEAD PLATES OF SEA TURTLES

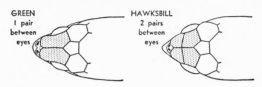

GREEN
1 pair
between
eyes

HAWKSBILL
2 pairs
between
eyes

ATLANTIC HAWKSBILL
Eretmochelys imbricata imbricata p. 79

Identification: 17–22; record 36+; weight 30–100 lbs., record 280 lbs. The large scutes of the carapace overlap, except in very old individuals in which they lie side by side as in most other turtles. A keel down center of carapace. General coloration brown. Some specimens, smaller ones especially, show a "tortoise-shell" pattern. Four costal plates, the 1st *not* touching the nuchal; *2 pairs* of prefrontals between eyes (Fig. 11, above). *Young:* Black or very dark brown above and below except for raised ridges, edges of shell, and areas on neck and flippers — all of which are light brown; 1 middorsal and 2 plastral keels; about 1½" to 1¾" at hatching.

Source of the tortoise shell of commerce, now less in demand since the advent of plastics.

Similar species: Green Turtle has only *1 pair* of prefrontals between eyes, and scutes do not overlap (except in very young). In Loggerhead and Ridley there are 5 or more costals, the 1st of which touches the nuchal.

Range: Warmer parts of Atlantic, especially in shallow waters along coasts; straggling north to Massachusetts and south to s. Brazil.

ATLANTIC LOGGERHEAD *Caretta caretta caretta* p. 79

Identification: 28–84±; weight to 900 lbs. or more, but usually less than 300. Reddish-brown coloration offers quickest clue, but also check arrangement of the scutes. Number of costals is 5 or more, and the 1st one always *touches* the nuchal. There are *three* large scutes on bridge between shells (see Figs., p. 79). There is also a middorsal keel, but this becomes low and inconspicuous in large specimens. *Young:* Light brown above and whitish beneath; 3 dorsal keels and 2 plastral keels; 1⅝" to 1⅞" at hatching.

Similar species: The Ridley is gray and usually has *four* large scutes on bridge. In both Hawksbill and Green Turtles the 1st costal does *not* touch the nuchal.

Range: Warm waters of Atlantic Ocean, but straggling north to Newfoundland and south to Argentina; nests north to North Carolina.

ATLANTIC RIDLEY *Lepidochelys kempi* p. 79
Identification: 20–25; record 27⅝. Gray coloration and 5 costals, the 1st one *touching* the nuchal. Usually *four* enlarged scutes on bridge (see Figs., p. 79). A middorsal keel. *Young:* Almost completely black; a short streak of light gray along rear edge of front flipper; 3 tuberculate dorsal ridges and 4 plastral ones; about 1⅝″ at hatching.

Smallest of the Atlantic sea turtles and widely known as the "bastard turtle" because of the erroneous belief it is a cross between the Loggerhead and Green Turtle.
Similar species: Loggerhead is reddish brown and has *three* enlarged scutes on bridge. In both the Hawksbill and Green Turtle the 1st costal does *not* touch the nuchal.
Range: Gulf of Mexico; casual north to Nova Scotia.

ATLANTIC LEATHERBACK
Dermochelys coriacea coriacea p. 79
Identification: 48–96; weight 700–1600 lbs., possibly a ton. Largest of all living turtles. *Seven prominent longitudinal ridges on carapace.* Five similar ridges on plastron. Carapace and plastron show no scutes, being covered instead by a smooth, slaty-black or dark brown skin. Irregular patches of white may appear almost anywhere. *Young:* Much more conspicuously marked than adults; covered with great numbers of small scales, which later are shed; tail keeled above; about 3″ at hatching.
Range: Open seas — warmer waters of Atlantic Ocean, but on rare occasions nesting on Florida coast and appearing as far north as Nova Scotia.

SOFTSHELL TURTLES:
FAMILY TRIONYCHIDAE

THESE animated pancakes belie the traditional slowness of the turtle. They are powerful swimmers and they can run on land with startling speed and agility. The shell is soft and leathery, bends freely at the sides and rear, and is completely devoid of scales or scutes. Vague outlines of the underlying bony structure often show through the skin of the carapace.

All species are thoroughly aquatic. They may bask ashore, but only where they can slide or dash into the water in literally a split second. A frequent habit is to lie buried in mud or sand in shallow water with only the eyes and snout exposed and where, when the long neck is extended, the nostrils can reach the surface for a breath of air. The Florida Softshell lives chiefly in lakes; all the others are river turtles to a large degree.

Identification is hampered by changes associated with age and sex. Young Softshells are about as well patterned as they will ever be. Males tend to retain the juvenile pattern and coloration, but the females, which grow very large in comparison with their mates, undergo marked changes, the original pattern being replaced and eventually obliterated completely by mottlings and blotches. Similar, but not such marked changes, may take place in old males. An exception to the general rule is the Florida Softshell, in which both sexes become drab and retain only traces of pattern. Males have much longer and stouter tails than females. The young in all our species average about 1½″ at hatching time.

Handle Softshells with caution. Their sharp claws and mandibles deserve respect.

The Softshell Family occurs in Africa, Asia, and Malaysia, as well as in North America.

SMOOTH SOFTSHELL *Trionyx muticus*   pp. 46, 94
  Identification: Adult females 7–14; males 5–7. Sometimes called the "spineless softshell," which is not very complimentary to a turtle that can bite and scratch with vigor, but this is a good way to remember an important fact. Our only Softshell *without* spines, bumps, or sandpapery projections on carapace. Shell is quite smooth. Also, only Softshell *without* ridges in nostrils (see Figs., p. 94). To complete the roster of negative characters, the feet are *not* strongly streaked or spotted. *Male and young:* Carapace olive-gray or brown, marked with dots and dashes only a little darker than ground color. *Adult female:* Mottled with various shades of gray, brown, or olive. *Young:* Plastron paler than underside of carapace (see Plate 5).

  Essentially a river turtle, an inhabitant of streams ranging in size from creeks to the mighty Mississippi. Occurs in lakes less frequently than the several members of the Spiny Softshell group, and often is missing where they are abundant, and vice versa.
  Similar species: The several races of Spiny Softshell (Eastern, Western, Gulf Coast, and Texas) all have rough shells, either sandpapery, with spines on front edge of carapace, or both, and all have a ridge in each nostril.
  Range: W. Pennsylvania to extr. w. Florida; west to Minnesota, South Dakota, and Texas; an isolated record in New Mexico.   Map 33

EASTERN SPINY SOFTSHELL
Trionyx spinifer spinifer   pp. 46, 94
  Identification: Adult females 7–17; males 5–8⅛. Check three

items: (1) feet strongly streaked and spotted; (2) a ridge in each nostril (Fig., p. 94); and (3) look or feel for projections on upper surface of carapace as described for the two sexes. *Male:* Dark eyelike spots (ocelli) on carapace, especially toward center. These quite variable in size — on same turtle and from one specimen to the next. Ground color olive-gray to yellowish brown. Tiny projections from surface of carapace in adult males make shell feel like sandpaper. *Female:* The circular markings, characteristic of juveniles, begin to break up as female approaches maturity; they are replaced by blotches of brown or olive-brown of varying sizes that produce a camouflage effect. Spines or enlarged tubercles are present on and near the forward edge of carapace (Fig., p. 94), and raised protuberances may appear on other parts of shell. *Young:* (Plate 5) Small dark spots or circular markings on a pale yellowish-brown ground color.

Essentially a river turtle, but also occurring in lakes and other quiet bodies of water where sand and mud bars are available. Sometimes floats at surface, where shape identifies it as a Softshell. Over a large part of the range this is the only member of the group, but in areas where Smooth Softshells also occur it is usually necessary to capture specimens to be sure of identification.

Similar species: See Smooth Softshell (p. 70).

Range: Lake Champlain (Vermont) west through St. Lawrence, Great Lakes, and Mississippi drainages to Wisconsin, Illinois, and Tennessee. Map 35

WESTERN SPINY SOFTSHELL
Trionyx spinifer hartwegi p. 94
Identification: Adult females 7–18; males 5–7¼. A western subspecies characterized by the smallness of the dark markings on the carapace; these are only slightly enlarged toward the center of shell. In other characteristics like Eastern Spiny Softshell.

In western parts of range, where arid or semi-arid conditions prevail, rivers offer the only suitable natural habitats for Softshells. Farther east a variety of bodies of water are utilized.

Similar species: See Smooth Softshell (p. 70).

Range: Minnesota to Montana and south to Oklahoma and Arkansas. This race intergrades with Eastern Spiny Softshell through a broad area paralleling the Mississippi River. Map 35

GULF COAST SOFTSHELL *Trionyx spinifer asper* p. 94
Identification: Adult females 7–17⅞; males 5–8. The southern representative of the Spiny Softshells. Two items of pattern set this off from other subspecies: (1) 2 or more dark lines (or broken lines) parallel the rear margin of shell — in all other races there is only a single dark line; (2) the 2 light bands on head, one extending backward from eye and other from jaw,

usually unite on side of head (Fig. 12, below) — in Eastern Spiny
Softshell the light bands normally fail to join. All these markings are best seen in juveniles and male specimens; they are
obscure or even lacking in old females. In many of the latter,
spines on the forward part of shell are developed to a remarkable degree.

A resident of southern rivers and ponds or oxbows associated
with rivers.

Similar species: Florida Softshell has bumps on carapace in
form of flattened hemispheres; general coloration dark in both
sexes; the carapace, proportionately, is considerably longer than
wide; young Florida Softshell is patterned with large dark spots
separated by a network of light lines (see Plate 5). Also see
Smooth Softshell (p. 70).

Range: North Carolina to Mississippi and Florida panhandle.
All four races of the species (Eastern, Western, Texas, and Gulf
Coast) come together in the great plexus of rivers and bayous of
the lower Mississippi Valley in Arkansas, Louisiana, and Mississippi, and all contribute their characters to a general Spiny
Softshell melting pot. Specimens from that area should be considered as intergrades. Map 35

Fig. 12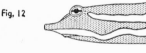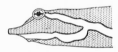

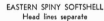

EASTERN SPINY SOFTSHELL
Head lines separate

GULF COAST SOFTSHELL
Head lines meet

TEXAS SOFTSHELL *Trionyx spinifer emoryi* p. 94
Identification: Adult females 6½–14½; males 5–8½. The southwestern member of the Spiny Softshell group. The small white
spots on the brown or olive carapace are a big help to identification, but they are subject to considerable variation. they are
often confined to hind part of shell and may be reduced to a few
rows of spots or virtually none. At best, the spots can be seen
only in males and young; females become mottled like females
of other Softshells. This, however, is the *only* Softshell Turtle
over a very large part of its range, so there is not much chance of
confusing it with others. Males may be quite sandpapery, but
females usually do not have the spines so well developed as in
other members of the Spiny Softshell group.

One might think this turtle was adept at threading its way
through arid country by following the streams. The opposite is
probably the case, for geological evidence indicates that much

of its range formerly was far more moist than at present. The turtle has survived only in the more permanent streams and by estivating in mud during periods of drought.

Similar species: See Smooth Softshell (p. 70).

Range: W. Louisiana to Colorado River (of California). There is indication that the species was introduced into the Gila-Colorado drainage system by man.   Map 35

FLORIDA SOFTSHELL   *Trionyx ferox*   pp. 46, 94

   Identification: Adult females 8–18; males 6–11⅛. Largest and bulkiest of North American Softshells, but the one with the smallest range. General appearance is dark brown or dark brownish gray, nearly uniform in coloration or with vague suggestions of large dark spots. There are numerous small bumps on the carapace (Fig., p. 94), usually occupying a crescentic area involving the front of the shell and back along its sides as far as the front legs. The bumps are flattened hemispheres — *not* spines or conical projections. A ridge in each nostril (Fig., p. 94) just as there is in the various members of the Spiny Softshell group. *Young:* Carapace with large dark round spots separated by network of light lines; bright lines and spots on an otherwise dark head (see Plate 5).

   The "lake dweller" among the Softshells — at home in lakes, ponds, big springs, canals, and roadside ditches, and occasionally in quiet portions of rivers. Largely because of the nature of its habitat, this Softshell is the most conspicuous member of the group, at least when submerged. Often seen moving about in clear water.

   Similar species: Gulf Coast Softshell has spines or cone-shaped projections on carapace, and in large individuals these may be present well back on shell; males and young are easily identified by yellowish-brown carapace and dark lines or broken lines paralleling rear margin of shell.

   Range: All of Florida, except panhandle and Keys; s. Georgia and s. South Carolina.   Map 34

VII

Lizards

IGUANIDS: FAMILY IGUANIDAE

To THIS very large family belong the Anoles (*Anolis*), and the Collared (*Crotaphytus*), Earless (*Holbrookia*), Spiny (*Sceloporus*), Tree (*Urosaurus*), and Horned (*Phrynosoma*) Lizards. The family as a whole ranges from New York and extreme southwestern Canada southward throughout the Americas. It is also represented in the West Indies, Bermuda (introduced), the Galápagos Islands, Madagascar, and the Fiji and Tonga Islands in Polynesia.

Anoles: Genus *Anolis*

THE ANOLES, with more than 300 named species and subspecies, constitute the largest genus of reptiles in the Americas. They are especially abundant in the tropics. Only one species, the Green Anole, is native to continental United States; another occurs at Key West, and at least two West Indian species have established themselves in Florida.

A striking feature is the throat fan. A flap of skin, attached to the throat and sometimes extending onto the chest, is swung forward and downward by a flexible rod of cartilage attached near the middle of the throat. As the fan flares out, the scales become widely separated and a bright color (red, orange, or yellow) flashes into view. Males have large throat fans; in females they are small or rudimentary. The fan is displayed, often to the accompaniment of push ups and head bobbing, during courtship and in defense of territory.

The ability to change color is well developed. The changes are the result of rearrangement of pigment cells in the skin and in response to such stimuli as temperature, humidity, emotion, and exercise. Our native (and introduced) species, taken collectively, are capable of exhibiting browns, grays, and greens.

Anoles have pads on their toes that aid in climbing, but they are less adept at negotiating smooth vertical surfaces than some of the Geckos. All our Anoles are quite arboreal, but they also forage on the ground. Their food consists largely of insects and spiders.

GREEN ANOLE *Anolis carolinensis carolinensis* p. 127
  Identification: 5–7½ (head–body max. 2¾). The "chameleon"

sold in pet shops and at the circus. The plain *green* hue and *pink* throat fan (Fig. 13, below) distinguish it from all our other lizards. Coloration varies, individuals being green at one time, mottled green and brown at another, and brown at still another. There may be indications of pattern in form of dark streaks or spots. Color-changing abilities are poor compared with true Chameleons of Old World.

An abundant lizard in the South; often seen on fences, around old buildings, on shrubs and vines, or on ground. Green Anoles climb high into trees, out of which they may tumble — especially when chasing one another — without harmful effects. Most easily caught at night when, asleep on leaf or vine, the bright green coloration stands out vividly in the beam of a flashlight.
Range: Extr. se. Virginia to Key West; west to se. Oklahoma and cent. Texas; subspecies in Cuba and the Bahamas.   Map 37

KEY WEST ANOLE *Anolis sagrei stejnegeri*   p. 127
Identification: 5–7 (head–body max. 2⅛); males considerably larger than females. *Male:* A brown lizard with a *white streak* down center of throat (Fig. 13, below). The streak is the under-side of the throat fan, which when extended is brilliant orange-red with a whitish border. Both throat fan and white streak are good field marks easily seen through binoculars. General colora-tion and pattern variable; same individual may change from pale to very dark brown. Small yellow spots usually visible on body, these arranged in 6 or more roughly vertical rows. *Female:* Narrow yellowish stripe down center of back, flanked toward each side by a row of dark brown half-circles.

Abundant in many parts of Key West on shrubs and trees and walls of buildings; frequently forages on ground. When cornered, these Anoles make short erratic hops in their efforts to escape.
Similar species: Green Anoles turn bright green; Key West Anoles are always some shade of brown.
Range: Key West and nearby Keys.
Subspecies: Two related subspecies have become established in Florida. Both resemble Key West Anole in most details, but vary in their generally darker coloration, stronger tendency

Fig. 13. HEADS OF ANOLES

GREEN
Pink throat fan

KEY WEST
Longitudinal light
streak on throat

KEY WEST
Orange-red throat fan
with light border

toward longitudinal striping, and as mentioned below. CUBAN BROWN ANOLE, *Anolis sagrei sagrei*. Throat fan orange-red, sometimes with flecks of dark brown. Cuba; introduced in or near St. Petersburg, Tampa, and Miami, Florida; also into Jamaica and British Honduras. BAHAMAN BROWN ANOLE, *Anolis sagrei ordinatus*. Throat fan more orange and with numerous flecks of dark gray, its white edge heavily spotted with dark pigment (edge is unspotted or virtually so in both Key West and Cuban Brown Anoles). Fan may be almost entirely dark gray in some individuals. Males of this race tend to have a pronounced crest along top of tail. The Bahamas; introduced at Lake Worth and Miami, Florida.   Map 36

BAHAMAN BARK ANOLE   *Anolis distichus*   Fig. 14
Identification: 3½–4½ (head–body max. 1¾). A piece of lichen-covered "bark" that scurries away when approached. The general coloration, variable from pale gray to very dark brown, tends to match background on which lizard is resting. Dorsum with 4 poorly defined dark chevrons that point toward the rear; a straight dark line between eyes (Fig. 14, below). Throat fan pale yellow.
   This species is gecko-like in its actions and is the most arboreal Anole found in the United States.
Range: Established in Miami; Hispaniola, Bahamas. Map 37

Fig. 14

BAHAMAN BARK ANOLE
Faint chevron-like
dorsal pattern

(EASTERN) COLLARED LIZARD
Crotaphytus collaris collaris   p. 127
Identification: 8–12; record 14 (head–body max. 4½). The "mountain boomer," a gangling, big-headed, long-tailed lizard that runs on its hind legs like a miniature dinosaur. The 2 black collar markings (often broken at nape) are constant, but coloration and pattern are variable. Body scales very small. *Male:* General coloration yellowish, greenish, brownish, or bluish, dorsal pattern consisting of a profusion of light spots and (at least in younger specimens) a series of dark crossbands. Very old specimens may lose all their markings except for the black collars and light spots. *Female:* Similar, but less brilliantly colored; in gravid specimens a suffusion of orange or reddish is often present toward rear of body and on hind limbs and tail. *Young:* Broad dark crossbands or rows of dark spots; colors dull; about 3½" at hatching.

This reptile has no voice. The name "mountain boomer" may have originated from seeing a Collared Lizard atop a rock while some other animal, possibly a Barking Frog, called from beneath the same rock. A resident of hilly, rocky, often arid or semi-arid regions. Seldom found on the plains, except in rocky canyons or gullies traversing them. Limestone ledges or rock piles, both offering an abundance of hiding places, are favorite habitats. Collared Lizards are wary and quick to take cover. When surprised in the open, however, they run first on all fours, not assuming the upright, bipedal type of locomotion until they have attained some speed. They are pugnacious, nip hard when caught, and males when on the defense hold their mouths open in readiness to bite, exposing the black interior to view. Insects of various kinds are eaten; so also are small lizards, including "horned toads." Don't cage Collared Lizards with other reptiles smaller than themselves.

Similar species: Both Blue and Crevice Spiny Lizards have only *one* black band (collar) across the neck, and their dorsal scales are very large and spiny.

Range: Cent. Missouri to cent. New Mexico, cent. Texas, and Coahuila. Western subspecies. Map 42

RETICULATE COLLARED LIZARD
Crotaphytus reticulatus   p. 127

Identification: 8–13 (head–body max. 4½). Reticulate means netlike, and the light markings on the dorsum of this large lizard form an open, though often broken, network. This, in conjunction with series of large black spots across back, makes identification easy. Females lack vertical black bars on neck.

An alert, active lizard most often seen sunning atop a rock or found hiding beneath stones or debris or in packrat nests. Netlike pattern temporarily disappears in specimens chilled by cold weather.

Range: Rio Grande Valley in s. Texas and adj. Mexico. Map 42

Earless Lizards: Genus *Holbrookia*

THESE lizards are modified for life in regions of loose, dry, sandy soil. Their long legs and toes are useful for running on the surface and their heads are shaped for quick burrowing into the sand. They dive in head first and quickly bury themselves with a shimmying motion. One species prefers rocky areas. There are no visible ear openings. Sexual dimorphism is pronounced, and males of most species are marked with a pair of bold black bars on their sides. Such bars are lacking on females, or only slightly indicated.

MUSK AND MUD TURTLES; GOPHER TORTOISES

	Map	Text

STINKPOT   7   36
  2 light lines on head; plastron small. *Male:* Large areas
  of skin between plastral scutes; large, stout tail. *Female:*
  Plastral scutes close together.

STRIPE-NECKED MUSK TURTLE   9   38
  Head and neck striped; a dorsal keel (Fig. 5, p. 38).

RAZOR-BACKED MUSK TURTLE   8   37
  Head spotted; strong dorsal keel (Fig. 5, p. 38).

FLATTENED MUSK TURTLE   8   39
  Netlike head pattern; shell flattened (Fig. 5, p. 38).

LOGGERHEAD MUSK TURTLE   9   38
  Male: Very large head. *Female:* Head moderate; shell
  streaked, spotted, or blotched. *Young:* Shell streaked;
  3 keels (Fig. 5, p. 38).

STRIPED MUD TURTLE   11   39
  Shell and head striped.

MISSISSIPPI MUD TURTLE   12   41
  2 light lines on head; plastron large.

EASTERN MUD TURTLE   12   40
  Nondescript; rounded shell; large plastron, rear lobe large.

FLORIDA MUD TURTLE   12   41
  Rear lobe of plastron short.

YELLOW MUD TURTLE   10   39
  Throat plain yellow; 9th marginal higher than 8th.

GOPHER TORTOISE   32   66
  Foot elephant-like; shell relatively long.

TEXAS TORTOISE   31   66
  Foot elephant-like; shell relatively short.

♂ means male, ♀ female.

STINKPOT

Plastron ♀ Plastron ♂

STRIPE-NECKED MUSK

RAZOR-BACKED MUSK

FLAT MUSK

Young

Old ♀

♂

LOGGERHEAD MUSK

STRIPED MUD

MISSISSIPPI MUD

EASTERN MUD

Plastron

YELLOW MUD

Plastron

FLORIDA MUD

GOPHER TORTOISE

TEXAS TORTOISE

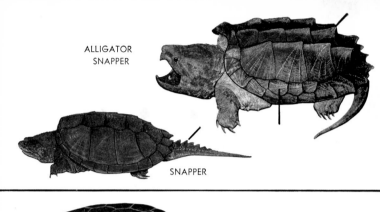

ALLIGATOR SNAPPER

SNAPPER

LOGGERHEAD

GREEN

RIDLEY

HAWKSBILL

LEATHERBACK

Plate 10   79

SNAPPERS AND SEA TURTLES

	Map	Text
ALLIGATOR SNAPPING TURTLE	2	35

ALLIGATOR SNAPPING TURTLE
Extra row of scutes at side of carapace; 3 prominent
ridges along back; head very large.

SNAPPING TURTLE   3   34
Long, saw-toothed tail.

ATLANTIC LOGGERHEAD   68
Reddish brown; 5 (or more) costal plates, 1st touching the
nuchal; *3 bridge scutes*.

ATLANTIC RIDLEY   69
Gray; 5 costal plates, 1st touching the nuchal; usually
4 bridge scutes.

ATLANTIC GREEN TURTLE   67
4 costal plates, 1st *not* touching the nuchal; 1 pair of plates
between eyes (Fig. 11, p. 68).

ATLANTIC LEATHERBACK   69
Prominent longitudinal ridges; no scutes; smooth skin.

ATLANTIC HAWKSBILL   68
Tortoise-shell pattern; scutes overlap (varies — see text).
2 pairs of plates between eyes (Fig. 11, p. 68).

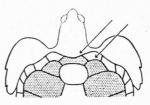

GREEN TURTLE
Nuchal separated from costal scute

LOGGERHEAD AND RIDLEY
Nuchal touches first costal scute

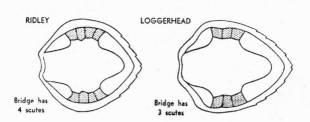

RIDLEY

LOGGERHEAD

Bridge has
4 scutes

Bridge has
3 scutes

Females heavy with eggs may bear an overwash of orange, orange-red, pink, or other pastel tints. Food includes insects and spiders. The range of the genus embraces the western United States and northern Mexico.

GREATER EARLESS LIZARD *Holbrookia texana* p. 127

    Identification: Males 3⅛–6¼ (head–body max. 3¼); females 2¾–5¼ (head–body max. 2¾). The black bars under the tail (Fig. 15, p. 82) offer a conspicuous field mark, for this lizard often holds its tail curled over the back, especially when perched atop a boulder. The bars are "flashed" when running, the tail being curled and waved from side to side as the lizard slows for a halt, or immediately after it stops. Intensity of dark dorsal markings varies in same individual and from one lizard or one geographical locality to the next. Also there is a tendency for the general coloration to resemble that of the habitat, those living in regions of gray soil being grayish, those living on reddish soil being reddish, etc. *Male:* The 2 bold black lines are near the groin and are much longer than in other Earless Lizards. The blue field surrounding them on the belly is usually very prominent. *Female:* Smaller in size; no black lines or blue field. *Young:* About 2″ at hatching.

    Rocky streambeds, sandstone or limestone outcrops, and rocky desert flats are typical habitats. This lizard tends to remain in its own home-range territory, and may dash from one boulder to another and then back again when pursued. The protective coloration of the dorsum is spectacularly evident when one of these lizards runs just a short distance, settles down on a pale-colored rock or sand, and virtually disappears.

Similar species: Spot-tailed Earless Lizard has rounded dark spots under tail instead of cross bars (Fig. 15, p. 82).

Range: Cent. Texas to Arizona and n. Mexico.

Subspecies: TEXAS EARLESS LIZARD, *Holbrookia texana texana* (illustrated on Plate 16). Only race occurring east of 100th meridian. Cent. and w. Texas and ne. Mexico. Western subspecies. Map 39

KEELED EARLESS LIZARD

Holbrookia propinqua propinqua p. 127

    Identification: 4½–5⁹⁄₁₆ (head–body max. 2⅜). This is a *long-tailed* Earless Lizard. The full original tail is noticeably longer than the head–body length in males and as long or longer in females. Dorsal scales distinctly keeled, but so small that a lens is necessary to see them. No dark spots under tail (Fig. 15, p. 82). *Male:* 2 black lines on side of body (behind armpit) *not* surrounded by blue; dorsal pattern variable and not clear-cut — usually a combination of dark blotches and dark longitudinal stripes covered by many small light dots. *Female:* Specimens from near the coast lack any prominent markings, but inland females are darker and with blotches. *Young:* Well-defined pattern of paired blotches; about 1½″ long at hatching.

A lizard indigenous to loose sandy soils and barrier beach islands of southern Texas and the Mexican coast.

Similar species: Tail in Lesser Earless Lizard is shorter — about as long as head and body combined, or a little shorter. (*Caution:* Be sure the tail has not been regenerated. Comparisons must be made upon basis of full original tail and not on invariably shorter, newly grown replacement.) Lesser Earless males usually have a small patch of blue touching or surrounding the black bars near the armpit. Some Lesser Earless Lizards have keeled scales. The two species (*propinqua* and *maculata*) are most easily separated on basis of range. If in doubt, also check the femoral pores (10 to 21, average 14 or 15, under each hind leg in Keeled Earless Lizard; 5 to 15, average 11 or 12, in Lesser Earless Lizard).

Range: S. Texas and ne. Mexico. Mexican subspecies. Map 40

LESSER EARLESS LIZARD *Holbrookia maculata* p. 127
Identification: 4–5 (head–body max. 2 7/16). Best identified by two negative characters: (1) no bars or spots under tail as in Greater and Spot-tailed Earless Lizards (Fig. 15, p. 82); (2) tail not so long as in Keeled Earless Lizard (only about as long as head and body combined, or a little shorter). *Male:* A pair of black lines near armpit that are often touched or surrounded by a small patch of blue; dorsal pattern blotched, but not clear-cut; a light stripe from head to near the groin and running between a series of blotches; dorsum usually sprinkled with small white specks. *Female:* Smaller in size and with black lines near the armpit much reduced; dorsal spots well defined but *not* surrounded by light pigment. *Young:* Like female in pattern and coloration; about 1½″ at hatching.

More or less sandy areas, open or with scant vegetational cover, are preferred. Specific habitats include sand prairies, dry sandbars in streambeds, fields under cultivation, chalk beds, and shortgrass-cactus-mesquite country. These lizards are diurnal and during the heat of the day they keep to shade afforded by bushes (or other vegetation) or take refuge in mammal or other burrows. They are particularly adept at "shimmy burial," diving into and then shimmying beneath the sand or loose soil.

Similar species: See Keeled Earless Lizard.

Range: S. South Dakota to Texas, Arizona, and n.-cent. Mexico.

Subspecies: NORTHERN EARLESS LIZARD, *Holbrookia maculata maculata* (male illustrated on Plate 16). As described above. South Dakota to nw. Texas and adj. New Mexico. EASTERN EARLESS LIZARD, *Holbrookia maculata perspicua* (female illustrated on Plate 16). Similar, but males lack white speckling; in both sexes there is a strong tendency for the dark dorsal blotches to fuse together so that there is only a *single* row down each side of the body. (In Northern Earless Lizard normally a *double* row on each side.) Se. Kansas to n.-cent. Texas.   Western and Mexican subspecies.   Map 38

Fig. 15. UNDERSURFACES OF TAILS OF EARLESS LIZARDS

GREATER   SPOT-TAILED   KEELED AND LESSER
Black crossbars   Dark spots   No markings

SPOT-TAILED EARLESS LIZARD   *Holbrookia lacerata* p. 127
Identification: $4\frac{1}{2}$–5 $^{11}\!/_{16}$ (head–body max. 2 $^{11}\!/_{16}$). Most conspicuously spotted of all Earless Lizards and with three separate sets of markings that can be checked: (1) dark dorsal spots *surrounded* by light pigment; (2) about 7 rounded dark spots under tail (Fig. 15, above); and (3) dusky to black oval streaks at edge of abdomen (these variable in number — from 4 to only 1, or even absent). Sexes patterned alike.   *Young:* Marked as adults; about $1\frac{1}{2}''$ at hatching.

A species of arid, dark-soil flats, mesquite-prickly pear associations, and uplands of Edwards Plateau in central Texas.
Similar species: Greater Earless Lizard has black *bars* extending completely across the underside of tail. In female Lesser Earless Lizards the light pigment does *not* surround the dorsal spots and there are *no* dark spots under tail.
Range: Cent. and s. Texas and adj. Mexico.
Subspecies: SOUTHERN SPOT-TAILED EARLESS LIZARD, *Holbrookia lacerata subcaudalis* (illustrated on Plate 16). Two distinct rows of dark blotches down each side of back; femoral pores average 16 under each hind leg. S. Texas and adj. Mexico, but not in lower Rio Grande Valley. PLATEAU SPOT-TAILED EARLESS LIZARD, *Holbrookia lacerata lacerata*. Dark blotches usually fused together in pairs and producing the effect of a single row on each side of back; femoral pores average 13. Edwards Plateau region of cent. Texas.   Map 41

Spiny Lizards: Genus *Sceloporus*

A LARGE and distinctive genus of lizards with *keeled* and pointed dorsal scales. Some species are so rough that they seem almost like pine cones with legs and tails. Several were formerly called "swifts." In gross appearance they resemble the Tree Lizard

(Urosaurus), but in the latter the dorsal scales are irregular in size and there is a fold of skin across the throat (Fig., p. 142).

Most species within our area are arboreal, at least to some extent. Rock outcrops or boulders and large rotting stumps or logs are also favorite habitats. They are best stalked by two persons working toward them from opposite directions, for they are adept at keeping a tree trunk or rock between themselves and a single observer.

These lizards are chiefly insectivorous, but they also eat spiders and other arthropods, and even smaller lizards, baby mice, etc. Most kinds reproduce by laying eggs; a few bear living young.

Sexual differences are usually well marked. Males of most species have a prominent blue patch at each side of the belly, and in many there is also some blue on the throat. Under certain conditions, such as during cool weather or before skin shedding, the blue may turn black. Females lack the blue areas or have them only slightly developed. Middorsal dark markings, which are often faint or reduced in size (or both) in males, are normally rather prominent in females.

The genus ranges from extreme southern British Columbia and extreme southern New York to Panama.

(TEXAS) ROSE-BELLIED LIZARD
Sceloporus variabilis marmoratus　　　　　　　　　　　　　　　p. 142

Identification: 3¾–5½ (head–body max. 2⅛). Unique in two ways. Our only Spiny Lizard with (1) pink belly patches and (2) a skin pocket behind the thigh (Fig. 16, below). Neither one is a good field mark, however, for the reptile usually must be caught to see them. The light dorsolateral stripe and double row of brown spots down back are best points to check. General coloration buffy- to olive-brown. *Male:* Large area of pink at each side of belly bordered fore and aft and toward center of belly by dark blue; the dark color extends upward onto sides of body to form a prominent dark spot in armpit and another much smaller one in groin. *Young:* About 2″ at birth.

An essentially terrestrial lizard of arid southern Texas. Often seen on fence posts and in clumps of cactus; occasionally on rocks or in mesquite or other scrubby trees.

Similar species: Southern Prairie Lizard has *blue* belly patches, and it lacks the skin pocket behind the thigh. Mesquite Lizard

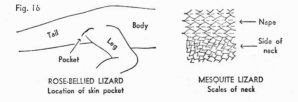

Fig. 16

Tail　　Body　　Leg

Pocket

ROSE-BELLIED LIZARD
Location of skin pocket

Nape
Side of neck

MESQUITE LIZARD
Scales of neck

has no dorsolateral light line, and scales on side of its neck are abruptly smaller than those on nape (Fig. 16, p. 83). Texas Spiny Lizard grows very large and has only 33 or fewer dorsal scales from back of head to base of tail (58 or more in Rose-bellied Lizard). Tree Lizard (*Urosaurus*) has fold of skin across throat (Fig., p. 142).

Range: S. Texas and ne. Mexico; other races occur in Mexico and to Costa Rica. Map 48

MESQUITE LIZARD *Sceloporus grammicus disparilis* p. 142
Identification: 4–6⅞ (head–body max. 2⅞). An arboreal and remarkably camouflaged Spiny Lizard, best identified (at a distance) by habitat and habits. When caught, scalation can be checked. Our only Spiny Lizard with scales on sides of neck abruptly *much* smaller than those on nape (Fig. 16, p. 83). General coloration gray or olive-gray. *Female:* 4 or 5 dark wavy lines across back; foreleg distinctly barred. *Male:* Dorsum sometimes with a metallic greenish luster; markings obscure; a dark vertical line in front of arm; sides of belly pale blue, the blue bordered by black (toward center of belly); throat mottled with black except the center, which may be flesh color or pale blue. *Young:* About 1¾″ at birth.

Most quiet and unobtrusive of the Spiny Lizards. Protective coloration and the habit of dodging to the opposite side of tree limb or bole are so well developed that few people ever see this reptile. Usually retreats to uppermost branches while observer is still far away. Found chiefly in mesquite, but also on other small scrubby trees.

Similar species: Rose-bellied and Southern Prairie Lizards have a light dorsolateral stripe; Prairie Lizard also is largely terrestrial. Texas Spiny Lizard grows big and has large dorsal scales, numbering 33 or fewer from back of head to base of tail; dorsal scales are 50 or more in Mesquite Lizard. Tree Lizard (*Urosaurus*) has a fold of skin across throat (Fig., p. 142).

Range: Extr. s. Texas and n. Mexico. Mexican subspecies.
Map 47

CREVICE SPINY LIZARD *Sceloporus poinsetti* p. 142
Identification: 5–11½ (head–body max. 4⅝). The dark band across the neck is an excellent field mark. Tail strongly barred, especially *near tip*. Young, at birth, boldly cross-banded with black from head to tip of tail. Females tend to retain these markings, but in adult males they may virtually disappear, except across neck and on tail. General dorsal coloration gray or greenish gray to reddish. *Male:* Throat bright blue; sides of belly bright blue, the blue bordered on its inner side by a broad black band. *Young:* Sometimes a narrow dark stripe connecting crossbands down center of back; 2½″ to 3″ at birth.

Boulders and rocky outcrops are favorite habitats, and on these the lizards may stand out conspicuously — at binocular range. Extremely difficult to approach and capture in such places, quickly darting to opposite side or into crevices to hide. **Similar species:** In the Blue Spiny Lizard the tail markings are *not* conspicuous toward tip; light spots are present on nape of neck and on back. In the Collared Lizard, there are *two* black lines on the neck, the scales very small and smooth.

Range: Cent. Texas to sw. New Mexico; south to Durango.

Map 45

BLUE SPINY LIZARD *Sceloporus cyanogenys* p. 142
Identification: 5–13½ (head–body max. 5½). Largest and bluest of the Spiny Lizards. The dark band across neck, bordered by white and in combination with light spots on nape and back, is a good field mark. Tail markings not conspicuous at tip. *Male:* A brilliant metallic greenish blue over a ground color of brown; upper sides of legs bronzy; entire throat bright blue; a large light blue patch at each side of belly bordered by a black band on inner side. *Female* (and young male): Gray or brown. *Young:* 2½″ to 2¾″ at birth.

Habitats include boulders, rocky or earthen cliffs, stone bridges, and abandoned houses.

Similar species: In Crevice Spiny Lizard the black bands are conspicuous near *tip* of tail. Collared Lizard has *two* black lines across neck. and scales are smooth and very small.

Range: S. Texas and ne. Mexico. Map 44

TEXAS SPINY LIZARD *Sceloporus olivaceus* p. 142
Identification: 7½–11 (head–body max. 4¾). The "rusty lizard." Conspicuous field marks are lacking, but this is our only very large, very spiny, tree-inhabiting lizard. A rather vague dorsolateral light stripe (stronger in males) and wavy dark lines across the back (more conspicuous in females). General dorsal coloration gray- to rusty-brown. The very large dorsal scales, counted from back of head to base of tail, are 33 or fewer (average 30). *Male:* Narrow light blue area at each side of belly and *without* a black border. *Young:* 2⅛″ to 2⅝″ at hatching.

Usually seen in trees — mesquite, live oak, cottonwood, cedar, etc. They are inconspicuous against the bark and are usually discovered when they move or by the noise they make in climbing. Although essentially arboreal, Texas Spiny Lizards also may be seen on fences, old bridges, abandoned houses, in patches of prickly pear, or in other places that offer shelter in the form of cracks or cavities.

Similar species: Fence Lizard usually has a fairly complete black line running down rear surface of thigh. In Northern Fence and Prairie Lizards the dorsal scales are small; from back of head to base of tail they number 35 or more (average 40 or more).

Range: Extr. s. Oklahoma to ne. Mexico; s. New Mexico.

Map 46

FENCE LIZARD *Sceloporus undulatus*
(subspecies *hyacinthinus* and *undulatus*)   p. 142
Identification: 4–7¼ (head–body max. 3¼). A small gray or brown Spiny Lizard with strong arboreal tendencies. Females chiefly gray and most conspicuously patterned on top; males usually brown and most heavily marked on bottom. Both sexes have a more or less complete dark line running along rear side of thigh. *Male:* Sides of belly hyacinth- to greenish-blue, the bright color bordered by black toward center of belly; a broad bluish area at base of throat, the blue surrounded by black and often split in 2 parts; dorsal crosslines indistinct or absent. *Female:* A series of dark wavy (undulating) lines across back; yellow, orange, or reddish at base of tail; belly whitish with scattered black flecks; small amounts of pale blue at sides of belly and throat. *Young:* Patterned as female but darker and duller; averaging 1⅝" to 2¼" at hatching.

Often seen on rail fences or on rotting logs or stumps. The only Spiny Lizard occurring throughout most of its range. (No other members of genus are found north of Florida or east of Texas.) When surprised on the ground, Fence Lizards usually dash for a nearby tree, climb upward for a short distance, and then remain motionless on the opposite side of the trunk. If approached, they dodge to the opposite side again, but higher up. The performance may be repeated several times, and the lizard soon ascends out of reach. Often called "pine lizard" because of its frequent occurrence in open pine woods.

Similar species: Florida Scrub Lizard has a distinct *dark brown* lateral stripe. Prairie Lizards have light longitudinal stripes, and are largely terrestrial in habits. Texas Spiny Lizard grows much bigger, has very large dorsal scales, and lacks a dark line on rear of thigh.

Range: Se. New York to cent. Florida; west to e. Kansas and cent. Texas.

Subspecies: NORTHERN FENCE LIZARD, *Sceloporus undulatus hyacinthinus* (illustrated on Plate 17). As described above. All of general range except the deep Southeast. SOUTHERN FENCE LIZARD, *Sceloporus undulatus undulatus*. Similar, but averaging slightly larger and with black markings more intense. Under surfaces of males may be almost entirely black, except for patches of blue. In females the black flecks are more numerous and some of them may form a broken black line down center of belly. Dorsal scales larger. Counting from the back of the head to a point opposite posterior margin of thighs, the scales are usually 37 or fewer in number. In Northern Fence Lizard they are usually 38 or more. S. South Carolina to cent. Florida and cent. Louisiana, and intergrading with Northern Fence Lizard where their ranges meet. The two Prairie Lizards are subspecifically related to the Fence Lizards. Map 50

PRAIRIE LIZARD *Sceloporus undulatus*
(subspecies *garmani* and *consobrinus*) p. 142

Identification: 3½–5⅜ (head–body max. 2⅛). The light longitudinal stripes, bold and usually clear-cut, are excellent field marks. (The lower stripe on each side may be less conspicuous than in the specimens illustrated.) Dark dorsal markings, so prominent in other subspecies, are reduced to spots bordering the light dorsolateral stripe. Ground color light brown to reddish brown; a light brown stripe down center of back. *Male:* A long narrow light blue patch at each side of belly; throat markings absent or represented by 2 inconspicuous dark spots. *Female:* Uniform white below, and without the black flecks of the Fence Lizards. *Young:* About 1¾" to 2" at hatching.

Essentially terrestrial, but occupying a wide variety of habitats — sand dunes and other sandy areas, brushy flatlands, cliffs, bases of buttes, etc. Forages widely for food but scurries back to cover of clumps of vegetation or rock crevices when approached. Occasionally climbs high into weeds and small trees, and is often found under shocks of wheat.

Similar species: A dorsolateral light stripe is sometimes evident in the Fence Lizard, but it is not well defined and is crossed by the dark markings of the back. Male Fence Lizards are conspicuously marked with black on throat and belly. Racerunner, Whiptail Lizard, and many of the Skinks have prominent light stripes, but none have large keeled scales. Texas Spiny Lizard grows much bigger, and its very large dorsal scales number only 33 or fewer from back of head to base of tail (35 or more in Prairie Lizards).

Range: S. South Dakota to n. Mexico; west to se. Arizona.

Subspecies: NORTHERN PRAIRIE LIZARD, *Sceloporus undulatus garmani* (illustrated on Plate 17). As described above. S. South Dakota to cent. Oklahoma. SOUTHERN PRAIRIE LIZARD, *Sceloporus undulatus consobrinus*. Similar but with the light stripes less prominent. Males have 2 patches of blue on throat (joined into 1 in some specimens), and these blue areas, as well as those on the belly, may be bordered by dark pigment. Averages considerably larger than the northern subspecies, and attains a total length of about 7" and a head–body maximum of 2¾". A lizard of the plains and mountains, and especially common in rocky terrain that furnishes abundant hiding and basking places. Sw. Oklahoma and most of the Texas panhandle to se. Arizona and n. Mexico. Intergrades with Northern Prairie Lizard where their ranges meet, and with Northern Fence

Lizard over a rather broad area through e.-cent. Texas. Western and Mexican subspecies. Map 50

FLORIDA SCRUB LIZARD *Sceloporus woodi* p. 142
Identification: 3½–5⅜ (head–body max. 2³⁄₁₆). A Spiny Lizard with a *dark brown* lateral stripe. General coloration pale brown or gray-brown. Many specimens, females especially, have 8 to 10 pairs of dark brown wavy spots on back. *Male:* A long blue area on each side of belly, bordered by black on inner side; a pair of blue spots at base of throat; rest of throat black except for a median white stripe. *Female:* Dark spots on chest and under surface of head; traces of blue on throat and sides of belly; rest of venter white.

A lizard of pine ridges and the Florida rosemary scrub. Usually dashes away over the ground like a Racerunner instead of dodging around tree trunks and logs like a Fence Lizard. Climbs readily, however, when closely pursued.

Similar species: In Southern Fence Lizard the under surfaces are marked with considerable black pigment, and there may be a *black* lateral stripe, but it is not so clear-cut as the *brown* stripe in the Florida Scrub Lizard. Dorsal scales in Florida Scrub Lizard average more than 40; in Southern Fence Lizard the average is 34.

Range: Cent. and s. Florida. Map 49

(EASTERN) TREE LIZARD *Urosaurus ornatus ornatus* p. 142
Identification: 4–5⅜ (head–body max. 2). A small gray or grayish-brown lizard with arboreal tendencies. Back with irregular dark spots or crossbands, some narrowly edged with blue. Check for three things: (1) a fold of skin across throat (Fig., p. 142); (2) dorsal scales variable in size — some large, some tiny; and (3) 2 long folds of skin on each side of body. The folds give the Tree Lizard a somewhat wrinkled appearance, as though the skin were a little too large for it. *Male:* 3 blue patches — one centered under the throat and another at each side of the belly. *Young:* About 1¼″ to 1¾″ at hatching.

Almost always seen in trees or on rocks and usually resting in a *vertical* position — "heads up" with tail dangling, or the reverse with head pointing down. Trips aground, either to forage or to move from one tree or rock to another, are usually brief. A difficult lizard to observe or catch. When motionless, camouflage is nearly perfect, but the lizard often may reveal itself by indulging in bobbing movements. When pursued, it is adept at dodging, keeping on opposite side of tree trunk or rock and climbing quickly out of reach. A member of a large genus with numerous species in the Southwest and Mexico.

Similar species: Various members of the Spiny Lizard genus (*Sceloporus*), although very similar to Tree Lizard in gross ap-

pearance, have following distinctive features: (1) *no* fold across throat; and (2) dorsal scales all approximately *same size.*
Range: Cent. Texas to Rio Grande Valley. Western and Mexican subspecies.   Map 43

Horned Lizards: Genus *Phrynosoma*

THE "horned toads," the majority of them adorned like cactus plants, are the most bizarre of all our lizards. The arrangement of the spines, especially on the head, and the fringe scales at the sides of the abdomen offer the best clues to identification.

Horned Lizards are diurnal. They eat spiders, sowbugs, and insects — ants especially — but high temperatures are required to stimulate their appetites. Even when a heat lamp is used, they are difficult to keep in captivity in the North; most of them refuse food during the winter months and die either during cold weather or after their first meal in the spring.

An extraordinary habit is the occasional squirting of blood from the forward corners of the eyes for a distance of several feet. This is associated with an ability to increase blood pressure in the head. Some species lay eggs; others give birth to living young. Despite their spiny garb, Horned Lizards are eaten by certain birds, such as hawks and roadrunners, and by such reptiles as Whipsnakes and Collared Lizards. The genus ranges from southern Canada to Guatemala and is particularly well represented in the Southwest and in Mexico.

TEXAS HORNED LIZARD *Phrynosoma cornutum*   p. 127
    Identification: 2½–4; record 5⅛ (head–body max. 4¼). The "horned toad" of the pet trade and the species most frequently carried home by tourists or visitors to the Southwest. The 2 central head spines are *much longer* than any of the others (Fig. 17, p. 90). *Two rows* of fringe scales at each side of abdomen. The general coloration is usually some shade of brown — yellowish, reddish, grayish, or tan — but may sometimes be gray. Dark dorsal spots usually conspicuous and with light posterior borders. *Young:* About 1⅛″ to 1¼″ at hatching.
    A lizard typically of dry, flat, open terrain with sparse plant cover; in areas of mesquite, prickly pear, etc., on sandy, rocky, or loamy soil. Occurs from sea level to at least 6000 feet. Specimens are usually evident only on very warm days. They run surprisingly fast and seek shelter, when pursued, in mammal burrows, in rock piles or ledges, or in clumps of vegetation.
    Similar species: In Round-tailed Horned Lizard the tail is slender and rounded but broadens abruptly near base, all the longer horns are about of equal length, and there are *no* fringe

scales at edge of abdomen. In Short-horned Lizard the horns are greatly reduced in size (Fig. 17, below), and there is *one row* of fringe scales.

Range: Kansas to se. Arizona and n. Mexico; introduced in Florida and other s. states. Map 52

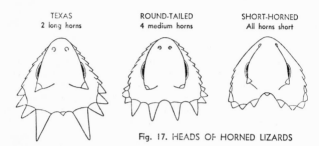

TEXAS
2 long horns

ROUND-TAILED
4 medium horns

SHORT-HORNED
All horns short

Fig. 17. HEADS OF HORNED LIZARDS

(EASTERN) SHORT-HORNED LIZARD

Phrynosoma douglassi brevirostre p. 127

Identification: 2½–3¾; record 4½ (head–body max. 2½). Short, stubby horns (Fig. 17, above) and only a *single row* of fringe scales along each side of abdomen. Ground color brown or gray. *Young:* Born alive, about 1¼″ at birth.

Indigenous to semi-arid, short-grass portions of the northern Great Plains; usually found in rather rough terrain.

Similar species: See Texas Horned Lizard (p. 89).

Range: Kansas to cent. Montana and adj. Canada. Western subspecies. Map 51

ROUND-TAILED HORNED LIZARD

Phrynosoma modestum p. 127

Identification: 3–4⅛ (head–body max. 2¾). Three distinct items to check: (1) tail round and slender but broadened abruptly near base; (2) 4 horns at back of head, all about equal in length (Fig. 17, above); and (3) *no* row of fringe scales along side of abdomen. Coloration variable: general tone may be yellowish gray or ash-white or any of several shades of light brown, but usually it closely matches the dominant soil color of the immediate habitat. The ability to change color is marked, and the intensity of the dark blotches may vary from black to pale hues only a little darker than ground color. *Young:* About 1″ at hatching.

This "horny toad" is so well camouflaged that it can easily be overlooked. Normally it remains motionless when approached, body flattened against the ground, and may be almost stepped on before it moves. After a short dash, it stops abruptly, virtually vanishing against the background, with which it blends so well. Habitats include desert flats and washes and arid and semi-arid plains with shrubby vegetation.

Similar species: See Texas Horned Lizard (p. 89).

Range: W.-cent. Texas to se. Arizona and cent. Mexico.

Map 53

GECKOS: FAMILY GEKKONIDAE

A LARGE FAMILY, widespread through the tropics and subtropics of both New and Old Worlds. Geckos are notorious for their ability to establish themselves in tropical seaports, and at least two (and probably three) of our five species are immigrants that were transported fortuitously, in cargoes of fruit, produce, lumber, etc., into Key West and other localities in the Far South.

Most of our species have vertical pupils and nonmovable eyelids, the eyes, like those of snakes, remaining open all the time. All but one are chiefly nocturnal or crepuscular; under cover of darkness they move actively about in pursuit of insects and spiders, their natural food.

Many kinds of Geckos are as good as flies at walking up and down smooth walls and even some types of ceilings. This they can do by virtue of the pads upon their toes, the under surface of each pad being equipped with a series of long narrow plates (lamellae) that bear microscopic hairlike processes. These are pressed into every minute inequality of the surface upon which the lizard is moving. On rough surfaces, the claws are also useful in climbing.

Some kinds of Geckos give voice to squeaky notes, and the group derives both its common and scientific names from an oriental species whose cry sounds like *geck-o*. Coloration in the individual specimen may vary greatly, the tones and hues changing, sometimes quickly, in response to such factors as temperature, humidity, amount of light, and degree of activity. The tails of these lizards are *very* easily detached, but are soon regenerated.

MEDITERRANEAN GECKO

Hemidactylus turcicus turcicus p. 111

Identification: 4–5 (head–body max. 2⅜). Eyes very large. Toe pads broad and extending nearly full length of toes; pads larger than those of any other gecko of our area (Fig., p. 111). Small wartlike bumps on head, body, legs, and tail. Both light and dark spots on a light ground. Dark spots may be brown or gray; light areas variable from bright pinkish ivory to whitish.

Almost completely nocturnal. On warm evenings look for it on buildings, window screens, or near lights where insects congregate. It makes itself quite at home around human habitations.

Voice: A faint mouselike squeak repeated at intervals. Our only lizard with a voice.

Range: Established at Key West, Miami, New Orleans, Browns-ville (Texas), and perhaps in other southern localities. An Old World Gecko ranging from w. India and Iran across North Africa to Morocco and Canary Islands. Also introduced into Cuba and e. Mexico. This is one reptile that has traveled widely by stow-ing itself away in shipments awaiting transportation.   Map 57

ASHY GECKO *Sphaerodactylus cinereus*   p. 111

Identification: 2¾–2⅞ (head–body max. 1⅜). A wraith of a lizard that appears on buildings walls, window screens, or near lights on warm evenings. There it searches for insects attracted by the illumination. Check dorsal pattern. Upper surfaces with a profusion of tiny white or yellow spots on a darker ground color that varies from reddish brown to pale grayish brown. The spots often tend to run together and form light lines on head. Snout pointed and slightly flattened. Dorsal scales *small and granular*. Small round pad at tip of each toe (Fig., p. 111). *Young:* The dark crossbands and reddish tail disappear with age.

Chiefly nocturnal; hides in crevices or under debris or vegeta-tion during daylight hours. Often found in or on walls of cisterns and outhouses.

Similar species: Reef Gecko is brown with *dark* markings, and its dorsal scales are strongly *keeled*.

Range: Key West; Cuba, Hispaniola, and adj. islands.   Map 56

REEF GECKO *Sphaerodactylus notatus*   p. 111

Identification: 2–2⅛ (head–body max. 1⅛). A tiny, chubby brown lizard with a pointed, slightly flattened snout. *Occurs in 2 color phases — striped and spotted.* In striped phase, there are 3 broad, dark, light-centered stripes on head that are pointed anteriorly and disappear toward middle of body; *2 light dots on nape.* In spotted phase, small dark spots are scattered over head and body. Some specimens are intermediate between these two extremes; others lack conspicuous dark markings entirely. Dorsal scales *strongly keeled*. Small round pad at tip of each toe (Fig., p. 111). *Young:* Like adults.

The Reef Gecko quickly scurries for the nearest cover when its shelter (a board, stone, coconut husk, trash, or other debris) is lifted. Chiefly nocturnal, but often crepuscular.

Similar species: Ashy Gecko has *light* spots on dark ground color and small *granular* dorsal scales.

Range: Florida Keys and extr. s. mainland Florida; Cuba and n. Bahamas.   Map 54

YELLOW-HEADED GECKO. *Gonatodes fuscus*   p. 111

Identification: 2½–3¼ (head–body max. 1½). *Adult males:*

Head yellow; body, legs, and tail uniformly dark, almost black in sunlight, but bluish (as illustrated) at night or in heavy shade. *Female and young:* Mottled with brown, gray, and yellow; *a narrow light collar* usually present on *one or both sides of neck.* In this species there are no expanded pads on toes (Fig., p. 111), and pupils of eyes are round. Tip of tail, unless regenerated, is whitish.

Largely diurnal, in contrast with our other Geckos. Occurs in and about abandoned buildings and docks and among debris on vacant land. A favorite habit is to hang upside down beneath a log, board, or other shelter.

Range: Introduced at Key West, on Jamaica and Cuba and in s. Mexico; El Salvador to Colombia. Map 58

(TEXAS) BANDED GECKO *Coleonyx variegatus brevis* p. 111
Identification: 4–4¾ (head–body max. 2¼). Our only Gecko with *functional eyelids.* No toe pads (Fig., p. 111). Scales tiny. A considerable *change in pattern* is associated with age. Juveniles are strongly marked by broad chocolate crossbands that alternate with narrower bands of cream or yellow. But as they grow older dark pigment appears in the light bands and, conversely, light areas develop in the chocolate bands. This produces a mottled effect that increases with age. In many adults the original pattern can be made out only with difficulty. *Young:* See above; about 1¾" at hatching.

Banded Geckos are terrestrial, climbing but little in comparison with their more acrobatic relatives. They prefer rocky areas, such as canyons, where they can take shelter during daylight hours beneath stones or in crevices. One of the thrills of night-time driving in Banded Gecko country is to see these pale delicate lizards standing out conspicuously against the dark macademized paving as they cross the highway during their nocturnal prowlings.

Range: S.-cent. Texas to New Mexico and Durango. Western subspecies. Map 55

WHIPTAILS: FAMILY TEIIDAE

A LARGE FAMILY, confined to the New World and especially abundant and diverse in South America. One genus (*Cnemidophorus*) in the United States, with many species in the West. The two occurring in our area are characterized by having thousands of tiny scales on their backs and 8 rows of large rectangular plates on their bellies (Fig. 18, p. 96). The tail is rough to the touch. Both species have bold longitudinal stripes, and could be confused only with the Skinks. They are extremely difficult to catch when on the prowl, running swiftly and dodging skillfully. When foraging they keep

SOFTSHELL TURTLES

(Consult text for descriptions of females not illustrated.)

	Map	*Text*

WESTERN SPINY SOFTSHELL   35   71
   Male: Shell with dark spots and small eyelike marks; feet
   strongly streaked and spotted. Top of shell rough; feels
   like sandpaper, at least toward rear.

SMOOTH SOFTSHELL   33   70
   Feet *not* strongly patterned. Shell smooth; no spines or
   bumps. No ridge in nostril. *Male:* Vague dots and dashes.
   Female: An indefinite mottled pattern.

EASTERN SPINY SOFTSHELL   35   70
   Feet strongly patterned. *Male:* Large eyelike spots; top
   of shell sandpapery. *Female:* Pattern vague (see text);
   spines at front of shell.

GULF COAST SOFTSHELL   35   71
   Male: 2 or more rows of curved black lines bordering rear
   edge of shell. Light lines on head usually meet (Fig. 12,
   p. 72).

TEXAS SOFTSHELL   35   72
   Male: Numerous light dots.

FLORIDA SOFTSHELL   34   73
   Shell proportionately longer than in other species. Surface of shell with numerous small bumps in form of flattened hemispheres.

♂ means male, ♀ female.

FRONT EDGES OF CARAPACES

SMOOTH
No projections

FLORIDA
Flattened hemispheres

SPINY GROUP
Spines or cones

SMOOTH SOFTSHELL
Nostrils round

ALL OTHER SOFTSHELLS
A ridge in each nostril

WESTERN
SPINY ♂

SMOOTH ♂ ♀

♀

EASTERN
SPINY

GULF COAST ♂

TEXAS ♂

FLORIDA ♂ ♀

PENINSULA
COOTER

♂

Plastron

♀

FLORIDA
RED-BELLIED
TURTLE

RIVER
COOTER

Plastron

♀

FLORIDA
COOTER

♂

SUWANNEE COOTER

TEXAS
SLIDER

♂

SLIDER

Plate 12   95

COOTERS AND SLIDERS

	Map	*Text*

PENINSULA COOTER   23   60
"Hairpins" on head; dark marginal smudges; plastron unmarked.

FLORIDA RED-BELLIED TURTLE   27   64
Light vertical band; few stripes on head, but including an
arrow.

RIVER COOTER   22   58
A figure "C"; under surfaces heavily marked.

FLORIDA COOTER   23   60
No "hairpins"; hollow circles on marginals; plastron as in
Peninsula Cooter.

TEXAS SLIDER   22   59
Broad head markings; under surfaces basically as in River
Cooter, but reduced to narrow dark lines.

SUWANNEE COOTER   22   58
A figure "C"; general appearance very dark; under surfaces as in River Cooter.

SLIDER   22   59
A figure "C"; shell pinched inward in front of hind legs;
under surfaces as in River Cooter.

Note: Patterns, often obscure in large specimens, are best seen if the
turtle is submerged in water. The illustrations of the River Cooter
and Texas Slider are of relatively young individuals, chosen to
show the distinctive markings that fade or even disappear in old
adults. These two turtles are reproduced at the scale of large
adults, however, and their heads are disproportionately large.

♂ means male, ♀ female.

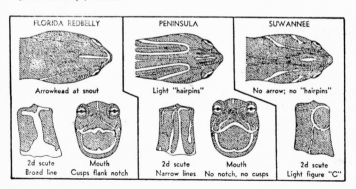

a minimum distance of several yards between themselves and an observer, but may be easily watched through binoculars.

Fig. 18. BACK AND BELLY SCALES OF WHIPTAILS AND SKINKS

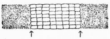

WHIPTAIL AND RACERUNNER
Rows of enlarged scales on belly

SKINKS
All scales approximately same size

SIX-LINED RACERUNNER *Cnemidophorus sexlineatus* p. 126
   Identification: 6–9½ (head–body max. 3). A dull (not shiny) lizard with a long whiplike tail. The 6 light stripes may be white, yellow, pale gray, or pale blue. Some specimens, especially from western part of range, have a greenish appearance. A short light stripe on side of tail, extending backward from hind leg and bordered below by a dark line. Eight rows of large plates on belly (Fig. 18, above). *Male:* Stripes less intense; belly washed with blue. *Young:* Light blue tail; stripes yellow and quite distinct; 3½″ to 4″ at hatching.

   An active lizard, conspicuous because of its boldness. Open, well-drained areas are preferred — those covered with sand or loose soil: fields, open woods, thicket margins, rocky outcrops, river flood plains, etc. Not arboreal. Racerunners are well named, usually winning the race with the would-be collector. Called "fieldstreaks" in some parts of their range. When pursued, they take refuge in vegetation, under boards or stones, or in burrows, sometimes of their own making.

   Similar species: Skinks are shiny, and their ventral scales are like dorsal scales in size and shape.

   Range: Maryland to Florida Keys; west to se. Wyoming, e. Colorado, and Texas; penetrates major stream valleys well outward from main part of range.   Map 72

(EASTERN) SPOTTED WHIPTAIL
Cnemidophorus sacki gularis   p. 126
   Identification: 6½–10½ (head–body max. 3⅜). *Rows of light spots in the dark stripes.* Six major light lines, plus a broader, less distinct light line down back. The brighter lines may be greenish on anterior part of body. No clearly-defined dark line at base of tail. Appearance dull (not shiny). Eight rows of large plates on belly (Fig. 18, above). *Male:* Throat bright orange or pink; large areas of bright blue on the venter. *Young:* Tail gray.

   A resident of open, more or less dry regions where vegetation is not dense and there is ample room for running. More deliberate in its movements than Six-lined Racerunner and not dash-

ing away from the observer so far before it stops. Completely
terrestrial.

Similar species: Skinks are shiny. In the Racerunner there is a
short light stripe on side of tail, extending backward from hind
leg and bordered below by a dark line.

Range: Cent. Oklahoma to n. Veracruz. Western and Mexican
subspecies.   Map 71

SKINKS: FAMILY SCINCIDAE

SMOOTH, SHINY, alert, and active lizards that are difficult to catch —
and to hold. Yet in most instances they *must* be caught and examined carefully for accurate identification. Watch the tails: they
break off *very* easily. The average Skink will try to bite, and large
ones can pinch painfully hard.

Most species are terrestrial, foraging actively by day but taking
shelter (at night, in bad weather, or from high temperatures) under
stones or in debris, decaying logs, abandoned packrat nests, etc.
The Broad-headed Skink and some others are often arboreal.
Habitats usually include some evidence of moisture, such as in the
form of nearby springs or swamps or underground humid retreats.
Insects and other arthropods are the chief food, but large skinks
can also manage such sizable prey as baby mice or birds in the
nest, or the eggs of such species as sparrows. Captives often do
well on a diet of live insects and spiders and will sometimes take
bits of meat dipped in raw beaten egg.

The family is very large and occurs in all the continents, but the
great majority of species are confined to the Eastern Hemisphere.
All but two of our skinks belong to the big genus *Eumeces*; the exceptions are the Ground Skink (*Lygosoma*) and the curious Sand
Skink (*Neoseps*). In some of the species of *Eumeces*, tones of red
or orange appear on the heads (of males only) during the breeding
season; in others the bright colors are retained throughout the year.
Females normally guard their eggs during the incubation period.

GROUND SKINK *Lygosoma laterale*   p. 126
  Identification: 3–4¾ (head–body max. 1⅞). The "brown-
backed skink." A small, smooth, golden-brown to blackish-
brown lizard with a *dark* dorsolateral stripe. Shade of brown
varies from one locality to another — from reddish or chocolate
to light golden brown. In darkest specimens the dark stripe
almost blends with ground color. Belly white or yellowish. A
"window" in lower eyelid in form of a transparent disc through
which lizard may see when eye is closed. *Young:* About 1¾′
at hatching.

An elfin reptile of the woodland floor, quietly but nervously searching for insects among leaves, decaying wood, and detritus, and taking refuge, when approached, beneath the nearest shelter. When running, it makes lateral, snakelike movements. Does not hesitate to enter shallow water to escape. Seldom climbs. Likely to appear almost anywhere in the Deep South, even in towns and gardens.

Similar species: Two-lined Salamanders are similar in coloration and pattern, but they lack claws and scales. Other small brown lizards either have rough scales, indications of *light* stripes, or both.

Range: Pine Barrens of s. New Jersey to Florida Keys; west to e. Kansas and cent. Texas.   Map 60

FIVE-LINED SKINK *Eumeces fasciatus*   p. 126
Identification: 5–7½ (head–body max. 3⅛). Highly variable, depending on age and sex. Hatchlings have 5 white or yellowish stripes on a black ground color, and their tails are bright blue. As they grow older and larger, pattern becomes less conspicuous — stripes darkening and ground color lightening; the tail turns gray. Females almost always retain some indications of striped pattern, the broad dark band extending backward from eye and along the side of body remaining most prominent. Adult males usually show traces of stripes, but they tend to become nearly uniform brown or olive in coloration, and in many parts of range they also develop orange-red pigment on their heads. *Young:* See above; about 2″ to 2½″ at hatching.

Two other species, Broad-headed and Southeastern Five-lined Skinks, are similarly patterned, undergo comparable changes, and have ranges broadly overlapping that of the Five-lined Skink. Therefore it is essential to check scale characters to be sure of identification. Eliminate Southeastern Five-line (*inexpectatus*) by looking under base of tail; all its scales are about same size (middle row enlarged in the other two species — see Fig. 19, below). This species (*fasciatus*) has: 26 to 30 longitudinal rows of scales around center of body, usually 4 labials anterior to the subocular, and 2 enlarged postlabial scales (Fig. 20, p. 99).

Cutover woodlots with many rotting stumps and logs, abandoned sawdust piles, rock piles, and decaying debris in or near woods are good places in which to look for these lizards. Habitat is usually damp. Over the greater part of its range, the Five-

Fig. 19. SKINKS: UNDERSURFACES OF TAILS

SOUTHEASTERN
FIVE-LINED
All scales about
same size

FIVE-LINED AND
BROAD-HEADED
Middle row
enlarged

Fig. 20. HEADS OF SKINKS

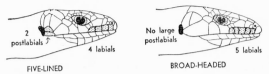

FIVE-LINED   BROAD-HEADED

lined Skink is essentially terrestrial, but it occasionally ascends trees, especially dead and decaying "snags" where insects are abundant. In Texas, it is distinctly arboreal.

Similar species: Broad-headed Skink usually has 30 to 32 rows of scales at midbody, 5 labials anterior to the subocular, and no enlarged postlabials (Fig. 20, above).

Range: S. New England to extr. n. Florida and west to Wisconsin and e. Texas; isolated colonies in South Dakota, Iowa, Minnesota, and the n. peninsula of Michigan.   Map 61

BROAD-HEADED SKINK   *Eumeces laticeps*   p. 126
  Identification: 6½–12⅜ (head–body max. 5½). The red-headed "scorpion" attains the greatest length of any Skink occurring within our area. Big olive-brown males, with their widely swollen jowls and orange-red heads, are impressive reptiles. Pattern and color variations parallel those of Five-lined Skink (*fasciatus*). Scale rows usually 30 or 32, usually 5 labials anterior to the subocular, and no enlarged postlabials (Fig. 20, above). Middle row of scales under tail wider than others (Fig. 19, p. 98). *Young:* Black with 5 yellow stripes and bright blue tail; in eastern part of range young may show 7 *light stripes*; about 2⅜" to 3⅜" at hatching.

  Habitats vary from swamp forests to empty urban lots strewn with debris. This is essentially a woodland species, however, and the most arboreal of our Skinks. The lizards make use of hollow trees and tree holes, and sometimes may be seen on rail fences or high among bare branches of dead or decaying trees.

  Similar species: Southeastern Five-lined Skink (*inexpectatus*) has the scales under tail all about same size. In Five-lined Skink (*fasciatus*) the scale rows at midbody are 26 to 30; usually 4 labials anterior to the subocular, and 2 enlarged postlabials (Fig. 20, above).

  Range: S. Pennsylvania to Florida; west to e. Kansas and cent. Texas.   Map 62

SOUTHEASTERN FIVE-LINED SKINK
Eumeces inexpectatus   p. 126
  Identification: 5½–8½ (head–body max. 3½). The only one of the three Five-lined Skinks in which the rows of scales under

the tail are all about the same size (Fig. 19, p. 98). (Be careful to check only on an original part of tail — not on a regenerated portion.) Pattern and coloration running a gamut of changes similar to those occurring in Five-lined Skink (*fasciatus*). Light stripes, especially middorsal one, tend to be quite narrow. Dorsolateral stripe is on the 5th (or 4th and 5th) row of scales, counting from midline of back. Dark areas between light stripes are black in young, but become brown in older specimens. *Young:* 5 very narrow light stripes that become brighter (often reddish orange) on head; often an additional faint light stripe at each side of belly; tail blue or purple. The juvenile coloration very frequently persists into adulthood, the orange head stripes remaining prominent and, in conjunction with the darker stripes, giving head an over-all orange-brown appearance; purplish hues may be seen on tails of even rather large specimens.

Found in a great variety of habitats, but able to tolerate drier conditions than the two other 5-striped species. Thrives on many small seashore islands in the Southeast which have no fresh water and little vegetation. Climbs well, but is also quite at home on the ground.

Similar species: In Five-lined Skink (*fasciatus*) and Broadheaded Skink (*laticeps*), middle row of scales under tail is distinctly wider than other rows (Fig. 19, p. 98). Also, the dorsolateral light stripe is on the 3d and 4th (or 4th only) rows of scales in both of those species.

Range: Virginia to Florida Keys; west to Louisiana.   Map 63

GREAT PLAINS SKINK   *Eumeces obsoletus*   p. 126
Identification: 6½–12¼ (head–body max. 5). Second largest of our Skinks, exceeded in size, and only slightly, by the Broadheaded Skink. Unique in having scales on sides of body arranged *obliquely* instead of in horizontal rows (Fig. 21, below). The ground color varies from light tan to light gray, and basically each scale is edged with black or dark brown. Distribution of the edging varies so that some specimens have strong indications of longitudinal stripes. *Young:* Jet-black; tail blue; white and orange spots on head; about 2½″ at hatching.

Chiefly in rough country, including limestone outcrops and grassy or partially wooded hillsides, but also on open plains, often in sandy area s, and where numerous mammal burrows offer shelter. Secretive; seldom seen except when rock slabs or other

Fig. 21
SKINKS:
SIDES OF
BODIES

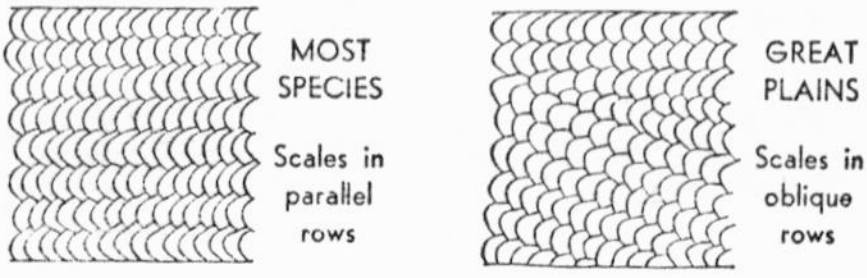

MOST SPECIES
Scales in parallel rows

GREAT PLAINS
Scales in oblique rows

places of concealment are overturned. Can inflict a painful bite, and does not tame readily.

Similar species: Young Southern Coal Skinks also may be virtually plain black; their snouts and lips may be reddish, but they lack bold white and orange spots.

Range: Nebraska to Arizona and n. Mexico.   Map 66

SHORT-LINED SKINK *Eumeces brevilineatus*   p. 126
Identification: 5–7 (head–body max. 2⅝). The light stripes terminate in the region of the *shoulder*. Dorsum varies from plain brown to olive-green. *Male:* Wash of orange at sides of throat. *Young:* Tail bright blue; dark band extending backward from eye; about 2″ at hatching.

At home in rocky or sandy areas in rough, hilly country or on the plains, but usually where moisture is in evidence — near springs, rivulets, or gullies with trickling water or intermittent pools. Hides in, and forages near, brush and trash piles, clumps of cactus, or abandoned packrat nests.

Range: Cent. and sw. Texas and ne. Mexico.   Map 69

FOUR-LINED SKINK *Eumeces tetragrammus*   p. 126
Identification: 5–7⅛ (head–body max. 3). Four light stripes that terminate in the region of the *groin*. Upper stripes fade out first, and they may be further obscured by an invasion of dark pigment. Traces of a light middorsal stripe near the head are sometimes present. *Male:* Wash of orange at sides of jaw. *Young:* Tail bright blue; the dark band between the light stripes darker than the middorsal area.

Abundant in lower Rio Grande Valley, but rare in more arid parts of range. Hides under all manner of debris, but sometimes may be found by peeling away the dried frond husks at bases of palm trees.

Similar species: Light stripes terminate near shoulder in Short-lined Skink. In Southern Prairie Skink, light stripes extend onto tail.

Range: S. Texas to extr. n. Veracruz.   Map 68

COAL SKINK *Eumeces anthracinus*   p. 126
Identification: 5–7 (head–body max. 2¾). A 4-lined Skink, but with the light stripes extending *onto tail*. Broad dark lateral stripe 2½ to 4 scales wide. *No light lines on top of head.* Dorsolateral light stripe is on the edges of the 3d and 4th scale rows, counting from midline of back. One postmental scale (Fig. 22, p. 102). *Young:* Plain black in one subspecies; patterned as adults in the other; about 1⅞″ at hatching.

The more humid portions of wooded hillsides are favorite habitats; also vicinity of springs and rocky bluffs overlooking creek valleys. When pursued, these lizards (as well as Skinks of some other species) do not hesitate to take refuge in shallow water, going to the bottom and hiding under stones or debris.

Similar species: In the two Prairie Skinks the dark lateral stripe is not more than 2 scales wide, and the dorsolateral light stripe is on the 4th (or 4th and 5th) row of scales. Light stripes do not extend onto the tail in Short-lined and Four-lined Skinks. In juveniles and young adults of the three species of Five-lined Skinks (*fasciatus*, *inexpectatus*, and *laticeps*) there are 2 light lines on head; in old adults of these, in which the stripes may have faded, check for presence of 2 *postmental scales* (Fig. 22, below). The black young of the Great Plains Skink have bold white and orange spots on their heads.

Range: Discontinuous — see subspecies below.

Subspecies: SOUTHERN COAL SKINK, *Eumeces anthracinus pluvialis* (illustrated on Plate 15). Usually one or more faint dark stripes or rows of spots down center of back. Rows of scales around body 26 or more. Young, black and unpatterned or with faint suggestions of light stripes; snout and lips reddish; tail bluish. Kansas and Missouri to n. Louisiana; s. Mississippi and adj. areas; intergrades with Northern Coal Skink in uplands of the Southeast. NORTHERN COAL SKINK, *Eumeces anthracinus anthracinus*. Usually no dark lines down center of back. Rows of scales around body usually 25 or fewer. Young with blue tails, but otherwise patterned as adults. New York to Kentucky.   Map 65

NORTHERN PRAIRIE SKINK
Eumeces septentrionalis septentrionalis   p. 126

Identification: 5¼–8⅛ (head–body max. 3¼). A many-striped Skink, but with the dorsolateral *light* stripes strongly bordered *both above and below* by dark stripes and extending onto the tail. This light stripe is on the 4th (or 4th and 5th) row of scales counting from midline of back. A pair of relatively faint dark lines down center of back, or a pale middorsal stripe, or both. Broadest dark stripe not more than 2 scales wide. Dorsal ground color olive to olive-brown. Two postmental scales (Fig. 22, below). *Male:* Deep reddish orange on sides of head during breeding season. *Young:* Tail bright blue; about 2″ at hatching.

Fig. 22. CHINS OF SKINKS

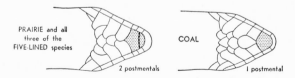

PRAIRIE and all three of the FIVE-LINED species

2 postmentals

COAL

1 postmental

Seldom seen in the open, but uses shallow burrows and excavations, often of its own making. Usually occurs in areas of soft soils, often in gravelly glacial deposits or their sandy outwash (in northern localities). Sometimes found in sawdust piles or by overturning objects left undisturbed long enough to be well settled into surface of sod or soil.

Similar species: In Many-lined Skink, the dorsolateral light stripe is *confined* to 3d row of scales. Coal Skink has: (1) broad dark lateral stripe, 2½ to 4 scales wide; (2) dorsolateral light stripe on edges of 3d and 4th scale rows; and (3) a single postmental scale (Fig. 22, p. 102).

Range: Extr. s. Manitoba to Wisconsin and Kansas.　　Map 59

SOUTHERN PRAIRIE SKINK
Eumeces septentrionalis obtusirostris　　　　　　　　　　p. 126
Identification: 5–7 (head–body max. 2 $\frac{15}{16}$). Similar to its subspecies, the Northern Prairie Skink, but with the middorsal markings greatly reduced or absent. In extreme cases the dark line above the light dorsolateral stripe may even be missing. Occasionally the light stripe along lower sides also is lacking. Dorsolateral light line is on the 4th (or 4th and 5th) row of scales, counting from middorsal line. The broad dark lateral stripe is not more than 2 scales wide. Two postmental scales (Fig. 22, p. 102).

Often seen foraging near bases of clumps of prickly pear or other vegetation into which it retreats at first sign of danger.

Similar species: Coal Skink has the dorsolateral light stripe on edges of the 3d and 4th scale rows, only one postmental scale, and the broad dark lateral stripe is 2½ to 4 scales wide. Light lines do not extend onto tail in Short-lined and Four-lined Skinks.
Range: S.-cent. Kansas to e.-cent. Texas.　　　　　　Map 59

MANY-LINED SKINK
Eumeces multivirgatus multivirgatus　　　　　　　　　　p. 126
Identification: 5–7⅝ (head–body max. 2⅞). Numerous light and dark stripes, some strong and well-defined, others weak and appearing merely as rows of dark dots. Our only skink with a prominent *light* stripe restricted to the 3d row of scales, counting from midline of back. A prominent *light* middorsal stripe flanked by prominent *dark* stripes. Tail swollen at base. Stripeless or virtually stripeless individuals occur as rare variants. *Young:* Darker than adults; only the prominent lines present, and these rather dim; the fainter secondary stripes develop later; tail brilliant blue; about 2½″ at hatching.

A species of the open plains and sandhills, often occurring in vacant lots and under debris in towns and settlements. Sometimes also found beneath cow chips, where it has taken shelter or is in search of insects.

Similar Species: In Northern Prairie Skink, dorsolateral light stripe is on the 4th (or 4th and 5th) row of scales.

Range: Sw. South Dakota to e.-cent. Colorado. Western subspecies. Map 64

STRIPED RED-TAILED SKINK

Eumeces egregius egregius p. 126

Identification: 3½–6 (head–body max. 2¼). A combination of red, pink, or orange tail plus light stripes that normally terminate *on tail*. Reddish color of tail *persists throughout life*; it does not fade as does the blue in other kinds of skinks. Ground color varies from gray-brown to dark chocolate-brown. Scales around middle of body usually 21 or more.

Highly secretive; often found in piles of stones or debris. Also in driftwood and tidal wrack along shores of Florida Keys.

Range: Florida Keys and Dry Tortugas.

Subspecies: GEORGIA RED-TAILED SKINK, *Eumeces egregius similis*. A northern race well separated geographically from the very similar Striped Redtail. Scales around middle of body 20. Found chiefly in dry sandy areas. S. Georgia and n. Florida to Mobile Bay, Alabama. Map 67

BROWN RED-TAILED SKINK

Eumeces egregius onocrepis p. 126

Identification: 3½–6⅛ (head–body max. 2 5/16). A pink or orange tail and light stripes that usually terminate *on body*. Reddish color of tail persists throughout life. Length of the stripes quite variable: they may fade out at shoulder, along body, or extend to groin. Stripes occupy the 2d row of scales toward front of body (counting down from midline of back), but *shift outward* to the 3d row farther back. Scales around middle of body 20 or fewer.

The Redtails are so slender and their legs so short that they seem almost snakelike in appearance and actions. Habitats include hammocks, pine woods, and Florida's rosemary scrub; but they are most often found in open areas of dry sand. They utilize burrows of beetles, Gopher Tortoises, and small mammals, and sometimes are plowed up from depths of a foot or more. Resting specimens may hold the tail coiled in corkscrew fashion above the back.

Range: Peninsular Florida. Map 67

SAND SKINK *Neoseps reynoldsi* p. 126

Identification: 4–5 (head–body max. 2⅜). The legs are greatly reduced in size and virtually useless. Each foreleg fits into a groove on lower side of body; it bears only a single toe and is so tiny as to be easily overlooked. Hind legs a little larger and each has 2 digits. Other characteristics include a wedge-shaped snout, lower jaw partially countersunk into upper one, a flat or slightly concave belly that meets sides of body at an angle, a tiny eye with built-in "window" in lower lid, and no noticeable external ear opening. Coloration varies from pale yellowish gray to light brown.

An adept burrower that literally "swims" through dry sand. The limbs, of little help underground, are in the evolutionary process of being lost.

Range: Rosemary scrub, high pine, old dune terrain, and other suitable sandy areas in cent. and s. Florida.   Map 70

GLASS LIZARDS AND ALLIGATOR LIZARD: FAMILY ANGUIDAE

MEMBERS of this family occurring in the United States are easily recognized by the presence of a deep, flexible groove running along each side of the body. The groove permits expansion when the body is distended with food or (in females) with eggs. The family ranges from southwestern Canada to Argentina and also is represented in the West Indies and the Old World.

Glass Lizards: Genus *Ophisaurus*

THESE SHINY, legless lizards are easily mistaken for snakes. But, *unlike* snakes, they have *movable eyelids* and *external ear openings* (see front endpaper). To the touch they feel stiff, almost brittle and lack the suppleness of the serpent. Their tails are very long (up to 2¾ times the length of the body) and fragile. Hence full-tailed specimens are not common. The regenerated tip, sharply pointed and of a different color from the remaining part of the original tail, earns them the name of "horn snake" among country folk. Some people even think such a tip is a "stinger." If hit with a flat object, the tail may break in two or more pieces. This is the origin of the "joint snake" legend in which the animal, after fragmentation, is supposed to grow back together again — an obvious impossibility.

Glass Lizards are good burrowers, and at least two of the kinds may spend much of their time below ground. Their food includes insects, spiders, snails, birds' eggs, and small snakes and lizards. Captives will usually accept a mixture of chopped raw meat and egg. They should have gravel or soil in which to hide, and should not be caged with other reptiles much smaller than themselves. The young vary from 4″ to 6″ at hatching.

We have three species of Glass Lizards. Other members of the genus occur in Mexico, Africa, Europe, and Asia.

EASTERN GLASS LIZARD *Ophisaurus ventralis* p. 111
Identification: 18–37½ (head–body max. 11½). *No* dark lengthwise stripes below the lateral groove or under the tail; *no* distinct middorsal dark stripe (Fig. 23, p. 107). White marks on neck, essentially vertical, but highly irregular in shape. White markings on *posterior corners* of scales. In older specimens there are numerous longitudinal dark lines or dashes on upper sides of body, and sometimes similar parallel lines occupy the entire middorsal area. An old adult (as shown on Plate 14) may be greenish above and yellow below. *Only* Glass Lizard that may look *green*. *Young:* Khaki-colored with a broad dark longitudinal stripe on each side of back.

Characteristically an inhabitant of wet meadows and grasslands and pine flatwoods.
Similar species: Slender Glass Lizards always have at least traces of dark stripes below lateral groove. Coastal Glass Lizard has dark stripe or series of dashes down center of back.
Range: North Carolina to Florida and west to Louisiana; isolated records in Oklahoma and Missouri. Map 77

ISLAND GLASS LIZARD *Ophisaurus compressus* p. 107
Identification: 15–24 (head–body max. 6⅝). The *single* dark solid stripe on each side of the body is situated on scale rows 3 and 4 above the lateral groove. A middorsal dark stripe, but this sometimes represented merely by a series of dark dashes (Fig. 23, p. 107). No dark stripes below the groove. Under surfaces pinkish buff or yellowish and unmarked. Numerous more or less vertical bars on neck, more numerous and usually more conspicuous than those of the Eastern Glass Lizard. In older specimens the top and sides of neck are mottled with bronze.
Similar species: Slender Glass Lizard has dark stripes below lateral groove. Also see Eastern Glass Lizard.
Range: Coastal areas and offshore islands of South Carolina, Georgia, and Florida; scrub pine regions and adj. flatwoods of peninsular Florida. Map 75

SLENDER GLASS LIZARD *Ophisaurus attenuatus* p. 111
Identification: 22–42 (head–body max. 11⅜). Narrow dark longitudinal stripes *below* the lateral groove and under the tail (Fig. 23, p. 107); these are black in the young, but paler and less prominent (sometimes considerably less) in adults. A dark middorsal stripe or series of dashes in young and medium-sized specimens. Old adults are brown with irregular light (but dark-bordered) cross-bands on the back and tail. White marks on scales occupy the *middle* of the scales.

Found chiefly in dry grasslands or dry, open woods. Seldom burrows, except for hibernation. Very active when held, vigorously trying to escape and sometimes whipping back and forth somewhat as Racers and Whipsnakes do. Glass Lizards of the other species are much less energetic in their efforts to escape.

Similar species: Both Eastern and Island Glass Lizards *lack* dark stripes below lateral groove and under tail.

Range: Se. Virginia to s. Florida; west to cent. Texas and north in Mississippi Valley to e. Kansas, s. Wisconsin, and nw. Indiana.

Subspecies: WESTERN SLENDER GLASS LIZARD, *Ophisaurus attenuatus attenuatus* (illustrated on Plate 14). Tail (when unregenerated) less than 2 $4/10$ times length from snout to vent. Chiefly west of Mississippi River, but crossing into Illinois and adj. states in the North. EASTERN SLENDER GLASS LIZARD. *Ophisaurus attenuatus longicaudus*. Tail longer (when unregenerated), 2 $4/10$ or more times length from snout to vent Se. Virginia to s. Florida and the Mississippi River. Map 74

Fig. 23. HEADS OF GLASS LIZARDS

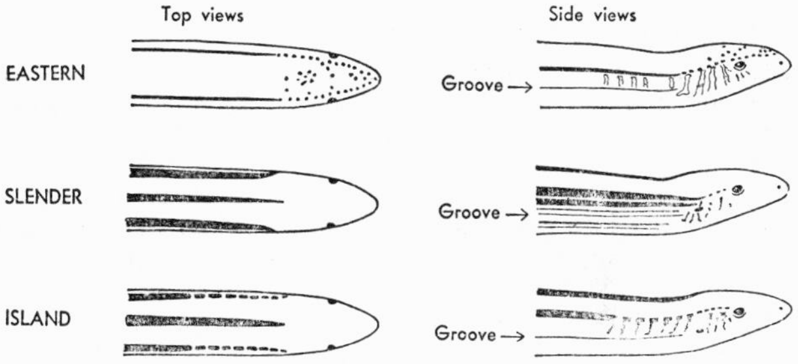

TEXAS ALLIGATOR LIZARD
Gerrhonotus liocephalus infernalis p. 111

Identification: 10–16; record 20 (head–body max. 8). Scales large and platelike (suggesting the Alligator). Coloration variable, from yellowish- to reddish-brown. Broken, irregular light lines cross back and tail. Check for flexible groove that runs along the side from neck to hind leg. Our only lizard with *both a lateral groove and legs*. (The Alligator Lizard illustrated on Plate 14 has puffed itself up with air — a common reptilian habit — so the groove is stretched out nearly flat.) *Young:* Much more vividly marked than adults; ground color dark brown to black and crossed by narrow whitish crossbands; head tan; 2″ to 4″ at hatching.

Essentially terrestrial and usually slow and deliberate in contrast with the quick, darting movements of most lizards. Tail is somewhat prehensile. The Alligator Lizard usually does well in terrariums. Insects, spiders, newborn mice, and small lizards and snakes are included on its menu. Never cage it with lizards smaller than itself. Some specimens resent being handled and will protest by biting, even though in other respects they are quite tame. They can pinch fingers painfully hard.

Range: Edwards Plateau and Big Bend regions of Texas to n. San Luis Potosí. Mexican subspecies.   Map 73

RINGED LIZARDS:
FAMILY AMPHISBAENIDAE

SNAKELIKE lizards with rings of flat scales encircling body and tail. There are no external ear openings, and only a very few members of the family possess visible limbs. Represented in Africa and adjacent parts of Europe and Asia, South America to Mexico, the West Indies, and Florida.

WORM LIZARD *Rhineura floridana*   p. 111

Identification: 7–11; record 15⅛. An extraordinary mimic of the common earthworm, both in coloration and gross appearance. Body looks segmented, like the worm's, but this reptile has scales and a well-defined, lizard-like head, even though both ends of the animal look superficially alike. Lower jaw counter-sunk into upper, facilitating burrowing. There are no limbs, no ear openings, and most specimens lack external eyes (internally there are remnants of eyes). Upper surface of the very short tail is flattened and covered with numerous small bumps (tubercles), forming an effective stopper for tunnels the lizard makes as it burrows through sand or soil. *Young:* About 4″ at hatching.

Worm Lizards remain underground virtually all their lives, but are sometimes plowed or dug up or may be forced to the surface by heavy rains. Dry, sandy habitats are preferred. Earthworms, spiders, and termites are the principal foods.

Range: Cent. and n. Florida.   Map 76

VIII

Snakes

SLENDER BLIND SNAKES:
FAMILY LEPTOTYPHLOPIDAE

A LARGE FAMILY containing only a single genus (*Leptotyphlops*) of small burrowing, wormlike snakes with vestigial eyes and the dentition reduced to a few teeth in the lower jaw. The family ranges from south-central United States to southern South America, and also occurs in the West Indies, Africa, southwestern Asia.

(TEXAS) BLIND SNAKE *Leptotyphlops dulcis*   p. 143
  Identification: 5–8; record 10¾. Which end is the head? The blunt, rounded tail strongly resembles the head, but the latter may be quickly recognized by 2 black dots. These are the eyes buried beneath translucent scales. Blind Snakes are unique among serpents of our area in having *belly scales same size as dorsal scales*. This is a shiny plain brown or reddish-brown "worm snake," smooth-scaled and slender as a knitting needle. Tail extremely short, only about 1/20 of total length.

  A chiefly subterranean resident of arid and semi-arid regions. Occurs on stony hillsides, prairies, and in sandy or rocky deserts, but usually in areas where some moisture is available. Frequently found beneath stones and boulders after rains. Most likely to prowl abroad in early evening. Food includes ant pupae and termites.

  Range: S. Kansas and se. Arizona to e. Mexico.

  Subspecies: PLAINS BLIND SNAKE, *Leptotyphlops dulcis dulcis* (illustrated on Plate 18). A *single* supralabial scale between the enlarged ocular scale (the one containing the eye) and the lower nasal scale (the one containing the nostril) — see Fig. 24, p. 112. Oklahoma to ne. Mexico. NEW MEXICO BLIND SNAKE, *Leptotyphlops dulcis dissectus*. *Two* supralabial scales between ocular and lower nasal scale (Fig. 24, p. 112). Sw. Kansas, cent. Oklahoma, and extr. n. Texas; a completely separate population farther southwest. Mexican subspecies. Map 78. NOTE: The Trans-Pecos Blind Snake, *Leptotyphlops humilis segregus*, is known to occur in Kinney County, Texas, and may eventually be found east of the 100th meridian. It has only a single scale on top of the head between the ocular scales. In the races of the Texas Blind Snake there are 3 scales between the ocular scales (Fig. 24, p 112).

PAINTED AND CHICKEN TURTLES; POND SLIDERS

(See Plate 5 for the young of many of these turtles.)

	Map	Text

MIDLAND PAINTED TURTLE — 21 — 54
Seam short; large scutes arranged in alternating fashion.

EASTERN PAINTED TURTLE — 21 — 54
Seam continuous across shell; large scutes with broad olive edges and arranged in rows *across* back.

WESTERN PAINTED TURTLE — 21 — 55
Light wormlike or netlike lines on carapace; bars on marginals.

SOUTHERN PAINTED TURTLE — 21 — 55
Broad red stripe (sometimes yellowish).

YELLOW-BELLIED TURTLE — 24 — 57
Yellow head blotch; vertical yellowish bars on shell; leg stripes *narrow;* has striped "pants."

CHICKEN TURTLE — 30 — 64
Long striped neck; light network on shell; leg stripe *broad;* has striped "pants."

RED-EARED TURTLE — 24 — 57
Female (and young): Reddish stripe behind eye. *Male:* Reddish stripe reduced; completely obscured in old specimens (see text).

RED-BELLIED TURTLE — 25 — 61
Female: Vertical reddish markings (persisting even in very dark specimens). *Male:* Dark; markings irregular (see text).

♂ means male, ♀ female.

YELLOW-BELLIED
Narrow leg stripes

BOTH
Striped "pants"

CHICKEN
Broad leg stripe

MIDLAND PAINTED

EASTERN PAINTED

WESTERN PAINTED

SOUTHERN PAINTED

YELLOW-BELLIED

CHICKEN

♂

♀

Old ♂

RED-EARED

♀

♂

RED-BELLIED

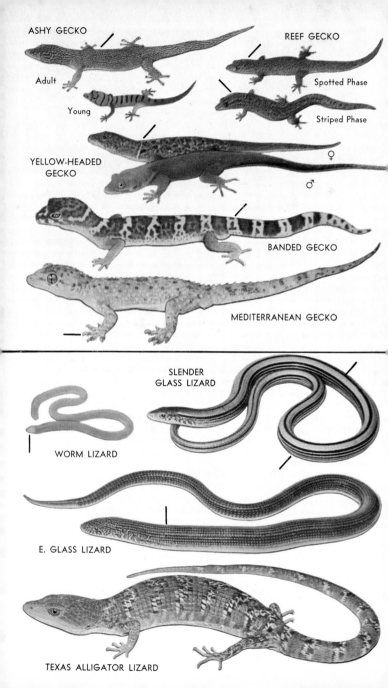

ASHY GECKO

Adult

Young

REEF GECKO

Spotted Phase

Striped Phase

YELLOW-HEADED GECKO

♀

♂

BANDED GECKO

MEDITERRANEAN GECKO

SLENDER GLASS LIZARD

WORM LIZARD

E. GLASS LIZARD

TEXAS ALLIGATOR LIZARD

Plate 14   111

GECKOS; GLASS, WORM, AND ALLIGATOR LIZARDS

	Map	*Text*

ASHY GECKO   53   92
  Adult: Tiny *light* spots on a dark ground color. *Young:*
  Dark crossbands; reddish tail.

REEF GECKO   54   92
  Dark markings on a lighter ground color.
  Striped phase: Dark head stripes; 2 light spots on nape.

YELLOW-HEADED GECKO   58   92
  Adult male: Yellowish head; body bluish (or black).
  Female and young: Light collar; body mottled.

BANDED GECKO   55   93
  Light crossbands (or mottlings) on a brown ground color;
  movable eyelids.

MEDITERRANEAN GECKO   57   91
  Toe pads *broad;* dorsum warty.

WORM LIZARD   76   108
  Like an earthworm; head scales distinctly evident when
  examined at close range.

SLENDER GLASS LIZARD*   74   106
  No legs; middorsal dark stripe; dark stripes on lower sides.

EASTERN GLASS LIZARD*   77   106
  No legs; no distinct middorsal dark stripe; greenish coloration. (Tip of tail regenerated.)

TEXAS ALLIGATOR LIZARD   73   107
  Large scales; irregular light crosslines.

♂ means male, ♀ female.

*There are three species of Glass Lizards, all confusingly alike. See text and
Fig. 23, p. 107.

TOES OF GECKOS

Side views   Bottom views

BANDED

REEF AND ASHY

YELLOW-HEADED   MEDITERRANEAN

Fig. 24. HEADS OF BLIND SNAKES

TEXAS BLIND SNAKE		TEXAS	TRANS-PECOS
NEW MEXICO subspecies	PLAINS subspecies	3 scales between	1 scale between
2 supralabials	1 supralabial	oculars	oculars

COLUBRIDS: FAMILY COLUBRIDAE

To THIS enormous family belong more than 70 per cent of all the living genera of snakes of the entire world. Its members predominate on all the continents save Australia, where relatives of the Cobra (Coral Snake) Family are most numerous. Of the 164 species and subspecies of snakes included in this book, a total of 141 (86 per cent) belong to the Colubridae (genera *Natrix*, below, to *Tantilla*, p. 182, inclusive). These vary in form and size from the stout-bodied Hognose Snakes to the slender Short-tailed or Rough Green Snakes, and from the 7-foot (or more) Rat or Indigo Snakes to the tiny Ground or Earth Snakes.

Most of our Colubrids have solid teeth, but some species are equipped with grooved fangs in the rear portion of the upper jaw. Some, like the Cat-eyed Snake, are venomous but scarcely dangerous to man; others, like the Black-headed Snakes, have grooved teeth but no well-developed venom system; still others, like the Night Snake, have venoms but no grooves or only slight indications of them. These represent various stages in the evolutionary development of the venom apparatus which, even in the dangerously poisonous snakes, functions chiefly in the procurement of food.

Water Snakes: Genus *Natrix*

HARMLESS, semi-aquatic snakes often seen basking on logs, branches, or brush from which they drop or glide into the water at the slightest alarm. They are adept at swimming and diving, and obtain most of their food, including frogs, salamanders, fish, and crayfish, in or near the water. Canned sardines or raw chopped fish (be sure to include the entrails) are readily accepted by captives of many species.

Water Snakes have been more maligned than any other non-poisonous serpents, partly because they strike and bite hard when cornered (even a rat would do as much), and partly because biased or uninformed persons resent their predation upon fishes. Research indicates they actually improve good fishing by culling out sick and less vigorous fish and helping to thin out overpopulated lakes and ponds in which the fish otherwise would remain stunted in size.

Most persons confuse the larger, stouter kinds of Water Snakes with the venomous Cottonmouth, and not without reason. They look much alike, and even the distinctive patterns may be obscured if the snake has been crawling in mud or is soon to shed its skin. Live Cottonmouths move more slowly, beating a more dignified retreat; cornered ones hold their mouths open widely in readiness to bite. Dead Cottonmouths can be checked for two things: (1) a single row of scales under the tail (double in Water Snakes); and (2) a deep pit between eye and nostril (absent in all harmless snakes — see Fig., p. 238). Be cautious about trying to catch any aquatic serpent within the range of the Cottonmouth (Map 143).

Many Water Snakes flatten their bodies when alarmed. When first seized, they discharge copious quantities of foul-smelling musk from glands at the base of the tail. Females grow larger than males; many that are heavy with young are enormous in girth. Besides occurring in eastern North America and Mexico, the genus is represented in Europe, North Africa, Asia, the Malay Archipelago, and northern Australia.

Dead or captive Water Snakes are often most quickly identified by flipping them over and examining their colorful and usually distinctive belly patterns. Most kinds are easily caught at night with the aid of a bright light.

GREEN WATER SNAKE. *Natrix cyclopion cyclopion*   p. 207
  Identification: 30–45; record 50. Although completely lacking in distinctive field marks, the two Green Water Snakes are unique among our *Natrix* in having a row of scales between the eye and lip scales (upper labials) — see Fig. 27, p. 119. This makes identification positive and final, but it means catching or killing the snake for close-up examination. General dorsal coloration may be greenish or brownish, but usually with at least some faint suggestion of a dark pattern on a lighter ground. Belly marked with *light* spots or half-moons on a ground color of gray or brown. Scales *keeled*; anal *divided*. *Young:* About 9" to 10" at birth.

  A species of quiet bodies of water — edges of lakes and ponds, of swamps, rice fields, or marshes, of bayous and other waterways. Occasionally found in brackish water.
  Similar species: Virtually all other large Water Snakes usually have strong indications of pattern — stripes, spots, or blotches — but these may not show well in a basking serpent unless it is wet. Cottonmouth usually moves sluggishly, not dropping or diving into water with alacrity of Water Snakes.
  Range: Mississippi Valley from extr. s. Illinois to the Gulf; Florida panhandle to se. Texas.   Map 95

FLORIDA GREEN WATER SNAKE
Natrix cyclopion floridana   p. 207

Identification: 30–55; record 74. A large greenish or brownish serpent (sometimes reddish in southern Florida) without any distinctive markings. Belly plain whitish or cream-colored, except near anus and under tail, where it is patterned like its western subspecies, the Green Water Snake. A row of scales between eye and upper lip plates (Fig. 27, p. 119). Scales *keeled*; anal *divided*. *Young:* Ground color brownish- or greenish-olive with about 50 black or dark brown bars on each side of body and similar but less conspicuous markings on back; belly yellow, but with black markings near and under tail; 8¾″ to 10½″ at birth.

Habitats include the Everglades and the Okefenokee region, as well as other swamps, marshes, and quiet bodies of water. Sometimes found in brackish water.

Similar species: Most other Water Snakes have distinctive patterns, either on their backs or bellies or both. Cottonmouth retreats slowly, and often holds mouth open in readiness to bite when closely approached.

Range: S. South Carolina to tip of Florida.   Map 95

BROWN WATER SNAKE   *Natrix taxispilota*   p. 207

Identification: 30–60; record 69. Often called the "water-pilot," and one of the easiest of all Water Snakes to mistake for the venomous Cottonmouth. The pattern consists of a series of large, squarish, dark brown blotches down middle of back and a similar but alternating row on each side (Fig. 25, p. 115). Many specimens are exceptionally dark, being deep chocolate-brown in gross appearance and with blotches only a little darker than ground color. Belly yellow to brown and boldly marked with spots and half-moons of dark brown or black. The head in this species is distinctly wider than the neck, producing a heart-shaped or "diamond-headed" appearance (viewed from above) that is erroneously alleged to occur only in venomous snakes. Scales *keeled*; anal *divided*. *Young:* 8½″ to 13″ at birth.

A species chiefly of quiet waters, and a characteristic resident of the great swamps and rivers of the South. An accomplished swimmer and climber, ascending trees to heights of 20 feet or more. Although they flee from man with alacrity, Brown Water Snakes are spirited fighters when seized or cornered.

Similar species: Eastern Cottonmouth is either virtually plain dark brown or marked with broad dark crossbands on a lighter (often greenish or olive) ground color; often holds mouth open in readiness to bite when approached. Green Water Snakes have a row of scales between eye and upper lip scales (Fig. 27, p. 119). Banded and Florida Water Snakes often have red in their patterns, and usually show a dark stripe from eye to angle of jaw (Fig. 27, p. 119).

Fig. 25. DIAGRAMMATIC DORSAL PATTERNS OF WATER SNAKES

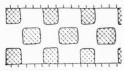

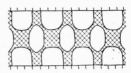

BROWN (Dark squares)   DIAMOND-BACKED (Dark chainlike pattern)

Range: Virginia to s. Alabama and south to tip of Florida; chiefly in Coastal Plain, but ascending some rivers into the Piedmont. Map 94

DIAMOND-BACKED WATER SNAKE

Natrix rhombifera rhombifera p. 207

Identification: 30–48; record 63. The light areas on the back may be vaguely diamond-shaped, but the pattern is best described as consisting of dark brown chainlike markings on a ground color of lighter brown or dirty yellow (Fig. 25, above). Belly yellow, marked with black or dark brown spots or halfmoons. *Adult male:* Unique among serpents of our area in having numerous raised protuberances (papillae) under chin (Fig. 26, p. 116). Scales *keeled*; anal *divided*. *Young:* Strongly patterned, belly often brightly tinged with orange; 9½″ to 12″ at birth.

Throughout most of its range this is an ubiquitous serpent, appearing in many types of aquatic habitats from big lakes and rivers to ditches and cattle tanks. Toward the west, it follows rivers far into otherwise arid terrain.

Similar species: Cottonmouth tends to move slowly and often holds mouth open when approached; adult Western Cottonmouths usually are plain black or dark brown, but younger ones are marked with dark crossbands on a lighter ground color.

Range: Mississippi Valley from extr. se. Iowa to the Gulf; w.-cent. Alabama to cent. Texas and ne. Mexico. Mexican subspecies. Map 92

RED-BELLIED WATER SNAKE

Natrix erythrogaster erythrogaster p. 206

Identification: 30–48; record 62. The "copperbelly." Venter plain red or orange-red. Dorsum normally plain brown (pale reddish brown to rich chocolate-brown), but often somewhat grayish or greenish on lower sides of body. Scales *keeled*; anal normally *divided* (single in about 5 per cent of the specimens of all subspecies of *Natrix erythrogaster*). *Young:* Boldly patterned, ground color usually pinkish as in young of Blotched Water Snake (top left figure, Plate 25); lateral blotches *alternate* with larger middorsal ones all the way *forward to head* (or nearly so.) Juvenile pattern disappears with age, but traces of it often persist well into young adulthood. About 8½″ to 11½″ at birth.

At home in the great river swamps and numerous other aquatic habitats of the Southeast. This snake often wanders well away from water in hot, humid weather, a habit shared by its several subspecies.

Similar species: Occasional Water Snakes of other species may be uniformly brown above, but they normally have strongly patterned bellies. Certain small serpents, such as the Red-bellied and Black Swamp Snakes, may have plain dark dorsal surfaces and crimson venters, but, when fully adult, they are of a size comparable with the well patterned young of the "copperbelly". Kirtland's Water Snake has a row of black spots down each side of belly.

Range: S. Delaware to n. Florida and se. Alabama.

Subspecies: NORTHERN COPPERBELLY, *Natrix erythrogaster neglecta*. Similar but darker above (sometimes black); belly often heavily invaded by dorsal ground color; young with the dorsal spots often irregular and running together. W. Kentucky north, chiefly in disjunct colonies in or near swampy woodlands or river bottoms, to s. Michigan and nw. Ohio. Map 89

Fig. 26. CHARACTERISTICS OF WATER SNAKES

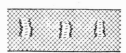

BLOTCHED
Traces of dark-bordered, but light,
crossbars in middorsal area

DIAMOND-BACKED
Projecting papillae
on chin of male

YELLOW-BELLIED WATER SNAKE

Natrix erythrogaster flavigaster   p. 206

Identification: 30–48; record 53⅛. A "redbelly" without the red — essentially like the Red-bellied Water Snake except in coloration. Dorsum gray or greenish gray, usually plain, but sometimes with traces of pattern persisting as light (but dark-bordered) transverse bars across center of back (Fig. 26, above). Belly plain yellow, often washed with orange; occasionally with dark pigment on bases or ends of ventral scutes. Scales *keeled*; anal *divided*. *Young:* Strongly patterned like young of Blotched Water Snake (Plate 25); about 9½″ to 12″ at birth.

A snake of the wetlands of the lower Mississippi Valley and adjacent areas. Usually found in or near the larger, more permanent, bodies of water — in river bottoms, swamps, marshes, edges of ponds and lakes, etc.

Similar species: Occasional adults of Water Snakes of other species are sometimes plain dark above, but their bellies are usually boldly marked.

Range: N.-cent. Georgia and se. Iowa to e. Texas and the Gulf.   Map 89

BLOTCHED WATER SNAKE
Natrix erythrogaster transversa   p. 206

Identification: 30–48; record 58. A race of the "redbelly" in which the blotched pattern of the young persists into adulthood, or even throughout life. An extremely variable snake; general coloration may be almost any shade of gray or brown, but with markings darker than background. Occasionally the blotched pattern may virtually disappear, but traces of it usually remain in the form of short, light, but dark-bordered, bars across center of back (Fig. 26, p. 116). Belly virtually plain yellow, often with an orange tinge; bases of belly scales may be dark, or the dark coloration of the dorsum may encroach onto edges of the scutes. Underside of tail unpatterned and usually *orange* or *reddish*. Scales *keeled*; anal *divided*. *Young:* Strongly blotched, lateral dark blotches (or spots) alternating with large middorsal blotches all the way forward to the head (or nearly so); about 9″ to 11″ at birth.

Likely to be found wherever permanent or semipermanent water occurs — in ditches, cattle tanks, and along streams. Follows rivers, in western part of its range, into what is otherwise decidedly arid country.

Similar species: In Northern Water Snake the lateral blotches unite with the middorsal ones to form dark crossbands on neck and forepart of body; belly is usually strongly patterned with half-moons or other dark markings, and underside of tail is patterned. In Broad-banded Water Snake dorsal markings are quite large, the venter is boldly patterned, and the head bears a dark stripe from eye to angle of jaw (Fig. 27, p. 119).

Range: W. Missouri and Kansas to ne. Mexico. Mexican subspecies.   Map 89

NORTHERN WATER SNAKE   *Natrix sipedon sipedon*   p. 206

Identification: 24–42; record 51. The only large Water Snake in most of the northern states, a fortunate thing for Northerners, for this reptile exhibits a bewildering array of variations. Farther south, where its range overlaps some of the other species of Water Snakes, one must check the chief diagnostic characters, which are: (1) dark crossbands on neck and forepart of body, but alternating dorsal and lateral blotches on rest of body; (2) dark markings wider than spaces between them; and (3) black or reddish half-moons on belly. Ground color varies from pale gray to dark brown, markings from bright reddish brown to black. Adults tend to darken so that the pattern becomes obscure; it may disappear altogether, resulting in a plain black or dark brown serpent. (Putting snake in water will often reveal pattern details in what seems like a virtually unicolored specimen.) Half-moons on belly may be arranged in a regular pattern, scattered at random, represented merely by dusky areas, or be entirely absent. Some specimens have their bellies almost uniformly stippled with gray except for a yellow, orange, or pinkish midventral stripe. Underside of tail patterned virtually to tip. Scales *keeled*; anal *divided*. *Young:* Strongly patterned, black on a ground of pale gray or light brown; about 7½″ to 9″ at birth.

A resident of virtually every swamp, marsh, or bog, of every stream, pond, or lake border within its range. Quiet waters may be preferred, but swift-flowing streams and the environs of waterfalls also have their quota of Water Snakes — unless they have been exterminated there by man!

Similar species: Banded Water Snake has crossbands throughout length of body, a dark stripe from eye to corner of mouth (Fig. 27, p. 119), and squarish spots on belly. Northern Copperbelly has bright red belly marked only with black or dark brown at edges of ventral scales. Blotched Water Snake has virtually plain yellowish belly, and underside of tail is unpatterned and usually orange or reddish.

Range: S. Maine and extr. s. Quebec to North Carolina and southern uplands; west to Colorado. Intergrades with Midland Water Snake over a broad area where their ranges meet.

Subspecies: LAKE ERIE WATER SNAKE, *Natrix sipedon insularum*. A pale race in which the pattern is much reduced or completely lacking. General coloration gray (often greenish or brownish); belly white or yellowish and sometimes with a pink or orange tinge down center. Pattern elements, when present, are like those of Northern Water Snake. Islands of Put-in-Bay Archipelago, Lake Erie.   Map 85

MIDLAND WATER SNAKE   *Natrix sipedon pleuralis*   p. 206
Identification: 2?–40; record 51½. Patterned basically like the Northern Water Snake — dark crossbands on the neck and alternating blotches farther back. But the dark markings are *smaller* than the spaces between them. Older specimens tend to darken and lose their patterns, but traces, at least of the lateral markings, usually show when snake is submerged in water. Occasionally crossbands continue throughout length of body. General coloration may be brown or gray instead of red, and blotches may even be black. The belly markings tend strongly to be in pairs, and do not so often break up and disappear as they do in Northern Water Snake. Scales *keeled*; anal *divided*. *Young:* 7½″ to 12″ at birth.

Throughout the bulk of its range this snake utilizes a wide variety of habitats — streams, ponds, swales, marshes, etc. Toward the south, however, it follows river valleys, in some cases all the way to the Gulf Coast.

Similar species: In the Banded Water Snake, crossbands are present throughout length of body, belly markings tend to be squarish and most prominent at sides, and there is a dark stripe from eye to angle of jaw (Fig. 27, below).

Range: Midland America, from Indiana to Oklahoma and the Gulf, and (south of the mountains) to the Carolinas.   Map 85

BANDED WATER SNAKE *Natrix sipedon fasciata*   p. 206

Identification: 24–42; record 60. Distinguished by three characteristics: (1) dark crossbands (often black-bordered); (2) squarish spots at sides of belly; and (3) dark stripe from eye to angle of jaw (Fig. 27, below). There is great variation in coloration; crossbands may be red, brown, or black, and ground color gray, tan, yellow, or even reddish. Most specimens darken with age, and black pigment tends to obscure the markings, resulting, in extreme cases, in a virtually all-black snake. Even in one of these, however, patches of red or of other light colors usually appear on lower sides of body. Scales *keeled*; anal *divided*. *Young:* Crossbands very dark, usually black, and in strong contrast with ground color; 7½″ to 9½″ at birth.

Occupies virtually all types of fresh-water habitats, and also occurs on many offshore, coastal islands.

Similar species: Northern and Midland Water Snakes normally have dark crossbands only on *forepart* of body; their belly markings include dark or reddish half-moons. Also see Cottonmouth (p. 186).

Range: Coastal Plain, North Carolina to Mississippi.   Map 84

Fig. 27. HEADS OF WATER SNAKES

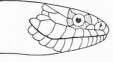

GREEN AND FLORIDA GREEN   BANDED, BROAD-BANDED, AND FLORIDA
Scales between eye and lip plates   Dark stripe from eye to angle of jaw

BROAD-BANDED WATER SNAKE
Natrix sipedon confluens   p. 206

Identification: 22–36; record 45. None of our other Water Snakes have such *broad* dark crossbands or so few. They number only 11 to 17 on body; every other North American *Natrix* has at least 19 and normally many more than that. The dark crossbands are separated by areas of yellow, irregular in shape and arrangement, and they frequently run together; in coloration they vary from black through brown to rich red-brown (or combinations of these). In some parts of range, either the yellow or red may be exceptionally prominent, as is reflected in such colorful local names as "yellow moccasin" and "pink flamingo snake." In lower Mississippi Valley, dark hues predominate, and even the belly markings are usually black or very dark brown. A dark stripe from eye to angle of mouth (Fig. 27, p. 119). Scales *keeled;* anal *divided. Young:* More brightly patterned; 7" to 9½" at birth.

A snake of the great watery wilderness of the Mississippi River delta region and of marshes, swamps, and shallow bodies of water in general throughout its range. Occurs to very edge of salt or brackish water along Gulf Coast.

Similar species: Cottonmouth has broad head and is a stouter, heavier snake.

Range: Central lowlands, extr. s. Illinois to cent. Texas and Gulf Coast.   Map 84

FLORIDA WATER SNAKE
Natrix sipedon pictiventris   p. 206

Identification: 24–42; record 62½. The Florida member of the "banded" Water Snake group. As in the others, there are dark crossbands and a dark stripe from eye to angle of jaw (Fig. 27, p. 119). But it differs in often having secondary dark spots on sides of body (between the prominent crossbands) and in possessing *wormlike* red or black markings across belly. Coloration and pattern highly variable — black, brown, or reddish markings on a ground color of gray, tan, or reddish. In the redder specimens, black pigment is reduced or even lacking; in darker ones, black obscures the other colors, and virtually plain black specimens are not rare. Scales *keeled;* anal *divided. Young:* Red or black crossbands in bold contrast with a light ground color; 7½" to 10½" at birth.

A snake chiefly of shallow-water habitats, of Florida's swamps, marshes, flatwoods ponds, cypress bays, borders of lakes and ponds, rivers, and fresh water in general.

Similar species: Florida Green Water Snake has a row of scales between eye and lip plates (Fig. 27, p. 119). Also see Eastern Cottonmouth (p. 186).

Range: Extr. s. Georgia to s. tip of Florida.   Map 84

GULF SALT MARSH SNAKE *Natrix sipedon clarki*   p. 207

Identification: 15–30; record 36. The only *striped* Water Snake normally occurring in a salt- or brackish-water habitat. There are *two* dark brown stripes and *two* tan or yellowish ones on *each* side of body. The very distinctive belly pattern consists of a central row of large white or yellow spots on a ground color of brown or reddish brown; in some specimens there is an extra, smaller row of light spots on each side, making 3 rows in all. Dorsal scale rows 21 or 23. Scales *keeled;* anal *divided. Young:* 7¾" to 9¾" at birth.

An abundant snake of coastal beaches, swamps, and marshes; only rarely enters fresh-water habitats.

Similar species: Other Striped Water Snakes (Queen and Graham's) do not have more than 19 scale rows. Garter Snakes have *single* anal plates and only *one* light stripe on each side of body.

Range: Gulf Coast from w.-cent. Florida to s. Texas. Intergrades with Banded and Broad-Banded Water Snakes in many areas where their fresh-water habitats blend into brackish ones.

Subspecies: ATLANTIC SALT MARSH SNAKE, *Natrix sipedon taeniata.* Dorsum striped anteriorly as in Gulf Salt Marsh Snake, but pattern on remainder of body consisting of dark blotches on a light ground color. A row of broad light spots down center of belly. N.-cent. portion of Florida's east coast. Map 87

MANGROVE WATER SNAKE
Natrix sipedon compressicauda p. 207

Identification: 15–30; record 36¾. A small Water Snake of the mangrove swamps of Florida's lower coasts. Pattern and coloration extremely variable. Commonly there are dark spots or crossbands on a greenish ground color. Stripes may appear on the neck. Some specimens are almost plain black, others straw-colored, and one fairly common phase is virtually plain red or orange-red. Scales *keeled;* anal *divided. Young:* 7″ to 9½″ at birth.

Identification is often best accomplished on basis of habitat. Although it occasionally enters fresh water, such as in some ponds on the Florida Keys, this is chiefly a serpent of salt and brackish water, an environment not often invaded by other Water Snakes native to southern Florida.

Similar species: Cottonmouth, which also sometimes occurs in brackish waters, is stout-bodied and has a broad head distinctly wider than neck; often opens mouth in readiness to bite when alarmed.

Range: S. Florida, especially on w. coast and the Keys; n. coast of Cuba. Intergrades with Gulf Salt Marsh Snake north of Tampa Bay and with Florida Water Snake where salt- and fresh-water habitats meet. Map 87

KIRTLAND'S WATER SNAKE *Natrix kirtlandi* p. 222
Identification: 14–18; record 22. The reddish belly with a prominent row of round black spots down each side is the best check. The 4 rows of dark spots on the back are not always conspicuous. They show best when the skin is stretched, when body, for example, is distended by food or by young (in pregnant females). In a relatively few specimens, the dark spots of the 2 central rows become small and indistinct, especially toward rear of body, and the reddish-brown ground color may appear as a light middorsal

stripe. Scales *keeled;* anal *divided.* *Young:* Dark and virtually unicolored above (unless skin is stretched); belly deep red; about 5″ to 6½″ at birth.

Flattening of the body when alarmed, a trait shared by other Water Snakes and their close allies, is developed to a remarkable degree in this species. Some specimens can make themselves almost ribbon-like, and may hold themselves rigidly immobile until touched or otherwise disturbed. Least aquatic of all Water Snakes; it swims well, but is usually found in a wet-meadow type of habitat. Feeds on earthworms and slugs. Named for Jared P. Kirtland, early Ohio physician and naturalist.
Similar species: Red-bellied Snake lacks conspicuous black spots, either above or below.
Range: W. Pennsylvania to cent. Illinois; s. Michigan to n. Kentucky.   Map 86

BRAZOS WATER SNAKE   *Natrix harteri*   p. 207
Identification: 20–30; record 35½. Within its range this is the only Water Snake with *4 rows of dark spots* on its back (2 rows on each side) and a row of dark dots down each side of a pinkish or orange belly. (Kirtland's Water Snake, of the north-central region, is similarly patterned.) Scales *keeled;* anal *divided.* *Young:* 8″ to 9″ at birth.

A river snake, locally abundant, but known only from a few of the streams of central Texas.   Map 88

QUEEN SNAKE   *Natrix septemvittata*   p. 207
Identification: 15–24; record 36¼. A slender brown aquatic snake with a yellow stripe along lower side of body (on 2d scale row and upper half of 1st). Belly yellow but boldly marked with 4 brown stripes: the 2 outer stripes are the larger and are situated on the edges of the belly plates (plus lower half of 1st row of scales). Ventral stripes most prominent toward neck; farther back they tend to run together, especially in adults, and to be obscured by a darkening of the ground color. Three additional very narrow dark stripes run down the back, but are difficult to see except in specimens that have recently shed their skins. Queen Snakes from the South tend to be nearly unicolored, with indications of pattern remaining only in the neck region. Scales *keeled;* anal *divided.* *Young:* Belly stripes clearly defined, usually all the way to tail; about 7½″ to 9⅛″ at birth.

The "willow snake" or "leather snake," as it sometimes is called, likes small stony creeks and rivers, especially those abounding in crayfish, but it is by no means confined to such habitats. Queen Snakes are not usually such conspicuous baskers as some of the other (and larger) Water Snakes, and they are more likely to be seen swimming or discovered beneath rocks or debris at water's edge. They feed very largely upon soft-shelled crayfish (ones that have just shed), and so are difficult to keep in captivity.

Similar species: Garter Snakes have *single* anal plates, and usually a *middorsal light stripe*. Graham's Water Snake has a broader yellow stripe (on scale rows 1, 2, and 3 — see front endpaper); its belly is either plain yellow or with a single dark area or row of spots down the center. Glossy Water Snake and Lined Snake each have a *double* row of black belly spots. Gulf Salt Marsh Snakes have brown or black bellies with 1 or 3 rows of yellow spots down center.

Range: S. Great Lakes region and se. Pennsylvania to Gulf Coast; an isolated population in Arkansas and sw. Missouri.

Map 91

GRAHAM'S WATER SNAKE *Natrix grahami*   p. 207
Identification: 18–28; record 47.   Look for two pattern characteristics: (1) broad yellow stripe on scale rows 1, 2, and 3 (see front endpaper); and (2) narrow black stripe where lowermost row of scales meets belly plates (stripe often zigzag or irregular). Sometimes a dark-bordered, pale stripe down center of back. Belly yellowish, either plain or marked with dark dots or a dull dark area down center. A dark color phase of this snake occurs in Iowa in which entire dorsal surface is brown, and pattern details can be made out only with difficulty; belly is deep olive-buff, chin and throat yellow. Scales *keeled;* anal *divided.   Young:* About 8″ to 10″ at birth.

Found at margins of ponds and streams, along sloughs and bayous, and in swamps. Sometimes basks, but is more apt to be found by overturning stones and debris at water's edge. May hide in holes in muddy streambanks or in crayfish chimneys. Food includes crayfish and other crustaceans, plus small amphibians and fishes.

Similar species: Queen Snake has 4 brown stripes down belly, and yellow side stripe is on scale rows 1 and 2.   Garter Snakes have *single* anal plates and usually a prominent light stripe down center of back.

Range: Iowa and Illinois to Louisiana and Texas.   Map 90

GLOSSY WATER SNAKE *Natrix rigida*   p. 207
Identification: 14–24; record 29. Shiniest of all the Water Snakes. A more or less plain brown or olive-brown snake, but dark stripes may be faintly evident on back or (more strongly so) on lower sides of body. The 2 rows of black spots down the belly are bold and distinct even in large specimens, wherein the center portion of belly may become clouded with dark pigment. Scales *keeled;* anal *divided.*

A secretive snake of the southern lowlands, rarely seen in the open except at night or after heavy rains.   Decidedly aquatic, its habits resembling those of the Swamp Snakes.   Food includes small fishes, frogs, salamanders, and crayfish.

Similar species: Garter Snakes, Lined Snakes, Striped Swamp Snake, and striped kinds of Water Snakes have prominent *light* stripes.

Range: Coastal Plain; Virginia to n.-cent. Florida and west to e.-cent. Texas.   Map 93

BLACK SWAMP SNAKE *Seminatrix pygaea*   p. 222

Identification: 10–15; record 18 ⁵⁄₁₆. A shiny black aquatic snake with a red belly. Scales *smooth*, but each scale of the 3 to 5 lowermost rows bears a light, longitudinal line that *looks* like a keel. Anal *divided*.   *Young:* Like adults; 4¼″ to 5⅜″ at birth.

Often common in areas where water hyacinths abound, the snakes concealing themselves among the roots of these floating plants.   Dragging hyacinths ashore is one way to search for them.   They often hide under boards and debris at water's edge, and on rainy or dewy nights may wander overland. The environs of cypress ponds are a natural habitat and probably were one of the most important before the pestiferous hyacinth was introduced from South America. Food includes leeches, small fishes, worms, tadpoles, dwarf sirens, and other small salamanders.

Similar species: Red-bellied Snake has *keeled* scales.

Range: Coastal North Carolina to s. Florida.

Subspecies: NORTH FLORIDA SWAMP SNAKE, *Seminatrix pygaea pygaea* (illustrated on Plate 27). Belly plain red or with a pair of black bars on base of each ventral scale; ventrals 118 to 124. N. Florida and s. Georgia. SOUTH FLORIDA SWAMP SNAKE, *Seminatrix pygaea cyclas*. A short triangular black mark at forward edge of each ventral scale; ventrals 117 or fewer. Southern half of peninsular Florida. CAROLINA SWAMP SNAKE, *Seminatrix pygaea paludis*. A pair of black bars on each ventral scale; ventrals 127 or more. Coastal Plain of South Carolina and se. North Carolina.   Map 80

Brown Snakes: Genus *Storeria*

THESE ARE small secretive snakes, usually brown, but sometimes gray or reddish in dorsal coloration. Scales *keeled*, anal *divided*, and no loreal plate (Fig., p. 222).   Several other small brown or gray snakes of other genera resemble them, so recourse to scale counting is often necessary.

Brown Snakes, like the Garter and Water Snakes to which they are related, may flatten their bodies when alarmed.   They also use their anal scent glands when picked up, but the odor is not particularly offensive. Food includes slugs, earthworms, and soft-bodied insects. The genus ranges from Canada to Honduras.

NORTHERN BROWN SNAKE *Storeria dekayi dekayi*   p. 222
  Identification: 9–13; record 18⅜. Formerly called "DeKay's snake" after James Edward DeKay, an early naturalist of New York. This is the little brown snake with 2 parallel rows of blackish spots down the back. A few of the spots may be linked with their partners across the back by narrow lines of dark pigment. General coloration varies from light yellowish brown or gray to dark brown or deep reddish brown. Almost always the middorsal area, for a width of about 4 scales, is lighter in color than sides of body. The small dark lateral spots may be inconspicuous unless skin is stretched. A dark downward streak on side of head (Fig. 28, p. 128). Belly pale yellowish, brownish, or pinkish, unmarked except for 1 or more small black dots at side of each ventral scale. Scales *keeled* and in 17 rows; anal *divided*. *Young:* Conspicuous yellowish collar across neck; general coloration darker than in adults and with spotted pattern scarcely evident; 3⅜″ to 4½″ at birth.
  This could almost be called the "city snake" because of the frequency with which it turns up in parks, cemeteries, and beneath trash in empty lots, even in our largest urban areas. Despite its abundance, it is so adept at hiding that few persons know it, and those who encounter it for the first time mistake it for a baby Garter Snake. Habitats (away from cities) include environs of bogs, swamps, fresh-water marshes, moist woods, hillsides, etc.
  Similar species: Earth Snakes have a long, horizontal loreal scale, whereas Brown Snakes have a vertical preocular scale — see Fig., p. 222. Ground Snakes (*Sonora*) and Worm Snakes (*Carphophis*) have *smooth* scales. Red-bellied Snakes have 15 scale rows and (normally) red bellies. Garter Snakes have *single* anal plates and (usually) a light stripe on each side of body. Ringneck Snakes (easily confused with young Brown Snakes) have *smooth* scales.
  Range: S. Maine to Virginia. Intergradation among the several races of this species occurs over such enormous areas that accurate delineation of the ranges of subspecies is virtually impossible. (Florida Brown Snake an exception.) In some instances it may be practical simply to designate specimens as Brown Snakes without attempting to assign them to subspecies.
  Subspecies: MIDLAND BROWN SNAKE, *Storeria dekayi wrightorum*. Very similar, but with numerous dark crosslines (Fig. 28, p. 128); sum of ventrals and subcaudals 176 or more (175 or fewer in Northern Brown Snake). Wisconsin to the Carolinas and Gulf Coast. TEXAS BROWN SNAKE, *Storeria dekayi texana*. Similar to the northern subspecies, with 2 rows

SKINKS AND WHIPTAILS

| | *Map* | *Text* |

GREAT PLAINS SKINK   66   100
  Dark-edged scales; suggestion of striping. *Young:* Black;
  bright head spots; blue tail.

SAND SKINK   70   104
  Tiny legs; only 1 or 2 toes.

GROUND SKINK   60   97
  Dark stripe; no light stripes.

BROWN RED-TAILED SKINK   67   104
  Tail reddish; stripes end on body.

STRIPED RED-TAILED SKINK   67   104
  Tail reddish; stripes extend onto tail.

SHORT-LINED SKINK   69   101
  Light stripes end at shoulder. *Young:* Blue tail.

FOUR-LINED SKINK   68   101
  Light stripes end near hind legs.

COAL SKINK   65   101
  Light stripes extend onto tail; broad dark stripe 2½ to 4
  scales wide.

SOUTHERN PRAIRIE SKINK   59   103
  Middorsal area plain or only weakly patterned; broad
  dark stripe not more than 2 scales wide.

NORTHERN PRAIRIE SKINK   59   102
  Stripes in middorsal area; broad dark stripe not more than
  2 scales wide.

MANY-LINED SKINK   64   103
  Middorsal light stripe flanked by bold dark stripes; tail
  swollen at base.

FIVE-LINED SKINK   61   98
  Female: 5 broad light stripes. *Male:* Traces of stripes;
  reddish on head. *Young:* Blue tail.

SOUTHEASTERN FIVE-LINED SKINK   63   99
  Female: 5 light stripes, middle one narrow. *Male and
  young:* Similar to Five-lined Skink.

BROAD-HEADED SKINK   62   99
  Male: Body olive-brown; head reddish; grows very large.
  Female and young: Like Five-lined Skink.

SIX-LINED RACERUNNER   72   96
  6 light stripes; dark stripes solid.

SPOTTED WHIPTAIL   71   96
  Dark stripes interrupted by light spots.

♂ means male, ♀ female.

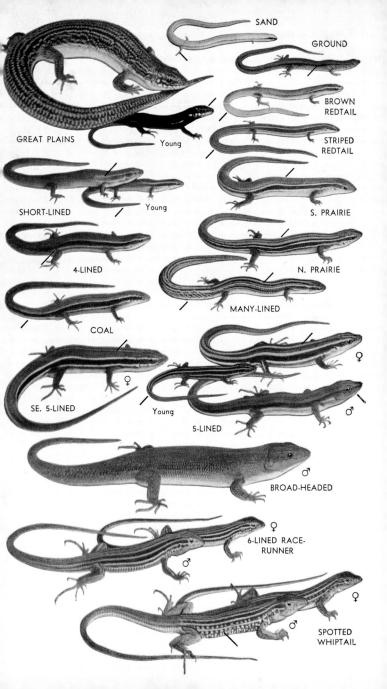

SAND

GROUND

GREAT PLAINS

Young

BROWN REDTAIL

STRIPED REDTAIL

SHORT-LINED

Young

S. PRAIRIE

4-LINED

N. PRAIRIE

MANY-LINED

COAL

SE. 5-LINED ♀

♀

♂

Young

5-LINED

BROAD-HEADED ♂

♀

♂

6-LINED RACE-RUNNER

♀

♂

SPOTTED WHIPTAIL

KEY WEST ANOLE ♂ ♀

GREEN ANOLE
Color Variations

Venter ♀ GREATER
EARLESS ♂ Venter

KEELED EARLESS ♂ ♀

LESSER EARLESS ♂ ♀

SPOT-TAILED
EARLESS

ROUND-
TAILED HORNED

SHORT-
HORNED

TEXAS HORNED

RETICULATE ♂ ♀

COLLARED ♂

Plate 16   127

IGUANA FAMILY

	Map	Text

KEY WEST ANOLE   36   75
  Male: Vertical rows of yellowish spots; extends orange-
  red throat fan (Fig. 13, p. 75). *Female:* Light middorsal
  stripe with scalloped edges.

GREEN ANOLE   37   74
  Green or brown or mottled with both. *Male:* Extends
  pink throat fan (Fig. 13, p. 75).

GREATER EARLESS LIZARD   39   80
  Black crossbars under tail. *Male:* 2 black lines on lower
  side near groin and invading a blue field on belly.

KEELED EARLESS LIZARD   40   80
  Tail long. *Male:* 2 short black lines near armpit. *Female:*
  Markings absent or indistinct; variable (see text).

LESSER EARLESS LIZARD   38   81
  Tail short. *Male:* 2 short black lines near armpit. *Female:*
  Distinct blotches or spots on back; suggestion of black
  lines near armpit.

SPOT-TAILED EARLESS LIZARD   41   82
  Dark dorsal blotches with light borders; dark streaks at
  edge of abdomen; dark spots under tail (Fig. 15, p. 82).

ROUND-TAILED HORNED LIZARD   53   99
  Tail cross-banded and round in cross section; large horns
  all about same length (Fig. 17, p. 90).

SHORT-HORNED LIZARD   51   90
  Horns little more than nubbins (Fig. 17, p. 90).

TEXAS HORNED LIZARD   52   89
  2 central horns greatly elongated (Fig. 17, p. 90).

RETICULATE COLLARED LIZARD   42   77
  Conspicuous black spots.

COLLARED LIZARD   42   76
  2 black "collars" across neck.

♂ means male, ♀ female.

of dark spots down back; no dark line on temporal scale, but a large dark spot under eye. Also, spot behind head is large and extends downward to belly scales (Fig. 28, below). Minnesota to Texas and ne. Mexico. MEXICAN BROWN SNAKE, *Storeria dekayi temporalineata*. Lip scales virtually without markings; a horizontal dark mark on temporal scale (Fig. 28, below). Eastern Mexico, but many specimens in the populations of Brown Snakes inhabitating coastal portions of Texas and Louisiana show the markings of this Mexican race.   Map 83

Fig. 28. CHARACTERISTICS OF BROWN SNAKES

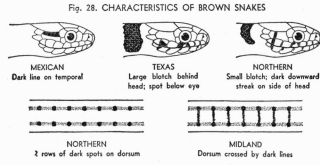

MEXICAN
Dark line on temporal

TEXAS
Large blotch behind head; spot below eye

NORTHERN
Small blotch; dark downward streak on side of head

NORTHERN
2 rows of dark spots on dorsum

MIDLAND
Dorsum crossed by dark lines

FLORIDA BROWN SNAKE *Storeria dekayi victa*   p. 222
Identification: 9–13; record 17⅛. The broad light band across the back of the head, heavy dark pigment on the lip scales below the eye, and a double row of small black spots at each side of the belly are all present in typical specimens, but this Brown Snake is subject to many variations. Some individuals closely resemble Midland Brown Snake in pattern and coloration, but others have the markings greatly reduced. *Most constant character* is number of scale rows — 15 as opposed to 17 in all other subspecies of *Storeria dekayi*. Florida Brown Snake also tends to be more slender than the others. Scales *keeled;* anal *divided. Young:* Similar to adults, but much darker; a prominent light band across back of head; 3¾″ to 4¼″ at birth.

A resident of bogs and marshes, of river-bottom swamps, and environs of ponds and sloughs, but also occurring in upland hammocks and the pineland-prairie region of southern Florida. Often hides among water hyacinths. Most likely to be seen abroad on warm, rainy, or humid nights on roads traversing or paralleling marshy bodies of water.
Similar species: Yellow-lipped Snake and Crowned Snakes have *smooth* scales. Earth Snakes have a horizontal loreal scale (Fig., p. 222). Florida Red-bellied Snakes (some of them do not have red bellies) show a light collar across neck (not back of

head) and there is a light spot on the 5th upper lip (labial) scale.
Range: Se. Georgia and peninsular Florida; lower Keys.

Map 83

RED-BELLIED SNAKE *Storeria occipitomaculata* p. 222
  Identification: 8–10; record 16. The two key characters — a
  plain red belly and light spots at the back of the head — are usually present, but this snake is subject to great variation. Dorsum
  normally plain brown except for indications of 4 narrow dark
  stripes or a broad, fairly light middorsal stripe, or both. Many
  specimens are gray; a few are black, and in extreme cases the
  belly may be blue-black. The belly color, normally bright red,
  may vary through orange to pale yellow. The 3 light spots may
  fuse together (especially in the Florida subspecies) to form a light
  collar across neck. Two preoculars. Scales *keeled* and in 15 rows;
  anal *divided*. *Young:* Similar but darker than adults; 2¾″ to
  4″ at birth.
  A secretive snake of spotty distribution, common in some
  localities but rare or lacking in others that seemingly offer identical habitats. Particularly abundant in many mountainous or
  upland parts of the Northeast. Often found in or near open
  woods, but also occurs in or near sphagnum bogs from sea level
  to high in the mountains.
  Similar species: Kirtland's Water Snake has double row of
  black spots down belly. Black Swamp Snake has *smooth* scales.
  Range: Nova Scotia to cent. Florida; west to the Dakotas,
  Oklahoma, and Louisiana.
  Subspecies: NORTHERN RED-BELLIED SNAKE, *Storeria
  occipitomaculata occipitomaculata* (illustrated on Plate 27). The
  3 light nape spots are usually well defined; moderate amount of
  black pigment on back and sides of head; a light mark on the 5th
  upper lip scale which is *bordered below by black.* All of range
  except parts of Florida and Georgia. FLORIDA RED-
  BELLIED SNAKE, *Storeria occipitomaculata obscura.* Spots
  fused to form a light collar across neck; top and sides of head
  black; a light spot on the 5th upper lip scale extending downward
  to edge of mouth. N. Florida and s. Georgia. Map 82

Garter Snakes: Genus *Thamnophis*

LIKE THE fancy garters that were once fashionable for supporting
a gentleman's socks, most of these snakes are longitudinally striped.
The positions of the light lateral stripes and whether they are en-
croached upon by the dark pattern are useful in telling one species
from another. To locate the stripe accurately, count upward from
the large belly scales (the ventrals). "Stripe on rows 3 and 4," for

example, means that the light lateral stripe is on the 3d and 4th rows of scales above the ventrals. (See Fig., p. 223). Count ¼ of the way back on the body. Most Garter Snakes have 2 very small white or yellow spots on top of their heads.

When alarmed, many specimens will flatten out their bodies, making the pattern seem particularly vivid. When first captured they discharge musk from glands at the base of the tail which has an unpleasant, sweetish odor. Many are docile, but others may strike and bite vigorously in self-defense.

Natural foods consist chiefly of frogs, toads, salamanders, fish, tadpoles, and earthworms, but other items, including leeches, small mammals, birds, and carrion, are eaten occasionally. Captives usually learn to accept chopped raw fish.

Garter Snakes are closely allied to the Water Snakes (*Natrix*), but unlike Water Snakes, they have *single* anal plates and *no scale pits*. (See drawings on front endpaper.) Very rarely, a Garter Snake may have a divided anal plate. Toward the west, members of the group are often found near water, with the inevitable result of being called "water snakes" by persons not acquainted with representatives of the genus *Natrix*. In the more humid East, Garter (sometimes called "garden") Snakes may occur almost anywhere, from virtually sea level to high in the mountains. The genus ranges from coast to coast across southern Canada and the United States and southward to Costa Rica.

(EASTERN) BLACK-NECKED GARTER SNAKE

Thamnophis cyrtopsis ocellata   p. 223

Identification: 16–20; record 29½. The *single row* of large dark spots on the neck sets this apart from our other Garter Snakes. The light lateral stripe on rows 2 and 3 is wavy from being partly invaded by the black spots both above and below it. Scales *keeled;* anal *single*.

An inhabitant of rocky hillsides, limestone ledges, and cedar brakes.

Range: Edwards Plateau of s.-cent. Texas west to the Big Bend. Western and Mexican subspecies.   Map 96

CHECKERED GARTER SNAKE *Thamnophis marcianus* p. 223

Identification: 18–24; record 42½. The snake with the checkerboard pattern. Black "squares" often strongly invade the light stripes. On each side of head behind mouth there is a yellowish curve or triangle, followed by a large dark blotch. Lateral stripe on row 3 near head; on rows 2 and 3 farther back. Scales *keeled;* anal *single*. *Young:* 8″ to 9¼″ at birth.

A snake of the arid Southwest, but one that seldom strays far from streambeds, springs, or other places where water may be present — at least beneath the surface.

Similar species: Plains Garter Snake may have a suggestion of

a yellowish curve behind head, but its side stripe involves row 4.
Range: Sw. Kansas to n. Mexico and west to California.
Subspecies: EASTERN CHECKERED GARTER SNAKE, *Thamnophis marcianus marcianus* (illustrated on Plate 28). Ventral scales usually 155 or fewer. S.-cent. Oklahoma to ne. Mexico. WESTERN CHECKERED GARTER SNAKE, *Thamnophis marcianus nigrolateris*. Ventrals usually 156 or more. Kansas to Chihuahua and California.   Map 97

EASTERN GARTER SNAKE
Thamnophis sirtalis sirtalis   p. 223

Identification: 18–26; record 48. The *only* Garter Snake throughout most of its range with lateral stripes *confined to rows 2 and 3.* Extremely variable in coloration and pattern; either stripes or spots may predominate. Normally 3 yellowish stripes, but they may be brownish, greenish, or bluish instead. Ground color black, dark brown, green, or olive. Usually a double row of alternating black spots between stripes, the spots sometimes very prominent and invading stripes; occasional specimens are virtually stripeless. Belly greenish or yellowish, with 2 rows of indistinct black spots partially hidden under overlapping portions of ventrals. Some individuals, especially from toward western part of range, have red or orange on skin between the dorsal scales. Jet-black (melanistic) specimens are found occasionally, especially near shores of Lake Erie. In the Chicago area many of these Garter Snakes exhibit a pattern variation in which the lateral stripe is interrupted at intervals in neck region by dark vertical crossbars. Scales *keeled;* anal *single.* *Young:* 5″ to 9″ at birth.

A well-known and common snake occupying a wide variety of habitats — meadows, marshes, woodlands, hillsides, along streams and drainage ditches, and even in city lots and dumps where there is moisture, or at least the ground is damp.
Similar species: All other Garter Snakes within the range have side stripes involving row 4, at least on neck — except Short-headed Garter Snake which is distinguished by small head and low number (17) of scale rows (19 in Eastern Garter). The striped Water Snakes (Queen, Graham's, and Glossy) and Gulf Salt Marsh Snake all have *divided* anal plates, and most of them have *strongly patterned* bellies. Brown Snakes lack light *lateral* stripes and loreal scale (Fig., p. 222).
Range: S. Canada to Gulf of Mexico and west to Minnesota and e. Texas.   Map 100

RED-SIDED GARTER SNAKE
Thamnophis sirtalis parietalis   p. 223

Identification: 20–26, record 46. The red or orange bars vary in size and intensity, so some specimens are redder than others. In many, red is largely confined to skin between scales. General ground color olive, brown, or black, the dark pigment sometimes invading much of belly. Lateral stripes on rows 2 and 3; all 3 stripes may be yellow, orange-yellow, bluish, or greenish. Scales *keeled;* anal *single. Young:* 7" to 8" at birth.

In the eastern part of the range, this snake is widespread and common in such habitats as prairie swales, along ditches paralleling railroads, the environs of ponds, etc. Farther west it may occur wherever water is found, and it follows watercourses, even intermittent ones, far into arid country.

Similar species: Checkered Garter Snake lacks red bars. Plains Garter and Western Ribbon Snakes have light stripes on rows 3 and 4.

Range: Prairie provinces of Canada to Oklahoma and New Mexico. Western subspecies.   Map 100

TEXAS GARTER SNAKE
Thamnophis sirtalis annectens   p. 223
Identification: 18–25; record 34½. The unusually broad orange stripe is characteristic. On forward third of body the lateral stripes involve row 3, *plus* adjacent parts of rows 2 and 4. Scales *keeled;* anal *single.*

Similar species: In Eastern and Red-sided Garter Snakes the lateral stripes do not include row 4. Black-necked Garter Snake has *single* row of large black spots on each side of neck. Western Ribbon Snake is more slender, and lateral stripes do not involve scale row 2. Checkered Garter Snake has a light band behind mouth followed by a broad dark band.

Range: E.-cent. Texas.   Map 100

PLAINS GARTER SNAKE   *Thamnophis radix*   p. 223
Identification: 20–28; record 40. This one may be troublesome. First check the stripe — it is on rows 3 and 4. Then look for black markings — black bars on lips, a double alternating row of spots between stripes, a row of black spots *below* side stripe, and a row of dark, often indefinite, spots down each side of belly. Some specimens are so dark that part of the markings may be obscured. Dorsal stripe may be bright yellow or orange, lateral ones greenish or bluish. Scales *keeled* in a maximum of 21 rows; anal *single. Young:* About 7½" at birth.

An extremely abundant snake throughout much of its range, being especially common in river valleys and near prairie ponds and sloughs. Frequently found in and near large cities, and is little disturbed by civilization or agriculture.

Similar species: Lateral stripe involves row 2 and the maximum number of scale rows is only 19 in most other Garter Snakes (Eastern, Red-sided, Butler's) occurring within the range of this one. Checkered Garter Snake has a yellow curve or triangle behind mouth followed by a broad black band. The Ribbon

Snakes, with the stripe on rows 3 and 4, are slender and their tails are long — $\frac{1}{4}$ or more of total length. (Other Garter Snakes normally have tails less than $\frac{1}{4}$ their lengths.)

Range: N.-cent. Ohio and nw. Indiana to Rocky Mountains and from n. New Mexico to s. Alberta.

Subspecies: EASTERN PLAINS GARTER SNAKE, *Thamnophis radix radix* (illustrated on Plate 28). Ventral scales usually 154 or fewer; scale rows on neck usually 19. Cent. Ohio; nw. Indiana to Iowa and adj. states. WESTERN PLAINS GARTER SNAKE, *Thamnophis radix haydeni.* Similar, but with black spots between stripes somewhat smaller. Ventral scales usually 155 or more; scale rows on neck usually 21. Minnesota to Missouri and west to Rockies. Map 99

BUTLER'S GARTER SNAKE *Thamnophis butleri* p. 223
Identification: 15–20; record 27$\frac{1}{4}$. A curious method of crawling when excited — as when trying to escape — is a good field character. The body wriggles vigorously from side to side, but the rather meager forward progress is out of all proportion to the amount of energy expended. Head small; lateral stripe (on neck) on row 3 and adjacent halves of rows 2 and 4. Lateral stripes may be orange. Dorsal ground color variable — olive-brown to black — and it may or may not show a double row of black spots between the stripes. Scales *keeled;* anal *single.* *Young:* 5″ to 7″ at birth.

Chiefly a snake of open, prairie-like areas. Very common in some localities, but rare or completely lacking over many parts of its range. Named for Amos Butler, early Indiana naturalist. **Similar species:** Eastern Garter Snake has stripe on rows 2 and 3. Plains Garter Snake has stripe on rows 3 and 4, and there are usually prominent black spots both above *and below* the lateral stripes. Also see Short-headed Garter Snake.
Range: Ohio and extr. s. Ontario to cent. Indiana; se. Wisconsin. Map 98

SHORT-HEADED GARTER SNAKE
Thamnophis brachystoma p. 223
Identification: 14–18; record 22. Smallest of the eastern Garter Snakes, and the one with the most restricted range. Head is quite short and no wider than neck. A tendency for each lateral stripe to be bordered by a narrow dark line. Lateral stripe (on neck) on rows 2 and 3, but occasionally involving lower part of row 4. Dark spots between the stripes, so common in many other kinds of Garter Snakes, are lacking or only faintly indicated. Scales *keeled;* anal *single. Young:* From 5″ to 6″ at birth.

A snake of the uplands and sometimes unbelievably abundant; where colonies occur, dozens or even hundreds may be seen on optimum days in spring.
Similar species: Butler's Garter Snake has the lateral stripe on

same scale rows, but head is somewhat larger and a trifle wider than neck; also, dark spots may appear between the stripes. If any doubt remains, count dorsal scale rows; maximum number normally is 17 in Short-headed and 19 in both Butler's and Eastern Garter Snakes. The stripe in the latter does *not* involve row 4.
Range: Sw. New York and nw. Pennsylvania. Map 98

EASTERN RIBBON SNAKE
Thamnophis sauritus sauritus p. 223

Identification: 18–26; record 38. Ribbon Snakes are the slimmest, trimmest members of the Garter Snake group. The 3 bright stripes are well set off against the dark slender body and tail; stripes normally yellow, but dorsal one sometimes with an orange or greenish tinge. A double row of black spots may appear, usually vaguely, between the stripes. Lateral stripes on rows 3 and 4. Lips unpatterned; belly plain yellowish or greenish. *Tail exceptionally long,* ¼ to ⅓ total length of snake. Scales *keeled;* anal *single. Young:* 7¼" to 9" at birth.

This agile, nervous serpent is semi-aquatic, seldom wandering far from streams, pools, bogs, or swamps. Swims at surface instead of diving as Water Snakes do. Deep water normally is avoided, and fleeing Ribbon Snakes skirt the shore, threading their way through vegetation and getting lost from sight with amazing rapidity. Unlike other Garter Snakes, Ribbon Snakes usually will not eat earthworms but are fond of salamanders, frogs, and small fishes. Captives remain nervous and may dart out of their cages the instant the lids are opened.

Similar species: The stripes of several other Garter Snakes also involve row 4, but no other kinds are so thin and have such long tails. The tail in other species and in the striped Water Snakes is generally less than ¼ total length.
Range: Nova Scotia to Michigan and south to Georgia and Mississippi. Map 102

WESTERN RIBBON SNAKE
Thamnophis sauritus proximus p. 223

Identification: 20–30; record 44. Very similar to the Eastern Ribbon Snake, but stouter as well as longer. Coloration more variable, also. Ground color may be olive, brown, or black; middorsal stripe may be yellow, orange, red, or brown. There is also a scale difference — usually 8 upper labials instead of 7 (as in Eastern Ribbon Snake). Scales *keeled;* anal *single. Young:* About 9" to 10" at birth.

Semi-aquatic and remaining close to streams and other bodies of water in more arid parts of range.
Similar species: Other Garter Snakes with a stripe on rows 3 and 4 have shorter tails that are generally less than ¼ total length.
Range: S. Wisconsin to se. Colorado and south to Louisiana,

Texas, and e. Mexico.   Mexican subspecies and to Costa Rica.
Map 102

SOUTHERN RIBBON SNAKE
Thamnophis sauritus sackeni   p. 223
Identification: 18–25; record 30. A less well patterned counterpart of the other Ribbon Snakes. The general impression is of a
brown or olive snake with a light stripe on each side. Dorsal
stripe less distinct than lateral ones and, occasionally, it may be
lacking altogether or represented only by a short line on neck.
Belly plain yellowish white; the edges of the plates brownish.
Tail very long. Scales *keeled;* anal *single.*

This abundant southern subspecies is semi-aquatic and, like
other Ribbon Snakes, often basks on vegetation overhanging
water, dropping in at the slightest alarm.
Similar species: Queen Snake and Glossy Water Snake have
divided anals and series of dark markings on their bellies.
Range: Extr. s. South Carolina to s. Mississippi and south to
tip of Florida; the lower Keys.   Map 102

LINED SNAKE   *Tropidoclonion lineatum*   p. 223
Identification: 8¾–15; record 21. It's "bottoms up" for checking this snake. The double row of bold black half-moons down
belly plus *single* anal plate should clinch identification. Middorsal stripe variable in coloration — whitish, yellow, orange,
or light gray. Lateral stripe on rows 2 and 3. Scales *keeled*.
Young: Averaging 4″ to 4¾″ at birth.

A very abundant snake throughout much of its range, appearing frequently in city lots, abandoned trash dumps, or public
parks. Also occurs on open prairies and in sparsely timbered
areas. Usually found by overturning stones, boards, and debris,
but it prowls at night or during the breeding season in spring.
Earthworms are the favorite food.
Similar species: Some of the Garter Snakes have dark spots on
their bellies, but these are not so large, dark, or clearly defined
as in the Lined Snake. Glossy Water Snake bears similar belly
markings, but its dorsal pattern, if any shows at all, consists of
dark stripes, and its anal plate is *divided*. Graham's Water Snake
also has *divided* anal.
Range: Cent. Illinois to Colorado and New Mexico; se. South
Dakota to cent. Texas.
Subspecies: NORTHERN LINED SNAKE, *Tropidoclonion
lineatum lineatum.* Ventrals 143 or fewer; caudals more than
32 in females and more than 40 in males.   CENTRAL LINED
SNAKE, *Tropidoclonion lineatum annectens.* Ventrals more
than 143; caudals more than 33 in females and more than 40 in
males. TEXAS LINED SNAKE, *Tropidoclonion lineatum
texanum.* Ventrals 143 or fewer; caudals fewer than 34 in

females and fewer than 41 in males. See map for individual ranges. Map 103

Earth Snakes: Genus *Haldea*

THESE ARE small gray, brown, or reddish-brown snakes virtually devoid of any distinctive markings. They must be caught and examined closely to verify identification. Any small nondescript serpent of an "earthy" color *may* belong to this genus. Earth Snakes are highly secretive and, in the North at least, seldom appear above ground except after cool, heavy rains, when they may be found, in addition to other places, hidden beneath stones that have been warmed by the sun. Food includes earthworms and soft-bodied insects and their larvae. The genus occurs only in the eastern United States, and a variety of names have been applied to its members — "ground snakes," "gray snakes," "little brown snakes," etc.

ROUGH EARTH SNAKE *Haldea striatula* p. 222
Identification: 7–10; record 12¾. A cone-headed snake with a distinctly pointed snout. Plain light brown to reddish brown in coloration. Upper labials 5 in number; a horizontal loreal scale (Fig., p. 222); internasals fused together into a single scale. Scales *keeled;* anal *divided. Young:* About 4″ at birth.

This small secretive snake is locally common in the South, but is normally found only when such shelters as boards and stones are overturned or logs and decaying trash piles are torn apart.
Similar species: Smooth Earth Snakes have 6 upper labials and *smooth* or *weakly keeled* scales. The Brown Snakes have no loreal scale (Fig., p. 222). The Worm Snakes and the Yellow-lipped Snake have *smooth* scales.
Range: Virginia to n. Florida; west to Kansas and Texas.
Map 79

SMOOTH EARTH SNAKE *Haldea valeriae* p. 222
Identification: 7–10; record 12⅝. Any small gray or reddish-brown snake virtually without markings may be this one (within its geographical range, of course). There may be an indication of a faint light stripe down the back, and many scales may have faint light lines upon them that look like keels but aren't. Often a dark "shadow" from eye to nostril. Belly plain white or yellowish. Upper labials 6 in number; a horizontal loreal scale (Fig., p. 222). Scales *smooth or weakly keeled* and in 15 or 17 rows (see subspecies below). Anal plate *divided. Young:* Without markings; about 3¾″ to 4½″ at birth.

Although considered a rare reptile over much of its range, the Smooth Earth Snake is locally common, and may be much more abundant than it seems. Adept at keeping out of sight. Habitats include abandoned fields, environs of trails and back roads, especially those in or near deciduous forests.

Similar species: Brown Snakes have *strongly keeled* scales and no loreal (Fig., p. 222). Rough Earth Snake has *strong keels* and only 5 upper labials. Worm Snakes have *smooth* scales and a maximum of 13 scale rows. Yellow-lipped Snake has a dark band running from snout through eye and to angle of jaw.

Range: New Jersey to n. Florida; west to Iowa, Kansas, and Texas.

Subspecies: EASTERN EARTH SNAKE, *Haldea valeriae valeriae* (illustrated on Plate 27). Scale rows 15; scales mostly *smooth*, but faint keels are usually discernible on back near tail. Often there are tiny black spots on dorsum, more or less scattered or arranged in 4 rows. Coloration gray or light brownish gray. New Jersey to n. Florida; west to Ohio, cent. Tennessee, and Alabama. MOUNTAIN EARTH SNAKE, *Haldea valeriae pulchra*. Scales *weakly keeled*, in 15 rows anteriorly and 17 at midbody and posteriorly. Dorsum reddish brown to dark gray. Unglaciated mountains and high plateaus of w. Pennsylvania and adj. Maryland and West Virginia. WESTERN EARTH SNAKE, *Haldea valeriae elegans*. Scales *weakly keeled*, in 17 rows. Reddish- to grayish-brown. (Great Plains Ground Snake, range of which overlaps range of Western Earth Snake has *smooth* scales in 15 rows.) S. Indiana to e. Kansas; south to the Gulf; disjunct colonies in Iowa.   Map 81

STRIPED SWAMP SNAKE *Liodytes alleni*   p. 222
Identification: 13–20; record 25¾. A shiny, brown, aquatic snake with a broad yellowish stripe along lower side of body. Belly normally yellowish and virtually unmarked, but it may be orange or orange-brown instead, and the same color may also replace the yellow of the lateral stripe. Dark midventral markings often present, but they may vary from a few scattered smudges to a long, well-defined row of spots. Head small in proportion to size of body. Scales *smooth* except in anal region and atop tail, where they are keeled. Anal *divided*. *Young:* Like adults; 6¼″ to 7″ at birth.

Thoroughly aquatic and at home in dense vegetation in shallow water. Sometimes found by hauling masses of water hyacinths ashore and then sorting through them. Habitats include sloughs and marshes, bayheads and sphagnum bogs. At twilight, especially on rainy or humid evenings, Striped Swamp Snakes sometimes travel overland and may be seen on roads paralleling or traversing wet prairies, marshes, etc. Food consists of crayfish, dwarf sirens, and frogs. Captives of this species and Black Swamp Snake survive best in aquariums well supplied with aquatic vegetation and several inches of water.

Similar species: Garter and Ribbon Snakes have *keeled* scales and *single* anal plates.

Range: S. Georgia and peninsular Florida.   Map 101

Hognose Snakes: Genus *Heterodon*

SERPENTS of extraordinary behavior. These are the "spreadheads" that flatten their heads and necks, hiss loudly, and inflate their bodies with air, producing a show of hostility that has earned them a bad reputation. If the intruder fails to retreat or prods the snake with a stick, it will soon roll on its back, open its mouth, give a few convulsive movements, and then lie still as though dead. Turn the snake right side up, and it promptly rolls over again, giving the bluff away.

As a result of their behavior these harmless snakes have earned such dangerous-sounding names as "hissing adder," "blow viper," "spreading adder," "hissing sand snake," and "puff adder."

The upturned snout (in combination with keeled scales) is also a good identification point. The tail is often held in a tight, flat coil. Toads are the prinicipal food. The genus occurs only in North America.

EASTERN HOGNOSE SNAKE   *Heterodon platyrhinos*   p. 191
  Identification: 18–30; record 43.   The hissing, head-spreading, and playing 'possum are usually sufficient. Check for the upturned snout, which is keeled above. General coloration quite variable — yellow, brown, gray, orange, or red may predominate. Normally a spotted snake, but jet-black specimens or nearly plain gray ones are common in some areas. Belly mottled, gray or greenish (rarely black) on yellow, light gray, or pinkish. Underside of tail *lighter than belly* — easily checked when the snake is playing 'possum (see Fig. 29, p. 139). Scales *keeled;* anal *divided. Young:* 6½″ to 8″ at hatching.

  Sandy areas are a favorite habitat. After a short period in captivity, most Hognose Snakes fail to "perform" any longer. Although toads are the mainstay, frogs and tadpoles also are eaten; so are some types of insects, especially by the young snakes.

  Similar species: In Southern Hognose Snake, underside of tail is *not* lighter than belly. In all three races of the western species the entire ventral surface is black with white or yellow patches (see Fig. 29, p. 139).

  Range: New Hampshire to s. Florida; west to South Dakota and Texas.   Map 108

Fig. 29. CHARACTERISTICS OF HOGNOSE SNAKES

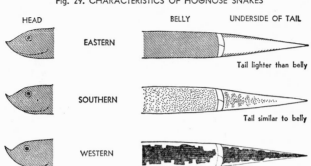

WESTERN HOGNOSE SNAKE   *Heterodon nasicus*   p. 191
  Identification: 16–21; record 31⅛. The sharply upturned snout,
  normally with a keel on top, marks this as a Hognose Snake, but
  the belly must be checked to distinguish it from the two eastern
  species (Fig. 29, above). Large jet-black ventral areas, interspersed with white or yellow, are characteristic. Scales *keeled;*
  anal *divided.*
    Partial to relatively dry prairie areas, especially sandy ones.
  The habit of rolling over and playing dead is not so well developed as in the Eastern Hognose Snake. Called "prairie
  rooter" in some parts of range.
  Similar species: The two kinds of Hook-nosed Snakes have
  smooth scales and there is a depression instead of a keel behind
  the "hook." Belly light in Southern Hognose. Underside of tail
  lighter than belly in Eastern Hognose (Fig. 29, above).
  Range: Illinois to Alberta; south to se. Arizona and cent.
  Mexico.
  Subspecies: DUSTY HOGNOSE SNAKE, *Heterodon nasicus
  gloydi* (illustrated on Plate 24). Dark middorsal blotches,
  counted from head to a point directly above anus, are fewer than
  32 in males; fewer than 37 in females. Se. Kansas to most of
  Texas; an isolated colony in Missouri. PLAINS HOGNOSE
  SNAKE, *Heterodon nasicus nasicus.* Similar but with markings
  darker and in sharper contrast with ground color. Dark body
  blotches more than 35 in males; more than 40 in females. Minnesota to Alberta and south to New Mexico; isolated colonies
  in sand prairies of w. Illinois. MEXICAN HOGNOSE SNAKE,
  Heterodon nasicus kennerlyi. Like Dusty Hognose in coloration
  and pattern but distinguished by scalation. Two to 6 small
  scales in the group on top of head directly behind rostral plate.

The Plains and Dusty subspecies have 9 or more. (These are called azygous scales.) Extr. s. Texas to se. Arizona and cent. Mexico.   Map 107

SOUTHERN HOGNOSE SNAKE   *Heterodon simus*   p. 191
Identification: 14–20; record 24. Smallest of the Hognose Snakes. Snout sharply upturned (Fig. 29, p. 139) and keeled above. Coloration fairly constant; not highly variable as in Eastern Hognose Snake. Underside of tail *not* conspicuously lighter than belly (Fig. 29, p. 139). Scales *keeled;* anal *divided.*

Habitats include sandy woods, fields, and groves, dry river floodplains, and hardwood hammocks; occasionally plowed out of the ground. Upturned snout is used in burrowing and in digging for spadefoot and other toads.
Similar species: In Eastern Hognose Snake, underside of tail is lighter than belly (Fig. 29, p. 139).
Range: Se. North Carolina to s.-cent. Florida and s. Mississippi.   Map 110

YELLOW-LIPPED SNAKE   *Rhadinaea flavilata*   p. 191
Identification: 10–13; record 15⅞. Dorsal coloration varying from rich golden brown to light reddish brown, but becoming paler on the lower sides. Head darker. *Dark line through eye.* Often a suggestion of a narrow dark stripe down center of back and another on each side of body on the 3d row of scales. Belly plain yellow. Scales *smooth*; anal *divided. Young:* About 6½″ at hatching.

A snake of the damp lowlands; in flatwoods and hammocks and near borders of bogs and swamps. Secretive and found chiefly under logs and boards, beneath bark, or buried in loose soil. Food includes small frogs, toads, snakes, and lizards.
Range: Coastal strip, North Carolina to e. Louisiana and s. Florida.   Map 105

NORTHERN RINGNECK SNAKE
Diadophis punctatus edwardsi   p. 191
Identification: 10–15; record 22½. A plain dark slender snake with a golden collar. Dorsal coloration variable — bluish black, bluish gray, slate, or brownish. Belly uniform yellow (Fig. 30, p. 141) or occasionally with a row or partial row of small black dots down center. Scales *smooth;* anal *divided. Young:* Darker than adults; 4″ to 5½″ at hatching.

A secretive woodland snake, usually most common in cutover areas that include an abundance of hiding places in the form of stones, logs, bark slabs, or other rotting wood. Rocky wooded hillsides also favored. The musk is pungent, clinging, and unpleasant. Many people believe Ringnecks are young Racers. Small salamanders are an important food, but earthworms and small snakes, lizards, and frogs also are eaten.

Similar species: Juvenile Brown Snakes have neck rings, but they also have *keeled* scales; a lens may be necessary to see the keels in such small snakes.

Range: Nova Scotia to Wisconsin; south through uplands and central lowlands to n. Georgia.   Map 112

Fig. 30. BELLY PATTERNS OF RINGNECK SNAKES

PRAIRIE
Spots numerous, irregularly placed

NORTHERN
Unmarked or with a few small black dots

MISSISSIPPI
Paired black spots down the center

SOUTHERN
Row of bold black half-moons

SOUTHERN RINGNECK SNAKE

Diadophis punctatus punctatus   p. 191

Identification: 10–14; record 17½. A Ringneck with a spotted belly. The black spots are large, shaped like half-moons, and in a *central row* (Fig. 30, above). Neck ring normally interrupted by dark pigment. Small black spots on chin and lower lips. Dorsal coloration light brown to nearly black; venter yellow to deep red, uniform or with the red confined to underside of tail and rear portion of belly. Scales *smooth;* anal *divided. Young:* 3½" to 4" at hatching.

Although not aquatic, Ringnecks are most often found where there are evidences of moisture—near swamps, springs, on damp wooded hillsides, etc. — but almost invariably under stones, bark, or other shelters. When alarmed, Ringnecks of this subspecies and of the Prairie Ringneck sometimes twist their tails upward in a tight spiral, thus exposing the bright colors to view. This habit has earned them the names of "corkscrew" and "thimble snakes." This behavior is only occasionally seen in the other eastern races.

Range: S. New Jersey to Florida Keys; west to the mountains and to cent. Alabama. (The entire population in s. New Jersey and the Delmarva Peninsula is intermediate between the northern and southern races.)

Subspecies: MISSISSIPPI RINGNECK SNAKE, *Diadophis punctatus stictogenys.* Neck ring narrow, often interrupted; belly spots irregular but usually grouped along midline in attached or separate pairs (Fig. 30, above). Extr. s. Illinois to the Gulf; Alabama to e. Texas. PRAIRIE RINGNECK

TREE AND SPINY LIZARDS

(Males of most species have a blue patch at each side of belly.)

	Map	Text

TREE LIZARD   43   88
Irregular dark spots; dorsal scales variable — some large,
some tiny; a fold across throat.

ROSE-BELLIED LIZARD   48   83
Row of dark spots bordered below by a light stripe; a
pocket at rear of thigh (Fig. 16, p. 83). *Male:* Dark spot
above armpit; large *pink* patch on each side of belly.

MESQUITE LIZARD   47   84
Wavy dark crosslines; scales at sides of neck much smaller
than scales on nape (Fig. 16, p. 83).

FENCE LIZARD   50   86
Female: Wavy dark crosslines. *Male:* Nearly unicolored
above; blue throat patch surrounded by black.

PRAIRIE LIZARD   50   87
A row of small dark spots bordered below by a *bold* light
stripe; secondary light stripe along lower side of body.

FLORIDA SCRUB LIZARD   49   88
Prominent dark *brown* stripe.

TEXAS SPINY LIZARD   46   85
Light stripe not sharply defined; dorsal scales large and
spiny.

CREVICE SPINY LIZARD   45   84
Dark collar; tail strongly patterned near tip. *Female and
young:* Dark bands across back.

BLUE SPINY LIZARD   44   85
Dark collar; tail markings not clear-cut.

♂ means male, ♀ female.

SPINY LIZARD   ↑ No fold across throat   TREE LIZARD   ↑ Fold across throat

TREE

ROSE-BELLIED ♀ ♂

MESQUITE ♀ ♂

FENCE ♀ ♂

PRAIRIE ♀ ♂

FLORIDA SCRUB

TEXAS SPINY

CREVICE SPINY ♀ ♂

BLUE SPINY ♀ ♂

BLIND

WESTERN HOOK-NOSED

MEXICAN HOOK-NOSED

SE. CROWNED

PLAINS BLACK-HEADED

FLORIDA CROWNED

FLAT-HEADED

BLACK-STRIPED

NIGHT

CAT-EYED

SPECKLED RACER

Plate 18   143

BLIND SNAKE, REAR-FANGED SNAKES, AND SOME TEXAS RARITIES

(All have smooth scales except the Speckled Racer.)

	Map	*Text*

BLIND SNAKE   78   109
Wormlike; tail blunt; belly scales same size as dorsal scales.

WESTERN HOOK-NOSED SNAKE   134   178
Snout upturned; head strongly cross-banded.

MEXICAN HOOK-NOSED SNAKE   135   178
Snout upturned; head virtually unpatterned.

SOUTHEASTERN CROWNED SNAKE   138   180
Light band across rear of head.

FLORIDA CROWNED SNAKE   138   181
Black pigmentation with extensions downward to mouth and on sides of neck.

PLAINS BLACK-HEADED SNAKE   140   182
Black pigmentation rounded or pointed on nape and normally without dark downward extensions; upper labials usually 7.

FLAT-HEADED SNAKE   139   181
Head nearly same color as body or only slightly darker; upper labials usually 6.

BLACK-STRIPED SNAKE   111   145
3 black (or dark brown) stripes on a ground color of light brown; belly bright red or orange.

NIGHT SNAKE   137   179
Dark neck blotch; body profusely spotted.

CAT-EYED SNAKE   136   179
Light collar; body crossed by bold dark saddles.

SPECKLED RACER   116   153
Scales with light centers; dark stripe behind eye; a few middorsal rows of scales with faint keels.

SNAKE, *Diadophis punctatus arnyi.* Dark head coloration extending around or across angle of jaw and slightly forward on lower jaw; belly spots numerous and highly irregular (Fig. 30, p. 141); scale rows usually 17 on forward part of body (normally 15 on other Ringnecks). Extr. se. Minnesota and extr. se. South Dakota to s.-cent. Texas.   Map 112

EASTERN WORM SNAKE *Carphophis amoenus amoenus* p. 191
Identification: 7½-11; record 13. A serpentine imitation of the common earthworm. Plain brown above; belly and 1 or 2 rows of scales pink. Head pointed. Two prefrontal and 2 internasal scales (Fig. 31, below). Scales *smooth and opalescent;* anal *divided. Young:* Darker than adults; 3½″ to 4″ at hatching.

Almost never seen in the open, but discovered under stones or boards, in rotting logs, during digging operations, etc. Partial to moist earth and disappearing deep underground in dry weather. When held in the hand, Worm Snakes attempt to push their way between one's fingers with both the head and spinelike tail tip. Food includes earthworms and soft-bodied insects.
Similar species: Other small brown snakes either have keeled scales or the belly color doesn't extend upward to involve a full row of dorsal scales or more.
Range: S. New England to cent. Alabama.
Subspecies: MIDWEST WORM SNAKE, *Carphophis amoenus helenae.* Very similar, but with each prefrontal scale fused with corresponding internasal (Fig. 31, below). S. Ohio to s. Illinois and south to the Gulf.   Map 109

Fig. 31. HEAD SCALES OF WORM SNAKES

EASTERN   MIDWEST

Prefrontals and   Each prefrontal
internasals   fused with the
separate   corresponding
                                          internasal

WESTERN WORM SNAKE *Carphophis amoenus vermis* p. 191
Identification: 7½-11; record 14¾. Plain purplish black above; pink of belly extends upward on the sides to the 3d row of scales. Head pointed. Scales *smooth and opalescent;* anal *divided.*

Essentially a woodland snake that follows stream valleys westward through prairie areas. Secretive and usually found under moist logs, stones, etc.
Range: S. Iowa and se. Nebraska to Louisiana.   Map 109

RAINBOW SNAKE *Abastor erythrogrammus* p. 191
Identification: 36–48; record 60. An iridescent, glossy snake with red and black stripes. Often a row of small black spots between the 2 main rows on the belly. Prior to shedding, the

skin becomes a translucent blue that obscures the normal color pattern. Tongue small. Scales *smooth;* anal *divided. Young:* 7¾″ to 8½″ at hatching.

This handsome snake seldom appears in the open. It burrows in a variety of habitats, including swamps and sandy fields. In the water it is perfectly at home and well able to catch the eels and other aquatic animals on which it feeds. Specimens are inoffensive when handled, but when first caught the hind part of the body thrashes about violently, and the harmless, but sharp, tail spine scratches or stabs at the collector's hands, without, however, breaking the skin.

Range: S. Maryland to cent. Florida and extr. e. Louisiana.

Map 104

MUD SNAKE *Farancia abacura* p. 191

Identification: 40–54; record 80. A shiny, iridescent black and red (or pink) snake. Prior to shedding, the skin becomes a translucent blue that obscures the normal color pattern. Tongue noticeably small. Scales *smooth;* anal *divided. Young:* 6¼″ to 9½″ at hatching.

A snake of southern swamps and lowlands. A burrower, but also thoroughly at home in water. (Captive Mud and Rainbow Snakes live best in aquariums.) Feeds chiefly on eel-like salamanders (Amphiumas), which are maneuvered into better swallowing positions by being pricked with the snake's spinelike, albeit harmless, tail. When Mud Snakes are first caught, the tail also may press against the collector's hands. This behavior earns it the names of "horn snake" or "stinging snake," and the habit of lying in a loose horizontal coil associates this species with the fabled "hoop snake." Sirens, other amphibians, and fishes also are eaten.

Range: Southern lowlands (see subspecies below).

Subspecies: WESTERN MUD SNAKE, *Farancia abacura reinwardti* (illustrated on Plate 24). Belly color extends upward on lower sides to form 52 or fewer red bars with rounded tops. (Count on body only; omit tail.) Smaller than the eastern race; record length 72″. Alabama to e. Texas and north in Mississippi Valley to s. Illinois and (formerly) s. Indiana. EASTERN MUD SNAKE, *Farancia abacura abacura.* Like the western subspecies, but with red "bars" more numerous (53 or more), extending farther upward, and in the shape of triangles. In some, the young especially, the upward red extensions from the points of the triangles may cross back of neck. Se. Virginia to s. Florida and se. Alabama. Map 106

BLACK-STRIPED SNAKE
Coniophanes imperialis imperialis p. 143

Identification: 12–18; record 20. The broad black or dark brown stripes alternate with stripes of tan or brown that brighten abruptly at their front ends. A thin, whitish or yellowish line, extending from snout through top of eye, terminates near rear of head. These markings, plus bright red or orange venter, assure identification. Scales *smooth;* anal *divided.*

A secretive, rear-fanged snake best sought by overturning piles of debris, heaps of rotting cactus, palm fronds, etc. It also takes refuge in deep cracks that form when soil dries out quickly under the torrid sun. Food includes small frogs, toads, lizards, and baby mice.

Range: Extr. s. Texas to n. Veracruz. Other subspecies occur farther south. Map 111

Racers and Whipsnakes: Genera *Coluber* and *Masticophis*

THESE ARE slender, fast-moving snakes — often mere streaks in the grass as they dash away. Adults of most kinds are more or less uniformly colored or longitudinally striped. Young Racers are blotched or spotted, juvenile Coachwhips are crosslined, and baby Whipsnakes, in general, resemble their parents. The scales are *smooth;* anal *divided.*

When alarmed or on the defensive, many of these snakes rapidly vibrate the tips of their tails, and, if they are in dry weeds or leaves, they produce a buzzing sound suggestive of a Rattlesnake. When held by the neck, with the body dangling, they characteristically lash vigorously back and forth in an effort to shake themselves free. All are diurnal; many are partially arboreal, ascending into shrubs, cactus, or low trees. Rodents, small birds, lizards, snakes, frogs, and insects are included on their menus. Food is not constricted. A loop of the body is thrown over the struggling victim, pressing it down. Eggs of Whipsnakes, Racers, and Indigo Snakes are coated with small nodules resembling hard dry grains of salt. Racers range from about 10″ to 13″ at hatching; Coachwhips 12″ to 16″; and Whipsnakes 10″ to 16.″

These snakes are subject to considerable individual and local variation, especially in regions where two or more subspecies intergrade. The Whipsnakes (*Masticophis*) range from the United States to northern South America. The Racers (*Coluber*) occur from southern Canada to Guatemala; there is a related species in northeastern Asia.

NORTHERN BLACK RACER
Coluber constrictor constrictor p. 190
Identification: 36–60; record 73. A slender, satiny snake that is plain black *both* above and below. Usually very little white

on chin and throat. Iris of eye brown or dark amber. Scales *smooth;* anal *divided. Young:* Strongly patterned with a mid-dorsal row of dark gray, brown, or reddish-brown blotches on a ground color of gray or bluish gray; small dark spots on flanks and venter; tail virtually unpatterned. As snake grows older, pattern becomes less distinct and upper surface darkens; at length of 30 inches virtually all traces of pattern have usually disappeared.

An alert, active, locally abundant serpent that is quick to flee when approached but fights fiercely when cornered. Often retreats *upward* into bushes or low branches of trees when closely pursued. Normally makes a poor captive, seldom settling down and often falling victim to parasites and infections.

Similar species: Black Rat Snake has *keels* on middorsal scales and is shaped like a loaf of bread in cross section (Fig., p. 175). Black phase of Coachwhip may show slight indications of light pigment toward rear of dorsum, and sides of tail often are reddish; check number of scale rows just anterior to tail — 13 in Coachwhips, 15 in Racers. Black phase of Eastern Garter Snake has *keeled* scales and a *single* anal plate. Young Rat Snakes have conspicuous dark blotches on tails.

Range: Nova Scotia to n. Alabama.

Subspecies: SOUTHERN BLACK RACER, *Coluber constrictor priapus.* Very similar to Northern Black Racer, but with internal anatomical differences. (Enlarged basal hemipenial spine 3 or more times length of its predecessor in same row. Spine is less than 3 times as long in Northern Black Racer.) Florida specimens usually have considerable white on chin and throat, and their irises may be bright red or orange. Young also similar to those of Northern Black Racer, but juveniles from Florida may have reddish dorsal blotches and their bellies may be reddish or pinkish toward tail. Southeastern states and north in Mississippi Valley to s. Indiana. BROWN-CHINNED RACER, *Coluber constrictor helvigularis.* Uniform black above and below except for chin and lips, which are light tan or brown or mottled or suffused with those colors. Lower Chipola and Apalachicola river valleys in Florida panhandle and adj. Georgia. (Also see Everglades Racer, p. 148, which bears a strong resemblance to the Blue Racer of the North.) Map 113

BLUE RACER *Coluber constrictor foxi* p. 190

Identification: 36–60; record 72. Plain blue above, the head darker and very often with an even darker area extending backward from the eye. Shade of blue varies; it may be greenish, grayish, or much darker than in the illustration. Chin and throat white, unspotted. Belly bluish, paler than back. Scales *smooth;* anal *divided. Young:* Similar to young of Northern Black Racer.

Prairies, open woodlands, environs of lakes and tamarack-sphagnum bogs, and more or less open habitats in general.

Range: S. Michigan and nw. Ohio to e. Iowa and se. Minnesota. Intergrades through a broad area with Eastern Yellow-bellied Racer.

Subspecies: EVERGLADES RACER, *Coluber constrictor paludicola*. A pale bluish-, greenish-, or brownish-gray snake. Bluish ones look very much like Blue Racer, of the north-central region, and will check out to that subspecies when compared with Plate 23. Belly whitish and usually with pale cloudy markings of whitish gray or powder blue. Iris of eye red or (rarely) yellow or reddish brown. *Young:* Similar to those of Black Racers, but with a decidedly reddish cast; dorsal spots light chestnut, reddish, or pinkish; belly spots reddish or orange. The Everglades and the Miami rim rock of se. Florida; also Cape Canaveral region of e. Florida.   Map 113

EASTERN YELLOW-BELLIED RACER
Coluber constrictor flaviventris   p. 190

Identification: 30–50; record 70. Averages considerably smaller than the Black or the Blue Racer. Highly variable in coloration. Dorsum plain brown, gray, olive, or dull to dark blue. Belly plain yellowish, varying from pale cream in some parts of range to bright lemon-yellow in others. Scales *smooth;* anal *divided.* *Young:* Similar to young of the Northern Black Racer, except that in southeastern Louisiana there is a definite reddish cast, as in young of the Everglades Racer.

At home in fields and grasslands, brushy areas, and open woods. More likely to forage actively through the day than most other snakes. Like other small animals of plains and prairies, it takes refuge in clumps of vegetation, glides into mammal burrows, or hides in stone or rock piles.

Similar species: Could be mistaken for a Green Snake. Rough Green Snake has *keeled* scales. Smooth Green Snake has a maximum of 15 rows of dorsal scales (17 in the Racers). Most confusion will occur with young. Scales must be checked; combination of *smooth* scales, *divided* anals, and maximum of 17 scale rows will distinguish juveniles from any of the several other spotted snakes occurring within its range.

Range North Dakota and Iowa to Texas and s. Louisiana.

Subspecies: RIO GRANDE RACER, *Coluber constrictor stejnegerianus*. Maximum length about 40″. The "dwarf racer." Mid-dorsal area plain green, or greenish gray, sides of body much lighter; belly plain yellow to yellow-green. *Young* with scattered small dark spots on greenish ground color, the spots joining together to form dark crossbars on neck and forward part of body (Fig. 32, p. 149); body becoming uniform dark olive-green toward tail. Often arboreal, foraging in shrubs and bushes. S. Texas and Coahuila to Guatemala. Western sub-species.   Map 113

Fig. 32. PATTERNS OF RACERS AND WHIPSNAKES
(Each diagram shows a section of skin removed from the animal)

| YOUNG RACERS | YOUNG RIO GRANDE | SCHOTT'S WHIPSNAKE and |
of most subspecies. | RACER | RUTHVEN'S WHIPSNAKE
A middorsal row of blotches | Spots and crossbands | Scales of middorsal rows with light edges

BUTTERMILK SNAKE *Coluber constrictor anthicus*   p. 190

Identification: 36–60; record 70. This Racer looks almost as though it had been spattered by a bleaching compound. Numerous scales are the "wrong" color — white, yellow, buff, or dark blue — and scattered about indiscriminately. No two specimens are marked alike; some are only slightly spotted, but others are heavily speckled. Ground color may be black, bluish, olive, or tan. Scales *smooth;* anal *divided.*

Similar species: Speckled Kingsnake is shiny, has a *single* anal plate, and the specks are small (several would fit upon one scale). Speckled Racer has several rows of scales *weakly keeled.*

Range: W. Louisiana and adj. Texas.   Map 113

EASTERN COACHWHIP
Masticophis flagellum flagellum   p. 190

Identification: 42–60; record 102±. The marked change from black or dark brown "forward" to light brown "aft" is unique among our snakes, but the amount of dark pigment is variable. Some specimens have only their heads and necks dark, others may be half-and-half, and still others may show light pigment only on the tail and rear of body. Coloration of belly corresponds with that of back. Scalation of the long slender tail suggests a braided whip. *Black phase:* In parts of northwestern Arkansas and adjacent Oklahoma and Missouri, Coachwhips may be virtually plain black all over, or with tail and rear of body distinctly reddish. Even in the blackest specimens, however, sides of tail are often reddish, and there may be traces of lighter pigment toward rear of dorsum, plus a considerable light area under tail. Minimum number of scale rows (just anterior to anus) is 13 (15 in Black Racers). Scales *smooth;* anal *divided.* *Young:* Similar to young of Western Coachwhip (see Plate 23), but with dark crosslines closer together.

An active, fast-moving serpent that sometimes prowls with head raised well above ground. Normally escapes the would-be collector with a burst of speed, but fights savagely when cornered. Many habitats are utilized, ranging from dry, sandy flatwoods to swamps, creek valleys, and the rugged terrain of western Arkansas. Coachwhips make nervous captives and are prone to strike repeatedly at persons passing their cages. In biting, they embed their teeth and then yank away, producing lacerations instead of puncture wounds.

Range: North Carolina to s. Florida; west to Texas, Oklahoma, and Kansas.   Map 115

WESTERN COACHWHIP
Masticophis flagellum testaceus   p. 190

Identification: 42–60; record 80. Essentially a unicolored snake — light yellow-brown to dark brown — with head and neck same color as body and tail. Occasional individuals retain indications of the dark juvenile crosslines; in some areas, notably in Texas, specimens may be marked with several broad crossbands, 10 to 15 scales wide, somewhat darker than and alternating with similar broad bands of the ground color. Whole populations in parts of the range may be distinctly reddish. Scales *smooth;* anal *divided. Young:* Dark crosslines 1 or 2 scales wide and separated from one another by about the width of 3 or more scales.

A snake of grasslands, mesquite savannas, arid brushlands, and numerous other more or less open habitats. Called "prairie runner" in some parts of its range.

Similar species: Racers have 15 dorsal scale rows immediately in front of anus; Coachwhips have 13. Ruthven's Whipsnake has only 15 dorsal rows on forward part of body; Coachwhips have 17.

Range: Sw. Nebraska and e. Colorado to ne. Mexico. Western and Mexican subspecies.   Map 115

CENTRAL TEXAS WHIPSNAKE
Masticophis taeniatus ornatus   p. 190

Identification: 42–60; record 72. The only "black snake" with longitudinal white patches on the sides. These are about equally spaced, but are strongest on neck and become gradually less prominent farther back Effect is similar to that produced by an automobile tire that runs over a freshly painted white line on highway and then prints an ever weakening white spot with each turn of the wheel. Amount of white variable; it may cover a larger area than it does on snake depicted on color plate. Large scales atop head usually outlined with light pigment. General dorsal coloration variable from black to reddish brown. Underside of tail bright coral pink. Scales *smooth;* anal *divided.*

Young: No white patches, except for narrow light crossband just behind head; longitudinal stripes present on lower sides, the most prominent being a light one on scale rows 3 and 4; usually a reddish overwash.

Also called "cedar racer" and "ornate whipsnake." An alert, fast-moving snake of brakes and valleys of Edwards Plateau and mountains and basins of Trans-Pecos Texas; occurs up to 5800 feet. Retreats among rocks, thorny vegetation, or other shelter when approached.

Range: Cent. and w. Texas; southward on Mexican Plateau. Western subspecies. Map 114

SCHOTT'S WHIPSNAKE *Masticophis taeniatus schotti* p. 190
  Identification: 40–56; record 66. The only *strongly* striped Whipsnake east of the 100th meridian. The 2 light longitudinal stripes on each side, one at edge of belly scales and the other on scale rows 3 and 4, are the most conspicuous features of the pattern. General coloration varies from bluish- to greenish-gray. Sides of neck reddish orange. Belly whitish anteriorly, stippled with bluish gray farther back; underside of tail pink or salmon. The light anterior edgings of 7 or 8 middorsal rows of scales (Fig. 32, p. 149) are best seen when scales are spread slightly apart (easily checked on living specimens). Scales *smooth;* anal *divided. Young:* Like adults but with reddish overwash.

An alert, elusive resident of the arid brush country of southern Texas. Named for Arthur Schott, who collected the type specimen while a member of the U. S. and Mexican Boundary Survey soon after the termination of the Mexican War.
  Similar species: Texas Patch-nosed Snake has light *middorsal* stripe flanked by dark stripes. Ruthven's Whipsnake has only faint indications of light stripes.
  Range: Texas, south of San Antonio; west into adj. Mexico. Several other strongly striped Whipsnakes (of other species) occur west of 100th meridian. Map 114

RUTHVEN'S WHIPSNAKE
Masticophis taeniatus ruthveni p. 190
  Identification: 40–56; record 66⅛. Typical specimens show very little pattern, except for traces of narrow light stripes on neck or sides. Throat dotted with dark orange; belly bright yellow anteriorly, light bluish gray or olive at midbody, and pink posteriorly; underside of tail bright red. Light anterior edges on 7 or 8 of the middorsal rows of scales (Fig. 32, p. 149). Scales *smooth;* anal *divided. Young:* Like adult, but with neck stripes better indicated.

An agile serpent of arid brushlands. Named for Dr. Alexander Grant Ruthven, herpetologist and long-time president of the University of Michigan.

Similar species: Rio Grande Racer has maximum of 17 scale rows; Whipsnakes have only 15. Rough Green Snake has *keeled* scales.

Range: Extr. s. Texas and ne. Mexico. Intergrades with Schott's Whipsnake in lower Rio Grande Valley. (Specimen illustrated on Plate 23 is actually an intergrade, and shows more indications of stripes than do typical individuals from Mexico.)　　　Map 114

ROUGH GREEN SNAKE *Opheodrys aestivus* 　　　p. 191
Identification: 22–32; record 42. The "vine snake." This dainty, slender serpent is plain light green above and plain white, yellow, or pale greenish below. Dead specimens, preserved ones especially, soon turn dull blue. Scales *keeled;* anal *divided. Young:* Grayish green; about 7″ or 8″ at hatching.

An excellent climber that, when foraging amid vines or shrubs, blends with the background so well as to be virtually invisible. At times it is almost semi-aquatic, freely entering shallow bodies of water. A frequent habitat is in the dense growth of vegetation overhanging a stream or lake border. Crickets, grasshoppers, larvae of moths and butterflies, and spiders constitute the bulk of the food.

Similar species: The very similar Smooth Green Snakes have *smooth* scales. So also does the greenish Rio Grande Racer.

Range: S. New Jersey to Florida Keys; west to Kansas and Texas; south in Mexico to Tampico. Isolated records in western part of range.　　　Map 121

SMOOTH GREEN SNAKE *Opheodrys vernalis* 　　　p. 191
Identification: 14–20; record 26. The "green grass snake." A gentle little reptile that is plain bright green above and plain white or washed with yellow below. Specimens turn bluish after death. Scales *smooth;* anal *divided. Young:* Dark olive-gray; 4″ to 6½″ at hatching.

In eastern and far western parts of its range this is an upland snake, but it occupies the lowlands in the north-central part of the country. (See comments under subspecies below.) Largely terrestrial, showing little inclination to climb. Spiders and insects are eaten.

Similar species: Rough Green Snake is more slender, grows larger, and has *keeled* scales; its range is southern, barely overlapping that of Smooth Green Snake (except in Texas).

Range: Maritime Provinces to s. Manitoba; south in the East to n. New Jersey and in mountains to North Carolina; to Texas, New Mexico, and Utah in the West.

Subspecies: EASTERN SMOOTH GREEN SNAKE, *Opheodrys vernalis vernalis* (illustrated on Plate 24). Males have 130 or fewer ventrals; females 139 or fewer. A snake chiefly of high altitudes or latitudes. Often found in mountain glades and in grassy or rocky meadows. Eastern half of range. WESTERN

SMOOTH GREEN SNAKE, *Opheodrys vernalis blanchardi.*
Males have 131 or more ventrals; females 140 or more. In moist
grassy sections of plains and prairies, but now scarce over much
of its range because of destruction of habitat by civilization.
Ohio to Manitoba, Utah, New Mexico, and Texas. The isolated
populations in the West ascend into mountains. Specimens
taken in Black Hills of South Dakota and adj. Wyoming have
low ventral count of Eastern Smooth Green Snake.   Map 120

SPECKLED RACER
Drymobius margaritiferus margaritiferus   p. 143
Identification: 30–40; record 50. A black stripe behind the eye,
and a yellow spot near the center of each dorsal scale. Base of
each scale blue and this, in combination with the yellow spots,
produces the illusion of a greenish overwash. Outer part of each
scale black. Belly plain whitish or yellowish. Subcaudal scales
black-edged posteriorly; ventrals may be similarly marked.
Scales of several middorsal rows *weakly keeled;* outer rows
smooth. Anal *divided. Young:* Similar but with colors less vivid.
    A rarity north of the Rio Grande. Often found near water or
in thickets of dense natural vegetation. Frogs are relished.
Range: Extr. s. Texas and Coahuila to Central America. Mexican subspecies.   Map 116

EASTERN INDIGO SNAKE *Drymarchon corais couperi*   p. 158
Identification: 60–84; record 103½. This is the "blue bullsnake"
or "blue gopher" of the snake charmer and carnival "pit" show.
Entire serpent shiny bluish black, belly included, except that
chin and sides of head may be reddish- or orange-brown. Scales
smooth; anal *single.* Third from last upper labial wedge-shaped
and cut off above by contact between adjacent labials (Fig. 33,
below). *Young:* Like adults, but often with much more reddish
on head and forward part of belly; 19″ to 24″ at hatching.
    When cornered, the Indigo Snake flattens its neck vertically,
hisses, and vibrates its tail, producing a rattling sound. When
caught, it seldom attempts to bite, becoming tame almost at
once. Specimens often thrive as captives, but usually remain
restless and keep on the move when handled. Food includes
small mammals, birds, frogs, and snakes — even Cottonmouths

Fig. 33. HEADS OF INDIGO SNAKES

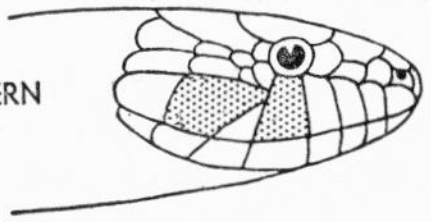

EASTERN

2 labials meet above
the third from last one

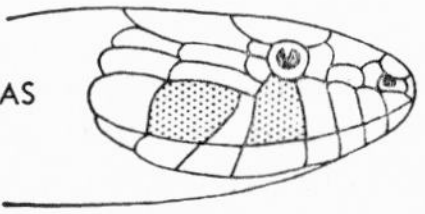

TEXAS

Third from last labial
reaches scale above it

and Rattlers are eaten. Not a constrictor. A snake chiefly of large unsettled areas.

Similar species: All other plain black snakes within its range have *keeled* scales, a *divided* anal plate, or both.

Range: Se. Georgia, peninsular Florida and lower Keys; disjunct colonies in w. Florida and s. Alabama.   Map 118

TEXAS INDIGO SNAKE

Drymarchon corais erebennus   p. 158

Identification: 60–78; record 93. Like the Eastern Indigo Snake except for: (1) prominent dark lines downward from eye; (2) tendency for forepart of body to be brownish and with some indications of pattern; (3) 3d from last upper labial reaching the scale above it (Fig. 33, p. 153); and (4) almost always 14 rows of dorsal scales on hindmost part of body instead of 15 as in eastern race. Scales *smooth;* anal *single.* Hisses, and vibrates tail.

Range: Arid s. Texas to Veracruz and Hidalgo. Other races in the American tropics.   Map 117

TEXAS PATCH-NOSED SNAKE   *Salvadora lineata*   p. 190

Identification: 26–42; record 47. The light *middorsal* stripe, flanked by distinct dark stripes, will distinguish this snake from any other smooth-scaled species east of the 100th meridian. Below each broad stripe is a narrow longitudinal dark line on the 3d row of scales (on 2d row toward tail). Snakes of the genus *Salvadora* are characterized by having the rostral (snout) plate enlarged and with free edges at the sides. Other species are found westward to Pacific Coast and southward to Guatemala. Scales *smooth;* anal *divided.* *Young:* Coloration and pattern similar to adults'; 8½″ to 10″ at hatching.

An essentially terrestrial relative of the Racers that utilizes a variety of habitats, including prairies, rugged, rocky terrain of the Balcones Escarpment in central Texas, arid brushlands farther south, and cultivated country of the lower Rio Grande Valley. Food includes snakes, lizards, and small rodents. The tail is vibrated when snake is alarmed.

Similar species: Garter and Ribbon Snakes have *keeled* scales and *single* anals.

Range: N.-cent. Texas and south into Mexico.   Map 122

Rat Snakes: Genus *Elaphe*

THESE LARGE handsome snakes in cross section are shaped like a loaf of bread, the flat belly meeting the sides of the body at an angle (Fig., p. 175). Adults have several of the middorsal rows of scales weakly *keeled* and the others smooth; keels are only slightly developed or lacking altogether in the young. Anal plate is *divided*.

At hatching time they are boldly marked with dark spots or blotches; some kinds retain the blotches throughout life, in others they disappear with age. Some develop 4 dark longitudinal stripes, and such markings may appear in individual specimens of kinds that normally are not striped at all.

There are three species in our area, each with two or more races. One species group (*guttata*), consisting of the Rosy and Great Plains Rat Snakes and the Corn Snake, characteristically has a light stripe down the underside of the tail flanked by a dark stripe (or broken stripe) on each side (Fig. 34, below). Most of these tame quickly and make good pets. So also do the Fox Snakes. Members of the remaining group (*obsoleta*) sometimes retain their belligerency in captivity; when cornered in the field many of them literally stand up and fight, rearing the fore portion of the body upward, the head drawn back in an S-curve, and the mouth held open in readiness to strike. Usually they hiss as they lunge forward from this position. All the Rat Snakes vibrate their tails rapidly when alarmed. All are good climbers, the angles in their belly scales helping to grip irregularities on the boles of trees, faces of cliffs, etc. With proper care most of them thrive in captivity. They constrict mice, young rats, or small birds in their strong coils. Young Rat Snakes also eat lizards and frogs, treefrogs especially. Young of the Fox and Corn Snake groups vary from about 9″ to 14″ at hatching; members of the other (*obsoleta*) group from about 11″ to 17″.

The genus *Elaphe* ranges southward to Costa Rica and is also represented in Europe, Asia, and the Malay Archipelago.

CORN SNAKE *Elaphe guttata guttata* p. 175
Identification: 30–48; record 72. A beautiful red or orange snake, but subject to considerable individual variation in color. Some specimens trend strongly to browns, especially those from upland habitats. Ground color variable from orange to gray. Dorsal spots and blotches boldly outlined with black. First

Fig. 34. UNDERSURFACES OF YOUNG RAT SNAKES

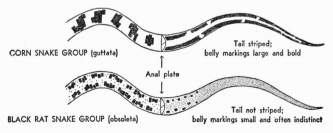

CORN SNAKE GROUP (guttata)

Tail striped;
belly markings large and bold

Anal plate

BLACK RAT SNAKE GROUP (obsoleta)

Tail not striped;
belly markings small and often indistinct

blotch on neck divided into 2 branches that extend forward and meet in a spear point between eyes (Fig. 35, below). Belly whitish, strongly checkered or cross-banded with black. Underside of tail striped (Fig. 34, p. 155). Dorsum occasionally with 4 dusky longitudinal stripes. Scales weakly *keeled;* anal *divided.* *Young:* Blotches dark, usually rich reddish brown; patches of orange between blotches along middorsal line. The dark stripe extending backward from eye usually continues past mouth line and onto neck (Fig. 36, p. 161).

Fig. 35. HEADS OF ADULT RAT SNAKES

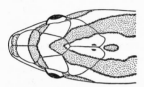

CORN AND GREAT PLAINS RAT SNAKE
Dark neck lines unite to form
a spear point between the eyes

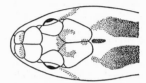

FOX SNAKE
No spear point; head brown
or reddish

This is the "red rat snake," a species much in demand as a pet for small boy, camp, or classroom. Its attractive coloration and usually gentle nature have done much to break down the marked antipathy toward snakes that was characteristic of older human generations and fortunately is now rare among our younger people. The Corn Snake climbs well, but is most likely to be found in terrestrial habitats — in pine barrens or wood lots, on rocky hillsides, etc. More common in many areas than it appears, spending much time underground, resting in or prowling through rodent burrows or other subterranean passageways.

Similar species: Milk Snakes and Mole Snake have *single* anal plates and *smooth* scales, and *lack* striping under tails. Young Rat Snakes of the races of *Elaphe obsoleta* (Black, Yellow, Gray, etc.) lack a dark spear point between the eyes, and the postocular dark stripe stops at the mouth line (Fig. 36, p. 161).

Range: S. New Jersey to s. Florida and s. Louisiana.   Map 126

ROSY RAT SNAKE *Elaphe guttata rosacea*   p. 175
Identification: 30–48; record 66. A subspecies of the Corn Snake in which the black pigment is greatly reduced, both on the back and belly. Amount of black in pattern varies from specimen to specimen, but is never so intense or extensive as in Corn Snake, nor is belly so heavily checkerboarded. General dorsal coloration usually reddish orange. Scales weakly *keeled;* anal *divided.*
Besides hiding beneath logs and debris, the Rosy Rat Snake

both climbs and burrows. When we tried to photograph a young specimen in the field against a background of coral rock sand, it persisted in pushing its head into the sand and then gliding down out of sight. Often ascends trees in search of food.

Range: Florida Keys; Key Largo to the Marquesas.   Map 126

GREAT PLAINS RAT SNAKE *Elaphe guttata emoryi*   p. 175
Identification: 24–36; record 57. A small western and rather drab subspecies of the Corn Snake, but quite similar in all essentials of pattern, including a spear point between eyes (Fig. 35, p. 156) and striping under tail (Fig. 34, p. 155). In very old adults the head markings are usually faint. Four dusky longitudinal stripes may be present. Blotches dark gray, brown, or olive-brown on a ground color of light gray. (In northern part of range blotches are much more numerous and so narrowed that they resemble transverse bands.) Scales weakly *keeled;* anal *divided.*

Secretive and essentially nocturnal during warm weather; hides beneath stones and in rock crevices, caves, etc., by day. More likely to be found in canyons or on rocky draws or hillsides than on open plains or prairies.
Similar species: Bullsnake has *strongly keeled* scales and a *single* anal plate. Prairie Kingsnake and Glossy Snake have *single* anals plus *smooth* scales. Black, Texas, and Baird's Rat Snakes and Fox Snake all lack a spear point between eyes (Fig. 35, p. 156).
Range: Sw. Illinois to Utah, New Mexico, and ne. Mexico.
Map 126

FOX SNAKE *Elaphe vulpina*   p. 175
Identification: 36–54; record 65. A boldly blotched snake of the north-central region. Ground color varies from yellowish to light brown, and the dark spots and blotches from chocolate to black. The head, usually devoid of any really conspicuous markings, varies from brown to distinctly reddish. Belly yellow, strongly checkered with black. Scales weakly *keeled;* anal *divided.*
Young: Ground color paler than in adults; blotches rich brown and narrowly edged with black or dark brown; head markings bold, including a dark line across in front of eyes and a dark line from eye to angle of jaw. Dark lines on head fade and become difficult to define as the snake approaches adulthood.

A serpent with many aliases — a "timber snake" in Ohio and parts of Michigan, a "pine snake" in Wisconsin and adjacent states, and a "spotted adder" to many who cannot think of a better name. The reddish head frequently causes it to be killed as a "copperhead," and the black and yellowish coloration plus the habit of vibrating the tail cause it to be slain as a "rattler." Actually harmless and normally quite inoffensive

PINE, BULL, GLOSSY, AND INDIGO SNAKES
(All have single anal plates.)

| | Map | Text |

GLOSSY SNAKE   119   163
  Brown blotches on ground of cream or buff; superficially
  like Bullsnake; scales *smooth*.

NORTHERN PINE SNAKE   123   164
  Black spots on white, yellowish, or pale gray; scales *keeled*.

BLACK PINE SNAKE   123   165
  Uniform black or dark brown; scales *keeled*.

FLORIDA PINE SNAKE   123   165
  Pale brown or brownish gray; blotches obscure toward
  front of body; scales *keeled*.

LOUISIANA PINE SNAKE   123   165
  40 or fewer dark body blotches, these obscure and dark
  toward front of body, but clear-cut and often reddish on
  and near tail; no conspicuous head markings; scales
  keeled.

BULLSNAKE   123   166
  Dark line from eye to angle of jaw; 41 or more black or
  brown body blotches on a ground color of yellow; scales
  keeled.

TEXAS INDIGO SNAKE   117   154
  Black lines on upper lip; traces of pattern on forepart of
  body; scales *smooth*.

EASTERN INDIGO SNAKE   118   153
  Plain shiny bluish black (chin and sides of head may be
  reddish or orange-brown); scales *smooth*.

GLOSSY SNAKE — 2 prefrontals

BULL AND PINE SNAKES — 4 prefrontals

GLOSSY

NORTHERN PINE

BLACK PINE

LOUISIANA PINE

FLORIDA PINE

BULL

TEXAS INDIGO

EASTERN INDIGO

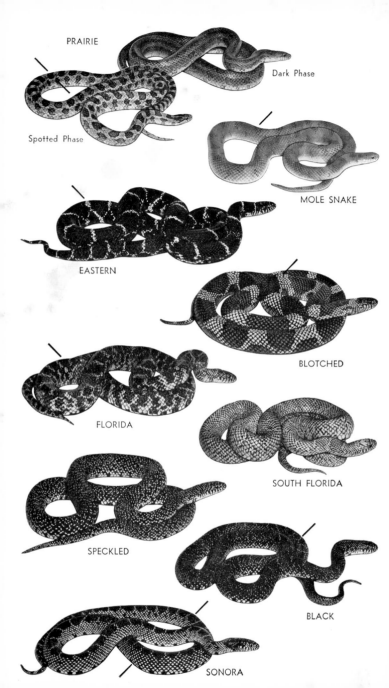

PRAIRIE

Spotted Phase

Dark Phase

MOLE SNAKE

EASTERN

BLOTCHED

FLORIDA

SOUTH FLORIDA

SPECKLED

BLACK

SONORA

Plate 20   159

KINGSNAKES

(All have smooth scales and single anal plates.)

Map Text

PRAIRIE KINGSNAKE   132 173
Spotted phase: Brown or reddish-brown blotches arranged
in middorsal and flanking rows.
Dark phase: Pattern similar but obscure; a slight suggestion of dark longitudinal stripes.

MOLE SNAKE   132 173
Uniform brown or with well-separated dark spots; variable (see text).

EASTERN KINGSNAKE   133 167
Shiny black or dark brown with a bold chainlike pattern.

BLOTCHED KINGSNAKE   133 168
Light bands very wide; dark blotches broad and few in
number.

FLORIDA KINGSNAKE   133 167
Dark blotches small and numerous; variable (see text).

SOUTH FLORIDA KINGSNAKE   133 168
Pale coloration; pattern only faintly indicated.

SPECKLED KINGSNAKE   133 169
Salt-and-pepper effect.

BLACK KINGSNAKE   133 168
Shiny black with a chainlike pattern faintly or incom-
pletely indicated by white or yellow dots.

SONORA KINGSNAKE   133 169
Black or dark brown dorsal blotches; sides of body
speckled.

Toward the west, it occurs in farmlands, prairies, stream valleys, woods, and dune country, but the eastern subspecies is essentially a resident of the extensive marshes bordering Lakes Erie and Huron and their immediate environs.

Similar species: A Corn Snake or Great Plains Rat Snake has a spear point atop head (Fig. 35, p. 156). Milk Snakes and Prairie Kingsnake have *smooth* scales and *single* anal plates. The Bullsnake, a great hisser, has pointed snout, *strongly keeled* scales, and a *single* anal. Hognose Snakes have upturned snouts. Juvenile Black Rat Snakes will be troublesome, for they are as strongly spotted as young Fox Snakes; only safe check is to count ventral scutes — 221 or more in Rat Snakes and 216 or fewer in Fox Snakes.

Range: S. Ontario to Nebraska; upper peninsula of Michigan to cent. Illinois and n. Missouri.

Subspecies: WESTERN FOX SNAKE, *Elaphe vulpina vulpina* (illustrated on Plate 22). Somewhat shorter in length than eastern race; record 61″. Large dorsal blotches average 41 in number (counted on body only). Most of range outlined above. EASTERN FOX SNAKE, *Elaphe vulpina gloydi.* Dorsal blotches bigger and fewer, averaging 34. Head very likely to be reddish. S. Ontario, e. Michigan, and n.-cent Ohio.   Map 124

BLACK RAT SNAKE   *Elaphe obsoleta obsoleta*   p. 175
Identification: 42–72; record 101. Typically a plain shiny black snake, but sometimes showing traces of a spotted pattern when the skin is distended (as after a heavy meal) or in portions of the range near where intergradation takes place with related subspecies. Light areas, chiefly confined to *skin between scales,* may be white, yellow, orange, or red. Belly diffused or clouded with gray or brown on white or yellowish, but usually with some indications of checkerboarding, at least toward head. Chin and throat plain white or cream. Scales weakly *keeled;* anal *divided.* *Young:* Strongly patterned dorsally on body *and tail* with gray or brown blotches on a pale gray ground color and looking like the adult Gray Rat Snake illustrated on Plate 22. Darkening occurs rapidly as the animal grows, and a 3-foot specimen may have only traces of pattern remaining. The dark stripe extending backward from eye terminates at mouth line (Fig. 36, p. 161). Some young Black Rat Snakes may have indications of dark stripes beneath the tail, but these are not so prominent as those in Corn Snake group (Fig. 34, p. 155), and usually fade out rapidly as snake grows older and larger.

The so-called "pilot" or "mountain black snake." Occurs virtually at sea level and to considerable altitudes in parts of the Appalachian mountain chain. Habitats range from rocky, timbered hillsides to flat farmlands of the Coastal Plain. An excellent climber, sometimes establishing residence in cavities high up in hollow trees.

Fig. 36. HEADS OF YOUNG RAT SNAKES

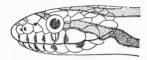

CORN SNAKE GROUP (guttata)
Postocular dark stripe
extends onto neck

BLACK RAT SNAKE GROUP (obsoleta)
Postocular dark stripe
stops at mouth line

Similar species: Black Racers and Coachwhips have smooth scales and their bodies are round in cross section — not shaped like a loaf of bread (Fig., p. 175). Juvenile Racers have no pattern on tail, or only traces of one. Water Snakes have *strongly* keeled scales, and many of them flatten their bodies when alarmed. Most confusion will occur in trying to identify young Black Rat Snakes. In young (and adults) of Corn Snake and Great Plains Rat Snake there is a spear point on head (Fig. 35, p. 156), and the postocular stripe continues onto neck (Fig. 36, above). Fox Snakes have 216 or fewer ventrals (221 or more in Black Rat Snake). Milk Snakes and Kingsnakes have *smooth* scales and *single* anal plates. (Also see Hognose Snakes, p. 138).
Range: Sw. New England to Georgia in the East; sw. Wisconsin to Oklahoma and Arkansas in the Midwest.   Map 125

YELLOW RAT SNAKE *Elaphe obsoleta quadrivittata*   p. 175
Identification: 42–72; record 84. The dark stripes are always strongly defined, but the ground color is subject to considerable variation. The brightest, most golden-yellow specimens come from peninsular Florida; from farther north they are darker, less brilliant yellow. The "Greenish Rat Snake" on Plate 22 is an intergrade between the Black and Yellow Rat Snakes from along the extreme northern portion of latter's range. Scales weakly *keeled;* anal *divided. Young:* Strongly blotched and similar in general appearance to an adult Gray Rat Snake (Plate 22); stripes absent or only slightly indicated. Blotches fade and the dark stripes develop as the young serpent grows.
   A common and characteristic snake of the great river swamps of the South, foraging high into cypress and other trees. Also occurs in a wide variety of other habitats, including live-oak hammocks, cutover woods, fallow fields, and around barns and abandoned buildings.
Similar species: For ways of telling the blotched young from other blotched or spotted snakes see Black Rat Snake (p. 160).
Range: Coastal strip from s. North Carolina to s.-cent. Florida.
          Map 125

EVERGLADES RAT SNAKE *Elaphe obsoleta rossalleni* p. 175
Identification: 48–78; record 87. "Orange rat snake" would be
a good alternate name for this handsome serpent. The ground
color, usually bright orange, may be orange-yellow or orange-
brown instead. The grayish longitudinal stripes are not clear-cut
and are often vague or almost lacking. Belly bright orange or
orange-yellow. Tongue *red*. Scales weakly *keeled;* anal *divided*.
Young: Ground color pinkish buff or pinkish orange; blotches
light grayish brown and not sharply in contrast with ground
color.

Occupies a wide variety of habitats in the Everglades and the
Big Cypress Swamp to the west—in the great waving seas of
sawgrass, on open prairies within the 'Glades, in trees or shrubs,
and along the waterways, taking readily to the water and
swimming skillfully when alarmed. Often seen in the Australian
"pine" (*Casuarina*) trees that have been planted along many
roads of the region.
Range: S. Florida, chiefly in the Everglades.
Subspecies: KEY RAT SNAKE, *Elaphe obsoleta deckerti*.
Averages smaller but attains nearly as great a length as Everglades
Rat Snake. A striped *and* spotted race, stripes gray-brown to
blackish and better defined than in Everglades Rat Snake;
dorsal ground color tan, dull orange, or some shade of brown;
dark dorsal spots, remnants of juvenile pattern, are usually distinctly evident; belly suffused with light gray, at least posteriorly. Tongue *black*. Extr. s. Florida and upper Keys. Map 125

GRAY RAT SNAKE *Elaphe obsoleta spiloides* p. 175
Identification: 42–72; record 84. Called the "oak snake" in
some parts of the South. This Rat Snake retains the strongly
blotched juvenile pattern throughout life, but there is much
variation in its intensity. The ground color may be dark or
medium gray in some specimens but pale brown or gray, sometimes almost white, in others. Blotches may be either brown or
gray and varying from pale to very dark, but always in contrast
with the lighter ground color. Scales weakly *keeled;* anal *divided*.

Habits of this serpent are similar to those of the Black Rat
Snake, which it replaces in the South. The two intergrade over a
fairly broad zone where their ranges meet except in parts of the
Southeast, where they may occur virtually side by side (but in
different habitats) and still retain their full identities. Intergrades in some areas are often chocolate-brown with the blotches
not much darker than ground color.
Similar species: See Black Rat Snake (p. 160) and general discussion of Rat Snakes (p. 154).
Range: Sw. Georgia to Louisiana and north in Mississippi
Valley to extr. s. Indiana.
Subspecies: GULF HAMMOCK RAT SNAKE, *Elaphe obsoleta williamsi*. Blotched like Gray Rat Snake, but also with 4

dark longitudinal stripes; ground color whitish and with dark markings standing out strongly against it. Nw. portion of peninsular Florida.   Map 125

TEXAS RAT SNAKE   *Elaphe obsoleta lindheimeri*   p. 175
Identification: 42–72; record 84. A blotched Rat Snake but often with less contrast between pattern and ground color than in Gray Rat Snake. Blotches usually brownish- or bluish-black; ground color gray or yellowish. Head often black. There may be red on the skin between scales, and this color often encroaches upon edges of the scales themselves. This race is subject to considerable individual variation in both coloration and pattern. Scales weakly *keeled;* anal *divided. Young:* A pattern of bold dark blotches that are considerably larger than the spaces between them. Ground color light gray — much darker than in the young of other races of *Elaphe obsoleta.*
A snake with a variety of habitats, ranging from bayou and swampy country of western Louisiana and adjacent Texas through woods and stream valleys to rocky canyons in western part of range.
Similar species: See Black Rat Snake (p. 160) and general section on Rat Snakes (p. 154).
Range: W. Louisiana and e. half of Texas.   Map 125

BAIRD'S RAT SNAKE   *Elaphe obsoleta bairdi*   p. 175
Identification: 33–54; record 60¼. The 4 longitudinal stripes, all rather vague but with the 2 center ones the darkest, are the most conspicuous markings in large adults. Traces of dorsal and lateral spots, remnants of the juvenile pattern, are often faintly discernible. The general dorsal coloration is grayish brown, but edges of the scales are yellow or orange-yellow on forepart of body and deeper orange toward rear, giving snake a rich overwash of bright coloration. Scales weakly *keeled;* anal *divided. Young:* 50 or more brown crossbands on back, and additional ones on tail; an alternating row of smaller dark spots along each side of body.
A resident of rocky, wooded canyons and of forested uplands (as in Chisos Mountains of the Big Bend). Named for Spencer Fullerton Baird, distinguished zoologist and administrator of the Smithsonian Institution during the nineteenth century.
Range: Cent. Texas to the Big Bend and south into Mexico.
                                                      Map 125

GLOSSY SNAKE   *Arizona elegans*   p. 158
Identification: 27–36; record 54½. A shiny, brownish "bullsnake" with *smooth* scales and only 2 prefrontals (Fig., p. 158). Blotches brown and dark-edged. Ground color cream or buff. In large adults the sides of the body become heavily suffused with brown. In extreme cases, the dark suffusion may obscure

the lateral spots and so overrun the pale ground color that the latter becomes restricted to small middorsal patches between the large blotches. Belly white or pale buff, *unmarked*. Pupil of eye slightly elliptical. Anal *single*. *Young:* About 11″ at hatching.

Nocturnal or crepuscular, but sometimes found abroad by day. Partial to sandy areas, and adept at burrowing. Food includes small mammals and lizards.

Similar species: Great Plains and Texas Rat Snakes have *keeled* scales and *divided* anals. In Prairie Kingsnake belly is normally marked with squarish blotches of brown or yellowish, but sometimes it is plain *except* that the lowermost lateral spots encroach upon the ends of the ventral scales.

Range: Sw. Nebraska to ne. Mexico and west to California.

Subspecies: TEXAS GLOSSY SNAKE, *Arizona elegans elegans* (illustrated on Plate 19). Usually with 53 or fewer large body blotches; ventrals usually 211 or more in males and 222 or more in females. N.-cent. Texas to ne. Mexico. KANSAS GLOSSY SNAKE, *Arizona elegans blanchardi*. Usually with 54 or more large body blotches; ventrals usually 210 or fewer in males and 221 or fewer in females. Sw. Nebraska to the Texas panhandle. Western subspecies.   Map 119

Pine Snakes and Bullsnake: Genus *Pituophis*

LARGE, POWERFUL, constricting snakes that hiss loudly, vibrate their tails rapidly, and are likely to strike vigorously when first encountered. The head appears disproportionately small, especially among the Pine Snakes. In our species there are 4 prefrontal scales (Fig., p. 158) instead of 2 as in most other snakes of the family Colubridae. The snout is somewhat pointed and the rostral plate extends upward between the internasals. Scales *keeled;* anal *single*. Snakes of this group eat small mammals and birds (and their eggs), and are useful in helping to control rodents. Some make good captives, but they tend to be nervous and wriggly when handled. The genus is confined to North America (including Mexico).

NORTHERN PINE SNAKE
Pituophis melanoleucus melanoleucus   p. 158

Identification: 48–66; record 83. A large black and white snake with a noisy hiss. Dark blotches are black toward front of body, but they may be brown near and on tail. Ground color dull white, yellowish, or light gray. Scales *keeled;* anal *single*. *Young:* Patterned as adults, but with ground color paler and with a pink or orange tinge; 15″ to 18″ at hatching.

A snake of flat, sandy pine barrens, sandhills, and dry mountain ridges, usually in or near pine woods. Climbs trees occasionally, but is much addicted to burrowing and is so secretive that its presence may be unsuspected even by persons who may have lived in same region with it for years.

Similar species: Gray Rat Snake has broader and blunter head and *divided* anal. Juvenile Black Rat Snakes also have *divided* anals, but their dorsal keels may be so poorly developed that the scales look smooth.

Range: S. New Jersey; Coastal Plain and Piedmont in the Carolinas; mountain areas from Virginia to Georgia; west into Kentucky and Tennessee. Intergrades with Florida Pine Snake over broad area in South Carolina and along the Fall Line in Georgia.   Map 123

FLORIDA PINE SNAKE *Pituophis melanoleucus mugitus* p. 158
   Identification: 48–66; record 90. A tan or rusty-brown snake with an indistinct pattern. Might be likened to a Northern Pine Snake coated with a thin layer of dried mud and through which dark markings are vaguely visible. Amount of pattern quite variable, but the markings are never so clean-cut and sharply defined as in the northern race. The dark blotches are clearly distinct on only the hind part of the body and on the tail. *Hisses loudly.* Scales *keeled;* anal *single.* *Young:* Patterned much as in the Northern Pine Snake, but with the blotches brown instead of black; 19″ or 20″ at hatching.

   Often found in dry, sandy areas, in stands of oak or pine, abandoned fields, etc. An accomplished burrower, adept at pursuing pocket gophers, a favorite food.

   Similar species: Eastern Coachwhip has *smooth* scales and *divided* anals. Eastern Indigo Snake has *smooth* scales.
   Range: S. South Carolina to Alabama and s. Florida. Map 123

BLACK PINE SNAKE *Pituophis melanoleucus lodingi* p. 158
   Identification: 48–64; record 74. A melanistic Pine Snake. Plain (or nearly plain) black or dark brown, both above and below. Faint indications of blotches may be evident on or near tail, and a few irregular white spots may be present on throat or belly. Snout and lips often dark russet-brown. *Hisses loudly.* Scales *keeled;* anal *single.*
   Similar species: Racers and Whipsnakes have *smooth* scales and *divided* anals. Eastern Indigo Snake has *smooth* scales.
   Range: Chiefly in sandy areas of longleaf pine belt from sw. Alabama to extr. e. Louisiana.   Map 123

LOUISIANA PINE SNAKE
Pituophis melanoleucus ruthveni   p. 158
   Identification: 48–56; record 60½. Markings conspicuously

different at opposite ends of body: (1) blotches *near head* dark brown, obscuring ground color and often running together, and (2) blotches *near and on tail*, brown or russet, clear-cut, and well separated. Total number of *body* blotches (in middorsal row) 40 or less. Ground color buff, changing to more yellowish on and near tail. Head buff and profusely spotted or splotched with dark brown. Belly boldly marked with black. *Hisses loudly.* Scales *keeled;* anal *single.*

Range: Chiefly sandy, longleaf pine woods from cent. Louisiana to e. Texas. Map 123

BULLSNAKE *Pituophis melanoleucus sayi* p. 158

Identification: 50–72; record 100. A large yellowish snake marked with a series of black, brown, or reddish-brown dorsal blotches. General appearance darkest in eastern part of range; much more pallid in arid regions. *Body* blotches (in middorsal row) 41 or more. Belly yellow with bold black spots, especially toward sides. Usually a *dark band* extending from eye to angle of jaw, and with a parallel yellow band above it. *Hisses loudly.* Scales *keeled;* anal *single.* *Young:* About 15″ to 20″ at hatching.

A resident of the plains and prairies, occurring in sand prairies in Illinois and Indiana to the near-desert country of southern Texas and adjacent Mexico. Clumps of vegetation and mammal burrows are favorite lurking places, both for the Bullsnake and its rodent food. Birds and their eggs are also eaten.

Similar species: Texas Rat Snake, Glossy Snake, Prairie King-snake, and other blotched or spotted species have *smooth* scales, *divided* anals, or both.

Range: W. Indiana and Wisconsin to s. Alberta, south to Texas and e. Mexico. Western subspecies. Map 123

Kingsnakes and Milk Snakes: Genus *Lampropeltis*

THESE ARE shiny snakes with *smooth* scales and *single* anal plates. All are powerful constrictors, and their killing and eating of other serpents, including venomous ones, is well known. They should not be kept with other reptiles smaller than themselves, even of their own species. In fact, they must be fed in separate cages or watched very carefully. Otherwise two of them may start to eat at opposite ends of the same bit of food and when their heads meet one snake will engulf the other! Besides snakes, they also eat lizards, rodents, small birds and their eggs, and turtle eggs.

The Kingsnakes are essentially black (or dark brown) with white or yellowish spots on their scales, but the size and arrangement of the spots vary from one subspecies to the next. When first encountered they vibrate their tails rapidly and may hiss and strike but, once caught, the majority become tame almost immediately. Contrary to popular opinion, they do not prowl about looking for Rattlers to fight. Any snake is simply a meal, but they apparently are immune to the venoms of our *native* poisonous snakes. Young Kingsnakes vary from about 9″ to 12″ at hatching.

The Milk Snakes are basically tricolored, with red (or brown), black, and white (or yellow) in the form of transverse rings. In some kinds there are rows of blotches instead of bands, but in all cases the reddish parts of the pattern are surrounded by black. Milk Snakes also vibrate their tails and hiss and strike, but many do not readily tame; some have a habit, when handled, of biting without warning. The name of the group derives from the nonsensical old-wives' tale that snakes milk cows. Milk Snakes feed largely upon mice and are among our most beneficial serpents; small snakes and lizards also are eaten. Young Milk Snakes are about 7″ to 8″ at hatching.

The Prairie Kingsnake and the Mole Snake are marked with brown or reddish-brown blotches outlined with black on a ground color of light brown or tan.

The genus ranges from southeastern Canada to Ecuador.

EASTERN KINGSNAKE *Lampropeltis getulus getulus* p. 159
Identification: 36–48; record 82. The "chain snake" — a shiny black serpent clad with large, bold links of white or cream. Specimens from southern part of range may be dark brown instead of black. Scales *smooth*; anal *single*.

A handsome serpent of the eastern seaboard's pine belt, but one that also crosses the Piedmont and even enters mountain valleys. Habitat is chiefly terrestrial, but it shows a distinct liking for streambanks and borders of swamps, possibly because Water Snakes and turtle eggs, two important foods, may be abundant there. Kingsnakes swim readily. They are often secretive, hiding under boards, logs, or debris; they bask in the open occasionally in spring or autumn, and may prowl by day, especially in early morning or at twilight, but are largely nocturnal in hot weather. Other vernacular names are "thunder snake" and "swamp wamper."
Similar species: Northern Pine Snake has black or dark brown blotches on a *whitish* ground color and *strongly keeled* scales. Young Black Rat Snakes and young Black Racers have *divided* anals.
Range: S. New Jersey to n. Florida; west to Appalachians and s. Alabama.   Map 133

FLORIDA KINGSNAKE *Lampropeltis getulus floridana* p. 159
Identification: 36–48; record 77. A dull black, brown, or olive snake marked with cream or yellow and with a highly variable

pattern. This race is intermediate between the boldly marked Eastern Kingsnake and the virtually unpatterned South Florida Kingsnake, with both of which it intergrades. Pattern may be: (1) chainlike; (2) with a series of light vertical bars alternating with yellowish middorsal crossbands; or (3) dark areas may be so invaded by light pigment as to obscure basic pattern. Dark blotches, when countable, number 50 or more (fewer than 50 in Eastern King). Scales *smooth;* anal *single.* *Young:* Like adults but usually darker and often with reddish or orange pigment on skin between scales.

Similar species: Florida Pine Snake and Corn Snake both have *keeled* scales; Corn Snake also has *divided* anal plate. Young Rat Snakes and young Whipsnakes and Racers also have *divided* anals.

Range: S.-cent. Florida.   Map 133

SOUTH FLORIDA KINGSNAKE
Lampropeltis getulus brooksi   p. 159
Identification: 36–52. Palest of the large Kingsnakes. Each individual dorsal scale is yellowish or cream-colored at base and brown at apex. Indications of light crosslines are sometimes present, especially in neck region. Belly is cream to pale yellow with spots of tan or pinkish brown. Scales *smooth*; anal *single.* *Young:* A blotched pattern, with yellow or light tan on black or dark brown; many scales in the dark dorsal areas have reddish-brown centers; light areas on sides have bright red centers.
Range: Extr. s. Florida.   Map 133

BLOTCHED KINGSNAKE *Lampropeltis getulus goini*   p. 159
Identification: 36–60. A Kingsnake with a restricted range and characterized by the considerable width of the white bands and the very low number of dark blotches (fewer than 25). Ground color brown, but almost all of the dark scales have light centers. Scales *smooth;* anal *single.*
Similar species: Pine Snakes and Rat Snakes both have *keeled* scales; Rat Snakes also have *divided* anal plates.
Range: Chipola and Apalachicola river valleys in Florida panhandle.   Map 133

BLACK KINGSNAKE *Lampropeltis getulus niger*   p. 159
Identification: 36–45; record 56. Similar to the Eastern Kingsnake, but with the chainlike pattern greatly reduced and indicated only by small yellowish spots. Some specimens are almost plain black; others, especially those from near the region of intergradation with the Speckled Kingsnake, may have numerous yellowish spots on sides of body. Scales *smooth;* anal *single.* *Young:* Chainlike pattern clearly distinct.

Habitats include dry, rocky hills, open woods, dry prairies, and stream valleys.

Similar species: Black Racers and Black Rat Snakes both have *divided* anal plates; Rat Snakes also have *keeled* scales.
Range: S. Ohio and se. Illinois to cent. Alabama.   Map 133

SPECKLED KINGSNAKE *Lampropeltis getulus holbrooki* p. 159
Identification: 36–48; record 66. The "salt-and-pepper snake" with a profusion of white or yellowish spots scattered more or less at random over all the black or dark brown dorsal surfaces. Scales *smooth;* anal *single.*
This Kingsnake makes use of a greater variety of habitats than any of the related subspecies. It is at home in the great river swamps of the lower Mississippi Valley, in upland wooded areas like the Ozarks, and in stream valleys across the open plains and prairies. Shelters, such as logs, rocks, ledges, thick clumps of vegetation, etc., are utilized as hiding places.
Similar species: Buttermilk Snake has light spots that vary both in coloration and size, and its anal plate is *divided.*
Range: Illinois to Nebraska; south to e. Texas and sw. Alabama.
Map 133

SONORA KINGSNAKE *Lampropeltis getulus splendida* p. 159
Identification: 36–45; record 60. A profusion of white or yellowish dots on the sides, but with a middorsal series of plain black or dark brown spots. Each such spot is separated from its neighbor by a row of light dots across the back. *Belly chiefly black.* Scales *smooth;* anal *single. Young:* Less dark pigment; middorsal dark spots boldly outlined with yellow; a row of dark spots on each side of body. The speckled flanks and over-all dark appearance develop with age.
A Kingsnake of the arid Southwest which, in order to avoid high temperatures and desiccation, has to be largely nocturnal — like other serpents of the region. Most often to be found near streams or irrigation ditches.
Similar species: Speckled Racer has *divided* anal plate and the middle rows of dorsal scales are *weakly* keeled. Also, Speckled Racer has conspicuously large eyes and a black stripe extends backward from eye.
Range: Cent. Texas to Sonora and n.-cent. Mexico. Western and Mexican subspecies.   Map 133

SCARLET KINGSNAKE
Lampropeltis doliata doliata   pp. 174, 238
Identification: 14–20; record 27. An extraordinary "mimic" of the venomous Coral Snake. But the snout is *red,* and the yellow rings are separated from the red by black. Rings normally continue across belly (Fig. 37, p. 170). Scales *smooth,* in 19 rows at midbody; anal *single. Young:* About 5″ at hatching.
Secretive and adept at working its way beneath bark, logs, or other hiding places; seldom seen in the open except at night

or after heavy rains. Commonly found in or near woodland habitats, pine especially. Food includes small snakes and lizards, baby mice, small fishes, and earthworms.

Similar species: In Coral Snake (see Plate 29) the 2 warning colors — red and yellow — touch each other; also the snout is *black*. In Scarlet Snake the belly is plain white. Ringed varieties of Milk Snakes have 21 or more scale rows at midbody.

Range: North Carolina to the tip of Florida (also Key West) and west to Mississippi River, thus chiefly in Coastal Plain but also occurring in more inland localities and to elevations of at least 2000 feet around edges of Appalachians; penetrates north into Tennessee and to s. Kentucky. Map 130

EASTERN MILK SNAKE
Lampropeltis doliata triangulum p. 174

Identification: 24–36; record 47¼. A rather slender, strongly blotched snake with a *Y*-shaped or *V*-shaped light patch on the nape. There are 3 (sometimes 5) rows of brown or reddish-brown, black-bordered blotches down the body, the middle ones quite large and alternating in position with those on sides. Ground color gray to tan. Belly checkerboarded (often very irregularly) with black on white (Fig. 37, below). Not too much trust should be placed in the *Y* or *V* marking, for it is subject to variation; in extreme cases it may even be replaced by a light collar like those found in other races of Milk Snakes. Scales

Fig. 37. DIAGRAMMATIC VENTRAL PATTERNS OF SNAKES
BOLDLY RINGED OR BLOTCHED
WITH RED, YELLOW, AND BLACK

Red (or orange) Yellow (or white) Black

CORAL
Danger! Red and yellow touch

EASTERN MILK
Checkerboard effect

SCARLET KING
Red and yellow separated by black

WESTERN MILK
H-shaped effect

LOUISIANA MILK
Pattern may not cross belly

MEXICAN MILK
Black predominates

SCARLET
Belly plain whitish

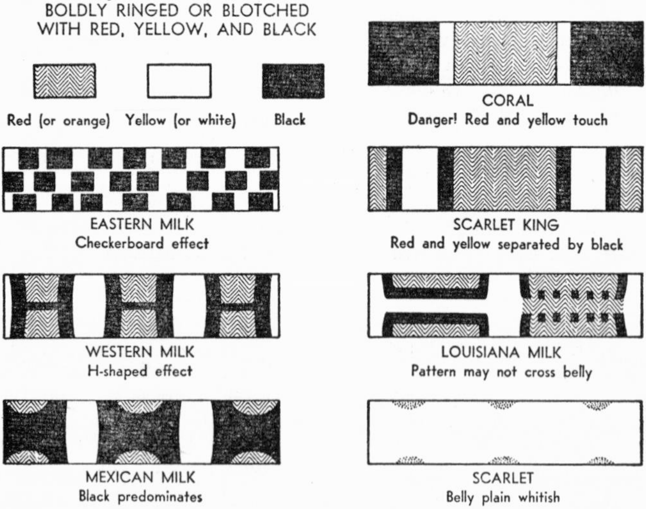

smooth; anal *single.* *Young:* Blotches bright red and forming basis for the name "red adder."

A frequent victim of the ridiculous belief that it milks cows. Also killed because of its superficial resemblance to the Copperhead — and the vernacular name "adder" doesn't help matters. Sometimes called "house snake," but "barn snake" would be more descriptive, for it would reflect the frequency with which farm buildings are entered in search of rodents. Many habitats are utilized — fields, woodlands, rocky hillsides, river bottoms, etc., from virtually sea level to high up in mountains. Usually secretive and found hiding under logs, boards, stones, etc.

Similar species: Copperhead has coppery, virtually unmarked head, single row of dorsal crossbands, and a belly that is *not* checkerboarded. Water Snakes have *keeled* scales and *divided* anals. Well-patterned young of the Racers and Rat Snakes have *divided* anals. Scarlet Snake has plain (unpatterned) belly. Dark markings of Mole Snake are well separated from one another (see pp. 159 and 174).

Range: Maine to Minnesota; south in uplands to n. Alabama.
Map 130

COASTAL PLAIN MILK SNAKE
Lampropeltis doliata temporalis   p. 174

Identification: 21–35; record 39⅜. The middorsal blotches are very large and, at least in the neck region, extend downward to the edges of the belly scales. This is usually a reddish snake, with red or reddish-brown, black-bordered blotches on a ground color of gray, tan, or yellowish. Collar across neck usually conspicuous. Belly with bold black spots on a whitish ground color; red sometimes extends onto edges of ventrals. Scales *smooth,* usually in 21 rows at midbody; anal *single.* *Young:* Patterned as adults, but with bright red blotches; belly boldly marked with black. Viewed from above, juveniles resemble Scarlet Snakes or Scarlet Kingsnakes.

Found in pine woods and barrens and other lowland habitats. Intergrades between it and Eastern Milk Snake occur in and near cities of Washington, Baltimore, and Philadelphia.

Similar species: Scarlet Snake has *plain* whitish belly. In Scarlet Kingsnake the pattern rings continue across belly (Fig. 37, p. 170). Middorsal blotches of Mole Snake are quite small, and are separated from belly plates by width of several scales.

Range: Coastal Plain, New Jersey to North Carolina. Map 130

RED MILK SNAKE *Lampropeltis doliata syspila*   p. 174
Identification: 21–28; record 42. Also called "red snake" and "candy-cane snake." A reddish serpent with larger and fewer markings than Eastern Milk Snake. The middorsal blotches extend well down onto sides of body and the lateral blotches are

small or virtually absent, at least in the neck region. Collar usually conspicuous. Belly boldly checked with black on white. Scales *smooth;* anal *single.*

Habitats vary from woodlands and rocky hillsides to open farming country.

Similar species: In Corn Snake and Great Plains Rat Snake there is a spear point between the eyes (Fig. 35, p. 156), and underside of tail is striped (Fig. 34, p. 155). In the Prairie Kingsnake, blotches are brown, and belly markings are brown or yellowish. Also see "Similar species" under Eastern Milk Snake (p. 170). The Coastal Plain Milk Snake and Red Milk Snake are strikingly alike but their ranges are widely separated.

Range: Midland America from s. Indiana and w. Kentucky to se. South Dakota and e. Oklahoma. Map 130

LOUISIANA MILK SNAKE *Lampropeltis doliata amaura* p. 174
  Identification: 16–22; record 25. A brilliantly marked "mimic" of the venomous Coral Snake with 18 to 25 broad red crossbands (include those on tail when counting). The red areas may cross the belly or may be encircled by black (Fig. 37, p. 170); in the latter case they are best described as black-bordered red "saddles" extending downward well onto edges of the belly plates. Snout basically red, but usually mottled or speckled with black and white; rarely it may be as black as a Coral Snake's snout. Scales *smooth* and in 21 rows at midbody; anal *single.*
  Similar species: The warning colors — red and yellow — touch in Coral Snake; in Louisiana Milk Snake the black separates the other colors. Scarlet Snake has plain whitish belly. Scarlet Kingsnake has plain red snout and only 19 rows of scales at midbody.
  Range: S. Arkansas and se. Oklahoma to Gulf Coast. Map 130

MEXICAN MILK SNAKE *Lampropeltis doliata annulata* p. 174
  Identification: 24–30; record 39. A ringed Milk Snake with an abundance of black pigment. Black rings rather wide and not narrowing on the 1st row of scales. Red rings broad (19 to 25 in number, including those on tail). Belly mostly black (Fig. 37, p. 170). Snout black (or virtually so). Scales *smooth;* anal *single.*
  Found in a variety of habitats ranging from sand dunes to cultivated fields.
  Similar species: Coral Snake has 2 warning colors — red and yellow — touching each other. Black separates the other colors in Mexican Milk Snake.
  Range: S. Texas and ne. Mexico. Map 130

WESTERN MILK SNAKE *Lampropeltis doliata gentilis* p. 174
  Identification: 16–24; record 36. In counting the reddish rings

be sure to include those on the tail. This race has a consistently higher number (26 to 38) than either the Louisiana Milk Snake or Mexican Milk Snake. The light rings vary from pale gray to yellow or greenish yellow, or are sometimes nearly white. The black in many specimens invades the reddish areas, completely cutting across them along middle of back. Black pigment normally occupies less than ½ of belly (Fig. 37, p. 170). Scales *smooth*, in 21 or more rows at midbody; anal *single*.

Occupies a wide range of habitats — open prairies, wooded stream valleys, rocky canyons, mountain slopes, etc.

Similar species: The 2 warning colors — red and yellow — touch in Coral Snake. Scarlet Snake has plain whitish belly. Ground Snake has 15 rows of scales at midbody.

Range: Most of Kansas and Oklahoma to e. Colorado.

Subspecies: PALLID MILK SNAKE, *Lampropeltis doliata multistrata.* Similar but paler, the black areas reduced in size and the red replaced by orange; venter immaculate or with only a few black markings. An inhabitant of sand dunes, open prairies, and high plains. Most of Nebraska to s. Montana. Western subspecies. Map 130

PRAIRIE KINGSNAKE *Lampropeltis calligaster calligaster* p. 159
Identification: 30–42; record 50. A blotched snake and one that may be troublesome to identify. Typically, back and tail are patterned with about 60 brown, reddish, or greenish, black-edged markings. Occasionally these are split in two down the back. There are 2 alternating rows of smaller dark markings on each side, but pairs of these may fuse together. The ground color is brownish gray to tan. In many older specimens the ground color darkens and the pattern becomes quite obscure, producing the *dark phase* that often is further characterized by the development of 4 longitudinal dusky stripes. Belly yellowish with squarish brown blotches. Scales *smooth;* anal *single. Young:* Strongly spotted; about 9″ to 11″ at hatching.

A resident of grassland prairies, open woodlands, and (farther east) patches of prairie and savanna in the midst of essentially forested country.

Similar species: Prairie Kingsnake bears a strong superficial resemblance to Great Plains Rat Snake, but Rat Snakes have *keeled* scales and *divided* anals. Glossy Snakes have plain white bellies. In Milk Snakes the reddish blotches or rings are boldly surrounded by black, and there are *black* markings on belly.

Range: Indiana, Kentucky, and n. Mississippi to se. Nebraska, Oklahoma, and e. Texas. Map 132

MOLE SNAKE
Lampropeltis calligaster rhombomaculata pp. 159, 174
Identification: 30–40; record 45. A shiny, *smooth*-scaled serpent

MILK SNAKES AND RELATED SPECIES

(All have smooth scales and single anal plates, except as noted.)

Map Text

GROUND SNAKE   131 177
Small, shiny, and with extremely variable pattern (see text). Anal *divided*.

SHORT-TAILED SNAKE   127 176
Dorsal blotches separated by areas of orange, red, or yellow; body very slender.

MOLE SNAKE (young)   132 173
Dark markings small, well separated, often red.

EASTERN MILK SNAKE   130 170
A light *Y* or *V* at back of head; large dorsal blotches alternating with smaller lateral ones. *Young:* Blotches red.

RED MILK SNAKE   130 171
A light collar; lateral blotches greatly reduced or absent. (Midwest)

COASTAL PLAIN MILK SNAKE   130 171
A light collar; dorsal blotches reach belly scales on forepart of body. (Mid-Atlantic region)

WESTERN MILK SNAKE   130 172
Reddish rings narrow (26 to 38), head black, snout light.

SCARLET KINGSNAKE   130 169
Body completely ringed as in Coral Snake (see Plate 29); snout red.

LOUISIANA MILK SNAKE   130 172
Red rings broad (18 to 25); head black, snout light.

MEXICAN MILK SNAKE   130 172
Red rings broad (19 to 25); snout black; belly chiefly black.

SCARLET SNAKE   129 176
Snout red; belly whitish, unpatterned.

LONG-NOSED SNAKE   128 177
Red areas speckled with black; black areas speckled with yellow.

GROUND Three Variations

MOLE
Young

SHORT-TAILED

Young

Adult

EASTERN MILK

RED MILK

COASTAL PLAIN MILK

WESTERN MILK

SCARLET KING

LOUISIANA MILK

MEXICAN MILK

SCARLET

LONG-NOSED

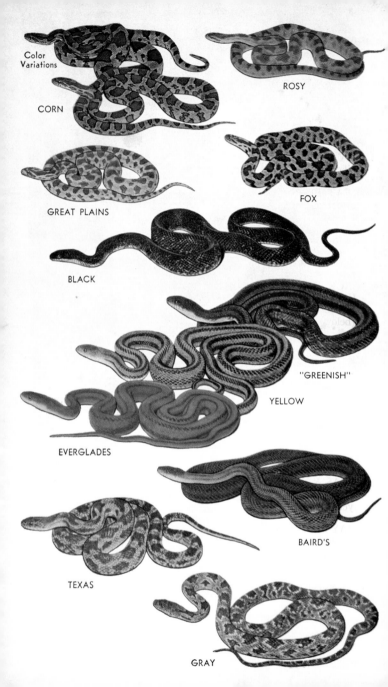

Color
Variations

ROSY

CORN

GREAT PLAINS

FOX

BLACK

"GREENISH"

YELLOW

EVERGLADES

BAIRD'S

TEXAS

GRAY

Plate 22   175

RAT SNAKES

(All have weakly keeled scales and divided anal plates.)

| | *Map* | *Text* |

CORN SNAKE — 126 155
  Reddish blotches with black borders on a ground of gray,
  tan, yellow, or orange.

ROSY RAT SNAKE — 126 156
  Like Corn Snake but with black greatly reduced or absent.

GREAT PLAINS RAT SNAKE — 126 157
  Brown blotches on a gray ground; neck lines unite to form
  a spear point on head (Fig. 35, p. 156).

FOX SNAKE — 124 157
  Dark brown blotches on a yellowish ground; no spear
  point on head (Fig. 35, p. 156).

BLACK RAT SNAKE — 125 160
  Uniform black or with faint traces of spotted pattern;
  throat light. *Young:* Patterned as Gray Rat Snake
  (below).

"GREENISH RAT SNAKE" — 161
  An intergrade between Black and Yellow Rat Snakes.

YELLOW RAT SNAKE — 125 161
  4 dark stripes on a ground of yellow to olive.

EVERGLADES RAT SNAKE — 125 162
  4 dark stripes on a ground of orange.

BAIRD'S RAT SNAKE — 125 163
  4 poorly defined dark stripes on a dark ground.

TEXAS RAT SNAKE — 125 163
  Brownish- or bluish-black blotches on a ground color of
  yellow or gray.

GRAY RAT SNAKE — 125 162
  Grayish in general appearance, but coloration variable
  (see text).

CROSS SECTIONS
OF SNAKES

RAT SNAKES
Like a
loaf of
bread

MOST OTHER
SNAKES
Body more
rounded

that may be patterned or not! Typical specimens have about 55 rather small, *well-separated*, reddish-brown, dark-edged spots down back and tail, and smaller and fainter spots on sides of body. The ground color is light to dark brown, sometimes with a greenish tinge, but changing to a more yellowish hue on sides of body. Older specimens may lose virtually all their markings, resulting in a plain "brown kingsnake." Dusky lengthwise stripes may also develop, as in Prairie Kingsnake. Belly white or yellowish and checked, spotted, or clouded with brown. Scales *smooth;* anal *single.* *Young:* Boldly marked with well-separated brown or red spots (see Plate 21); 2 lengthwise dark streaks on neck; about 8″ or 9″ at hatching.

An accomplished burrower often turned up by the plow or during excavation operations. Occasionally appears on the surface, especially after heavy spring or summer rains. Ranges from Coastal Plain to at least the lower parts of Appalachians. Habitats include thickets, woodlots, cultivated fields, and even back yards in some suburban areas.

Similar species: Corn Snake has *divided* anal, *keeled* scales, and stripes under tail (Fig. 34, p. 155). In Milk Snakes the dorsal blotches are large and close together, and belly is boldly marked with black.

Range: Vicinity of Baltimore, Maryland, to n.-cent. Florida; west to e. Tennessee and s. Mississippi.   Map 132

SHORT-TAILED SNAKE *Stilosoma extenuatum*   p. 174

Identification: 14–20; record 24. An exceptionally slender spotted snake with a tail only 7 to 10 per cent of total length. The small dark blotches, black or brown in coloration, are separated along midline of back by areas of yellow, orange, or red. Belly strongly blotched with brown or black. Scales *smooth;* anal *single.*

A secretive burrower occurring chiefly in the dry "high" pine woods of central Florida. Similar in habits to the Milk Snakes—vibrates tail when alarmed, strikes with a sneezelike hiss, is a constrictor, and eats small snakes and lizards.

Range: Florida from Alachua County to Polk County.

Subspecies: EASTERN SHORT-TAILED SNAKE, *Stilosoma extenuatum extenuatum.* Lower labials 6 on one or both sides of head and/or internasals and prefrontals fused. WESTERN SHORT-TAILED SNAKE, *Stilosoma extenuatum arenicolor.* Lower labials 7; internasals and prefrontals separate; body blotches 68 or fewer. NORTHERN SHORT-TAILED SNAKE, *Stilosoma extenuatum multistictum.* Like western race, but with body blotches 69 or more. See map for individual ranges.   Map 127

SCARLET SNAKE *Cemophora coccinea*   pp. 174, 238

Identification: 14–20; record 32¼. The Coral Snake "mimic" with the plain whitish (or yellowish) belly. Snout *red* and pointed. Scales *smooth;* anal *single. Young:* About 5½″ at hatching.

Usually found in or near soils suitable for burrowing (sandy, loamy, etc.), in logs, beneath bark, etc.; seldom seen above ground except at night or after heavy rains. Occasionally unearthed during plowing or excavation work. Young mice and small snakes and lizards are killed by constriction; contents of snake and turtle eggs also are devoured.

Similar species: Red and yellow rings touch and there is a *black* snout in the venomous Coral Snake (see Plate 29); also, its belly is invaded by black pigment, and so are the bellies of all Milk Snakes (except Pallid) and the Scarlet Kingsnake (Fig. 37, p. 170).

Range: S. New Jersey to tip of Florida; west to Louisiana and e. Oklahoma; disjunct colonies in Texas and as far north in Mississippi Valley as southern parts of Indiana, Illinois, and Missouri.

Map 129

(TEXAS) LONG-NOSED SNAKE

Rhinocheilus lecontei tessellatus   p. 174

Identification: 22–32; record 41. A red, black, and yellow snake with a strongly speckled appearance. Snout red or pink and pointed, protruding, or even upturned; belly yellow or whitish with a few dark spots. Only a *single row of scales under tail.* Scales *smooth;* anal *single. Young:* Speckling on sides of body only partially developed or virtually absent; about 7½″ to 8½″ at hatching.

A resident chiefly of deserts and dry prairies. Nocturnal to a large extent, spending daylight hours secreted among rocks or debris or in mammal burrows or other underground retreats. Captives should be given shelters beneath which to hide, or sand in which to burrow. Lizards are the chief food, but small rodents, lizard eggs, and insects are also eaten.

Similar species: Pattern of Scarlet Snake consists of red "saddles" with black borders. In the ringed Milk Snakes, black pigment strongly invades belly and there is no speckling on sides of body. Also, in *all* of these snakes there is a *double* row of scales under the tail.

Range: Sw. Kansas to ne. Mexico and west to New Mexico. Western subspecies.   Map 128

GROUND SNAKE *Sonora episcopa*   p. 174

Identification: 9–12; record 15. The most strikingly variable snake within our area. A collector may find plain, cross-banded, black-collared, or longitudinally streaked specimens under the same rock, and all of this one species. Three common variations are shown on Plate 21. Crossbands usually black or orange; the ground color may be gray or brown, often with a strong red or orange tinge. Belly plain white or yellowish; underside of tail plain or with suggestions of crossbands. Collared and cross-banded individuals are easily identified, but plainer ones will be troublesome. The head is slightly wider than the neck, and this will help in distinguishing the Ground Snake from some of the other small brown or gray snakes. If a series of specimens is available (including well-patterned ones), use them to compare head and body shapes, belly color, etc. Scales usually must be checked, however. The loreal scale is present 90 per cent of the time (Fig., p. 222), but it may be fused with one of the adjacent scales. Scales *smooth*, in 15 rows; anal *divided*.

Found chiefly in the "great open spaces" — in terms of general environment; actually a secretive snake most often discovered by overturning stones on rocky hillsides or boards or trash in suburban areas. Feeds upon small scorpions, centipedes, spiders, and insects.

Similar species: Flat-headed Snake has: (1) bright pink venter; (2) distinctly small head no wider than neck; and (3) no loreal scale. Western Earth Snake, Rough Earth Snake, and Brown Snakes have keeled scales. In Texas Blind Snake, ventral scales are same size as dorsal scales.

Range: Kansas to ne. Mexico and the Big Bend.

Subspecies: GREAT PLAINS GROUND SNAKE, *Sonora episcopa episcopa* (described above and illustrated on Plate 21). All of range except extr. se. part. SOUTH TEXAS GROUND SNAKE, *Sonora episcopa taylori.* Like the nearly plain brown form of the Great Plains Ground Snake, but sometimes with a darkening across back of head; scales in 13 rows, occasionally 14 at midbody. S. Texas and extr. ne. Mexico.   Map 131

WESTERN HOOK-NOSED SNAKE *Ficimia cana*   p. 143
   Identification: 7–11; record 14. Check for three things: (1) upturned snout; (2) *smooth* scales; and (3) a strongly marked pattern with the crossbands on head particularly prominent. There are 30 or more brown or yellowish-brown, dark-edged crossbars on body and 8 to 12 on tail. Ground color grayish brown or yellowish. Anal *divided*.

   A burrowing snake with the extraordinary habit of anal "popping." When touched in the field, it may undergo a series of gyrations as though writhing in agony, meanwhile extruding and retracting the lining of the cloaca through the vent to the accompaniment of a bubbling or popping sound.

   Similar species: Hognose Snakes have *keeled* scales. Mexican Hook-nosed Snake has narrower, but more numerous, crossbands, and its head markings are meager or virtually absent.

   Range: Arid Southwest from w.-cent. Texas to se. Arizona and south into Mexico.   Map 134

MEXICAN HOOK-NOSED SNAKE
Ficimia olivacea streckeri   p. 143
   Identification: 7–11; record 19. A combination of upturned

snout, *smooth* scales, and relatively little head pattern identifies this species. Ground color light to medium gray, and the narrow crossbands (37 to 45 on body and 11 to 16 on tail) are olive or greenish. In both Hook-nosed Snakes the snout, posterior to the "hook," is flattened or somewhat concave instead of bearing a dorsal keel as it does among the Hognose Snakes. Anal *divided*.

This burrowing serpent occasionally is seen above ground after rains, on freshly sprinkled lawns, along irrigation ditches, or in other places where water is present. Hook-nosed Snakes (of both species) make rather unsatisfactory captives. They should be provided with an inch or more of dry sand, into which they will promptly burrow out of sight. Food consists largely of spiders, but centipedes are also eaten.

Similar species: Hognose Snakes have *keeled* scales. In Western Hook-nosed Snake dorsal markings are fewer but more prominent, the head being conspicuously patterned.

Range: Extr. s. Texas to Veracruz. Mexican subspecies; other species of this genus also occur in Mexico and in n. Central America. Map 135

(TEXAS) NIGHT SNAKE

Hypsiglena torquata texana p. 143

Identification: 14–16; record 20. A spotted snake with a bold elongated blotch on each side of the neck and another on the nape. A dark band backward and downward from eye. Pupil *vertically elliptical*. Body spots brown or dark gray; ground color light brown or grayish. Belly immaculate white or yellowish. Scales *smooth*; anal *divided*. *Young:* About 6" at hatching.

A resident of arid or semi-arid country, prowling chiefly at night and often frequenting rocky regions. Small lizards are the principal food. Captives should be given sand or fairly dry soil in which to burrow, or stones or bark under which to hide.

Range: Sw. Kansas and se. Colorado to New Mexico and ne. Mexico. Western subspecies. Map 137

(TEXAS) CAT-EYED SNAKE

Leptodeira septentrionalis septentrionalis p. 143

Identification: 18–24; record 38¾. The broad crossbands (saddles) of dark brown or black extend completely across the back, and are usually in strong contrast with the tan or yellowish ground color. Head broad, much wider than neck. Eye with a *vertically elliptical* pupil (cat-eyed). Scales *smooth;* anal *divided.* *Young:* More boldly patterned than adults; ground color orange-tan; about 8½" to 9½" at hatching.

This snake is equipped with grooved fangs toward the rear of the upper jaw for introducing venom into prey that has been seized and partly swallowed; the venom tends to benumb and immobilize prey. The Cat-eyed Snake is big enough so that theoretically it might cause trouble if it swallowed a person's finger far enough to bring the fangs into play — a quite unlikely occurrence. It is best to handle it with care, however. A con-siderable number of snakes, both in the New and Old Worlds and especially in the tropics, are rear-fanged. Chiefly nocturnal, and likely to be found prowling in search of frogs near streams or other bodies of water. Sometimes climbs into bushes.

Range: Extr. s. Texas to Veracruz. Related subspecies, more slender in body and with dorsal markings much reduced in size occur farther south. Specimens of these tropical Cat-eyed Snakes sometimes are inadvertently imported in shipments of bananas.

Map 136

Black-headed Snakes: Genus *Tantilla*

THESE SMALL secretive snakes have 15 rows of *smooth* scales throughout the length of the body, no loreal scale, and most of them wear black "caps" on their heads. Their food includes small centipedes and the larvae of insects that live underground. The genus ranges from the southern United States to South America.

SOUTHEASTERN CROWNED SNAKE
Tantilla coronata coronata   p. 143

Identification: 8–10; record 13. This Black-headed Snake not only has a black head cap but also a light band (or collar) across rear of head, followed in turn by a black band 3 to 5 scales wide (Fig. 38, below). Rest of dorsum is plain brown or reddish brown; belly white or with a pinkish or yellowish tinge. Dark pig-ment usually extends downward from the head cap to or almost to the mouth, both under the eye and near back of head. Scales *smooth;* anal *divided.*

Habitats vary, running the gamut from environs of swamps to dry wooded hillsides, and from wilderness areas to back yards. This snake is where you find it, and then almost always in hid-ing — under stones, in rotting logs, etc.

Similar species: Florida Brown Snakes and juveniles of other

Fig. 38. BLACK-HEADED SNAKES

MEXICAN	PLAINS	FLAT-HEADED	SE. CROWNED	FLA. CROWNED

| Rear of cap straight; close to head scales | Rear of cap convex or pointed | Cap pale; concave at rear | Light collar | Cap extends far beyond head scales |

Brown Snakes have dark heads and light collars but they also have *keeled* scales. Ringneck Snakes have yellow, orange, or red bellies boldly marked with black spots (at least in southern races).

Range: Virginia and s. Indiana to n. Florida and se. Louisiana.

Subspecies: APPALACHIAN CROWNED SNAKE, *Tantilla coronata mitrifer.* A montane race, darker in coloration and with dark pigmentation at rear of head *not* extending down to mouth line. At elevations of 1000 to 2000 feet or more in Appalachians of western parts of Carolinas and adj. Tennessee and Georgia.

Map 138

FLORIDA CROWNED SNAKE
Tantilla coronata wagneri   p. 143

Identification: 7–9; record 10. A Florida subspecies of the Crowned Snake in which the white collar is suppressed or completely obliterated (Fig. 38, p. 180). Dark pigment extends backward from the head to a width of 4 or 5 scales behind the parietals. Scales *smooth;* anal *divided.*

Similar species: See Southeastern Crowned Snake (p. 180).

Range: Most of peninsular Florida and Key Largo.   Map 138

FLAT-HEADED SNAKE *Tantilla gracilis*   p. 143

Identification: 7–8; record 9⅛. A Black-headed Snake that usually doesn't have a black head! Head normally slightly darker than body, but occasional specimens do have quite dark heads; when a black cap shows, it is *concave* at its posterior end (Fig. 38, p. 180). A slender, shiny snake with a plain (unpatterned) dorsum of some shade of brown — golden- or gray-brown to reddish brown. *Belly salmon pink.* Upper labial scales 6. Scales *smooth;* anal *divided. Young:* About 3″ to 3½″ at hatching.

A small, secretive, almost wormlike snake, completely inoffensive but adept at forcing its way through the fingers when held in the hand. Normally found under rocks below which there is at least some moisture.

Similar species: Lack of dorsal pattern makes this snake easy to confuse with several other plain brown species. Brown Snakes and the Rough Earth Snake have *keeled* scales; Western Earth Snake has weak *keels* on at least some middorsal scales. Ground Snake has cream or whitish belly and also usually has a loreal scale (Fig., p. 222). Blind Snake has belly scales same size as dorsal scales (unique among serpents of our area). Plains Black-headed Snake has 7 upper labials and the black cap, almost invariably prominent, is *convex* or pointed at rear.

Range: Missouri and e. Kansas to s. Texas.

Subspecies: SLENDER FLAT-HEADED SNAKE, *Tantilla*

gracilis gracilis (illustrated on Plate 18). Ventrals usually 127 or fewer in females and 119 or fewer in males; caudals usually 41 or fewer in females and 50 or fewer in males. Sw. Arkansas and se. Oklahoma to s. Texas. NORTHERN FLAT-HEADED SNAKE, *Tantilla gracilis hallowelli*. Ventrals usually 128 or more in females and 120 or more in males; caudals usually 42 or more in females and 51 or more in males. Most of Missouri and e. Kansas and south into Arkansas and Oklahoma; an isolated record in the Texas panhandle. Map 139

PLAINS BLACK-HEADED SNAKE *Tantilla nigriceps* p. 143
Identification: 7–10; record 14⅝. The black cap is convex or even pointed at the rear, and it extends backward 2 to 5 scale lengths from the parietals (Fig. 38, p. 180). Dorsum plain yellowish brown to brownish gray; belly whitish or pink. Upper labial scales 7. Scales *smooth;* anal *divided.*

The Black-headed Snake of the southern Great Plains and arid lands to the south and west. Found under rocks, debris, etc., and only rarely in the open.
Similar species: In Flat-headed Snakes upper labials are 6, and in the few Flatheads with black caps the rear of the dark area is *concave.*
Range: Sw. Nebraska to Arizona and extr. n. Mexico.
Subspecies: TEXAS BLACK-HEADED SNAKE, *Tantilla nigriceps fumiceps* (illustrated on Plate 18). Ventrals usually 145 or fewer. Sw. Oklahoma to extr. s. Texas. PLAINS BLACK-HEADED SNAKE, *Tantilla nigriceps nigriceps*. Ventrals 146 or more. Sw. Nebraska and Kansas to w. Texas and se. Arizona. Map 140

NOTE: The Mexican Black-headed Snake, *Tantilla atriceps*, is known from Terrell County, Texas, and it may occur farther east. Also, two specimens are alleged to have come from Drumright, Oklahoma, but confirmation of the presence of the species in the latter state is needed. In *atriceps* the black cap extends only the width of 1 or 2 scales behind the parietals and its posterior border runs straight across or is very slightly convex (Fig. 38, p. 180). Also, the 1st lower labials usually do not meet under the chin. (In *nigriceps* the 1st lower labials usually touch each other behind the mental scale.)

CORAL SNAKES: FAMILY ELAPIDAE

THESE SNAKES are dangerously poisonous. Although their small mouths and relatively short fangs make it difficult for them to bite most parts of the human anatomy (fingers or toes, of course, are quite vulnerable), their venoms are potent. They are strongly ringed with red, yellow, and black, or in the tropics with black and red or black and yellow. Coral snakes range from the southern United States to Argentina. The family is also widespread in the Old World, where it includes such notorious members as cobras, mambas, kraits, and tiger snakes.

EASTERN CORAL SNAKE *Micrurus fulvius* p. 238
Identification: 20–30; record 47½. A shiny, "candystick" snake, the colored rings completely encircling the body. *Red and yellow rings touch.* End of snout black, followed by a broad yellow band across head. *Young:* Similarly patterned and colored; 7" to 9" at hatching.

Coral Snakes are usually secretive, but when they prowl it is normally by day, especially in early morning. Sometimes they may be discovered hiding under leaves or debris, in logs, palmetto stumps, etc. Habitats vary from well-drained pine woods and open, dry, or sandy areas to such moister environments as pond and lake borders and in the (often) dense and jungly growths of hardwoods known in the South (Florida especially) as hammocks. Coral Snakes eat snakes, lizards, and frogs. When suddenly restrained, a Coral Snake may thrust its tail upward with the tip curled into a ball that may momentarily be mistaken for the head.

Similar species: The venomous Coral Snakes are well imitated serpents. Several of our harmless snakes also sport rings (or near-rings) of red, black, and yellow (or white). In all of them, however, black separates red from yellow. Think of a traffic light: red means *stop*, yellow means *caution*. If these two warning colors touch on the snake's body, it is poisonous. "Mimics" include the Scarlet Snake, Scarlet Kingsnake, and several of the Milk Snakes. The cross-banded phase of the Ground Snake (Plate 21) bears a remote resemblance to a Coral Snake, but the rings do not cross the belly.

Range: Southern states, North Carolina to Texas.

Subspecies: EASTERN CORAL SNAKE, *Micrurus fulvius fulvius* (illustrated on Plate 29). Red rings dotted or spotted with black, the dark markings often concentrated into a pair of fairly large black spots in each red ring. E. North Carolina south, chiefly in lowlands, to s. Florida; west through Gulf states to Mississippi River. SOUTH FLORIDA CORAL SNAKE, *Micrurus fulvius barbouri.* Similar, but with little or no black in the red rings. On upper Florida Keys the yellow rings may be absent, but yellow crossband remains on head. Smaller, maximum length about 37½". Extr. s. Florida (but not on lower Keys). TEXAS CORAL SNAKE, *Micrurus fulvius tenere.* Like eastern races, but with more and widely scattered black pigment in the red rings. In addition to inhabiting lowland areas, this subspecies ascends onto the Edwards Plateau of central Texas, where it may be found in cedar brakes, rocky canyons, or on rocky hillsides. S. Arkansas and Louisiana to w.-cent. Texas; south into Mexico.   Map 141

FAMILY VIPERIDAE

Pit Vipers: Subfamily Crotalinae

ALL OUR dangerously poisonous serpents except the Coral Snakes belong to this group. Copperheads, Cottonmouths, and Rattlesnakes are members.

The subfamily name is derived from the deep facial pit on each side of the head situated a little below midway between eye and nostril (Fig., p. 238). It is a sensory organ that helps the snake to aim in striking at warm-blooded prey. *Any serpent with such a pit is poisonous*, but this can be checked only on dead or caged specimens. Don't approach live ones in the field close enough to see the pit. Also beware of handling freshly killed snakes. Reflex action is marked; even decapitated heads have been known to bite!

The scales under the tail are in only 1 row, at least anteriorly; the heads are distinctly wider than the necks; and the pupils of the eyes are vertically elliptical. A few nonpoisonous and rear-fanged snakes also have one or more of these characteristics.

Pit Vipers range from southern Canada to Argentina and from extreme southeastern Europe through southern and central Asia and Malaysia. They and the True Vipers of the Old World constitute the Family Viperidae.

Copperheads and Cottonmouths: Genus: *Agkistrodon*

THESE ARE the venomous "moccasins" — Copperheads being the "highland moccasins" and Cottonmouths the "water moccasins." In refering to these snakes, however, the name "moccasin" should be studiously avoided, for it is misleading. Ignorant or uninformed persons apply the same term to the nonpoisonous Water Snakes. Members of the genus *Agkistrodon* have facial pits and all the other characteristics of the Pit Vipers. Scales are *weakly keeled;* anal *single*. When alarmed they rapidly vibrate their tails, producing a lively tattoo against a leaf, vegetation, or even the ground — whatever the tail may touch. The young at birth have bright yellow tail tips. The genus is represented in North and Central America, Asia, Malaysia, and extreme southeastern Europe.

NORTHERN COPPERHEAD
Agkistrodon contortrix mokeson   p. 238

Identification: 24–36; record 53. A coppery-red head and an hourglass pattern. Viewed from above, the dark chestnut markings are wide on the sides and narrow at the center of the back. Dark rounded spots at sides of belly. Scales *weakly keeled;* anal *single;* a single row of scales under tail, at least anteriorly. *Young:* Paler; tail tip yellow; a *narrow* dark line through eye that divides the dark head from the pale lips; 8″ to 9¾″ at birth.

The Copperhead has many aliases — "chunkhead," "highland moccasin," "pilot," "adder," etc. Natural camouflage renders it inconspicuous. Normally a quiet, almost lethargic snake, content to lie motionless or beat a dignified retreat. Once aroused, it strikes vigorously and may rapidly vibrate the tail. Rocky, wooded hillsides and mountainous areas are favorite habitats. Abandoned and rotting sawdust piles, left in the wake of the itinerant, portable sawmill, are another; in these, Copperheads as well as other reptiles find shelter, food, and moisture. Copperheads are gregarious, especially in autumn, when they assemble at hibernating dens or denning areas, often in company with other species of snakes. Mice are the principal food, but small birds, frogs, and insects also are eaten.

Similar species: In Milk Snakes the large dorsal markings are *wide* at center of back; belly markings black and squarish. Eastern Milk Snake usually has *checkerboard* belly. Hognose Snakes, besides having turned-up snouts, hiss and flatten their heads and necks. Water Snakes seldom wander far from water and retreat into it when alarmed; their scales are *strongly* keeled. In Fox Snakes the markings consist of a series of large dark blotches flanked by a series of smaller blotches on each side. Great numbers of harmless snakes are killed in mistaken belief they are Copperheads. If snake is dead check for the facial pits. (Also see "Young" under Cottonmouth, p. 186.)

Range: Massachusetts to e. Kansas; south in uplands to Alabama; south through Ozarks and adj. areas to ne. Texas.

Map 142

SOUTHERN COPPERHEAD
Agkistrodon contortrix contortrix   p. 238

Identification: 24–36; record 52. A paler, pinker counterpart of the Northern Copperhead. The dark markings are quite narrow across the back, giving the "hourglasses" a more wasp-waist appearance than in the northern race. Very often they are broken at middorsum, the two halves failing to meet. Scales *weakly keeled;* anal *single. Young:* Similar to young of Northern Copperhead, but with pinched, often-broken markings.

This is mainly a snake of the lowlands, of low ground near swamps and cypress-bordered streams, but it also ascends into the hilly Piedmont region.

Similar species: Baby Cottonmouths have a *broad* dark band through eye, and their body hues consist largely of dark browns.
Range: Extr. se. Virginia to Florida panhandle and west to Arkansas and e. Texas; north in Mississippi Valley to s. Illinois and se. Missouri where it intergrades with Northern Copperhead northward to Iowa.   Map 142

BROAD-BANDED COPPERHEAD
Agkistrodon contortrix laticinctus   p. 238
Identification: 22–30; record 34. The rich reddish-brown or chestnut-brown crossbands are almost as broad on the back as on the sides of the body. Tip of tail greenish gray (yellow in newborn young). Scales *weakly keeled;* anal *single. Young:* Tip of tail yellow or greenish yellow; 8⅝″ to 10″ at birth.
Range: Extr. s. Kansas through Oklahoma and cent. Texas to the Gulf. Western subspecies.   Map 142

EASTERN COTTONMOUTH
Agkistrodon piscivorus piscivorus   p. 238
Identification: 30–48; record 74. A large aquatic snake. Olive, brown, or black above; belly lighter. Crossbands with dark, more or less distinct borders; centers of crossbands often invaded by the lighter ground color. Details of pattern most evident in young and sub-adults; old adults may be completely dark and unpatterned. *Snout light in color* and usually with a vertical dark line at each side of rostral. A dead specimen is easily identified by facial pits, *single* anal plate, and *single* row of scales under tail (Fig., p. 238). Dorsal scales *weakly keeled. Young:* Strongly patterned with light-centered dark brown to brilliant reddish-brown crossbands; tip of tail yellow; a *broad* dark band through eye; 10″ to 13″ at birth.

Beware of any aquatic serpent within the range of the Cottonmouths. These very dangerous snakes closely resemble several of the nonpoisonous Water Snakes (*Natrix*) and are difficult to tell from them in the field. Behavior offers some of the best clues. Cottonmouths often stand their ground or crawl slowly away. Water Snakes usually flee quickly or drop with a splash into the water. Cottonmouths vibrate tails when excited; Water Snakes do not. A thoroughly aroused Cottonmouth throws its head upward and backward and holds its mouth wide open, revealing a white interior — origin of the name Cottonmouth.

This is a snake of southern lowlands, a denizen of swamps, lakes, and rivers, of rice fields and ditches. Suns itself on branches, logs, or stones at water's edge and sometimes wanders away from its normal habitat in pursuit of food. Fish, frogs, salamanders, snakes, lizards, small turtles, baby alligators, birds, and small mammals are included in the list.

Similar species: The nonpoisonous Water Snakes (*Natrix*) have *divided* anal plates, a *double* row of scales under tail, and *no* facial pits (Fig., p. 238). Young Copperheads are more reddish and have a *narrow* dark line through eye.

Range: Se. Virginia to Key West and Alabama.　　Map 143

WESTERN COTTONMOUTH
Agkistrodon piscivorus leucostoma　　　　　　　　p. 238

Identification: 30–42; record 54. A smaller, darker, less well patterned subspecies of the Eastern Cottonmouth. Belly dark brown or black, the dark crossbands (when evident) uniform or with dusky centers, and snout without clear-cut markings. Many specimens are plain black or dark brown with little or no trace of markings. *Young:* Strongly and brightly patterned; tip of tail yellow; 6″ to 11″ at birth.

Behavior the same as in Eastern Cottonmouth. The habit of holding the mouth open has earned it the names of "gapper" and "trapjaw," the latter in reference to speed with which mouth snaps shut if anything touches it. These names are prevalent in Ozarks and other regions. An extremely abundant snake in the swamps and bayous of Louisiana and other southern states. Also invades certain more upland areas of the central highlands and may be found in company of or hibernating with Rattlesnakes and Copperheads.

Similar species: See Eastern Cottonmouth.

Range: Extr. s. Illinois to extr. sw. Alabama; west to extr. se. Kansas, e. Oklahoma, and cent. Texas. An isolated colony in n.-cent. Missouri and several old records from Rio Grande Valley, Texas.　　　　　　　　　　　　　　　　　　　　Map 143

Rattlesnakes: Genera *Sistrurus* and *Crotalus*

THE RATTLE is the hallmark of these snakes. In adults it is an organ of loosely attached horny segments that strike against one another to produce a buzzing sound when the tail is vibrated rapidly. In the very young the rattle is represented by a "button." Later a new segment is added at each shedding time, the segments becoming progressively larger until the snake reaches adult size. Two to 4 new segments are normally added each year. The button remains at the end of the string unless it is lost through wear or breaking of the rather fragile rattle (see Fig., p. 239).

Because of the great disparity in size, the sounds made by the different species vary greatly. In general, the largest rattlesnakes produce the loudest, most sonorous tones. Buzzing is the best way to describe them, but the sounds have also been likened to those of escaping steam and the noise produced by cicadas ("lo-

custs"). Rarely, a Rattlesnake may have no rattle — if the end
of the tail has been chopped off by a man wielding a hoe or by some
other enemy. Many other snakes, including Cottonmouths,
Copperheads, and numerous nonpoisonous species, vibrate their
tails rapidly when brought to bay. If their tails brush against dry
leaves or other vegetation, the resultant sound is suggestive of a
Rattlesnake.

The Pigmy Rattlers and Massasaugas (*Sistrurus*) have a set of 9
plates on the crowns of their heads, as do most nonpoisonous
snakes. All our other Rattlers (*Crotalus*) have their heads largely
covered with small scales (see Fig. 39, below).

Fig. 39. TOPS OF HEADS OF RATTLESNAKES

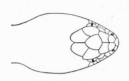 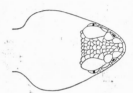

PIGMIES AND MASSASAUGAS (Sistrurus)   RATTLESNAKES (Crotalus)
A group of 9 large scales (plates)   Crown of head covered by a mixture
on the crown of the head   of large and small scales

Rodents and birds are the chief foods, but frogs, lizards, etc.,
are also eaten, especially by the smaller kinds. Rattlesnakes occur
only in the New World. There are nearly 30 species distributed
from southern Canada to northern Argentina. They are found in
all states save Maine and Delaware.

In measuring Rattlesnakes the length of the rattle is *not* included.

EASTERN MASSASAUGA *Sistrurus catenatus catenatus* p. 239
  Identification: 20–30; record 37½. The "swamp rattler" or
  "black snapper." A spotted Rattler with a row of large black or
  dark brown blotches down the back and 3 rows of smaller or
  lighter spots on each side of body. Ground color gray or brownish gray. Belly black, irregularly marked with white or yellowish (Fig. 40, p. 189). Some adults are jet-black, both above and
  below, with no trace of pattern save for a few light marks on chin
  and throat. Nine *plates* on crown of head (Fig. 39, above).
  Young: Well-patterned but paler than adults; 7″ to 9½″ at
  birth.

   Wet prairies are the preferred habitat toward the western part
  of the range and bogs and swamps toward the east, but these
  snakes also occur in dry woodlands. Many individuals are mild-
  mannered, seldom rattling until thoroughly aroused. They may

hide in crayfish holes or other underground cavities. At harvest times Massasaugas often turn up, sometimes in numbers, under shocks of grain where mice have congregated. Other food includes small birds, frogs, and snakes.

Similar species: Timber Rattlesnake has small scales on crown of head (Fig. 39, p. 188).

Range: Cent. New York and s. Ontario to Iowa and Missouri.

Map 145

WESTERN MASSASAUGA

Sistrurus catenatus tergeminus p. 239

Identification: 18–26; record 32¼. Similar to Eastern Massasauga, but lighter in coloration, the dark brown blotches in strong contrast with the light gray or tan-gray ground color. Belly light with a few dark markings (Fig. 40, below). *Young:* 7″ to 9½″ at birth.

A snake of the plains and prairies, taking advantage of boggy areas where they exist.

Similar species: Western Pigmy Rattlesnake has a tiny rattle, slender tail, and usually a reddish stripe down center of back. From all other Rattlers within its range, the Western Massasauga may be distinguished by the group of 9 *plates* on the crown of its head (Fig. 39, p. 188).

Range: Se. Nebraska and adj. Missouri to s.-cent. Texas.

Subspecies: DESERT MASSASAUGA, *Sistrurus catenatus edwardsi.* Smaller and more slender; max. about 21″. Similarly patterned but paler, and with ventral surface nearly white and virtually (or completely) unmarked. Scale rows at midbody 23 (25 in Western Massasauga). Chiefly desert grasslands from se. Arizona and New Mexico to extr. s. Texas. Map 145

Fig. 40. BELLIES OF MASSASAUGAS

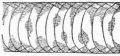

WESTERN
Light in coloration

EASTERN
Chiefly black

DUSKY PIGMY RATTLESNAKE

Sistrurus miliarius barbouri p. 239

Identification: 15–22; record 31. The tiny rattle, sounding like the buzz of an insect, is scarcely audible more than a few feet away. It and the slender tail identify the Pigmy or "ground rattlers." This one has a "dusted" appearance caused by dark

WHIPSNAKES, RACERS, AND PATCH-NOSED SNAKE
(All have smooth scales and divided anal plates.)

Map Text

NORTHERN BLACK RACER (young)   113 146
  Dark middorsal blotches.

WESTERN COACHWHIP (young)   115 150
  Dark crosslines.

TEXAS PATCH-NOSED SNAKE   122 154
  Orange (or yellow) stripe bordered by broad dark stripes;
  narrow dark stripe on side of body.

EASTERN YELLOW-BELLIED RACER   113 148
  Belly yellow; dorsal coloration variable (see text).

BLUE RACER   113 147
  Blue above, belly paler; dark area on side of head.   (Everglades Racer may be very similar —see p. 148).

NORTHERN BLACK RACER   113 146
  Plain black above and below; some white on chin.

BUTTERMILK SNAKE   113 149
  Irregular white, buff, or blue spots.

WESTERN COACHWHIP   115 150
  Essentially plain brown above, but varying (see text);
  tail like a braided whip.

EASTERN COACHWHIP   115 149
  Head and part of body black, changing to light brown
  posteriorly.
  Black phase: Traces of light pattern; reddish on tail
  (see text).

CENTRAL TEXAS WHIPSNAKE   114 150
  Longitudinal white patches on sides.

SCHOTT'S WHIPSNAKE   114 151
  Striped on sides; reddish on neck; dorsal scales with light
  edges (Fig. 32, p. 149).

RUTHVEN'S WHIPSNAKE   114 151
  Suggestion of stripes on sides; dorsal scales with light
  edges (Fig. 32, p. 149).

YOUNG

N. BLACK RACER

W. COACHWHIP

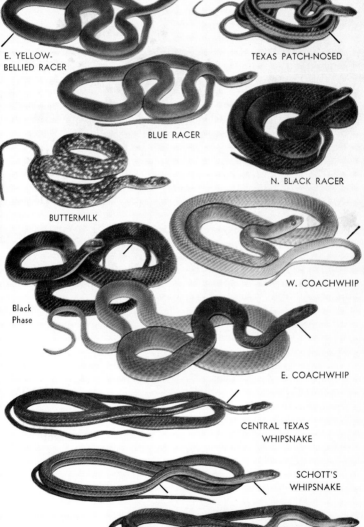

E. YELLOW-
BELLIED RACER

TEXAS PATCH-NOSED

BLUE RACER

N. BLACK RACER

BUTTERMILK

W. COACHWHIP

Black
Phase

E. COACHWHIP

CENTRAL TEXAS
WHIPSNAKE

SCHOTT'S
WHIPSNAKE

RUTHVEN'S
WHIPSNAKE

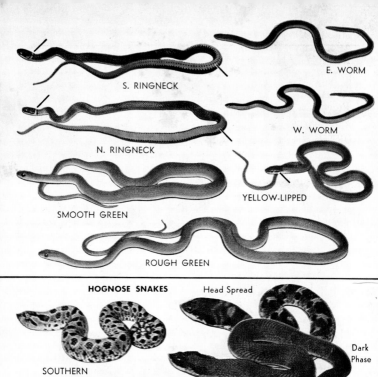

S. RINGNECK

E. WORM

N. RINGNECK

W. WORM

SMOOTH GREEN

YELLOW-LIPPED

ROUGH GREEN

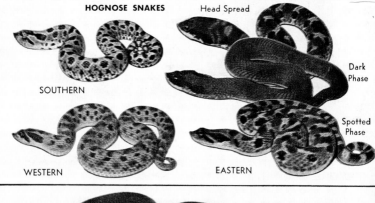

HOGNOSE SNAKES

Head Spread

SOUTHERN

Dark Phase

WESTERN

Spotted Phase

EASTERN

MUD

Chin and Neck

RAINBOW

Chin and Neck

Plate 24   191

WOODLAND, HOGNOSE, AND MUD SNAKES

Map Text

SOUTHERN RINGNECK SNAKE   112 **141**
   Prominent row of black spots; ring interrupted. (Hind
   part of snake turned upside down.)

NORTHERN RINGNECK SNAKE   112 **140**
   Belly plain yellow; ring complete. (Hind part of snake
   turned upside down.)

EASTERN WORM SNAKE   109 **144**
   Brown back; pink belly.

WESTERN WORM SNAKE   109 **144**
   Black back; pink belly.

SMOOTH GREEN SNAKE   120 **152**
   Plain green; *smooth* scales.

ROUGH GREEN SNAKE   121 **152**
   Plain green; *keeled* scales; body and tail very slender.

YELLOW-LIPPED SNAKE   105 **140**
   Lips whitish or yellowish; dark line through eye.

SOUTHERN HOGNOSE SNAKE   110 **140**
   Snout sharply upturned; belly unpatterned or mottled
   with grayish brown (Fig. 29, p. 139).

WESTERN HOGNOSE SNAKE   107 **139**
   Snout sharply upturned; belly chiefly black (Fig. 29, p.
   139).

EASTERN HOGNOSE SNAKE   108 **138**
   Spotted phase: Snout upturned; underside of tail lighter
   than belly (Fig. 29, p. 139).
   Dark phase: Dark gray to black; usually trace of dark
   neck stripes.

MUD SNAKE   106 **145**
   Dorsum: Shiny black or dark gray; pink of belly encroaches on sides.
   Chin and neck (at larger scale): Black spots continuous
   with black of dorsum.

RAINBOW SNAKE   104 **144**
   Dorsum: Red and black stripes.
   Chin and neck (at larger scale): Rounded black spots in
   double row.

stippling that may largely obscure the markings. Dark spots rounded. A reddish-brown middorsal stripe usually present, but varying in prominence from one specimen to the next. Belly dark. Nine *plates* on crown of head (Fig. 39, p. 188). *Young:* Tip of tail sulfur-yellow; 6¼″ to 7″ at birth.

Behavior varies, depending upon such factors as temperature and temperament. Some strike furiously; others are lethargic and don't sound the rattle. At home in flatwoods and in virtually all types of terrain where lakes and marshes abound. Especially abundant in the "prairie" portions of the Everglades. Food includes mice, lizards, snakes, and frogs.

Range: Extr. s. South Carolina to se. Mississippi and south throughout Florida (except on the Keys).

Subspecies: CAROLINA PIGMY RATTLESNAKE, *Sistrurus miliarius miliarius.* Similar, but smaller (21″ maximum); head and body patterns more distinct; belly pale, lightly flecked or mottled with dark pigment instead of heavily blotched as in Dusky Pigmy. Se. North Carolina to cent. Alabama. Map 144

WESTERN PIGMY RATTLESNAKE
Sistrurus miliarius streckeri   p. 239
Identification: 15–20; record 25⅛. Tiny rattle and skinny tail. Ground color light, usually pale grayish brown. The middorsal dark spots may be highly irregular in shape, but they often tend to form short transverse bars. One or 2 conspicuous rows of dark spots on each side of body. Reddish dorsal stripe sometimes absent. Nine *plates* on crown of head (Fig. 39, p. 188). *Young:* Tail bands less distinct; 5½″ to 7″ at birth.

Habitats are usually in areas where water is nearby — in river floodplains, swamps, marshes, and wet prairies.

Similar species: Western Massasauga has much larger rattle and a tail of moderate size. All other Rattlesnakes occurring within Western Pigmy's range have small scales on crown of head (Fig. 39, p. 188).

Range: S. Missouri and e. Oklahoma to the Gulf; an eastward extension into sw. Tennessee.   Map 144

TIMBER RATTLESNAKE *Crotalus horridus horridus*   p. 239
Identification: 36–54; record 74. Sometimes called the "banded" or "velvet-tail rattler." Two major color patterns: (1) *yellow phase* — black or dark brown crossbands on a ground color of yellow, brown, or gray; the crossbands, which may be *V*-shaped, break up anteriorly to form a row of dark spots down the back plus a row along each side of body; (2) *black phase* — a heavy stippling of black or very dark brown that hides much of lighter pigment; completely black specimens are not rare in uplands of the Northeast. *Young:* Always cross-banded as in yellow phase, but with colors more somber; 11″ or 12″ or birth.

The only Rattlesnake in most of the populous Northeast.

Still common in mountainous regions but completely extirpated in many areas where it once was numerous. During winter, Timber Rattlers may congregate in dens to hibernate, together with Copperheads and other snakes. Such dens, which may include a hundred or more Rattlers, usually are in or near wooded rocky ledges with southern exposures, where they can sun themselves in spring and autumn. During summer they scatter over the surrounding countryside but return to den in the fall. Make local inquiries when fishing, hiking, or camping so that infested areas may be avoided. This is a snake of timbered terrain, usually most common in second-growth where rodents abound. Toward the west it follows wooded stream valleys that extend out into the prairies.

Similar species: Eastern Massasaugas, sometimes completely black, have 9 plates on crowns of heads instead of numerous small scales (Fig. 39, p. 188).

Range: New Hampshire to s. New Jersey (formerly known also from s. Maine and Long Island); south in Appalachian highlands to n. Alabama and west through Ohio Valley; Minnesota and Wisconsin to ne. Texas; also n. Ohio and s. Ontario. Map 147

Fig. 41. SIDES OF HEADS OF RATTLESNAKES

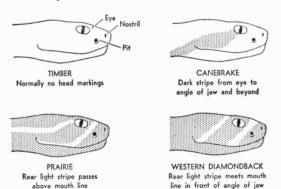

TIMBER
Normally no head markings

CANEBRAKE
Dark stripe from eye to
angle of jaw and beyond

PRAIRIE
Rear light stripe passes
above mouth line

WESTERN DIAMONDBACK
Rear light stripe meets mouth
line in front of angle of jaw

CANEBRAKE RATTLESNAKE

Crotalus horridus atricaudatus p. 239

Identification: 42–60; record 74½. The broad dark stripe, running backward from the eye, is one of the most reliable characters (Fig. 41, above). The reddish middorsal stripe splits the black spots in half on forward part of body. Ground color ranges from pale grayish brown to pinkish buff. *Young:* Strongly patterned but paler; 11″ to 16″ at birth.

A lowland counterpart of the Timber Rattler that is at home in cane thickets and swamplands of the South.

Similar species: Timber Rattler normally lacks dark stripe behind eye; eastern Timbers usually lack reddish-brown middorsal stripe, but specimens in western part of range may have it. The two Diamondback Rattlers have diamond markings instead of dark crossbands. Pigmies and Massasaugas have 9 plates on crowns of heads instead of small scales (Fig. 39, p. 188).

Range: Lowlands of se. Virginia to n. Florida and west to cent. Texas; north in Mississippi Valley to s. Illinois.   Map 147

(NORTHERN) BLACK-TAILED RATTLESNAKE
Crotalus molossus molossus   p. 239

Identification: 30–42; record 49½. The "green rattler" of the central Texas uplands and westward. Characterized by three unique features: (1) black of the tail ends abruptly at body; (2) patches of light scales in dark crossbands; and (3) each scale unicolored. In other Rattlers the pattern cuts across the scales, so that many individual scales may be half dark and half light, etc. *Young:* Similar, but with dark crossbands visible on tail; 9″ to 11¾″ at birth.

An inhabitant of rock piles and slides, wooded canyons, and the vicinity of cliffs.

Range: The Edwards Plateau of cent. Texas west to Arizona and n. Mexico. Mexican subspecies.   Map 149

(MOTTLED) ROCK RATTLESNAKE
Crotalus lepidus lepidus   p. 239

Identification: 18–24; record 30¼. A dusty-looking snake, the mottled effect being produced by a profuse stippling of dark pigment that may be so intense as to form pseudo-crossbands between the dark crosslines. General coloration may be gray, bluish gray, greenish gray, tan, brown, or pinkish. The dark crosslines, progressively more prominent toward tail, may be brown or black but they vary in intensity from one specimen to the next. *Young:* 6¾″ to 8″ at birth.

A montane, rock-inhabiting rattler. Its menu is extremely varied: small rodents, lizards, small snakes, frogs, salamanders, and insects are included.

Range: S.-cent. Texas west through Trans-Pecos region and south to San Luis Potosí; se. New Mexico. Western subspecies.   Map 146

EASTERN DIAMONDBACK RATTLESNAKE
Crotalus adamanteus   p. 239

Identification: 33–72; record 96. An ominously impressive snake to meet in the field; suddenly finding yourself in close proximity to the compact coils, broad head, and loud buzzing rattle is almost certain to raise the hair on the nape of your neck. The diamonds, dark brown or black in color, are strongly outlined by a row of cream-colored or yellowish scales. Ground color olive, brown, or almost black. Pattern and colors vivid in freshly shed specimens; dull and quite dark in those preparing to shed. Only Rattler within its range with 2 prominent light lines on face. *Young:* 12″ to 14″ at birth.

At home in the palmetto flatwoods and dry pinelands of the South. Occasionally ventures into salt water, swimming to outlying keys off the Florida coast. Individual dispositions vary. Some snakes will permit close approach without making a sound, whereas others, completely concealed in palmettos or other vegetation, will rattle when dogs or persons are 20 or 30 feet away. Many stand their ground, but when hard pressed they back away, rattling vigorously but still facing the intruder. Frequently they take refuge in burrows of Gopher Tortoises, in holes beneath stumps, etc. Rabbits, rodents, and birds are eaten.
Range: Coastal lowlands from the Sounds of North Carolina to extr. e. Louisiana; all of Florida, including the Keys. Map 151

WESTERN DIAMONDBACK RATTLESNAKE
Crotalus atrox p. 239

Identification: 30–72; record 83⅛. Great size, a tendency to stand its ground, and the loud, buzzing rattle usually are sufficient identification. When fully aroused it may raise the head and a loop of the neck high above the coils, gaining elevation for aiming and striking. The diamonds are not clear-cut, and entire head and body may have a dusty appearance. General coloration brown or gray, but sometimes with tones of reddish or yellowish. Light stripe behind eye reaches lip in *front* of corner of mouth (Fig. 41, p. 193). *Tail strongly ringed* with black and white or light gray ("coontail rattler"). *Young:* Diamonds more sharply defined; 10″ to 14″ at birth.

A snake of the arid Southwest, occurring chiefly in the lowlands, but also ascending into mountains to altitudes of 5000 feet or more. At home on desert flats as well as in rocky cliffs and canyons. Food includes rabbits and such rodents as rats, mice, gophers, and ground squirrels. The Western Diamondback is responsible for more serious snake bites and fatalities than any other North American serpent. It and the Eastern Diamondback rank among the world's most dangerous snakes.
Similar species: In Prairie Rattler light line behind eye passes *behind* corner of mouth (Fig. 41, p. 193).
Range: Cent. Arkansas and Texas to California; south into n. Mexico; isolated populations in s. Mexico. Map 150

PRAIRIE RATTLESNAKE *Crotalus viridis viridis* p. 239
Identification: 35–45; record 57. A blotched Rattlesnake with

the blotches broad anteriorly, but narrow and joining with the lateral markings to form crossbands near the tail. Ground color usually greenish gray, olive-green, or greenish brown, but sometimes light brown or yellowish. The dark brown blotches are narrowly bordered with white. Two oblique light lines on head, the one behind eye passing *behind* corner of mouth (Fig. 41, p. 193).

A very abundant Rattler (in some areas) that lives in the grasslands of the Great Plains, but retreats in winter to dens in rocky outcrops and ledges. This is the snake supposed to live in harmony with prairie dogs and burrowing owls, but, alas for the writers of fanciful fiction, young prairie dogs and owls make excellent meals for Prairie Rattlers. *Young:* 8½″ to 11″ at birth.
Similar species: In Western Diamondback light line behind eye reaches mouth in *front* of its back corner (Fig. 41, p. 193); also, tail of Diamondback is strongly ringed with black and white. Western Massasauga has 9 plates on crown of head instead of small scales (Fig. 39, p. 188). In Rock Rattlesnake the dark crossbands are far apart.
Range: Extr. w. Iowa to Rockies and beyond; s. Canada to n. Mexico. Western subspecies.   Map 148

IX

Salamanders

GIANT SALAMANDERS: FAMILIES CRYPTOBRANCHIDAE, PROTEIDAE, SIRENIDAE, AND AMPHIUMIDAE

NORTH AMERICA (including Central America) not only has more varieties of salamanders than all the rest of the world put together, but it boasts an assortment of big bizarre kinds that look more like bad dreams than live animals. Some are long, dark, and slender and resemble eels. Some permanently retain the larval form, bearing external gills throughout their lives. Others are flattened and smack of weird creatures crawling forth from the antediluvian slime. Since all are aquatic and nocturnal, few persons other than fishermen ever meet them in person. Periodically one or the other is reported in the press as an animal "new to science." The erroneous belief that they are poisonous is widespread.

Many of these salamanders thrive in aquariums, but they should be provided with shelter in the form of flat rocks under which to crawl, or aquatic vegetation in which to hide. As in the care of aquarium fishes, the water must be kept from fouling and free from chlorine. A screened lid, tied or weighted down, should be provided; many specimens are persistent in their efforts to escape, at least during the first day or two. Many soon learn to eat small pieces of meat or liver or canned dog food.

Two of the families (Amphiumidae and Sirenidae) are confined to North America. The Proteidae (Mudpuppies and Waterdogs) have a relative in Europe, and the Cryptobranchidae (Hellbenders) have a single representative in eastern Asia, the enormous Japanese Salamander that grows to a length of 5 feet. Not all members of these families are large: the Dwarf Sirens (*Pseudobranchus*) are tiny (about 6" long) compared with their close relative, the Greater Siren, that attains a length of 3 feet.

HELLBENDER *Cryptobranchus alleganiensis alleganiensis* p. 266
    Identification: 11½–20; records 22(♂) and 29⅛ (♀). A huge, grotesque, thoroughly aquatic salamander. Head flattened and each side of body with a wrinkled, fleshy fold of skin. Ground color usually gray, but varying from yellowish brown to almost black. Vague, scattered, and irregular dark or light spots may often be seen. No external gills in adult. *Young:* Numerous irregular dark spots that are conspicuous against light ground color;

usually between 4″ and 5″ when they lose their external gills.

Almost always found in rivers and larger streams where water is running and ample shelter is available in the form of large rocks, snags, or debris. Hellbenders sometimes may be caught by *slowly* overturning or moving large rocks in clear, relatively shallow streams, and taking them by dip net or by hand. Since they are exceedingly slimy, the fingers must encircle the neck *and* immobilize both front legs on the first grab. Quite harmless but many fishermen, believing them to be poisonous, will cut their lines and sacrifice their gear rather than unhook them. Captives will eat crayfish, earthworms, aquatic insects, and sometimes even pieces of meat.

Similar species: Adult Mudpuppies and Waterdogs have external gills, and so do larval specimens of other species.

Range: S. New York to n. Alabama; cent. Missouri.   Map 153

OZARK HELLBENDER
Cryptobranchus alleganiensis bishopi   p. 266

Identification: 11–17⅝. Like the wide-ranging Hellbender but with the dark markings on the back much more conspicuous and in the form of blotches rather than spots. Lower lips heavily spotted with black (only lightly spotted or not at all in Hellbender). There are also minor anatomical differences. This form is best identified on basis of geography.

Range: Black River system of se. Missouri and adj. Arkansas.
Map 153

MUDPUPPY   *Necturus maculosus*   p. 266

Identification: 8–13; record 17. The gills, at maximum development, are like miniature ostrich plumes, dyed maroon and waving gracefully in the current. This, like all other members of its genus is a permanent larva, retaining gills throughout life. *Four* toes on each of the 4 feet. Dark stripe through eye. General coloration gray to rust-brown, dorsum normally marked with rather indistinct, scattered, rounded, blue-black spots. Sometimes the spots are few in number, or, rarely, absent altogether. Belly pale, with dark spots (Fig. 42, p. 199) or sometimes plain gray. Tail fins often tinged with orange or reddish. *Young*: Normally striped; a broad middorsal dark stripe flanked on each side by a yellowish stripe; a conspicuous dark stripe on side of body from gills to tip of tail (Fig., p. 266). Occasionally the young are uniformly gray, without markings.

This salamander is a Mudpuppy in the North, but Southerners, not to be outdone in coining colorful names, refer to it and all its relatives as Waterdogs. Throughout much of Dixieland, Mudpuppy is also used by country folk, but they reserve that name for adults of any of the Mole Salamanders (*Ambystoma*). Both names owe their origin at least in part to the belief that these animals bark.

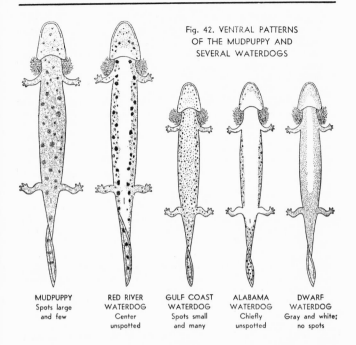

Fig. 42. VENTRAL PATTERNS OF THE MUDPUPPY AND SEVERAL WATERDOGS

MUDPUPPY	RED RIVER WATERDOG	GULF COAST WATERDOG	ALABAMA WATERDOG	DWARF WATERDOG
Spots large and few	Center unspotted	Spots small and many	Chiefly unspotted	Gray and white; no spots

Habitats include lakes, ponds, rivers, streams, and other permanent bodies of water. Essentially nocturnal, but may also be active by day in muddy or weed-choked waters. Almost any small aquatic animal may be taken as food — fishes, fish eggs, crayfish, aquatic insects, mollusks, etc. Size and condition of gills, although subject to individual variation, usually reflect environment. They are most likely to be large, bushy, and kept in motion if the water is foul or warm; usually they are small and contracted if the water is cool and contains considerable oxygen in solution.

Similar species: Hellbenders have flat heads, folds of skin along sides, and adults lack external gills. In the Gulf Coast Waterdog, dorsal spots are very numerous and the dark stripe through eye may be absent or poorly developed. Larvae of some of the Mole Salamanders (*Ambystoma*) grow large enough to be mistaken for Mudpuppies or Waterdogs (*Necturus*), but Mole Salamanders have *five* toes on each *hind* foot.

Range: W. New England to Manitoba and south to drainage systems of Tennessee and Missouri Rivers.

Subspecies: MUDPUPPY, *Necturus maculosus maculosus*

(illustrated on Plate 3). As described and with range indicated above. LAKE WINNEBAGO MUDPUPPY, *Necturus maculosus stictus*. A very dark race, dark gray to almost black, with dorsum, head especially, marked with scattered black or dark brown dots; tiny flecks of tan may partially obscure ground color; occasionally there may be a few large dark blotches on back and sides; record length 10⅛″ Ne. Wisconsin and adj. Michigan. RED RIVER WATERDOG, *Necturus maculosus louisianensis*. Similar, but with ground color light yellowish brown or reddish and with a broad, fairly distinct light stripe on each side of a darker middorsal area. These markings are remnants of the juvenile pattern, which is striped like that of a young Mudpuppy. Dark spots begin to develop at an early age. Dark stripe through eye; center of venter grayish white, unmarked but tinged with pink (Fig. 42, p. 199). Dorsum becomes gray in largest specimens, but dark spots remain clearly evident. Averages smaller than Mudpuppy; maximum length about 11″. Drainage systems of Red and Arkansas Rivers; w. Tennessee and w. Mississippi.   Map 154

GULF COAST WATERDOG   *Necturus beyeri*   p. 266
Identification: 6¼–8¾. A profusely spotted Waterdog. Ground color dark brown, but appearing much lighter because of a multiplicity of tan spots that form an overlying, fine-meshed, netlike pattern. The round or oval spots, dark brown to almost black in color, are arranged in irregular rows or scattered at random. Belly invaded by spots and by dorsal ground color (Fig. 42, p. 199). Dark stripe through eye in some specimens, absent in others. *Four* toes on all 4 feet. *Young:* Spotted, never striped (Fig., p. 266); dull yellow spots on head and body and in rows on edges of tail fin; dark spots develop as animal grows.

Chiefly in sandy, spring-fed streams.
Similar species: Two generalizations will be useful in separating the Mudpuppy (*maculosus*) and its races from the Gulf Coast Waterdog (*beyeri*). Mudpuppy attains large size and becomes very gray with age; young ones have relatively few dark spots. Contrariwise, Gulf Coast Waterdog is small and never gets gray; both adults and young are marked with great numbers of small spots. In addition, Mudpuppy and its races almost always have a dark stripe through eye; this may or may not be present in Gulf Coast Waterdog and its subspecies. The Mobile Waterdog is almost uniformly dark or with indistinct dark spots. In larvae of the Mole Salamanders there are *five* toes on each *hind* foot.
Range: Drainage of Gulf Coast streams from se. Texas to Mobile Bay, Alabama.
Subspecies: GULF COAST WATERDOG, *Necturus beyeri beyeri* (illustrated on Plate 35). As described and with range indicated above. ALABAMA WATERDOG, *Necturus beyeri*

alabamensis. Similar but with fewer dorsal spots and with center of belly unmarked (Fig. 42, p. 199). Streams of Gulf Coast drainage from ne. Mississippi to w. Georgia.   Map 154

NEUSE RIVER WATERDOG   *Necturus lewisi*   Fig. 43
Identification: 6–9; record 10⅞. This Waterdog is strongly spotted both above *and below*, but markings tend to be fewer and smaller on the under surfaces (Fig. 43, below). Spots dark brown or bluish black. Dorsal ground color rusty brown; ventral ground color dull brown or slate-colored. Dark line through eye. *Four* toes on each foot. *Young:* Spotted, never plain or striped.
Similar species: Dwarf Waterdog is almost uniformly dark above and plain bluish white down center of belly (Fig. 42, p. 199). Larvae of Mole Salamanders have *five* toes on each *hind* foot.
Range: Neuse and Tar river systems, North Carolina.   Map 154

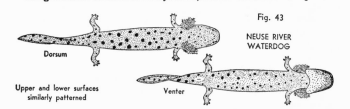

Fig. 43

NEUSE RIVER WATERDOG

Dorsum

Upper and lower surfaces
similarly patterned

Venter

DWARF WATERDOG   *Necturus punctatus*   p. 266
Identification: 4½–6¼; record 7¼. A southeastern Waterdog with no conspicuous markings of any kind. Dorsum is plain black (often purplish) or dark brown or with a few small pale spots. Throat whitish. Central portion of belly bluish white, plain or partly invaded by the dorsal color (Fig. 42, p. 199). *Four* toes on all 4 feet. *Young:* Colored as adults.
Found in sluggish streams, chiefly those with muddy or sandy banks and bottoms. Can sometimes be collected by stirring up bottom leaves and debris and then using a seine.
Similar species: Neuse River Waterdog and Alabama Waterdog are conspicuously spotted. Larvae of the Mole Salamanders have *five* toes on each *hind* foot.
Range: Coastal Plain from Virginia to Alabama.
Subspecies: DWARF WATERDOG, *Necturus punctatus punctatus* (illustrated on Plate 35). As described above. Streams of Atlantic drainage from extr. se. Virginia to cent. Georgia. MOBILE WATERDOG, *Necturus punctatus lodingi.* Similar but usually lighter in color, varying from russet to dark brown. Dorsum nearly uniform dark or with a marbled appearance (at least on sides). There may be dark spots, but these usually are vague and difficult to distinguish. Small scattered light spots usually present. Center of belly bluish white. Chin and sides of throat grayish brown. Maximum length about 6¾″. Streams

of Gulf drainage from w.-cent. Georgia to vicinity of Mobile, Alabama. Map 155

GREATER SIREN *Siren lacertina* p. 266
Identification: 20–30; record 36. An "eel" with forelegs and external gills; these appendages are crowded together instead of being spread out along the slender body. The legs, so small that they are easily hidden by the gills, have *four* toes each. General coloration olive to light gray, the back darker than sides, and the latter with rather faint greenish or yellowish dots and dashes. In some specimens circular, well-defined black spots may be seen on top of head, back, and sides. Belly with numerous small greenish or yellowish flecks. *Young:* A prominent light stripe on side of body plus a light dorsal fin make juveniles look superficially like Dwarf Sirens. Light markings disappear and young become almost uniformly dark as they approach maturity.

Lives in a large variety of essentially shallow water habitats — ditches, weed-choked or muddy ponds, rice fields, streams with clear to turbid water, lakes, etc. Often these salamanders may be observed at night with the aid of a flashlight as they forage about. Young ones sometimes abound amid roots of water hyacinths. Crayfish, worms, mollusks, etc., are eaten, but Sirens also engulf quantities of aquatic vegetation in the course of swallowing animal food.

Similar species: True eels (which are fishes) have a fin at each side of neck and no legs or external gills. Amphiumas also lack visible gills, but they have *four* small legs, a pair aft as well as forward. Dwarf Sirens have only *three* toes on each leg. Difficulty will inevitably arise in trying to distinguish small Greater Sirens from adults of Eastern Lesser Siren — even experts have trouble! Eastern Lesser Siren lacks any pronounced light markings; counting costal grooves will help, these being 36 to 39 in Greater Siren (from armpit to anus), and from 31 to 34 in Eastern Lesser Siren. Checking on costal grooves is always difficult on a live salamander. Let your Siren settle down in an aquarium and don't touch it when you count.

Range: Washington, D.C., to extr. s. Florida and s. Alabama. Map 157

LESSER SIREN *Siren intermedia* p. 266
Identification: 7–24½ (varies — see subspecies). Like the Greater Siren in general appearance and in having external gills and 2 tiny front legs, each with *four* toes. General dorsal coloration dark brown to bluish black, sometimes olive-green. Darker specimens are virtually without markings, but in the lighter ones irregularly scattered black dots are discernible. *Young:* A red band across snout and along the side of head. These markings disappear with age; older juveniles may be olive-green with tiny brown spots.

This eel-like salamander spends the daylight hours burrowed in debris that accumulates at bottoms of ditches, ponds, and other bodies of shallow water. When the water dries up it descends into the mud, and when that, in turn, dries over, the Siren becomes entombed and must wait in estivation, sometimes for months, until the coming of rains. Food similar to that of Greater Siren.

Similar species: See Greater Siren.

Range: South Carolina to cent. Florida; west to e. and s. Texas and north in Mississippi Valley to Indiana and Illinois.

Subspecies: EASTERN LESSER SIREN, *Siren intermedia intermedia* (illustrated on Plate 35). Plain black or brown above or with minute black dots sprinkled over dorsal surface and tail; venter uniformly dark but paler than dorsum; costal grooves 31 to 34; averages small, with a maximum length of 15″. S. Atlantic and Gulf Coastal Plains to extr. e. Louisiana. WESTERN LESSER SIREN, *Siren intermedia nettingi.* Olive or gray above with scattered, minute black spots; venter dark with numerous *light spots*; costal grooves 34 to 36; averages slightly larger — record 16⅞″. Mississippi Valley; west to e. Texas. RIO GRANDE SIREN, *Siren intermedia texana.* Gray or brownish gray above and marked with tiny black flecks; venter light gray but paler under gills and limbs, around vent, and behind the angles of jaws; costal grooves 36 to 38; size large — record 24½″. Lower Rio Grande Valley and n. Tamaulipas.

Map 156

Dwarf Sirens: Genus *Pseudobranchus*

THESE ARE small, aquatic, eel-like salamanders with external gills and tiny forelegs. Each foot bears *three* toes. All are patterned with longitudinal stripes. Just as is true among the Waterdogs, the size of the gills depends upon temperature and other conditions. This is one of the groups of animals that has prospered by the introduction of the water hyacinth, for Dwarf Sirens find food and shelter among the roots of these floating pests. A good collecting technique is to roll up masses of hyacinths or slide a large box-like sieve of fine-mesh wire under a patch of them and carry them ashore. Careful sorting through the lot often may reveal Dwarf Sirens. (There is a good chance of finding some small aquatic snakes at the same time.) The genus *Pseudobranchus* occurs only in the extreme southeastern United States. There is a single species, but there are several races.

NARROW-STRIPED DWARF SIREN
Pseudobranchus striatus axanthus p. 270

Identification: 4¾–7½; record 8¼. The only one of the Dwarf

Sirens in which there are no sharply defined light stripes (Fig. 44, below). Entire animal looks "muddy," and it may be difficult to make out pattern details. Body slender and elongate and head terminates in a bluntly rounded snout. *Three* toes on each foot.

Extraordinarily abundant in many of the marshes, ditches, and other shallow bodies of water choked with hyacinths.

Similar species: Both Greater and Lesser Sirens have *four* toes on each foot.

Range: N. and cent. Florida and into the Okefenokee region, Georgia. This subspecies intergrades with all four other races.

Map 158

SLENDER DWARF SIREN
Pseudobranchus striatus spheniscus   p. 270

Identification: 4–6. A tiny slender "eel" with a narrow, wedge-shaped snout, and 2 bright tan or yellow stripes on sides of body. Stripes on the various races of Dwarf Sirens are most easily seen when these salamanders are submerged in water. Put them in a flat-sided aquarium when trying to identify the various subspecies.

A resident of shallow lime-sink ponds of small or medium size, especially those containing numbers of black gum and cypress trees, but also occurring in a variety of other aquatic habitats. Best found by seining up and examining detritus from the pond bottoms. The other races occur in a wide variety of shallow fresh-water habitats.

Similar species: Greater and Lesser Sirens have *four* toes on each foot. Dwarf Sirens have only *three*.

Range: Sw. Georgia and e. half of Florida panhandle.

Fig. 44. PATTERNS OF DWARF SIRENS

(Each diagram shows a section of skin removed from the animal and flattened out — dorsum in center, venter at the sides)

BROAD-STRIPED
Dark middorsal stripe
flanked by broad yellow one

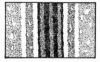

SLENDER
2 tan or yellow
stripes on each side

EVERGLADES
Lateral stripe buff;
belly gray

GULF HAMMOCK
3 narrow yellow
stripes in dark middorsal
region; belly blackish

NARROW-STRIPED
Dark stripes narrow,
subdued

Subspecies: All of these are strongly striped (Fig. 44, p. 204). BROAD-STRIPED DWARF SIREN, *Pseudobranchus striatus striatus*. Most strikingly patterned of all the races; a broad dark brown middorsal stripe with a vague light line down its center and flanked on each side by a broad yellow stripe; belly dark but heavily mottled with yellow; length up to 6". Extr. s. South Carolina and se. Georgia. GULF HAMMOCK DWARF SIREN, *Pseudobranchus striatus lustricolus*. A broad dark middorsal stripe containing *within itself* 3 narrow light stripes, the central one down ridge of back; 2 broad sharply defined light stripes on each side of body, upper one orange-brown in coloration and lower one silvery white; belly black with light mottling; body relatively stout, snout blunt; length up to 8½". Gulf Hammock region on nw. side of Florida peninsula. EVERGLADES DWARF SIREN, *Pseudobranchus striatus belli*. Similar in stripe pattern to Gulf Hammock race, but with the broad light stripes buff in color and belly gray; a small, slender subspecies with length up to 6". Southern third of Florida peninsula. Map 158

AMPHIUMA *Amphiuma means* p. 266

Identification: 13–30; record 40. An "eel" with 2 pairs of tiny, useless-looking legs. Dorsum dark brown to black. This is the "congo (conger) eel," "lamper eel," or "ditch eel" of fishermen and country folk. (The same names are often applied to both species of *Siren*.)

Almost completely aquatic, but occasionally moves overland through swamps on rainy nights. Habitats include ditches, sloughs, pools, ponds, rice fields, swamps, streams, etc. Many specimens utilize lairs in mud or jumbles of bottom debris, protruding their heads a short distance upward or outward from their hiding places while waiting for crayfish or other food to come along. Best sought at night in shallow water. A dip net with a deep bag, although rather awkward to use on such slippery, elongated animals, is the safest tool with which to catch them unharmed. They can bite savagely. Another technique is to cover your hand with burlap sacking or wear a stout glove, grab the Amphiuma at midbody, and sling it out on land where you can work it into a bag. Food includes worms, insects, mollusks, crustaceans, small fishes, snakes, frogs, and smaller Amphiumas.

Similar species: True eels (fishes) have a fin at each side of head and no legs. Sirens have external gills and *no hind legs*.

Range: Coastal Plain from Virginia to the s. tip of Florida and west to se. Texas; north to Missouri in Mississippi Valley.

Subspecies: TWO-TOED AMPHIUMA, *Amphiuma means means*. *Two toes* on each limb; no sharp change of color between back and belly; venter dark gray. Se. Virginia to extr. s. Florida and west to s. Mississippi. THREE-TOED AMPHIUMA,

WATER SNAKES (1)

(Keeled scales and divided anal plates. The rectangles show belly colors and patterns.)

Map Text

BLOTCHED WATER SNAKE (young)   89 117
  Dark spots on neck alternate with dorsal blotches.

NORTHERN WATER SNAKE (young)   85 117
  Dark spots on neck join dorsal blotches to form crossbands.

MIDLAND WATER SNAKE   85 118
  Dark markings *smaller* than spaces between them. *Belly:*
  Double row of half-moons or crescents.

NORTHERN WATER SNAKE   85 117
  Dark markings *larger* than spaces between them. *Belly:*
  Highly variable; half-moons paired, scattered, or virtually
  absent.

FLORIDA WATER SNAKE   84 120
  Eye stripe (Fig. 27, p. 119); black, brown, or red crossbands; often secondary dark spots on sides. *Belly:* Wavy,
  wormlike crosslines.

BANDED WATER SNAKE   84 119
  Eye stripe (Fig. 27, p. 119); black, brown, or red crossbands throughout length of body. *Black phase:* Usually
  some red showing on sides. *Belly:* Largest markings
  squarish.

BROAD-BANDED WATER SNAKE   84 119
  Eye stripe (Fig. 27, p. 119); dark crossbands *much* wider
  than light interspaces. *Belly:* Large squarish markings,
  red to black in coloration.

RED-BELLIED WATER SNAKE   89 115
  Plain brown above. *Belly:* Red or orange.

BLOTCHED WATER SNAKE   89 117
  Dark lateral spots alternate with dorsal blotches throughout length of body. *Belly:* Yellow with faint suggestions
  of spots.

YELLOW-BELLIED WATER SNAKE   89 116
  Plain gray or greenish above. *Belly:* Yellow.

BLOTCHED NORTHERN

MIDLAND

NORTHERN

Color Variations

Black Phase

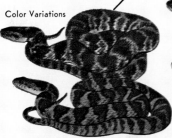

FLORIDA

BANDED

BROAD-BANDED

RED-BELLIED

BLOTCHED

YELLOW-BELLIED

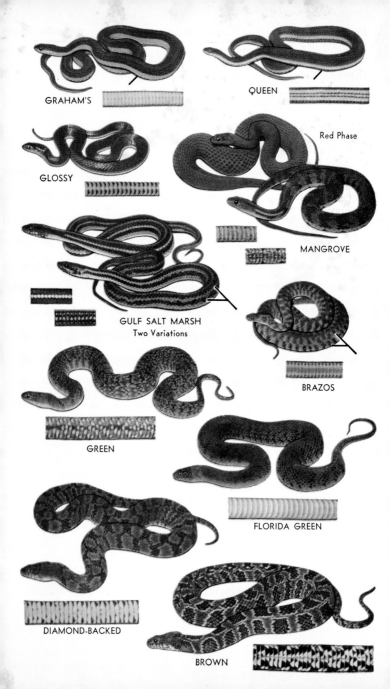

GRAHAM'S

QUEEN

GLOSSY

Red Phase

MANGROVE

GULF SALT MARSH
Two Variations

BRAZOS

GREEN

FLORIDA GREEN

DIAMOND-BACKED

BROWN

Plate 26   207

WATER SNAKES (2)

(Keeled scales and divided anal plates. The rectangles show belly colors and patterns.)

Map Text

GRAHAM'S WATER SNAKE   90   123
    Broad yellowish stripe. *Belly:* Plain or with a central row
    of dark dots.

QUEEN SNAKE   91   122
    Yellowish stripe. *Belly:* 4 brown stripes.

GLOSSY WATER SNAKE   93   123
    Shiny, often with traces of stripes. *Belly:* Double row of
    large black half-moons.

MANGROVE WATER SNAKE   87   121
    Irregular dark markings above and below; highly variable
    (see text). *Red phase:* Red or orange-red, both on back
    and belly.

GULF SALT MARSH SNAKE   87   120
    2 *dark* stripes on each side of body. *Belly:* A row of light
    spots (sometimes 3 rows).

BRAZOS WATER SNAKE   88   122
    2 rows of spots on each side of body. *Belly:* Pink center;
    row of dark dots down each side.

GREEN WATER SNAKE   95   113
    No distinctive pattern; a row of scales between lip plates
    and eye (Fig. 27, p. 119). *Belly:* Light half-moons on dark
    ground.

FLORIDA GREEN WATER SNAKE   95   114
    No distinctive pattern; a row of scales between lip plates
    and eye (Fig. 27, p. 119). *Belly:* Light, virtually uni-
    colored.

DIAMOND-BACKED WATER SNAKE   92   115
    Dark chainlike pattern (Fig. 25, p. 115). *Belly:* Yellow,
    largest dark spots concentrated chiefly at sides.

BROWN WATER SNAKE   94   114
    Dark middorsal blotches separate from lateral blotches
    (Fig. 25, p. 115). *Belly:* Heavy dark markings on yellow
    ground color.

Amphiuma means tridactylum. Three toes on each limb; dorsum dark brown and sharply set off from much paler (light gray) venter; a dark throat patch. Se. Missouri and extr. se. Oklahoma to Gulf of Mexico.   Map 152

MOLE SALAMANDERS:
FAMILY AMBYSTOMIDAE

LIKE MOLES, these amphibians stay underground most of their lives. But during the breeding season they congregate in numbers for courtship and deposition of eggs, activities that may be completed in one or just a few nights. Looking for them in the North usually requires donning hip boots, dressing warmly, and wading in icy water with seine or dip net. After the first early warm spring rains, examine any small shallow ponds in your neighborhood — woodland or pasture pools, etc. The eggs may be laid in large clusters or in small groups, floating at the surface of the water or submerged and attached to sticks or debris. The style depends upon the species. Some kinds breed in autumn; in the South, most egg-laying takes place in winter.

Finding specimens before or after the breeding season is largely a matter of chance. They may sally forth on rainy nights, prowling in the darkness but taking shelter before morning beneath boards or logs unless they accidentally tumble into cellar window wells or ditches.

The larvae of some kinds grow to large size, retain their gills, remain permanently aquatic, and breed without developing all the adult characteristics. Such specimens technically are said to be neotenic, but the Mexican Indians have given us the name axolotl for them (Fig., p. 259). Newly transformed salamanders of this genus are often difficult to identify.

Some of the Mole Salamanders bear a resemblance to certain of the Lungless Salamanders (Plethodontidae), but members of the latter family have a groove running from the nostril down to the lip (check with a lens) — see back endpaper.

The family Ambystomidae occurs throughout most of the United States and ranges from extreme southeastern Alaska, James Bay, and southern Labrador to the southern edge of the Mexican Plateau. Its members are widely studied as laboratory animals. In captivity they are easily maintained in terrariums equipped with a few inches of damp earth. They will eat live earthworms and other invertebrates, and some can be trained to accept small pieces of meat.

RINGED SALAMANDER *Ambystoma annulatum*   p. 259
   Identification: 5½–7; record 8. Any of the rings may be incomplete, interrupted across the back, or represented solely by

vertical light bars or elongated spots. Coloration variable from medium dark brown to almost black; rings may be buff, yellow, or whitish, sometimes not all same color on same animal. A light gray, rather irregular stripe along lower side of body.

Seldom encountered except during or following medium to heavy rains. These stimulate the salamanders into forming breeding congresses of scores or even hundreds in pools or shallow ponds.

Similar species: Marbled Salamander is a shorter, stouter amphibian, and its crossbands are broader and may have a silvery appearance.

Range: Cent. Missouri, w. Arkansas, and e. Oklahoma. Map 168

FROSTED FLATWOODS SALAMANDER
Ambystoma cingulatum cingulatum   p. 259

Identification: 3½–4¼. The dorsal markings, "frosted" or lichen-like in appearance, are grayish on a black ground color and show some tendency to form a netlike pattern. Belly black with *scattered* pearl-gray spots.

Both Flatwoods Salamanders are inhabitants of slashpine-wiregrass flatwoods. Look for them in or under objects near the small shallow cypress ponds characteristic of such areas.

Similar species: Mabee's Salamander is often brownish and with light flecks most conspicuous along the sides; not patterned "all over" as is the Frosted. If in doubt check jaw teeth; they are in a single row in Mabee's, in multiple rows in the two Flatwoods Salamanders. Slimy Salamander has a groove from nostril to lip.

Range: Extr. s. North Carolina to ne. Florida.   Map 166

RETICULATED FLATWOODS SALAMANDER
Ambystoma cingulatum bishopi   p. 259

Identification: 3½–4½. The dorsal markings vary from a completely netlike (reticulated) pattern to a series of narrow light rings. Ground color chocolate-black; markings gray or brownish gray. Belly black with a multitude of tiny gray flecks producing a *salt-and-pepper* appearance.

Similar species: The light spots are larger and well separated on belly of eastern subspecies, Frosted Flatwoods Salamander. Slimy Salamander has groove from nostril to lip and its skin-gland secretions stick like glue to one's fingers.

Range: Gulf Coastal Plain through the Florida panhandle to vicinity of Mobile, Alabama.   Map 166

JEFFERSON SALAMANDER *Ambystoma jeffersonianum* p. 259

Identification: 4¼–7; record 8¼. The long toes and relatively slender build are the best things to look for in this otherwise non-descript salamander. Dorsal ground color dark brown or gray, the belly lighter. Small pale bluish flecks, concentrated chiefly on sides of head, body, and tail and also on throat, are usually present. Bluish markings conspicuous in small specimens; they may be virtually absent in large adults.

An early spring breeder, and northernmost member of the Mole Salamander group in the East. Named for Jefferson College, Canonsburg, Pennsylvania, hence indirectly for the excellent naturalist who attained the Presidency — Thomas Jefferson.

Similar species: See Blue-spotted Salamander (below). In much of the area where ranges of Jefferson and Small-mouthed Salamanders overlap, the latter also is virtually unicolored. The Smallmouth is short and rather plump, has a short snout, and much shorter toes. Some of the Lungless Salamanders are also dark and unpatterned, but all bear the hallmark of their family—a groove from nostril downward to lip.

Range: S. Labrador to se. Manitoba and south to Virginia and Kentucky.   Map 162

BLUE-SPOTTED SALAMANDER *Ambystoma laterale*   p. 259
  Identification: 4–6; record 6¼. Many specimens would match the enamelware of yesteryear, of dishpans and pots, with their flecks and spots of white and blue on bluish black. The long toes, relatively long snout, blue to bluish-white flecks on back, and (often) bluish-white spots on sides of trunk and tail will usually distinguish this species from all others except the Jefferson Salamander (see below). Dorsal ground color dark brown to black; venter dark gray or grayish brown.

Breeds in spring in small ponds, ditches, etc.

Similar species: Small-mouthed Salamander has short snout and short toes. Slimy Salamander has groove from mouth to nostril.

Blue-spotted and Jefferson Salamanders are easily confused. Not only do they look very similar, but they also hybridize (almost 100 per cent of the hybrids are females). The Blue-spot normally is profusely marked with *spots*, whereas light markings in the virtually unicolored Jefferson are confined to bluish *flecks* along the sides. Markings in hybrids are intermediate, both in number and intensity. The Blue-spot is a dark animal (ground color black or dark brown); the Jefferson may also be dark brown, but it tends to be paler — brownish gray or lead-colored. Toes are much longer in the Jefferson, and it is a bigger, proportionately more slender animal when fully grown.

Range: The ease with which the Jefferson and Blue-spotted Salamanders may be confused makes it impossible to trust all the published records for them. A large number of specimens of *laterale* have been reported in the scientific literature as *jeffersonianum*. Therefore, no separate distribution map has been prepared. Map 162 is a composite of the two species whose ranges widely overlap. In general, the Blue-spotted Salamander is to be expected only in more western and northern portions of the range indicated.   Map 162

SMALL-MOUTHED SALAMANDER *Ambystoma texanum* p. 259
Identification: 4½–5½; record 9¼. Well-named; both mouth and head are small. Ground color black or very dark brown. Usually a pattern of grayish lichen-like markings, but these are extremely variable in intensity. Many specimens have the markings concentrated upon the back and upper sides. Some, especially toward northeastern part of range, are almost plain black. Texas specimens are very heavily speckled, with the light markings especially large and prominent on the lower sides.
   A spring breeder and frequently found at that season under logs, boards, or other debris near ponds or swamps, in river bottoms, or other situations where moisture is abundant.
Similar species: Jefferson Salamander has *much* longer toes and a longer snout and head. Rule out any Lungless Salamander that may be similarly marked or colored by checking for groove from nostril to lip.
Range: Ohio to s. Iowa and south to the Gulf.   Map 164

MABEE'S SALAMANDER. *Ambystoma mabeei*   p. 259
Identification: 3–4. The light specks are palest and most conspicuous along the sides. Dorsal ground color chiefly deep brown to black; belly dark brown or gray. Note long toes and small head. Jaw teeth are in a single row.
   Named for W. B. Mabee, who collected the first specimen made known to science.
Similar species: Mole Salamander has a conspicuously large head. Slimy Salamander has groove from nostril to lip. Frosted Flatwoods Salamander is "frosted" all over, not just conspicuously along sides; if in doubt, check jaw teeth, which (in the Frosted) are in multiple rows.
Range: Coastal Plain of the Carolinas.   Map 160

MOLE SALAMANDER *Ambystoma talpoideum*   p. 259
Identification: 3–4. Looks like a case of arrested growth, with head and feet too large for the rest of the animal. Ground color brown or gray; pale flecks bluish white.
   A confirmed burrower, but occasionally found under logs or other objects in damp places. Occasionally neotenic.
Range: South Carolina to n. Florida and Louisiana; disjunct colonies in se. Oklahoma, s. Illinois to w. Tennessee and Arkansas, and in valleys of w. North Carolina and adj. Tennessee.   Map 167

MARBLED SALAMANDER *Ambystoma opacum*   p. 259
Identification: 3½–4¼; record 5. "Silvery salamander" would

be a good alternate name. The light markings, basically cross-bands, are variable, being sometimes incomplete, running together, or enclosing dark spots. On rare occasions there may be a light stripe along or parallel to the middorsal line. Markings gray in females, white in males; in both sexes they contrast strongly with the black components of the pattern and the plain black belly. *Newly transformed juveniles:* Scattered light flecks on a dorsal ground color of dull brown to black.

This rather chunky salamander occurs in a variety of habitats, ranging from moist sandy areas to dry hillsides. Breeds in *autumn*, the female depositing her eggs in a low depression, which will be filled by the next good rain. Eggs, laid in a group but unattached to one another, do not hatch until covered with water. Until then they are guarded by female.

Similar species: Ringed and Reticulated Flatwoods Salamanders are more slender, and their light rings or crossbands are narrow.
Range: New England to n. Florida and west to e. Texas. Map 165

SPOTTED SALAMANDER *Ambystoma maculatum* p. 259
Identification: 6–7¾; record 9. The round light spots, yellow or orange in coloration, are arranged in an irregular *row* along each side of the back, from eye to tail tip. Dorsal ground color black, slate, or bluish black; *belly slate-gray.*

An early spring breeder which, under stimulus of warm rains, sometimes makes mass migrations to woodland ponds. Occasionally found (from spring to autumn) beneath stones or boards in moist environments or during wet weather.
Similar species: Light spots on Eastern Tiger Salamander are irregular, often elongated, and extend far down on sides. The Tiger also has an *olive-yellow belly.*
Range: Nova Scotia and Gaspé Peninsula to cent. Ontario; south to Georgia and e. Texas. Map 163

EASTERN TIGER SALAMANDER
Ambystoma tigrinum tigrinum p. 259
Identification: 7–8¼; record 13. The light spots, olive- or yellowish-brown, are highly irregular in shape and distribution, and extend well downward upon the sides. Dorsal ground color dull black to deep brown; *belly olive-yellow,* marbled with darker pigment.

A very early spring breeder, usually congregating in deeper water than does the Spotted Salamander. Larvae are often common in farm ponds — until such ponds are stocked with fish! **Similar species:** In the Spotted Salamander the light spots form an irregular *row* and belly is gray.
Range: Long Island to n. Florida; Ohio to Minnesota and south to the Gulf; absent from most of Appalachian uplands.
Map 169

BARRED TIGER SALAMANDER

Ambystoma tigrinum mavortium p. 259

Identification: 6–8; record 10. Typically with light vertical bars running upward from belly to midline of back. Highly variable, however, the light markings taking many shapes and forms, but in general being larger in size and fewer in number than the light markings on the Eastern Tiger. Ground color black or dark brown; markings yellowish, bright on sides but diffused with darker pigment on back. Belly black and yellow.

Often neotenic, especially toward the west, where the immediate environs of a pond may become completely dry and inhospitable. Neotenic (or larval) specimens may attain great size; one measuring almost 13″ is on record.

Similar species: Some specimens resemble Ringed Salamanders. In the Barred Tiger, dark pigment extends all the way from back to belly; in the Ringed, the black is interrupted by a light grayish stripe along lower side of body.

Range: Cent. Nebraska to ne. Mexico.

Subspecies: BLOTCHED TIGER SALAMANDER, *Ambystoma tigrinum melanostictum.* A race in which the dark ground color (brown to black) is reduced to a network; light areas dull yellow and with indefinite borders. Slightly smaller on the average than the Barred Tiger. Nebraska to Washington and s.-cent. Alberta. GRAY TIGER SALAMANDER, *Ambystoma tigrinum diaboli.* Ground color light olive; scattered circular black spots on back and sides. Large — up to 11¼″ and to 12¼″ in the larval form. Often neotenic. Sw. Minnesota to s. Manitoba and s. Saskatchewan. Western subspecies. Map 169

NEWTS: FAMILY SALAMANDRIDAE

NEWTS ARE not so slippery as most salamanders. Their skins are rougher and not slimy, and they do not slide easily through your fingers when you try to catch them. The costal grooves, that are prominent in most other salamanders, are indistinct.

Most Newts are essentially aquatic, but there is also a land stage, like the Red Eft form of the Red-spotted Newt. The larvae transform into efts, which remain ashore for one to three years; they then return to the water and change into the aquatic adults. Sometimes the land stage is omitted, and the larvae transform directly into adults, in which case remnants of the external gills may be retained. The tails of efts are almost round in cross section, and their skins are quite rough; the tails of adults are vertically compressed and their skins are much smoother.

Natural food includes insects, leeches, worms, tiny mollusks and crustaceans, young amphibians, and frogs' eggs. Captive aquatic adults will eat small pieces of meat, but crumbs of canned dog food make a better balanced diet. Efts respond most readily to live insects. Few predators will eat Newts, for their skin-gland secretions are toxic or at least irritating to mucous membranes.

There are three species in eastern North America. Other members of this large family occur in the Pacific states and provinces (southeastern Alaska to northwestern Baja California), in Europe, North Africa, and Asia.

RED-SPOTTED NEWT
Diemictylus viridescens viridescens   p. 270

Identification: 2⅞–4; record 5. The red spots are variable in number and position, but are present at all stages of the complex life history. The aquatic adults, although normally olive-green, may vary from yellowish brown to dark greenish brown. Their venters are yellow with small black spots. *Male:* Both the high tail fin and black excrescences on the legs disappear after the spring breeding season, but they may develop again as early as the following autumn. *Red Eft:* 1⅜″ to 3⅜″. Bright orange-red to dull red or orange, the most brilliantly colored ones usually occurring in moist forested mountains or other upland habitats. Individuals recently transformed from the larval to eft stage may be yellowish brown or dull reddish brown. Specimens transforming to adult form (or aquatic adults that have had to live out of water, as when ponds dry up) may be very dark, even almost black.

Ponds, small lakes, marshes, ditches, quiet portions of streams, or other shallow permanent or semipermanent bodies of water are the most frequent habitats during aquatic stages. Adults may be seen resting motionless or swimming about slowly in open water or crawling on bottom or through vegetation. Often they remain active all winter and may be observed through the ice. The terrestrial efts, although avoiding direct sunlight, are extraordinarily bold, often walking about in the open on the forest floor in broad daylight. After summer showers in mountainous regions they sometimes may be seen by scores or even hundreds. In many areas, notably on the Coastal Plain, the land stage may be omitted.

Similar species: Most other small salamanders have slimy skins and conspicuous costal grooves.

Range: Maritime Provinces to Great Lakes and south to Apalachicola drainage of Florida.   Map 159

CENTRAL NEWT
Diemictylus viridescens louisianensis   p. 270

Identification: 2½–4. A small, more slender race of the Red-spotted Newt, but normally *without red spots*. If such spots are present they are small or only partly outlined by black. The dorsal ground color varies from olive-green to yellowish- or olive-brown, and is sharply cut off from the yellow venter.

A newt of swales and swamplands, of woodland ponds and ditches, and of river bottoms in the South. The eft or land stage is usually uncommon in comparison with its abundance in the Red-spotted Newt.

Similar species: See Red-spotted Newt.

Range: Lake Superior to e. Texas and east to s. South Carolina. This race intergrades with the Red-spotted subspecies over a broad area from Michigan to and through the Deep South.

Map 159

PENINSULA NEWT *Diemictylus viridescens piaropicola* p. 270
Identification: 3–4⅛. This is a dusky newt from Florida with a dark olive, dark brown, or almost black dorsum, and a venter finely peppered with black specks on a ground color of yellow or orange-yellow.

An inhabitant of ponds, ditches, swamps, and virtually any other standing body of water. Often abundant in canals or sloughs choked with hyacinths, or in submerged aquatic vegetation of cypress-bordered ponds. Terrestrial individuals may be found ashore under logs or debris.

Range: Peninsular Florida. Map 159

BROKEN-STRIPED NEWT
Diemictylus viridescens dorsalis p. 270
Identification: 2½–3⅜. The black-bordered red stripe is broken in at least 1 or 2 places on head and trunk; it rarely extends onto tail. There may also be a row of small red spots on lower sides of body and a light line down center of back. *Eft:* Reddish brown; red stripes not so strongly bordered by black as in the adults.

Found in pools, ponds, ditches, quiet portions of streams, etc., the efts under logs, boards, or other shelters in damp places.

Range: Coastal Plain in the Carolinas. Map 159

STRIPED NEWT *Diemictylus perstriatus* p. 270
Identification: 2–3⅛. The red stripe is continuous on the head and trunk, but it may break into fragments on the tail. It varies in coloration from bright to dull red, but the red may be partly obscured by dusky pigment. The stripe is dark-bordered, but not so boldly and evenly as in Broken-striped Newt. There may be a row of red spots along the side of body and a faint light stripe down center of back. Dorsal ground color olive-green to dark brown. *Eft:* Orange-red but also with red stripes like those of the adults.

Generally to be found in almost any body of shallow, standing water; the efts remain ashore but near such habitats.

Range: N. Florida and s. Georgia. Map 161

BLACK-SPOTTED NEWT *Diemictylus meridionalis* p. 270
Identification: 3–4⅛. The large black spots — on both dorsum and venter — give this salamander its name. The yellowish stripes are wavy or uneven, and often there is a suggestion of a brown or russet stripe down the center of the back. No red spots. Venter orange or bright yellow.

A resident of ponds, lagoons, and swampy areas — habitats that are not abundant in its rather arid homeland.
Similar species: Central Newt has much smaller dark spots and *no stripes*.
Range: S. Texas and adj. Mexico. Map 161

LUNGLESS SALAMANDERS:
FAMILY PLETHODONTIDAE

LUNGS ARE absent and respiration is accomplished through the skin and the lining of the mouth. There is a groove extending downward from the eye to the edge of the mouth (the naso-labial groove — see back endpaper), but this is so small that a lens may be needed to reveal it. In some forms there are cirri, downward projections from the nostrils beyond the mouth line, and the groove follows these.

To this family belong such abundant groups as the Dusky, Brook, and Woodland Salamanders and their allies (genera *Desmognathus*, below, to *Manculus*, p. 251, inclusive). The family ranges from southern Canada to northern South America, and is also represented in Europe.

Some herpetologists split the family into two parts. One, the Subfamily Desmognathinae, would include only the Dusky Salamanders (*Desmognathus*) and the closely allied Shovel-nosed Salamanders (*Leurognathus*). In both, the lower jaw is immovable, thus stiffening the front part of the body so that the salamander can more readily force its way under things. The mouth is opened by lifting the upper jaw and head. All other members of the group would be classified in the Subfamily Plethodontinae.

Dusky Salamanders: Genus *Desmognathus*

IDENTIFYING these salamanders is like working with fall warblers — only worse! Added to changes in coloration and pattern, associated with age and size, are bewildering individual variations plus differences between one local population and the next.

Pay strict attention to ranges to eliminate those not found in your vicinity. If possible, do what professional herpetologists do — collect a small series to learn how much the population varies in your area. Among them may be a specimen or two that will match the illustrations closely enough to furnish a clue.

There is usually *a pale diagonal line from eye to angle of jaw* (Fig., p. 258). This may be absent, however, in old, dark adults or in those specimens where it is obscured by dark *or* light pigment. The hind legs are larger and stouter than the forelegs; the body is relatively short and stout. Dusky Salamanders are accomplished jumpers, often leaping several times their own length in their efforts to escape.

Members of this genus are found most commonly in or near brooks, rills, mountain cascades, springs, or seeps, but are usually absent from larger streams where predatory fishes occur. Collectively, they reach their greatest abundance in the Appalachian region. The Allegheny Mountain and Blue Ridge Mountain Salamanders frequently wander far out into humid forest areas, especially during wet weather. The Pigmy Salamander is terrestrial.

Similar species: In the Woodland Salamanders (*Plethodon*) the body is long and slender, and the hind legs are about the same size as the forelegs (Fig., p. 258). The Shovel-nosed Salamanders (*Leurognathus*) have smaller eyes and more wedge-shaped heads. The Mole Salamanders (*Ambystoma*) lack the naso-labial groove common to *Desmognathus* and all other Lungless Salamanders (Family Plethodontidae) — see illustrations on back endpaper.

NORTHERN DUSKY SALAMANDER

Desmognathus fuscus fuscus   p. 258

Identification: 2½–4½; record 5¼. An *extremely* variable salamander. General coloration gray or brown, markings often not much darker than ground color. Pattern changes with age. The very young have 5 to 8 pairs of round yellowish spots on the back bordered by a dark *wavy* band (Fig. 45, p. 218); similar markings continue onto tail. The pattern breaks up as the animal grows older, the darker remnants of it appearing as spots or streaks. Base of tail usually lighter (olive, yellowish, or bright chestnut) than rest of dorsum and bordered by dark scallops. Old adults may be almost uniform gray with markings reduced to scattered dark spots. Venter variable, but usually lightly mottled with gray or brown; dark pigment of sides of body may encroach on edges of belly. Tail compressed and knife-edged above; a little less than ½ total length.

A very abundant species, occurring in brooks, near springs, and in seepage areas. Perhaps most common along edges of small woodland streams where stones, chunks of wood, and miscellaneous debris provide ample shelter both for the salamanders and their food. Seldom wanders far from running or trickling water.

Similar species: See main heading for Dusky Salamander

(p. 216) for ways of distinguishing *Desmognathus* from species of other genera. Other members of Dusky group may be confusingly similar. In the Blue Ridge and Allegheny Mountain Salamanders the tail is round (not knife-edged on top). Also in the Allegheny, there is a light middorsal stripe with a *straight* dark border on each side. Seal Salamanders have heavy black or dark brown spots. Black-bellied Salamander not only has an ebony venter, but possesses 2 rows of light dots on each side of body. The Shovel-nosed Salamanders are strictly aquatic. Check ranges: Northern Dusky is the only member of its genus occurring in many parts of the North.

Range: S. New Brunswick to s. Illinois and Alabama; south through the Apalachicola drainage system to Gulf of Mexico. Altitudinally, from virtually sea level to high mountains of Appalachians.

Subspecies: BLACK MOUNTAIN DUSKY SALAMANDER, *Desmognathus fuscus welteri.* Size large — up to 6½″. Belly darker, with dark spots or irregular markings. Dorsum with numerous brown to black irregular blotches. E. Kentucky and adj. Virginia.   Map 171

Fig. 45. DORSAL PATTERNS OF YOUNG DUSKY SALAMANDERS

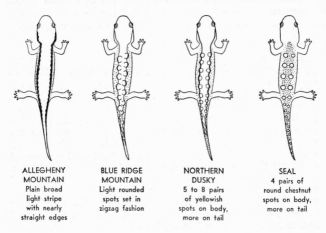

ALLEGHENY MOUNTAIN	BLUE RIDGE MOUNTAIN	NORTHERN DUSKY	SEAL
Plain broad light stripe with nearly straight edges	Light rounded spots set in zigzag fashion	5 to 8 pairs of yellowish spots on body, more on tail	4 pairs of round chestnut spots on body, more on tail

SOUTHERN DUSKY SALAMANDER
Desmognathus fuscus auriculatus   p. 221

Identification: 3–4¼; record 4¾. A dark subspecies, with a row of "portholes" along each side of body. These consist of whitish or reddish spots, but they may be irregular in placement, arranged in a double row, or even obscure in darkest specimens.

General dorsal coloration dark brown or black; belly black or very dark brown, but sprinkled with distinct white dots.

Often found near cypress ponds or in stagnant or nearly stagnant pools, the environment muddy and (chemically) slightly acid.

Range: Coastal Plain, Virginia to Louisiana.   Map 171

PENINSULA DUSKY SALAMANDER
Desmognathus fuscus carri   p. 221

Identification: 2½–3½. A dwarf Florida race. Dorsum usually dark gray or brown, but sometimes light orange-brown. A broad light middorsal stripe. Venter light anteriorly, darker posteriorly. Usually a conspicuous reddish or orange spot below and behind eye.

Found in and near clear, cool, slightly alkaline water characteristic of small streams and seepage areas near big springs.

Range: Big Scrub region (Ocala National Forest) of Florida, south to Polk and Hillsborough Counties.   Map 171

CENTRAL DUSKY SALAMANDER
Desmognathus fuscus brimleyorum   p. 221

Identification: 3⅛–5½; record 7. Like a dark and poorly patterned Northern Dusky Salamander. No conspicuous markings; usually a row of small pale dots along each side of body; traces of light dorsal spots may be seen in many younger specimens. General dorsal coloration gray or brown; belly uniformly but lightly pigmented.

Range: Ouachita Mountains in Arkansas to Gulf of Mexico; intergrading with allied subspecies to east.   Map 171

FLAT-HEADED SALAMANDER
Desmognathus planiceps   Not illustrated

Identification: 3–5. A stout-bodied, aquatic salamander with a broad, black-bordered dorsal stripe. Head broad and decidedly flattened, ending in a blunt (spatulate) snout. General coloration dark brownish gray. Dorsal stripe straight-edged, reddish brown in color, but becoming zigzag and abruptly reddish on tail. Snout light tan. Chin, throat, and last 3d of belly spotted with brown.

Lives in cool mountain streams, especially in rocky, fast-flowing shallows.

Similar species: In the other large aquatic or semi-aquatic species (Shovel-nosed, Black-bellied, Seal, and Northern Dusky Salamanders) of Blue Ridge Mountains there is no sharply defined, straight-edged dorsal stripe. From other species of the region, the Flat-headed Salamander may be distinguished by its aquatic habitat.

Range: Mountain streams of s. part of Blue Ridge in Virginia.
                                                  Map 176

WOODLAND AND DUSKY SALAMANDERS (1)

Map *Text*

ALABAMA SALAMANDER   173   227
  Row of dark smudges within the light middorsal stripe;
  variable (see text).

CHEROKEE SALAMANDER   173   227
  Narrow dark middorsal line meeting *Y* on head; variable
  (see text).

PIGMY SALAMANDER   173   226
  Herringbone pattern; terrestrial.

ALLEGHENY MOUNTAIN SALAMANDER   174   224
  Middorsal light stripe with nearly *straight* dark borders;
  a central row of dark spots or chevrons.

BLUE RIDGE MOUNTAIN SALAMANDER   174   224
  Middorsal light stripe wavy; variable (see text).

CENTRAL DUSKY SALAMANDER   171   219
  No conspicuous markings; general coloration gray or
  brown.

SOUTHERN DUSKY SALAMANDER   171   218
  Generally dark appearance; row of light "portholes"
  along side of body.

PENINSULA DUSKY SALAMANDER   171   219
  Light middorsal stripe; a reddish or orange spot below
  and behind each eye.

CLIFFSIDE SALAMANDER   176   225
  Long, threadlike tail; 4 pairs of light spots on back (count
  from rear of forelegs to front of hind legs).

ZIGZAG SALAMANDER   180   231
  Middorsal stripe zigzag or wavy for at least part of length;
  belly mottled with orange or reddish.

RED-BACKED SALAMANDER   179   230
  Belly "salt-and-pepper" (Fig. 48, p. 231).
  Red-backed: Straight-edged reddish or orange middorsal
  stripe, the bright colors in sharp contrast with their dark
  borders.
  Lead-backed: Dorsum nearly plain dark.

OZARK RED-BACKED SALAMANDER   180   231
  Stripe narrow, without sharp edges. Ozark region.

OUACHITA RED-BACKED SALAMANDER   179   230
  Stripe saw-toothed. Ouachita Mountain region.

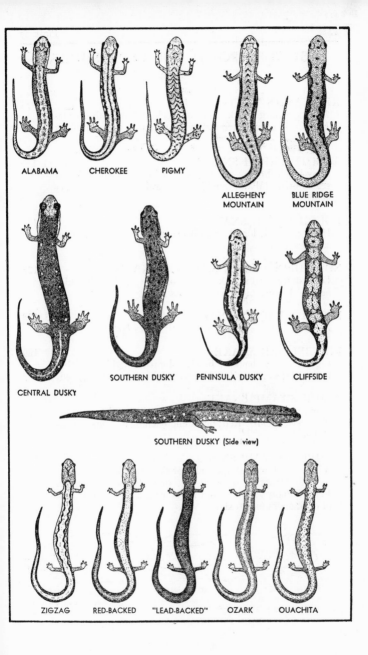

ALABAMA CHEROKEE PIGMY ALLEGHENY MOUNTAIN BLUE RIDGE MOUNTAIN

CENTRAL DUSKY SOUTHERN DUSKY PENINSULA DUSKY CLIFFSIDE

SOUTHERN DUSKY (Side view)

ZIGZAG RED-BACKED "LEAD-BACKED" OZARK OUACHITA

SWAMP, BROWN, AND EARTH SNAKES
(All have divided anal plates.)

Map Text

KIRTLAND'S WATER SNAKE   86 121
2 rows of large dark spots on each side of body; scales *keeled. Venter:* Brick-red with flanking rows of black spots.

SMOOTH EARTH SNAKE   81 136
Tiny black dots on a plain gray or brown dorsum; loreal scale horizontal and touching eye; scales *smooth* or *weakly keeled.*

ROUGH EARTH SNAKE   79 136
Head pointed; loreal scale horizontal and touching eye; scales *keeled.*

NORTHERN BROWN SNAKE (DEKAY'S)   83 125
Dark downward streak on side of head; no loreal; scales *keeled. Young:* Light band across neck.

FLORIDA BROWN SNAKE   83 128
Light band across head; no loreal; scales *keeled.*

RED-BELLIED SNAKE   82 129
Light spots at back of head; coloration highly variable (see text); scales *keeled. Venter:* Bright red or orange-red.

BLACK SWAMP SNAKE   80 124
Shiny black; scales *smooth* but with pale streaks that *look* like keels. *Venter:* Red; black encroaching on ends of ventral scales.

STRIPED SWAMP SNAKE   101 137
A broad yellowish stripe on lower side; a dark stripe down back and another on each side of body; scales *smooth. Venter:* Plain yellow or orange or with a midventral row of dark spots (see text).

EARTH SNAKE
Loreal scale horizontal
and touching eye

BROWN SNAKE
No loreal; postnasal
scale touches preocular

GROUND SNAKE
A loreal scale between
postnasal and preocular

Venter

Dorsum

KIRTLAND'S WATER

SMOOTH EARTH

ROUGH EARTH

Color Variations

FLORIDA BROWN

Young

NORTHERN BROWN

RED-BELLIED

Color Variations

Venter

Venter

Dorsum

BLACK SWAMP

Venter

Dorsum

STRIPED SWAMP

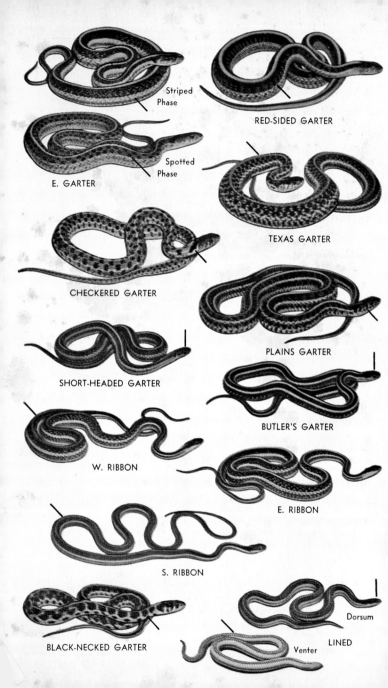

Striped Phase

RED-SIDED GARTER

E. GARTER

Spotted Phase

TEXAS GARTER

CHECKERED GARTER

PLAINS GARTER

SHORT-HEADED GARTER

BUTLER'S GARTER

W. RIBBON

E. RIBBON

S. RIBBON

BLACK-NECKED GARTER

Dorsum

Venter

LINED

Plate 28   223

GARTER SNAKES
(All have keeled scales and single anal plates.)

	Map	Text

EASTERN GARTER SNAKE   100   131
Stripe on rows 2 and 3; either spots or stripes may predominate.

RED-SIDED GARTER SNAKE   100   131
Red or orange bars; stripe on rows 2 and 3.

TEXAS GARTER SNAKE   100   132
Broad orange dorsal stripe; stripe on rows 2, 3, and 4.

CHECKERED GARTER SNAKE   97   130
Checkerboard of black spots; light band behind mouth followed by broad black blotch.

PLAINS GARTER SNAKE   99   132
Black bars on lips; stripe on rows 3 and 4.

SHORT-HEADED GARTER SNAKE   98   133
Very small head; scale rows 17.

BUTLER'S GARTER SNAKE   98   133
Small head; stripe on rows 2, 3, and 4; scale rows 19.

WESTERN RIBBON SNAKE   102   134
Occasionally with red stripe (see text).

EASTERN RIBBON SNAKE   102   134
Long, slender tail; stripe on rows 3 and 4.

SOUTHERN RIBBON SNAKE   102   135
Dorsal stripe fainter than lateral stripes or even lacking.

BLACK-NECKED GARTER SNAKE   96   130
Large black spots on neck; lateral stripe wavy.

LINED SNAKE   103   135
Double row of black half-moons on belly; small head; stripe on rows 2 and 3.

POSITIONS OF LATERAL STRIPES (Numbers refer to scale rows)

ALLEGHENY MOUNTAIN SALAMANDER

Desmognathus ochrophaeus ochrophaeus   pp. 221, 255

Identification: 2¾–4. A *straight-edged* light stripe down the back and tail. The stripe may be yellow, orange, olive, gray, tan, brown, or reddish; it is flanked by very dark, sometimes black, pigment that fades into the mottled lower sides. A row of dark, often *chevron-like*, spots down center of back. Old individuals may be nearly plain dark brown and virtually without pattern. Tail *round* (not knife-edged on top), slender, and tapering; about ½ total length. *Young:* Dorsal stripe bright orange, unmarked or with 1 or 2 dark spots on the nape (Fig. 45, p. 218).

More terrestrial than most other Dusky Salamanders, sometimes wandering far out into the woods during wet weather. Normally found under stones, logs, leaves, etc. near springs and streams, not actually in the water but where the ground is saturated. Often congregates in winter in large numbers in shaly seepage areas or near springs.

Similar species: Two-lined Salamander has bright yellow belly and compressed tail. Both it and Red-backed Salamander lack light diagonal line behind eye. Dusky and Seal Salamanders have irregular dorsal patterns and tails are *knife-edged* above.

Range: Upland areas from Adirondack Mountains, New York, to Tennessee.   Map 174

BLUE RIDGE MOUNTAIN SALAMANDER

Desmognathus ochrophaeus carolinensis   pp. 221, 255

Identification: 2¾–4⅜. A southern counterpart of the Allegheny Mountain Salamander, but with a *wavy* or *irregular* dorsal stripe instead of a straight-edged one. Coloration and pattern extremely variable. A dorsal stripe with scalloped edges (Fig. 46, p. 221) is typical of many individuals, but in others the edges are far less regular. In some, especially juveniles, there are dark-bordered light areas set in zigzag fashion down the back (Fig. 45, p. 218). The light dorsal areas may be yellowish, reddish, tan, greenish, or gray. An amazing variation of this amphibian, with cheek patches of yellow, orange, or reddish, is illustrated on Plate 32, p. 255, as the "Imitator Salamander." (Also see Red-cheeked Salamander, p. 235.) Tail round and about ½ total length.

Usually found in seepage areas, near springs, etc., where the ground is saturated. More likely to occur in a wet environment than the Woodland Salamanders, but decidedly less aquatic than the Eastern Dusky, Seal, and Black-bellied Salamanders.

Similar species: All Woodland Salamanders lack a light line from eye to angle of jaw. Eastern Dusky, Seal, and Black-bellied Salamanders have relatively short tails that are knife-edged on top, at least near tip; normally they also lack bright colors except that in the Dusky there may be yellowish or reddish pigment on the dorsal surface of the tail near its base.

Range: Mountains from sw. Virginia to n. Georgia.   Map 174

OCOEE SALAMANDER *Desmognathus ocoee*   Not illustrated
Identification: 2–3. A light middorsal area, greenish- to yellow-brown in coloration, its general appearance irregular or uneven. Coloration paler in juveniles; darker and overlaid with white specks in old males. There are pale dorsal markings usually consisting of paired light spots, the 1st pair opposite each other, the others alternating. Upper sides of body dark brown or black; belly light, flecked with dark pigment.

A dwarf relative of the Blue Ridge Mountain Salamander that lives amid the cliffs of rocky gorges, venturing out from deep crevices onto the rock faces when these are wet from seepages or spray.

Range: Ships Prow Rock, Ocoee Gorge in extr. se. Tennessee.
Map 176

CLIFFSIDE SALAMANDER *Desmognathus perlapsus*   p. 221
Identification: 2⅞–3½. Four pairs of spots on the back, these being yellowish to reddish or brown and surrounded by darker pigment; the spots sometimes irregular, zigzag, or fused with their partners across the midline of dorsum. Extensive white mottlings on lower sides. Belly mottled with white. Tail a little more than ½ total length, and ending in a slender, almost *threadlike* tip.

An inhabitant of wet, nearly vertical rock faces of mountain cliffs and gorges.

Range: Ne. Georgia and adj. North Carolina.   Map 176

SEAL SALAMANDER *Desmognathus monticola*   p. 258
Identification: 3¼–5; record 5¾. A robust salamander, boldly patterned above, but plain and quite pale below. Dorsum with strong black or dark brown markings on a ground of buff, gray, or light brown, the markings extremely variable — wormlike, netlike, or surrounding roughly circular areas of ground color. Some specimens patterned simply with scattered dark or light spots or streaks. Venter white in juveniles, but becoming lightly and *uniformly* pigmented with gray or brown in old adults. Sometimes a *single* row of light dots on sides between legs. Elderly specimens may be purplish brown, with dark markings few and obscure. Tail compressed and knife-edged above near tip; approximately ½ total length. *Young:* About 4 pairs of rounded chestnut or orange-brown spots down back (Fig. 45, p. 218).

Boggy spots in cool well-shaded ravines and banks of mountain brooks are among the varied habitats of this rather large, active species. Hides by day and may be found by overturning stones, bark, etc. At night, poised at the entrance to a burrow or perched atop a wet rock and illuminated by the collector's flashlight, its appearance suggests a miniature seal. The name Seal Salamander is derived from the specific name *phoca* (Latin for seal) that was incorrectly applied to this species for many years.

Similar species: Northern Dusky Salamander has a light but mottled under surface. Black-bellied Salamander (besides the black venter) has *two* rows of small white dots along each side of body.

Range: Mountainous and hilly regions from sw. Pennsylvania to n. Georgia and n. Alabama.

Subspecies: APPALACHIAN SEAL SALAMANDER, *Desmognathus monticola monticola* (illustrated on Plate 33). As described above and occurring throughout most of the range. VIRGINIA SEAL SALAMANDER, *Desmognathus monticola jeffersoni*. Similar but with dark markings much reduced, these being round, scattered, and about size of salamander's eye. Some adults virtually patternless. Blue Ridge Mountains of Virginia.   Map 170

BLACK-BELLIED SALAMANDER
Desmognathus quadramaculatus   p. 258

Identification: 4–6⅛; record 7⅜. A large robust salamander of cascading southern mountain streams. *Belly black* in adults; dark, but flecked with yellow in young. (Put your specimen in a bottle to see its underside.) Usually a double row of light dots along each side of body. Tail less than ½ total length; knife-edged above. *Young:* Snout and feet often light in color, especially in southern part of range.

This salamander, one of the largest and heaviest of the lungless group, is daring enough to pause in the open occasionally on a wet rock, even in sunshine! Abundant in boulder-strewn brooks; also found near waterfalls or other spots where cold water drips or flows. Usually seeks shelter under rocks during day, but when these are lifted it dashes off instantly to plunge beneath the next nearest stone or to swim vigorously away with *or against* the current. Trying to catch these agile amphibians is like going fishing with your bare hands.

Similar species: Old adults of other members of Dusky Salamander group may be almost uniformly dark (bellies included), but they do not attain so large a size and their tails are proportionately longer. Shovel-nosed Salamanders have long-sloping snouts and small eyes.

Range: S. West Virginia through mountains to n. Georgia.
                                                                  Map 172

PIGMY SALAMANDER *Desmognathus wrighti*   pp. 221, 255
Identification: 1½–2. A tiny, bronzy mite of a salamander; one of our smallest species and a strictly non-aquatic one. A broad light stripe down back, from reddish brown to tan in coloration; often with a dark *herringbone* pattern down center. Tail rounded; less than ½ total length.

Best sought by day beneath rotting wood on the forest floor. At night, especially in foggy or rainy weather, it may become "arboreal," ascending trunks of trees as much as 6 or 7 feet above ground.

Similar species: Young Blue Ridge Mountain Salamanders may also have light middorsal stripes, but their markings (if present) are irregular or suggestive of series of dark-bordered light spots.

Range: Elevations of 3500 to 6500 feet in Great Smoky Mountains and other mountains from sw. North Carolina to sw. Virginia.   Map 173

CHEROKEE SALAMANDER
Desmognathus aeneus aeneus   p. 221

Identification: 1¾–2. Tail rounded; about ½ total length. A wide, almost straight-sided dorsal stripe of reddish brown flecked with irregular dark spots, or with a narrow middorsal dark line that is continuous with a dark *Y*-shaped mark on head. Sides dark where they meet the light dorsal stripe, lighter toward belly. Under surfaces mottled brown and white.

Similar species: Pigmy Salamander usually has dark *herringbone* pattern down center of back. Both Blue Ridge Mountain Salamander and Alabama Salamander have light dorsal stripes with *irregular* edges.

Range: Extr. sw. North Carolina and n. Georgia.   Map 173

ALABAMA SALAMANDER
Desmognathus aeneus chermocki   p. 221

Identification: 1⅛–2¼. Tail rounded; about ½ total length. A wide dorsal stripe of tan or yellow, with somewhat *wavy* edges. Irregular dark smudges or small blotches within dorsal stripe; rarely, a faint suggestion of a herringbone pattern. Sides dark next to stripe, but fading to the pale, almost plain under surfaces.

Found in heavily shaded seepage areas where the uplands terminate near the Fall Line in Alabama.

Similar species: Resembles Pigmy Salamander that lives at high altitudes in southern Blue Ridge Mountains, but the Pigmy *usually* has a herringbone pattern. In the Blue Ridge Mountain Salamander belly is finely pigmented with black. Belly of Cherokee Salamander is mottled brown and white, and dorsal stripe has virtually straight edges.

Range: N.-cent. Alabama.   Map 173

NORTHERN SHOVEL-NOSED SALAMANDER
Leurognathus marmoratus marmoratus   p. 258

Identification: 3½–5; record 5¾. Pattern and coloration dull and variable, but blending beautifully with pebbles, leaves, and debris on bottoms of rocky streams. Dorsum gray, mixed with tan or olive, the markings usually arranged to form (1) an indefinite light zigzag pattern, or (2) a double row of light irregular blotches. Tail less than ½ total length, compressed and knife-edged above. Head flattened and wedge-shaped, the slope starting downward from a point *well behind* the rather small eyes.

An aquatic salamander preferring mountain brooks of large or medium size that offer an abundance of stones beneath which to hide. In quiet waters, if care is taken not to disturb it unduly (lifting rocks slowly, for example), the Shovelnose tends to remain still or walk slowly and deliberately to another shelter. The Black-bellied Salamander, often present in same streams, normally *dashes* away.

Similar species: Black-bellied Salamander and other members of Dusky group tend to be more "pop-eyed," and usually have a well-defined light line from eye to angle of jaws. (A similar but much fainter light line may occasionally be present in the Shovel-nosed Salamanders.) Check the roof of the mouth if in doubt. Internal openings of nostrils are clearly evident in Dusky Salamanders (*Desmognathus*); they are hidden behind folds at each side of mouth in Shovel-nosed Salamanders (Fig. 47, below). When opening the mouth, lift *upper* jaw; you will break the lower jaw if you try to force it downward.

Range: Elevations of 2000 to 4000 feet, east and north of French Broad River in w. North Carolina and adj. Tennessee and Virginia.

Subspecies: GOLDEN SHOVEL-NOSED SALAMANDER, *Leurognathus marmoratus aureatus*. Similar but with dorsal ground color lighter and more yellowish, the light markings usually with bright yellow centers. Headwaters of Chattahoochee and Tallulah river systems of Georgia and adj. North Carolina. HUSKY SHOVEL-NOSED SALAMANDER, *Leurognathus marmoratus roboratus*. A dark stout-bodied race in which the light dorsal markings are reduced to small spots. Headwaters of Chattooga River system of Georgia, South Carolina, and adj. North Carolina. Map 175

Fig. 47. ROOFS OF MOUTHS OF LUNGLESS SALAMANDERS

DUSKY
Internal openings
of nostrils
clearly visible

SHOVEL-NOSED
No openings
visible

SOUTHERN SHOVEL-NOSED SALAMANDER
Leurognathus marmoratus intermedius p. 258

Identification: 3½–5; record 5⅝. Typically, *2 rows of light spots* down the back. Dorsal ground color usually dark brown. Head shape, tail length, etc., similar to Northern Shovelnose.

An aquatic salamander, but one that tolerates smaller brooks and rills than the northern subspecies. Hence, it ascends considerably higher in mountains, where the streams, here near their headwaters, are not large in size. Occurs from elevations of 1700 to 5500 feet. Found under stones, often in the shallow layer of mud that may collect beneath them, or sometimes in mud in open places, but almost always where water is flowing.

Similar species: See "Similar species" section for Northern Shovelnose (opposite page). Same details apply.

Range: Streams immediately west and south of French Broad River, in southern Blue Ridge Mountains.

Subspecies: BLACK SHOVEL-NOSED SALAMANDER, *Leurognathus marmoratus melanius.* Similar but much darker; paired light spots sometimes visible in younger specimens, but this normally is an almost plain black salamander. Streams of w. North Carolina and adj. Tennessee.   Map 175

Woodland Salamanders: Genus *Plethodon*

THIS GROUP is widespread and abundant through the forested portions of eastern North America. In high, humid mountains in the South, specimens may be encountered at almost all seasons (except midwinter), but elsewhere they are easiest to find after spring or autumn rains. During hot, dry weather they either estivate or seek optimum conditions of moisture (as well as their food) in rock crevices or below the surface of the ground. They prowl only at night or during heavy rains; hence, during daylight hours, most specimens are found by raking through their habitats, overturning boards and stones, tearing moss from rocks, breaking open rotting logs, etc. Night collecting with flashlight or headlamp sometimes is very productive.

The Woodland Salamanders feed upon a large variety of invertebrates, including earthworms and many kinds of insects, among them beetles with hard shells, ants with sharp stings, and bugs with bad smells. Most captives readily accept tubifex worms, which are procurable at almost any tropical-fish supply store.

Eggs are laid in small clusters in damp logs, moss, etc., and complete development takes place within the egg; there is no aquatic larval stage as is the case among most other salamanders. Adult males of some species have a prominent large circular gland (the mental gland) under their chins.

The genus is strictly North American, with a large number of forms in our area and others in forested portions of far-western states.

Similar species: Mole Salamanders (*Ambystoma*) all *lack* the groove from nostril to lip (use a lens). Most confusion will come with Dusky Salamanders (*Desmognathus*), some of which wander far out into the woods. Dusky Salamanders usually have a light line from eye to angle of jaw, and their hind legs are larger and stouter than their forelegs. Woodland Salamanders lack the light line, and *all four* limbs are about the same size (Fig., p. 258).

RED-BACKED SALAMANDER

Plethodon cinereus cinereus   pp. 221, 255

Identification: 2¼–3⅝; record 5. *Two distinct colorations:* (1) *red-backed* — a straight-edged reddish stripe down back from base of head to tail, and bordered by dark pigment that extends downward onto sides of body; (2) *lead-backed* — uniformly dark gray to almost black. (Some individuals are intermediate between the two types.) In red-backed phase, the stripe may be orange, yellow, or even light gray instead of red. Usually the stripe *narrows* slightly on base of tail. In some areas, red-backed and lead-backed specimens are equally abundant; in others, one or the other may predominate; leadbacks may be rare or absent at high elevations. Both phases have one outstanding character in common — bellies mottled with black and white, producing a *salt-and-pepper* effect (Fig. 48, p. 231).

A terrestrial salamander, confined more or less to wooded or forested areas, but sometimes found far from streams or other bodies of water — even in fairly dry situations. Hides beneath all manner of objects, including chunks of tar paper or other trash, as well as logs, bark, stones, etc. The most ubiquitous salamander throughout the greater part of its range.

Similar species: Ravine Salamander (colored as a leadback) is more slender and its venter looks almost *uniformly dark* (Fig. 48, p. 231). Also see Zigzag Salamander.

Range: S. Labrador and the Maritime Provinces to Minnesota; south to North Carolina and se. Missouri.

Subspecies: GEORGIA RED-BACKED SALAMANDER, *Plethodon cinereus polycentratus*. Identical in appearance with Red-backed Salamander, and occurring in both red-backed and lead-backed phases; differs in having a greater number of trunk vertebrae (21 to 23) than other subspecies (19 or 20). Identify by range — Piedmont of nw. Georgia.   Map 179

OUACHITA RED-BACKED SALAMANDER

Plethodon cinereus serratus   p. 221

Identification: 2¾–4. A light middorsal stripe with saw-toothed edges; "teeth" corresponding with costal grooves (stripe widest above each groove and narrowest between them). Stripe may be orange or reddish, rest of body dark gray to almost black — coloration, in general, like Red-backed Salamander's; occasional individuals may be dark and unpatterned (lead-backed).

Range: Forested mountains of w.-cent. Arkansas and adj. Oklahoma.   Map 179

Fig. 48. VENTRAL PATTERNS OF SMALL LUNGLESS SALAMANDERS

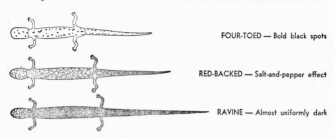

FOUR-TOED — Bold black spots

RED-BACKED — Salt-and-pepper effect

RAVINE — Almost uniformly dark

ZIGZAG SALAMANDER *Plethodon dorsalis dorsalis* pp. 221, 255

Identification: 2½–3½; record 3⅝. "Zigzag" well describes the light dorsal stripe in many specimens; in others the angles are not so sharp and "lobed" or "wavy" would be more accurate. The stripe varies from red to yellowish in coloration, and may be straight for at least part of its length; it is *broadly* continued on tail. Venter includes a mottling of orange or reddish pigment. This salamander also occurs in a dark phase.

Sometimes a woodland species, but more likely to be found in rock slides or in or near mouths of caves. Ascends to elevations of 2500 feet in western approaches to Blue Ridge Mountains.

Similar species: Red-backed Salamander has a straight dorsal stripe that *narrows* slightly on base of tail. Dark phases of Zigzag and Redback will offer difficulties. Unpatterned Zigzags have the dark pigment diffused, as though the dark borders of the light stripe had broken down and spread about. The dorsal coloration may be uniformly dark brown, reddish brown, or gray; dark Redbacks (leadbacks) are much darker, usually dark gray to black, and they have *salt-and-pepper* bellies without a mottling of red or orange pigment.

Range: Cent. Indiana to cent. Alabama. Map 180

OZARK RED-BACKED SALAMANDER
Plethodon dorsalis angusticlavius p. 221

Identification: 2⅜–3½. General coloration similar to that of the Zigzag Salamander. The slender orange or reddish middorsal stripe has indistinct edges, and it varies in width from one specimen to the next. Some individuals are uniformly dark.

Usually in or near caves of the Central Highlands.

Range: Sw. Missouri, n. Arkansas, and ne. Oklahoma. Map 180

RAVINE SALAMANDER *Plethodon richmondi richmondi* p. 258
Identification: 3–4½; record 5½. Like a lead-colored Red-

backed Salamander, but with a virtually plain dark venter (Fig. 48, p. 231). A longer, more slender, shorter-legged species — almost a worm with legs. Dorsal coloration seal-brown to nearly black, but sprinkled with minute silvery-white and bronzy specks; very small, irregular white blotches on lower sides.

Wooded *slopes* of valleys and ravines are preferred. It shuns hilltops and occurs only rarely on valley floors.

Similar species: Red-backed Salamander has a *salt-and-pepper* venter (Fig. 48, p. 231). Zigzag Salamander, even in its dark phase, usually has some reddish or orange pigment showing on the under surfaces. Metcalf's and Wehrle's Salamanders are much stouter-bodied and have proportionately larger legs.

Range: Cent. Pennsylvania to e. Indiana; south to w. Virginia and e. Kentucky.

Subspecies: SOUTHERN RAVINE SALAMANDER, *Plethodon richmondi popei*. Differentiated solely by fewer trunk vertebrae (usually 21 as opposed to 22 or more in *richmondi*). Identify on basis of locality. Extr. sw. Virginia and nearby portions of the three adjacent states. (Also see Cheat Mountain Salamander.)   Map 184

CHEAT MOUNTAIN SALAMANDER
Plethodon richmondi nettingi   p. 255

Identification: 3–4; record 4⅜. Dorsal surface strongly sprinkled with small brassy flecks, most numerous on or near the head and extending to tail. Dorsal ground color black; belly plain dark slaty gray to black; throat paler. Brassy flecks disappear in preserved specimens.

Found in cool, shady ravines and spruce forests at high elevations in the Cheat Mountains.

Similar species: Ravine Salamander has fewer and smaller brassy flecks, and is a longer, more slender animal, with 20 to 23 costal grooves (18 in *nettingi*). Red-backed Salamanders collected high in the Cheat Mountains have all been red-backed (not lead-backed), so reddish stripe will distinguish these.

Range: E.-cent. West Virginia.   Map 183

Subspecies: PEAKS OF OTTER SALAMANDER, *Plethodon richmondi hubrichti*. More elongated and slightly larger (to 4 13/16″), dorsal metallic pigment more abundant and in form of spots, blotches, or a roughly continuous stripe (instead of flecking or lacy mottling). Cool, moist ravines of Peaks of Otter region ne. of Roanoke, Virginia.   Map 184

WELLER'S SALAMANDER   *Plethodon welleri*   p. 255

Identification: 2½–3⅛. Like a small "leadback" (Red-backed Salamander) in size and shape. Upper surfaces with a profusion of dull golden or silvery blotches on a ground color of black. Venter plain black or spotted with white.

Named for Worth Hamilton Weller, a promising young Cincinnati naturalist who lost his life while collecting salamanders on Grandfather Mountain in 1931.

Range: Tri-state area — extreme ne. Tennessee, Whitetop and Mount Rogers, Virginia, and nw. North Carolina. From 2500 feet upward, but chiefly in spruce forests above 5000 feet.

Subspecies: SPOT-BELLIED SALAMANDER, *Plethodon welleri ventromaculatum* (illustrated on Plate 32). Venter and lower flanks of body spotted with white. All of range except Grandfather Mountain. WELLER'S SALAMANDER, *Plethodon welleri welleri*. Venter virtually uniform black. Grandfather Mountain, North Carolina.   Map 183

SLIMY SALAMANDER *Plethodon glutinosus glutinosus*   p. 258
Identification: 4¾–6¾; record 7⅜. A large black salamander generally well sprinkled with silvery-white flecks. Extent of sprinkling extremely variable; there are innumerable modifications, some confined to individual specimens and others evident throughout local populations. Specks may be restricted to certain portions of dorsum, concentrated along sides of body, greatly reduced in number, or even absent. Under surfaces normally plain slate color; chin and throat, although somewhat lighter, are definitely dark. *Young:* Flecks sometimes golden instead of white or silvery.

This is the "sticky salamander" whose skin-gland secretions cling to your hands like glue and almost have to wear off. (Some of the other large Woodland Salamanders are almost as bad.) Moist wooded ravines or hillsides are favorite habitats. Apparently the Slimy needs more moisture than its smaller compatriot, the Redback.

Similar species: Combination of dark throat and widely scattered light spots will usually distinguish this species from other dark salamanders that resemble it. Like all its relatives, it has a groove running downward from nostril to lip; the Jefferson and the other Mole Salamanders (*Ambystoma*) lack this.

Range: Cent. New York to cent. Florida and west to Missouri, Oklahoma, and Texas.   Map 181

WHITE-THROATED SLIMY SALAMANDER
Plethodon glutinosus albagula   p. 258
Identification: 5¼–6. The bulk of the light spotting is along the sides of this otherwise black salamander. Depend largely upon geography in making identification, because this same concentration of light pigment appears occasionally in populations of the wide-ranging eastern subspecies, the Slimy Salamander. The throat of the Western Slimy is lighter in coloration, but this character is not too helpful unless specimens of *both* subspecies are at hand for comparison.

Found in wooded ravines and in caves of the eastern part of the Edwards Plateau.

Range: S.-cent. Texas.   Map 181

WEHRLE'S SALAMANDER *Plethodon wehrlei wehrlei*   p. 258
Identification: 4–5¼; record 6⁵⁄₁₆. Black or dark brown with a row of irregular white or bluish-white spots and dashes along each side of body. The middorsal area may be unmarked or it may be patterned with small *red* or *orange-red* spots, these often arranged in pairs. Specimens from the northern and western parts of the range usually are plain-backed, but those from farther south, the young especially, tend to be red-spotted. *Throat white or blotched with white;* white spots frequently extending backward onto breast. Belly and underside of tail uniform gray.

At home in upland forests; found under stones, in rotting logs, in deep rock crevices, or the twilight zones of caves. Named for R. W. Wehrle, of Indiana, Pennsylvania, who collected many of the specimens from which the species was first described.

Similar species: Easily confused with the Slimy Salamander, which (at least within the range of Wehrle's Salamander) normally has white spots scattered all over dorsum — not just along sides. Also, Slimy's throat may be gray, but *not white.* Jefferson and other Mole Salamanders (*Ambystoma*) lack the groove from nostril to lip that is common to all Woodland Salamanders.

Range: Sw. New York to sw. Virginia.   Map 182

ROANOKE SALAMANDER *Plethodon wehrlei dixi*   p. 258
Identification: 3½–4½; record 4⅞. A dark purplish-brown salamander profusely covered with bronzy mottling and dotted with small light flecks. Lower sides of body marked with white or yellowish spots that blend into the mottled gray and yellow of the belly. *Young:* Light spots more numerous than in adults.

These troglodytes are most numerous where seepages occur in the twilight zone near entrances to caves. There they are found upon the formations, clinging to the vertical faces of stalactites and flowstone by the natural adhesion of their damp feet and bodies. Occasionally found during springtime in woods outside caves.

Range: Dixie Caverns and nearby caves in sw. Virginia.
                                                              Map 182

YONAHLOSSEE SALAMANDER *Plethodon yonahlossee* p. 255
Identification: 4½–6½; record 7. An extremely handsome salamander in life, but usually fading rapidly to almost uniform dull gray in preservatives. A broad *red or chestnut stripe* down back, extending from neck well onto base of tail. A stripe of light gray

or whitish pigment *directly below* red stripe. Head plain black or marked with light specks. Tail black. Underparts dark gray, belly often mottled with light spots. Black sometimes invades the red stripe to an appreciable extent. *Young:* 4 to 6 pairs of red dorsal spots on a dark ground color; belly light.

One of our most agile salamanders, darting away into the forest litter, under any nearby shelter, or down the long burrows it utilizes to move about beneath the surface. Named for the old Yonahlossee Road on Grandfather Mountain, North Carolina.

Similar species: Other red- or chestnut-backed salamanders (Red-backed and some individuals of Blue Ridge Mountain Salamander) occurring within the range of the Yonahlossee Salamander have the red flanked on each side by *dark* instead of light pigment.

Range: Southern Blue Ridge Mountains, east and north of French Broad River, from Iron Mountains (Comers Rock) in sw. Virginia to vicinity of Asheville, North Carolina; elevations from 2500 to 5700 feet. Map 182

RICH MOUNTAIN SALAMANDER *Plethodon ouachitae* p. 255
Identification: 3½–4½; record 5½. Extremely variable in coloration. A typical specimen has dark red or chocolate pigment overlying the black of the dorsal ground color, numerous small white specks, and a shiny, metallic-looking "frosting." Any one of these pattern elements may be lacking or, conversely, so profuse as to obscure the others. The throat is light, but usually suffused with gray.
Similar species: Slimy Salamander has a *dark* throat.
Range: Wooded slopes and crest of Rich Mountain and vicinity in Ouachitas of w. Arkansas and e. Oklahoma. Map 185

CADDO MOUNTAIN SALAMANDER
Plethodon caddoensis Not illustrated
Identification: 3½–4½. A black and white salamander similar to the Rich Mountain species, but lacking the reddish pigment and metallic "frosting" of the latter. A *diffuse* stripe of *white pigment* along each side of body. The black back and upper sides are profusely marked with pale white spots that stand out less than the Slimy Salamander's spotting and Rich Mountain Salamander's speckling. The throat is light.
Similar species: Slimy Salamander has *dark* throat. Also see Rich Mountain Salamander (above).
Range: Caddo Mountains of w. Arkansas. Map 185

RED-CHEEKED SALAMANDER
Plethodon jordani jordani p. 255
Identification: 4–5½; record 6. The rosy-red cheek patches, in contrast with the plain blue-black body, will identify most speci-

mens. The red is brightest among juveniles; in adults it may be pink or orange-red or (rarely) altogether lacking. Dark pigment may invade the bright colors.

Similar species: Some specimens of the Blue Ridge Mountain Salamander also have cheek patches of red, orange, or yellow (illustrated as the "Imitator Salamander" on Plate 32). These once were considered a distinct subspecies, to which the scientific name *imitator* was applied. The "mimics," which belong to the Dusky Salamander group, generally have some indications of a dorsal pattern and also of a line from eye to angle of jaw; and their hind legs are larger (Fig., p. 258). Habitat may also help. The Redcheek is a forest species that normally shuns water; the Blue Ridge (including the "Imitator") also occurs in woods, but is usually found near springs, edges of streams, in seepage areas, etc.

Range: Great Smoky Mountains, North Carolina and Tennessee, at elevations above 2500 feet. Map 178

RED-LEGGED SALAMANDER

Plethodon jordani shermani p. 255

Identification: 4–5½; record 6 1/16. The bright red on the legs contrasts strongly with the blue-black body. Amount of red variable; normally it is present in irregular blotches, but these may run together, forming large red areas, or may be reduced to small flecks. Small white spots sometimes present on body.

A woodland and forest species of mountain sides and tops.

Range: Nantahala Mountains, in sw. North Carolina, at elevations above 2500 feet. Map 178

CLEMSON SALAMANDER

Plethodon jordani clemsonae p. 255

Identification: 3½–5; record 6⅛. A black salamander with dull silvery, lichen-like patches on upper surfaces and white flecks along the sides. Extent of silvery coloration highly variable. It may consist of numerous separate small spots or these may run together over large areas, giving the salamander, in extreme cases, an almost completely metallic look. The lateral white flecks may be few or numerous. Named for Clemson College.

Range: Rich wooded hillsides in vicinity of Jocassee, in nw. South Carolina. Map 178

METCALF'S SALAMANDER *Plethodon jordani metcalfi* p. 255

Identification: 3½–4½; record 5¼. A plain, almost black salamander that may vary in tone from purplish to brownish. *Throat and belly light gray.* Occasional specimens have whitish spots on back and sides.

This is a high-forest amphibian that lives by day beneath rocks, logs, and moss on wooded slopes and mountain tops.

Named for Professor Z. P. Metcalf, the first person to collect this salamander in numbers.

Similar species: This and the subspecies listed below are often confused with the Slimy Salamander. The Slimy grows larger than the others (up to 7⅜" in length), has relatively shorter limbs, and may be well sprinkled all over the dorsum with silvery-white flecks.

Range: Southern Blue Ridge Mountains from extr. s. Virginia to Balsam Mountains in w. North Carolina at elevations from 3500 to 5800 feet; also in extr. s. West Virginia and adj. Virginia north of the Great Valley.

Subspecies: HIGHLANDS SALAMANDER, *Plethodon jordani melaventris.* Completely black, above and below, except for throat, which is gray; grows to larger size; record 6⅞". From Swannanoa, North Carolina, south to Greenville County, South Carolina, and west to Highlands, North Carolina; also in mountains of Burke County, North Carolina. RABUN BALD SALAMANDER, *Plethodon jordani rabunensis.* Black above, but with white spots on cheeks and sides of trunk; underside dark gray, throat paler; grows to a length of 6" or more. Mountainous areas of ne. Georgia. TEYAHALEE SALAMANDER, *Plethodon jordani teyahalee.* Black above and below, but with irregular greenish-yellow spots on cheeks and sides, tiny white spots on dorsum, and tiny red spots on legs. Teyahalee Bald, in Snowbird Mountains, sw. North Carolina.   Map 178

FOUR-TOED SALAMANDER *Hemidactylium scutatum* p. 255
Identification: 2–3½. Look for three things: (1) enamel-white belly boldly marked with *black spots* (unique among our salamanders — see Fig. 48, p. 231); (2) 4 toes on *hind foot* as well as forefoot (most salamanders have 5 on each *hind* foot); (3) *marked constriction* at base of tail (if an enemy seized the tail, this is where it would break away from body).

Usually associated with sphagnum. Sphagnaceous areas adjacent to woods are common habitats, and so are boggy woodland ponds. The Fourtoe is terrestrial when adult (like Woodland Salamanders); but its larvae are aquatic (like Dusky Salamanders').

Similar species: Dwarf Salamander also has 4 toes on all feet, but it lacks characteristics (1) and (3) above.

Range: Nova Scotia to Wisconsin and Alabama. Distribution spotty, especially in the South. Disjunct populations in Missouri, Arkansas, Louisiana, and Georgia.   Map 187

MANY-LINED SALAMANDER *Stereochilus marginatus* p. 254
Identification: 2½–3¾; record 4½. Nondescript except for a series of narrow, indistinct, dark longitudinal lines on sides of body, and even these may be reduced to a few dark spots. In

COPPERHEADS AND COTTONMOUTHS; CORAL SNAKE AND MIMICS

Map Text

SOUTHERN COPPERHEAD   142 185
Bands narrow along midline of back, often failing to meet;
ground color pale.

NORTHERN COPPERHEAD   142 185
Coppery-red head; bands wide at sides of body, narrow
across back.

BROAD-BANDED COPPERHEAD   142 186
Bands broad, nearly as wide across back as on sides.

EASTERN COTTONMOUTH*   143 186
Head markings well-defined.

WESTERN COTTONMOUTH*   143 187
Head markings obscure or absent.

EASTERN COTTONMOUTH (young)*   143 186
Yellow tail tip; *broad* dark band through eye.

NORTHERN COPPERHEAD (young)   142 185
Yellow tail tip; *narrow* dark line through eye.

EASTERN CORAL SNAKE   141 183
Red and yellow rings touch; snout black.

SCARLET SNAKE (nonpoisonous)   129 176
Red and yellow separated by black; belly whitish, unpatterned; snout red.

SCARLET KINGSNAKE (nonpoisonous)   130 169
Red and yellow rings separated by black; rings enter upon
or cross belly; snout red.

*Cottonmouths resemble many of the Water Snakes. On dead or captive speci-
mens check heads and under surfaces of tails.

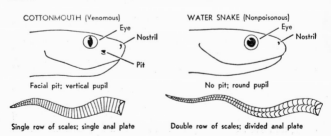

COTTONMOUTH (Venomous)   WATER SNAKE (Nonpoisonous)

Facial pit; vertical pupil   No pit; round pupil

Single row of scales; single anal plate   Double row of scales; divided anal plate

VENOMOUS

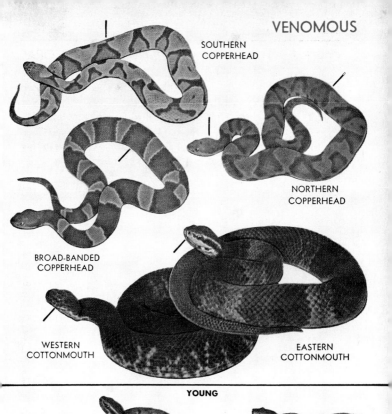

SOUTHERN
COPPERHEAD

NORTHERN
COPPERHEAD

BROAD-BANDED
COPPERHEAD

WESTERN
COTTONMOUTH

EASTERN
COTTONMOUTH

YOUNG

E. COTTONMOUTH

N. COPPERHEAD

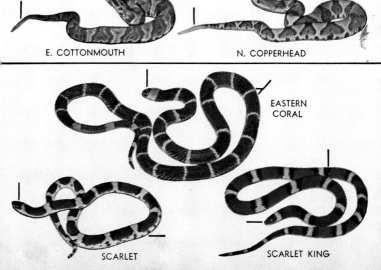

EASTERN
CORAL

SCARLET

SCARLET KING

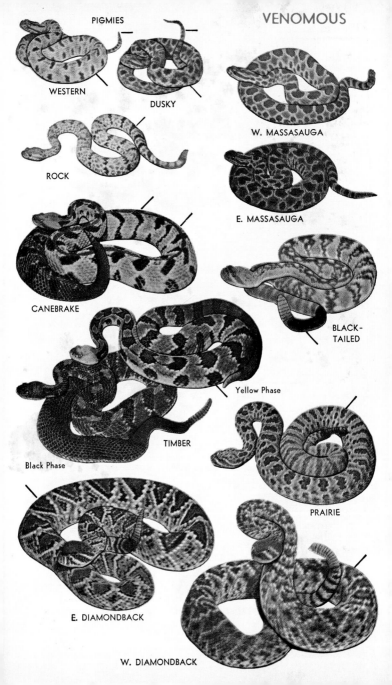

VENOMOUS

PIGMIES

WESTERN

DUSKY

W. MASSASAUGA

ROCK

E. MASSASAUGA

CANEBRAKE

BLACK-
TAILED

Yellow Phase

TIMBER

Black Phase

PRAIRIE

E. DIAMONDBACK

W. DIAMONDBACK

Plate 30   239

RATTLESNAKES

	Map	*Text*

WESTERN PIGMY RATTLESNAKE   144   192
Tiny rattle; slender tail; dark bars.

DUSKY PIGMY RATTLESNAKE   144   189
Tiny rattle; slender tail; rounded spots.

WESTERN MASSASAUGA   145   189
Large rounded spots on a *pale* ground color; belly light
(Fig. 40, p. 189).

EASTERN MASSASAUGA   145   188
Large rounded spots on a *medium to dark* ground color;
belly mostly black (Fig. 40, p. 189).

ROCK RATTLESNAKE   146   194
Dark crossbands; coloration variable (see text).

BLACK-TAILED RATTLESNAKE   149   194
Black tail in strong contrast with body coloration.

CANEBRAKE RATTLESNAKE   147   193
Reddish-brown stripe; dark crossbands; dark postocular
line (Fig. 41, p. 193).

TIMBER RATTLESNAKE   147   192
Yellow phase: Dark spots or crossbands; no head mark-
ings (Fig. 41, p. 193).
Black phase: Black predominates (often all black).

PRAIRIE RATTLESNAKE   148   195
Dark crossbars on rear of body; postocular light line
passes behind corner of mouth (Fig. 41, p. 193).

EASTERN DIAMONDBACK RATTLESNAKE   151   194
Diamonds clear-cut, strongly outlined.

WESTERN DIAMONDBACK RATTLESNAKE   150   195
Tail strongly ringed; diamonds not clear-cut; postocular
light line reaches mouth in front of its back corner (Fig.
41, p.193).

Button   Young rattle — tapering in   Old rattle — terminal   Cross section showing
              size, button still retained   joints broken off   interlinking arrangement

some specimens there are indistinct dark (or light) markings on the back. Most Many-lined Salamanders tend to be brown in general coloration, others may be dull yellow. Belly yellow with scattered dark specks. The small head and short tail are characteristic.

A denizen of pools and sluggish streams in swampy woodlands, best found by raking out dead leaves and other bottom debris. Essentially aquatic, but sometimes uncovered by overturning logs where the ground is damp.

Range: Coastal Plain of the Carolinas and se. Virginia. Map 177

Blind Salamanders:
Genera *Typhlotriton*, *Typhlomolge*, and *Haideotriton*

THESE ARE residents of caves or underground streams which live in perpetual darkness and have no need for functional eyes. They are white or pinkish with an iridescent overwash, and their skins are so translucent that outlines of the darker internal organs are readily apparent through at least the lower sides and belly. Occasionally they are pumped to the surface or appear in the outflow from deep wells or springs, but otherwise one must seek them by becoming a spelunker (cave explorer). Blind Salamanders of this family (Plethodontidae) have been found only in limestone regions of the southern United States. A similar-looking blind species of a different family (Proteidae) occurs in Europe.

GROTTO SALAMANDER *Typhlotriton spelaeus*   p. 270
  Identification: 3–4¾; record 5⁵⁄₁₆. The "ghost lizard" of Ozark caves and grottoes. The whitish or pinkish adults sometimes have faint traces of orange on tail, feet, and lower sides of body. Eyes show as dark spots beneath fused or partly fused lids. *No* external gills. *Young:* The larvae have functional eyes and external gills; they are rather strongly pigmented, being brownish- or purplish-gray with yellowish longitudinal flecks or dark streaks on the sides; the tail fin is high.

This is an extraordinary salamander that literally has two lives. First, as a larva it resides in mountain brooks and springs, and its activities are not unlike those of larvae of other species. Later it moves into a cave, loses fins and pigment, its eyes cease to function, the eyelids grow shut or nearly so, and it remains a blind troglodyte for the rest of its days.

Similar species: Larvae of several forms of Brook Salamanders (*Eurycea*) live in the same region but all have low tail fins, and their patterns tend to be in the form of stippling, networks, or lichen-like patches.

Range: Central uplands; sw. Missouri and adj. areas. Map 190

TEXAS BLIND SALAMANDER *Typhlomolge rathbuni*   p. 270
Identification: 3¼–4¼; record 5⅜. A ghostly salamander with toothpick legs and a strongly flattened snout (Fig. 49, below). Remnants of eyes appear as tiny dark dots buried under the skin.

This weird-looking amphibian occurs in underground streams along the sharp escarpment separating the Edwards Plateau of central Texas from the prairies and other flatlands to the east. A neotenic salamander — one that retains larval form and pink or red external gills throughout life.
Similar species: Other neotenic salamanders of same general region bear at least some dark pigment, and their snouts are not grotesquely flattened.
Range: Balcones Escarpment of cent. Texas.   Map 190

Fig. 49. PROFILES OF BLIND SALAMANDERS

TEXAS
Snout flattened

GEORGIA
Snout rounded; large gills; no eye spots

GEORGIA BLIND SALAMANDER *Haideotriton wallacei* Fig. 49
Identification: 3. A pinkish-white and slightly opalescent salamander. External gills long, slender, and blood-red in coloration. Head broad and long but not greatly flattened. No external indication of eyes or eye spots.

The single known specimen came from a well 200 feet deep at Albany, Georgia.   Map 190

Spring, Red, and Mud Salamanders:
Genera *Gyrinophilus* and *Pseudotriton*

THESE ARE chiefly red or salmon-colored salamanders, most of them patterned with black spots. All are at home in the water, as well as in damp or soggy terrain. The Spring Salamanders (*Gyrinophilus*) like clear, cool water, and their habitats run the roster from forested seepage areas to rushing mountain brooks. Formerly they were called "purple salamanders," a name more appropriate for a badly preserved specimen than one of the orange- or salmon-colored living animals. Both the Red and Mud Salamanders (*Pseudotriton*) are red or reddish, and details must be checked carefully to tell them apart. Age also is important; young adults are brilliantly colored, whereas older specimens darken and their patterns become obscure. The Reds prefer clear water, but the Muds usually are found in muddy places. Both genera occur only in eastern North America.

SPRING SALAMANDER *Gyrinophilus porphyriticus* p. 254

Identification: 4¾–7½; record 8⅝. The light line from eye to nostril is bordered below by gray pigment, but these markings usually are not overly conspicuous. The general dorsal coloration varies from salmon and light brownish pink to reddish. The ground color has a cloudy appearance, and the darker markings are vague — not clear-cut.

These are agile denizens of cool springs and mountain streams, but are also likely to be found in any wet depression beneath logs, stones, or leaves in the surrounding forests.

Similar species: In all the several races of the Mountain Spring Salamander there is a conspicuous light *and dark* line from eye to nostril. Such markings are completely absent in Red and Mud Salamanders. Also, members of the two latter groups have rounded heads that lack the distinct angle (canthus rostralis) along which the eye lines run in Spring Salamanders.

Range: S. Maine and s. Quebec to n. Alabama.

Subspecies: NORTHERN SPRING SALAMANDER, *Gyrinophilus porphyriticus porphyriticus* (illustrated on Plate 31). Salmon or light yellowish brown with reddish tinges, and with a mottled or clouded appearance; sides tend to be darker and to form a netlike pattern enclosing light spots; venter flesh-colored; small, scattered dark spots on belly and throat and especially on margin of lower jaw in old specimens. Recently transformed young are salmon-red and with the darker mottlings not well developed. Most of the range of the species. KENTUCKY SPRING SALAMANDER, *Gyrinophilus porphyriticus duryi*. Smaller; max. length about 6½". Dorsal coloration salmon-pink to light brownish pink; small black spots arranged in a row along each side of body, scattered along sides, or (in a few individuals) over all the dorsal surfaces. (Even when the black spots are widely distributed, they are most strongly concentrated along the sides.) Venter flesh-colored and unmarked except on lower lip and occasionally chin and throat. S. Ohio to extr. sw. Virginia. OHIO SPRING SALAMANDER, *Gyrinophilus porphyriticus inagnoscus*. Dorsum reddish and uniformly mottled with a dusky shade, the spots and flecks forming a chevron-like pattern down center of back; venter pinkish or flesh-colored. Se. Ohio. Map 186

MOUNTAIN SPRING SALAMANDER
Gyrinophilus danielsi p. 254

Identification: 5–7½; record 8 1/16. The white line from eye to nostril, *bordered below* by a conspicuous black or dark brown line, is the distinctive mark of this species. There also may be a dark line above the white line, and in many specimens this, too, is conspicuous. Dorsal coloration clear reddish, salmon, or orange-yellow marked with black or brown spots or flecks; chin and throat speckled or not (see subspecies below).

Turning over a stone at a mountain spring and revealing one of these brightly colored amphibians is a startling experience. Also found in seepage and wet forest areas, especially near edges of mountain brooks.

Similar species: Among the races of the Spring Salamander (*G. porphyriticus*), lines from eyes to nostril are much less prominent; a *light* line is present, but the dark line below it may be obscure or virtually lacking. Such markings are completely absent among Red and Mud Salamanders.

Range: Southern Blue Ridge Mountains and nearby areas.

Subspecies: BLUE RIDGE SPRING SALAMANDER, *Gyrinophilus danielsi danielsi* (illustrated on Plate 31). Reddish or rich salmon-colored with scattered black spots on the back; heavy dark speckling on chin, but little or none posteriorly to the fold of skin across the throat. The Blue Ridge Province from vicinity of Grandfather Mountain, North Carolina, to and including Great Smoky Mountains. MOUNT MITCHELL SPRING SALAMANDER, *Gyrinophilus danielsi polystictus.* Similar, but dark dorsal spots larger, more numerous, and frequently joined with one another; numerous small dark markings on chin and continuing *beyond* the fold of skin across the throat; a few dark spots on belly. Mount Mitchell and other high elevations of Black Mountains massif of w. North Carolina. CAROLINA SPRING SALAMANDER, *Gyrinophilus danielsi dunni.* Smallest of the races; max. length about 6⅜". Orange-yellow to light reddish, marked with numbers of small brown flecks; venter salmon-pink, usually immaculate except for margins of jaws, which are mottled with black and white. Southern portion of Blue Ridge Mountains and south into the Piedmont of Georgia and South Carolina; Cheaha Mountain, Alabama. Map 189

TENNESSEE CAVE SALAMANDER
Gyrinophilus palleucus p. 270
Identification: 2⅛–6⅛. A cave-dwelling and probably neotenic member of the Spring Salamander genus. Eyes much reduced in size, and eyelids lacking as in larval salamanders. Coloration normally pale flesh-pink, except for bright red external gills. Most specimens are paler than the one shown on Plate 37.
Range: Caves of se. Tennessee. Map 189

EASTERN MUD SALAMANDER
Pseudotriton montanus montanus p. 254
Identification: 3½–6; record 7. A red-colored salamander with a

brown eye. Black spots round and well separated. Dorsum with a definite "ground color" that doesn't blend directly into the reddish of the lower sides and belly. Young specimens brightly colored, with sharply distinct spots and virtually unmarked venters. Older ones vary from light reddish brown to chocolate; their dorsal spots are larger and more numerous but tend to be inconspicuous against the darker backgrounds; under surfaces often spotted or flecked with brown or black.

Occurs in the muddy environs of springs, muddy seeps along small streams, etc. It burrows into the muck in its efforts to escape, and may take refuge in crayfish or other holes.

Similar species: Mud and Red Salamanders are easily confused — even experienced herpetologists have trouble with them. Check color of iris; it normally is yellowish instead of brown in the Reds. Look at shape of head: in the Muds, snout is blunter and shorter in front of eyes. Habitat will help: Mud Salamanders usually live up to their names. Spring Salamanders have a light and dark line from eye to nostril.

Range: S. New Jersey to the Carolinas and ne. Georgia.

Subspecies: MIDLAND MUD SALAMANDER, *Pseudotriton montanus diastictus*. The ground color, coral-pink or red to brown, is clearer and brighter than in Eastern Mud Salamander; black spots fewer in number; under surfaces unmarked except occasionally for a dark line on rim of lower jaw. S. Ohio and West Virginia to n. Alabama. GULF COAST MUD SALAMANDER, *Pseudotriton montanus flavissimus*. Averages smaller and more slender; max. length about 4⅛". A large number of small, well-separated round spots on a ground of clear, light brownish salmon; underside of head and trunk clear salmon-pink. Extr. s. South Carolina to extr. e. Louisiana.   Map 192

RUSTY MUD SALAMANDER
Pseudotriton montanus floridanus   p. 254
Identification: 2⅞–4¼; record 4⅝. The rustiest and one of the smallest of the Mud Salamanders. The virtually plain dorsum may be slightly mottled with indistinct darker areas and a few small, irregular, light pinkish spots. *No dark dots on back*, but there may be a few scattered ones atop tail. Streaking on sides highly irregular — a mixture of pinkish buff and rust color and sometimes with streaks or specks of black. Under surfaces buffy and sparsely marked with small, irregular blackish spots.

Habitats include mucky seepage areas and small, shallow streams flowing through hardwood hammocks or mixed forests.
Range: N. Florida and s. Georgia.   Map 192

NORTHERN RED SALAMANDER
Pseudotriton ruber ruber   p. 254
Identification: 4¼–6; record 7⅛. A red or reddish orange sala-

mander with the upper surfaces profusely dotted with irregular, rounded black spots. Iris of eye normally *yellow*. Margin of chin often flecked with black. *Old adults:* Dull purplish brown, the ground color darker and the spots larger and running together; black or brown spots on under surfaces.

Look for the Red Salamander under moss, stones, or other objects in or near springs or rills, even mere trickles, provided water is clear, cool, and not stagnant. Occurs in streams that flow through open fields and meadows as well as those through woods; streams with bottoms of sand, gravel, or rock usually are preferred.

Similar species: Mud Salamanders have noticeably fewer and well-separated *circular* (or nearly circular) black spots, their dorsal ground color is more sharply set off from the ventral coloration, and their irises are *brown*. Spring Salamanders have a light and dark line from eye to nostril.

Range: S. New York and Ohio to n. Alabama (except in s. Blue Ridge, where related subspecies occur).

Subspecies: BLUE RIDGE RED SALAMANDER, *Pseudotriton ruber nitidus*. Small; max. length about 4⅝". Coloration and pattern similar to Northern Red Salamander's, but without black pigment on tip half of tail and little or none on chin; old adults retain their bright appearance. Elevations to more than 5000 feet, north and east of French Broad River, in southern Blue Ridge Mountains. Map 188

BLACK-CHINNED RED SALAMANDER
Pseudotriton ruber schencki   p. 254

Identification: 2¾–4¾; record 5. A red salamander with a strong concentration of black pigment under the chin. (Black area much heavier and broader than narrow black flecking seen in some individuals of its related subspecies.) Tail spotted almost to tip.

Under logs, stones, moss, etc., in habitats ranging from open pastures to forests.

Range: Elevations to more than 5000 feet, west and south of French Broad River, southern Blue Ridge Mountains. Map 188

SOUTHERN RED SALAMANDER
Pseudotriton ruber vioscai   p. 254

Identification: 3⅛–5¾; record 6⅜. A purplish, reddish, or salmon-colored salamander with a profusion of white flecks, these largely concentrated on snout and sides of head. The purplish effect is produced by numerous, fairly large blue-black blotches. Under surfaces light but with a profusion of small dark spots.

In and near springs, small streams, and in rotting, well-saturated logs.

Range: W.-cent. South Carolina to se. Louisiana and w. Tennessee.   Map 188

GREEN SALAMANDER *Aneides aeneus*   p. 254
Identification: 3¼–5; record 5½. Our *only really green salamander*. Green lichen-like markings on a dark ground color. Note square-tipped toes.

A cliff dweller. Narrow crevices on rock faces are a favorite habitat, provided rocks are damp but not wet, situated where the atmosphere is humid, and well protected from sun and direct rain. The flattened head and body are admirably adapted for getting about in tight places. Also sometimes found under stones, logs, or loose bark, or in rock crevices even in open fields. Occasionally arboreal.

Range: Appalachian region; s. Ohio and sw. Pennsylvania to n. Alabama. Other members of genus *Aneides* occur along Pacific Coast from s. California to Vancouver Island.   Map 191

Brook Salamanders: Genus *Eurycea*

THESE ARE salamanders of small brooks, rills, springs, seepage areas, river-bottom swamps, and other small bodies of water where fishes are absent or at a minimum. An alternate name might be "yellow salamanders," for yellowish pigment is found in most of them, at least on their under surfaces. In many there are well-pronounced, downward projections (cirri) from the nostrils, at least in males. All species have aquatic larvae. The genus occurs only in eastern North America.

The Brook Salamanders may be readily separated into three groups:

1. Typical "brook" salamanders, such as the Two-lined and Many-ribbed. These frequently wander well out into moist woodlands during wet weather and on humid nights.

2. The "long-tailed salamanders," which in the adult stage have tails considerably more than ½ their total lengths (juveniles have much shorter tails). These salamanders are essentially terrestrial but they swim readily; they include the Three-lined, Long-tailed, Dark-sided, and Cave Salamanders, the last three of which frequently are found in caves.

3. The "neotenic euryceas," which retain the larval form (with external gills) throughout life. These are completely aquatic, and are difficult to distinguish from the larvae of salamanders that normally transform into a gill-less adult form. Several occur in localities along or near the Balcones Escarpment in central Texas, where, fortunately, there are no other larval aquatic salamanders that could be confused with them.

NORTHERN TWO-LINED SALAMANDER

Eurycea bislineata bislineata p. 254

Identification: 2½–3¾; record 4½. The common yellow salamander of the Northeast. The 2 dark "lines" border a broad light middorsal stripe, but often tend to break up into dots or dashes on tail. The dorsal coloration, always essentially yellow, may be brownish, greenish, bronzy, or bordering on orange. The broad light stripe down back is usually peppered with small black spots that may join to form a narrow median dark line. Mottling on side of body varies in intensity from one specimen to the next; it may be so dark as to blend with dorsolateral line or, contrariwise, it may be much reduced or virtually absent.

Essentially a brookside salamander, hiding under all manner of objects at water's edge and running or swimming away vigorously when alarmed. Saturated areas near springs or seeps are also favorite habitats. In warm wet weather, it may wander far out into nearby woodlands.

Similar species: Populations of several kinds of Dusky Salamanders frequently include yellowish specimens, but in these there is often a light line from eye to angle of jaw; also, their hind legs are noticeably larger than their forelegs. Adult Salamanders of the long-tailed group have tails much more than ½ their total lengths. Ground Skinks superficially resemble Two-lined Salamanders, but Skinks, being lizards, are clad in scales and their toes are equipped with claws.

Range: S. Quebec to Virginia, Tennessee, and e. Illinois.

Subspecies: SOUTHERN TWO-LINED SALAMANDER, *Eurycea bislineata cirrigera.* Smaller; max. length about 4", but similar to Northern Twoline. The narrow black "lines" usually continue without interruption to tip of tail, and most specimens have a row of small circular light spots in the dark and light mottled area along the sides; dorsal coloration yellow to russet; adult males with well-developed projections (cirri) downward from nostrils, as in Blue Ridge Twoline. Chiefly a Coastal Plain and Piedmont race, secretive and hiding beneath all types of sheltering objects, including masses of wet leaves in creek or river swamps. North Carolina to n. Florida and west to Mississippi River. Map 194

BLUE RIDGE TWO-LINED SALAMANDER

Eurycea bislineata wilderae p. 254

Identification: 2¾–4¼; record 4¾. A montane salamander with the colors and pattern more vivid than in the Northern Twolined Salamander. "Lines" *broad* and black and normally breaking up into dots at about middle of tail. Most adult males have conspicuous projections (cirri) downward from nostrils.

Found in and near springs and rills, but wandering far out into the humid forests, at least at higher elevations. Most abundant above 2000 feet and to tops of tallest mountains.

Similar species: Yellowish examples of Blue Ridge Mountain Salamander usually have a light line from eye to angle of jaw (Fig., p. 258). Cave and Long-tailed Salamanders are *spotted*, and tails of adults are considerably more than ½ their total lengths.

Range: Southern Blue Ridge Mountain region from sw. Virginia to n. Georgia. Map 194

LONG-TAILED SALAMANDER
Eurycea longicauda longicauda p. 254

Identification: 4–6¼; record 7⅛. The only yellowish salamander with vertical black markings on the tail. These, although frequently varying from the herringbone or "dumbbell" theme, are usually conspicuous. The ground color also varies — from yellow to orange-red or even red. Some individuals, from scattered portions of the range, have the black markings larger and more conspicuous. *Young:* Yellow; tail relatively short.

Found in or under rotting logs, under stones, in shale banks near seepages, under rocks at streamside, and frequently in caves.

Range: S. New York to n. Alabama and w. Kentucky. Map 193

THREE-LINED SALAMANDER
Eurycea longicauda guttolineata p. 254

Identification: 4–6¼; record 7⅛. This is the southern member of the Long-tailed Salamander group and the only one with 3 dark stripes. Middorsal stripe may be broken into a series of elongated spots. Ground color varies from yellow to tan. Belly mottled with greenish gray on a ground color of dull yellow.

In river-bottom swamps, wet ditches, seepage areas at springs and streamside; sometimes at considerable distances from water.

Range: Virginia to Florida panhandle and Mississippi River.
Map 193

DARK-SIDED SALAMANDER
Eurycea longicauda melanopleura p. 254

Identification: 3⅝–5⅞; record 6⅝. The dark stripes, one along each side of the body, are in strong contrast with a broad middorsal stripe that is essentially light in color but well marked with dark spots. Coloration varies. Dark pigment on sides is grayish in juveniles but changes to deep reddish brown in old adults. The light flecks and spots in the dark bands vary from light gray to yellow. The middorsal stripe ranges from bright yellow in juveniles through greenish yellow to dull brownish yellow in the largest individuals.

This is a cave salamander, occurring in the twilight zone of caverns and grottoes, but also venturing far afield into the outer world.

Range: Central Highlands (Ozarks) and adj. areas; intergrading with the Long-tailed Salamander in Illinois and se. Missouri.
Map 193

CAVE SALAMANDER *Eurycea lucifuga* p. 254
Identification: 4–6; record 7⅛. A reddish salamander with a *long* tail. Ground color variable, however, and ranging from dull yellow through orange to bright orange-red. (Young tend to be yellow, the adults reddish.) The black spots are usually irregularly scattered, but sometimes they may form 2 to 3 longitudinal rows. Occasional specimens have the black markings especially large and conspicuous. Yellowish under surfaces normally unspotted. *Young:* Tail relatively short.

A favorite habitat is in the twilight zone of caves — near entrances, where the light is weak. There these salamanders — excellent climbers — move about on the formations and ledges, sometimes clinging solely by their prehensile tails. They also occur outside caves and may be discovered beneath logs, stones, or debris in wooded or fairly open places.

Similar species: Three-lined and Dark-sided Salamanders have dark longitudinal markings. Long-tailed Salamander usually has dark "dumbbells" or a herringbone pattern on sides of tail; also, its head is not so broad and flat as Cave Salamander's.

Range: Limestone areas, Virginia to Oklahoma. Map 195

MANY-RIBBED SALAMANDER
Eurycea multiplicata multiplicata p. 254
Identification: 2½–3¼; record 3 9/16. A yellowish salamander without strong longitudinal dark stripes. Sides of body somewhat darker than middorsal area and often with a row of faint light spots. Under surfaces plain bright yellow. Costal grooves 19 or 20. Often neotenic.

Essentially an aquatic amphibian, hiding beneath stones, logs, and various other objects, both in and out of caves. Wanders short distances afield in wet weather.

Similar species: Dwarf Salamander has only *four* toes on each *hind* foot. Two-lined Salamanders are superficially similar, but their ranges do not overlap range of Many-ribbed. They and Dwarf Salamander have 16 or fewer costal grooves. (See back endpaper for procedure on counting grooves.)

Range: N.-cent. Arkansas to se. Oklahoma. Map 197

GRAY-BELLIED SALAMANDER
Eurycea multiplicata griseogaster p. 254
Identification: 1⅞–3¼. A dark subspecies of the Many-ribbed Salamander, with a *gray* instead of yellow belly. Amount of tan

on back variable, and middorsal area may consist of a longitudinal stripe paler than the adjacent sides. Costal grooves 19 or 20.

Similar species: Central Dusky Salamander has light line from eye to angle of jaw. Darker specimens of Dwarf Salamander resemble Graybelly but they have only *four* toes on hind feet.

Range: Sw. Missouri and adj. Arkansas and Oklahoma.

Map 197

OKLAHOMA SALAMANDER *Eurycea tynerensis* p. 270

Identification: 1¾–3⅛. The grayish appearance is caused by a heavy stippling and streaking of black over a cream-colored ground. Amount of dark pigment variable; may be densest on sides, leaving a broad light stripe down back, or it may be heavy over all dorsal surfaces. Usually at least 1 row of small light spots appears along each side of body (as many as 3 rows in the larvae). Belly pale, except where viscera or eggs show through body wall. *External gills present.* Tail fin low.

This neotenic salamander lives in small gravelly creeks and springs, and may be found among stones or in vegetation growing in water.

Similar species: Larvae of Grotto Salamander have high tail fin and longitudinal streaks on sides of body.

Range: Ne. Oklahoma and adj. corners of Arkansas and Missouri.

Map 196

TEXAS SALAMANDER *Eurycea neotenes* p. 270

Identification: 2–4⅛. Light yellowish in coloration, but mottled with darker pigment; a double row of light flecks on each side of body, at least in smaller specimens (lower row fades out in older ones). Belly and lower sides plain light yellow, except where viscera or eggs may be seen through skin. *External gills present.*

This neotenic salamander is a resident of springs, seeps, small cavern streams, and other bodies of water along or near the Balcones Escarpment of central Texas.

Similar species: Texas Blind Salamander is virtually white and has a strongly flattened snout.

Subspecies: The several races are distinguished by minutiae or internal anatomy. Identify them by locality in which they are collected. FERN BANK SALAMANDER, *Eurycea neotenes pterophila* (illustrated on Plate 37). Fern Bank Spring, near Wimberley, Hays County, Texas. CASCADE CAVERN SALAMANDER, *Eurycea neotenes latitans.* Cascade Cavern, near Boerne, Kendall County, and Turtle Creek, Kerr County, Texas. BEXAR COUNTY SALAMANDER, *Eurycea neotenes neotenes.* Numerous localities from vicinities of Austin and San Antonio to Edwards and Uvalde Counties, Texas. Map 196

VALDINA FARMS SALAMANDER
Eurycea troglodytes   Not illustrated
Identification: 2–3⅛. About midway in general appearance between the Texas Blind Salamander and Texas Salamander. (It
may be a race of the latter.) This cave dweller looks white in
the beam of a flashlight, but it normally is grayish with white
specks and indistinct yellowish stripes along the sides of body
and upper surface of tail. Eyes partly or completely covered
with skin, legs long and slender, a somewhat flattened forehead,
and usually 13 costal grooves (14 to 16 in the subspecies of the
Texas Salamander). *External gills present.*
Range: Known only from the Valdina Farms Sinkhole, a cave in
northwestern Medina County, Texas.   Map 196

SAN MARCOS SALAMANDER   *Eurycea nana*   p. 270
Identification: 1½–2. Almost plain brown above, but with a row
of yellowish flecks down each side of back. Venter whitish or
yellowish except where viscera and eggs (of females in season)
show through translucent skin. *External gills present.*
    A tiny neotenic species known only from the shallow, weed-
choked border of the big spring forming the source of the San
Marcos River, at San Marcos, Texas.
Similar species: Texas Salamander is chiefly yellowish rather
than brown. Texas Blind Salamander is virtually white and has
a strongly flattened snout.   Map 196

DWARF SALAMANDER   *Manculus quadridigitatus*   p. 254
Identification: 2⅛–3; record 3⁹⁄₁₆. *Four toes on hind feet* as well
as forefeet. (Most other salamanders have *five* on each *hind*
foot.) The dark dorsolateral stripe ranges from black through
various shades of dark brown, and the amount of dark pigmentation on sides of body is quite variable. Many specimens have a
middorsal row of small dark spots; in others the row is short,
broken, or absent. *Male:* Often with downward projections
(cirri) from nostrils.
    A resident of low swampy areas, where it hides under all types
of shelter.
Similar species: Two-lined and Many-ribbed Salamanders are
superficially similar, but both have *five* toes on their *hind* feet.
Range: Chiefly in Coastal Plain from North Carolina to Florida
and west to e. Texas.   Map 198

X

Toads and Frogs

SPADEFOOT TOADS: FAMILY PELOBATIDAE

A SINGLE, sharp-edged, black "spade" on each hind foot enables a Spadefoot Toad to burrow vertically downward into sandy or other loose soil. This is the hallmark of the genus, but other characteristics include a rather smooth skin, parotoid glands absent or indistinct, and (normally) a vertically elliptical pupil (Fig. 50, below).

In contrast, the true Toads (*Bufo*) have *two* tubercles on the underside of each hind foot, one of which may be quite spadelike. They also have well-developed warts, ridges, and parotoid glands, and their pupils are horizontally oval (Fig. 50, below).

For distinguishing among the several Spadefoot Toads, two items should always be checked: (1) is there a raised area (boss) between the eyes; and (2) is the spade elongated and sickle-shaped or short and wedge-shaped? (See Fig. 51, p. 256).

Spadefoot Toads are "explosive" breeders, appearing suddenly, sometimes in great numbers, after heavy rains and at almost any time during the warm months of the year. They are adapted for life in arid regions and can remain underground for weeks or even months at a time, but they often venture forth on damp or rainy nights. Breeding males have black pads or excrescences on their thumbs and first 2 fingers.

The genus *Scaphiopus*, occurring throughout a large part of the United States and from southwestern Canada to southern Mexico, is the only group of the family in the New World. Other genera

Fig. 50. CHARACTERISTICS OF TOADS AND SPADEFOOT TOADS

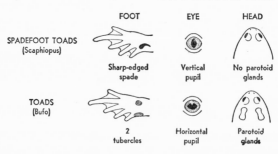

	FOOT	EYE	HEAD
SPADEFOOT TOADS (Scaphiopus)	Sharp-edged spade	Vertical pupil	No parotoid glands
TOADS (Bufo)	2 tubercles	Horizontal pupil	Parotoid glands

are found in Europe, extreme northwestern Africa, Asia, and the East Indies.

EASTERN SPADEFOOT *Scaphiopus holbrooki*   p. 267
 Identification: 1¾–2¼; record 2⅞. The only Spadefoot Toad occurring east of the Mississippi River. Spade elongate and sickle-shaped. No boss between eyes. Two yellowish lines, one originating at each eye and running down back, are usually well in evidence. The 2 lines together may form a lyre-shaped pattern or resemble the outline of a somewhat misshapen hourglass. Normally there is an additional light line on each side of body. Ground color some shade of brown (grayish- or blackish-brown or sepia). Some specimens may be almost uniformly dark gray to almost black.

 Although this is a species of the forested East and Southeast, it is usually found in areas characterized by sandy or other loose soils—habitats that in some respects resemble those of the Spadefoot Toads of more arid regions to the west.

 Voice: An explosive grunt, rather low-pitched, short in duration, but repeated at brief intervals. Some persons liken sound to call of a young crow.

 Range: S. New England to s. Florida (also Key West) and west to se. Missouri, Arkansas, and Louisiana; absent from most upland areas in the South.   Map 201

HURTER'S SPADEFOOT *Scaphiopus hurteri*   p. 267
 Identification: 1¾–2¼; record 3⅛. The only Spadefoot with a boss between the eyes (Fig. 52, p. 257) *and* an *elongate*, sickle-shaped spade. (The boss is actually a little farther back than the eyes.) General coloration often matches the "garrison green" uniforms of the U.S. Marine Corps, but it may vary from grayish green to a chocolate- or greenish-brown, or to almost black. The 2 curved light stripes on the back are often as conspicuous as those of Eastern Spadefoot.

 An inhabitant of wooded and savanna areas, but also occurring in arid terrain in southern Texas. Named for Julius Hurter, Missouri herpetologist.

 Similar species: In Couch's and Eastern Spadefoot Toads there is no boss between eyes (Fig. 52, p. 257). In the Plains and Western Spadefoot Toads the spade is *short*, rounded, and often wedge-shaped.

 Voice: A bleating note, slightly explosive, and short in duration, each bleat lasting less than ½ second.

 Range: Cent. Arkansas and w. Louisiana to cent. Oklahoma and s. Texas.   Map 200

COUCH'S SPADEFOOT *Scaphiopus couchi*   p. 267
 Identification: 2¼–2⅞; record 3½. A southwestern Spadefoot

RED, YELLOW, AND GREEN SALAMANDERS

	Map	*Text*

MOUNTAIN SPRING SALAMANDER   189   242
  Light *and* dark line, eye to nostril; black spots.

SPRING SALAMANDER   186   242
  Eye lines and pattern not clear-cut.

BLACK-CHINNED RED SALAMANDER   188   245
  Heavy black pigment on chin.

SOUTHERN RED SALAMANDER   188   245
  Small white flecks, especially on head.

NORTHERN RED SALAMANDER   188   244
  Black spots numerous, irregular, and often running together; *eye yellow. Old adult:* Spots large, but indistinct; ground color dark.

EASTERN MUD SALAMANDER   192   243
  Black spots round, few in number, and remaining separate; *eye brown.*

RUSTY MUD SALAMANDER   192   244
  Markings obscure; dark streaks on sides.

THREE-LINED SALAMANDER   193   248
  Tail long; a middorsal dark stripe.

LONG-TAILED SALAMANDER   193   248
  Tail long, with "dumbbells" or herringbone pattern.

DARK-SIDED SALAMANDER   193   248
  Tail long; sides marked with gray and yellow.

CAVE SALAMANDER   195   249
  Tail long; black spots on reddish ground color.

DWARF SALAMANDER   198   251
  4 toes on *hind* foot; dark dorsolateral stripe.

NORTHERN TWO-LINED SALAMANDER   194   247
  Belly yellow; dark line from eye to tail.

BLUE RIDGE TWO-LINED SALAMANDER   194   247
  Bright coloration; dark lines clear-cut. *Male:* Conspicuous downward projection from nostril.

MANY-RIBBED SALAMANDER   197   249
  Light spots in dark lateral stripe (see text).

GRAY-BELLIED SALAMANDER   197   249
  Dark venter; trace of tan on dorsum (see text).

GREEN SALAMANDER   191   246
  Green, lichen-like markings.

MANY-LINED SALAMANDER   177   237
  Light and dark streaks on lower sides.

♂ means male, ♀ female.

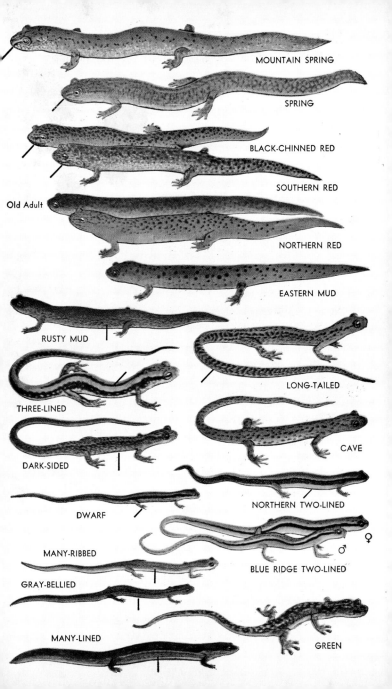

MOUNTAIN SPRING

SPRING

BLACK-CHINNED RED

SOUTHERN RED

Old Adult

NORTHERN RED

EASTERN MUD

RUSTY MUD

LONG-TAILED

THREE-LINED

DARK-SIDED

CAVE

NORTHERN TWO-LINED

DWARF

MANY-RIBBED

♀

♂

BLUE RIDGE TWO-LINED

GRAY-BELLIED

MANY-LINED

GREEN

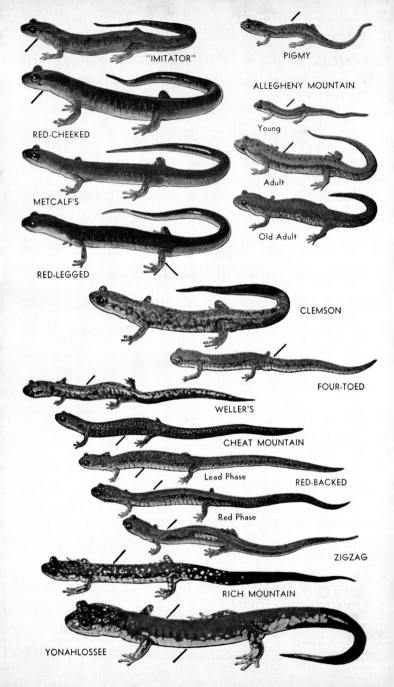

"IMITATOR"

PIGMY

ALLEGHENY MOUNTAIN

RED-CHEEKED

Young

Adult

Old Adult

METCALF'S

RED-LEGGED

CLEMSON

FOUR-TOED

WELLER'S

CHEAT MOUNTAIN

Lead Phase

RED-BACKED

Red Phase

ZIGZAG

RICH MOUNTAIN

YONAHLOSSEE

Plate 32   **255**

WOODLAND AND DUSKY SALAMANDERS (2)

Map Text

"IMITATOR SALAMANDER"   224
(A pattern phase of Blue Ridge Mountain Salamander.)
Light cheek patch; suggestion of line from eye to angle of
jaw. Seepage areas or wet environment.

RED-CHEEKED SALAMANDER   178 235
Rosy-red cheek patch; terrestrial.

METCALF'S SALAMANDER   178 236
Unmarked black or dark gray.

RED-LEGGED SALAMANDER   178 236
Red patches on legs.

PIGMY SALAMANDER   173 226
Tiny size; herringbone pattern; terrestrial.

ALLEGHENY MOUNTAIN SALAMANDER   174 224
Middorsal light stripe with nearly *straight* dark border;
coloration variable (see text). *Young:* Unpatterned
orange stripe. *Adult:* Row of dots or chevrons. *Old
adult:* Dark brown to black; pattern faint.

CLEMSON SALAMANDER   178 236
Metallic patches on dark ground; white flecks on sides;
variable (see text).

FOUR-TOED SALAMANDER   187 237
4 toes on *hind* foot; constriction at base of tail; belly white
with black spots (Fig. 48, p. 231).

WELLER'S SALAMANDER   183 232
Gold or silver blotches.

CHEAT MOUNTAIN SALAMANDER   183 232
Numerous small gold flecks; belly *black*.

RED-BACKED SALAMANDER   179 230
Belly "salt-and-pepper" (Fig. 48, p. 231).
Lead-backed: Dorsum nearly plain dark.
Red-backed: Straight-edged middorsal stripe.

ZIGZAG SALAMANDER   180 231
Zigzag or irregular middorsal stripe.

RICH MOUNTAIN SALAMANDER   185 235
Dark red or chocolate with white specks.

YONAHLOSSEE SALAMANDER   182 234
Red or chestnut dorsum; light lateral stripe.

with considerable yellowish pigmentation in the skin. Dorsal ground color varying from bright greenish yellow to dull brownish yellow; marked with a mottling or marbling of black, green, or dark brown. (Dark pattern may fade out during breeding season.) Spade *elongate* and often sickle-shaped. No boss between eyes. Diameter of eyelid about equal to distance between eyes (Fig. 51, below).

A species of short-grass plains and also of mesquite savannas and other arid or semi-arid regions. Named for Darius Nash Couch, a professional soldier who collected many natural-history specimens while serving in northern Mexico, and with the U. S. and Mexican Boundary Survey.

Similar species: Plains and Western Spadefoot Toads have *short* wedge-shaped spades and eyelids noticeably wider than distance between them (Fig. 51, below). Hurter's Spadefoot has boss between eyes.

Voice: A groaning bleat, suggestive of a goat or sheep unhappy at being tied. Each bleat fairly long, lasting ½ to 1 second.

Range: Cent. Texas and adj. Oklahoma to Arizona and south into Mexico.   Map 203

Fig. 51. CHARACTERISTICS OF SPADEFOOT TOADS

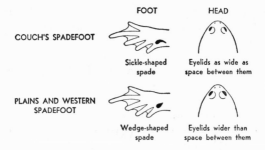

FOOT   HEAD

COUCH'S SPADEFOOT

Sickle-shaped spade   Eyelids as wide as space between them

PLAINS AND WESTERN SPADEFOOT

Wedge-shaped spade   Eyelids wider than space between them

PLAINS SPADEFOOT *Scaphiopus bombifrons*   p. 267
Identification: 1½–2; record 2¼. Our only Spadefoot with a pronounced boss between the eyes *plus* a *short*, rounded, often wedge-shaped spade. General coloration grayish or brownish, often with a greenish tinge; dark markings brown or gray. Small tubercles on the dorsum may be noticeably yellowish or reddish. Four rather vague longitudinal light lines often present on back. Eyelids wider than distance between them (Fig. 51, above).

At home on the Great Plains and in regions of low rainfall; a species of the open grasslands, avoiding river bottoms and wooded areas.

Similar species: Both Couch's and the Western Spadefoot

Toads lack a boss between eyes (Fig. 52, below). Also in Couch's Spadefoot the spade is *elongate* and space between eyes is about equal to width of an eyelid (Fig. 51, p. 256).

Voice: A short rasping bleat repeated at intervals of ½ to a full second, or a rasping snore, rather low-pitched and each trill lasting ½ to ¾ second.

Range: S. Alberta to n. Mexico; east to Nebraska, w. Missouri, Oklahoma, and s. Texas.   Map 199

Fig. 52   A raised boss between the eyes in the DAKOTA TOAD and PLAINS and HURTER'S SPADEFOOT TOADS   No raised boss in most other TOADS and SPADEFOOT TOADS

WESTERN SPADEFOOT *Scaphiopus hammondi*   p. 267
Identification: 1½–2; record 2½. The spade is *short* and wedge-shaped, and there is *no* boss between the eyes. General coloration dusky — gray, brown, or dusky green — with scattered spots and blotches of a darker color. The small tubercles on the dorsum may be reddish. Occasional specimens may have vague suggestions of longitudinal, light-colored lines. Eyelids wider than distance between them (Fig. 51, p. 256). Skin produces an odor like unroasted peanuts.

At home in short-grass plains and in playas and alkali flats of arid and semi-arid regions; absent from extreme deserts.

Similar species: Plains Spadefoot has boss between eyes (Fig. 52, above). In Couch's Spadefoot the spade is *elongate*, and space between eyes is about equal to width of eyelid (Fig. 51, p. 256).

Voice: A vibrant metallic trill like running a fingernail along the stiff teeth of a large comb. Each trill lasts about ¾ to 1½ seconds.

Range: W. Oklahoma, extr. s. Wyoming, and cent. Arizona south into Mexico; a disjunct population in the Californias.   Map 202

LEPTODACTYLID FROGS:
FAMILY LEPTODACTYLIDAE

A VERY LARGE family of the American tropics, but with several species ranging northward into Texas and another introduced into Florida. Many of its members lay their eggs on land, their tadpoles undergoing complete metamorphosis in the egg. Others beat the egg jelly into a froth, the larvae living in the liquefied center of the mass until rains wash them into nearby pools. Three genera occur within our area: Nest-building Frogs (*Leptodactylus*), Robber

WOODLAND AND DUSKY SALAMANDERS (3)

WOODLAND SPECIES
(Most of these are black with light markings.)

Map Text

ROANOKE SALAMANDER   182 234
Small white flecks and bronzy mottling on purplish-brown background.

WEHRLE'S SALAMANDER   182 234
White or bluish-white spots along sides.

RAVINE SALAMANDER   184 231
Long, slender body; no conspicuous markings; belly dark (Fig. 48, p. 231).

WHITE-THROATED SLIMY SALAMANDER   181 233
Bulk of white spots along sides; throat light.

SLIMY SALAMANDER   181 233
Numerous silvery-white spots; throat dark.

DUSKY AND ALLIED SPECIES
(Usually a diagonal light line behind eye.)

SEAL SALAMANDER   170 225
Heavy dark markings on dorsum; venter pale.

NORTHERN DUSKY SALAMANDER   171 217
Markings extremely variable (see text); venter lightly pigmented.

BLACK-BELLIED SALAMANDER   172 226
2 rows of light dots on sides; venter black.

SOUTHERN SHOVEL-NOSED SALAMANDER   175 228
A row of light spots on each side.

NORTHERN SHOVEL-NOSED SALAMANDER   175 227
Dorsum gray, mottled with tan or olive.

WOODLAND SALAMANDER
Legs approximately same size

DUSKY SALAMANDER
Hind legs larger than forelegs; light line from eye to angle of jaw

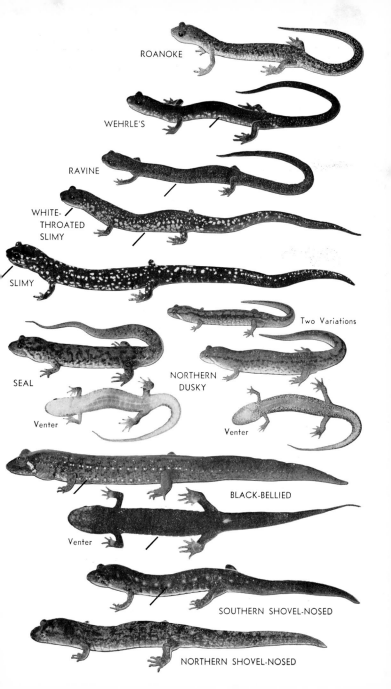

ROANOKE

WEHRLE'S

RAVINE

WHITE-
THROATED
SLIMY

SLIMY

SEAL

NORTHERN
DUSKY

Two Variations

Venter

Venter

BLACK-BELLIED

Venter

SOUTHERN SHOVEL-NOSED

NORTHERN SHOVEL-NOSED

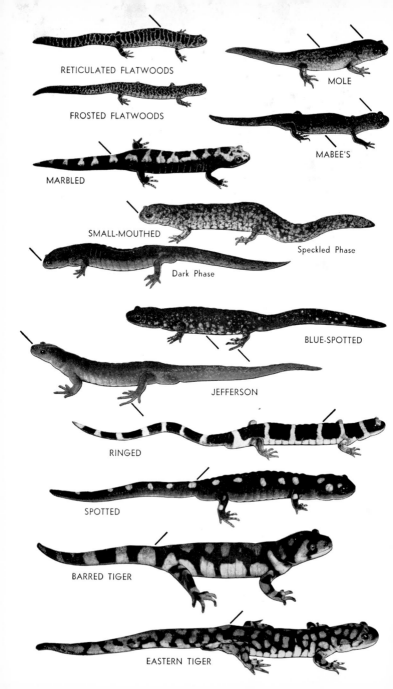

RETICULATED FLATWOODS

MOLE

FROSTED FLATWOODS

MABEE'S

MARBLED

SMALL-MOUTHED

Speckled Phase

Dark Phase

BLUE-SPOTTED

JEFFERSON

RINGED

SPOTTED

BARRED TIGER

EASTERN TIGER

Plate 34   259

MOLE SALAMANDERS

	Map	*Text*

RETICULATED FLATWOODS SALAMANDER   166 209
  Narrow light rings or a tendency to form a netlike pattern.

FROSTED FLATWOODS SALAMANDER   166 209
  Irregular "frosted" pattern.

MOLE SALAMANDER   167 211
  Short, chunky body; large head.

MABEE'S SALAMANDER   160 211
  Profuse light speckling on sides; small head.

MARBLED SALAMANDER   165 211
  White or silvery crossbars.

SMALL-MOUTHED SALAMANDER   164 211
  Very short snout. *Dark phase:* Markings indistinct.
  Speckled phase: Profuse lichen-like markings.

BLUE-SPOTTED SALAMANDER   162 210
  Long toes; numerous blue or bluish-white spots and flecks.

JEFFERSON SALAMANDER   162 209
  Long toes; long snout; a few bluish flecks on sides.

RINGED SALAMANDER   168 208
  Bold light crossbands.

SPOTTED SALAMANDER   163 212
  Round light spots in irregular dorsolateral row.

BARRED TIGER SALAMANDER   169 213
  Large light bars or blotches.

EASTERN TIGER SALAMANDER   169 212
  Light markings small, not forming definite pattern.

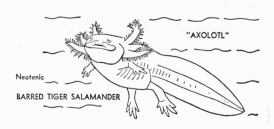

"AXOLOTL"

Neotenic

BARRED TIGER SALAMANDER

Frogs (*Eleutherodactylus*), and Chirping Frogs (*Syrrhophus*). The family is also abundantly represented in Australia.

MEXICAN WHITE-LIPPED FROG

Leptodactylus labialis   p. 271

Identification: 1⅜–2. A white or cream-colored line on the upper lip and a distinct ventral disc (Fig. 53, below). Dorsolateral folds present. Ground color varies from gray to chocolate-brown. Number and size of dark dorsal spots also variable.

One of the several Mexican amphibians and reptiles that barely enter the United States in extreme southern Texas. Found in a wide variety of habitats, including roadside ditches, irrigated fields, moist meadows, drains, etc.

Similar species: Spotted Chorus Frog has no dorsolateral folds and also lacks a ventral disc.

Voice: *Throw-up, throw-up* repeated continually and with a rising inflection at end of each call. Males call from cavities beneath hummocks of grass or clods of dirt or in small pits as much as 3 inches deep. Breeding season begins in spring or summer with onset of heavy rains. Eggs laid in a froth "nest."

Range: Lower Rio Grande Valley, Texas, to Panama. Map 204

BARKING FROG   *Eleutherodactylus augusti latrans*   p. 271

Identification: 2½–3; record 3¾. A frog that looks like a toad, but has a smooth, dry skin (no warts). There is a dorsolateral fold and a ventral disc similar to that of Mexican White-lipped Frog (Fig. 53, below). The general coloration may vary from tan to greenish and may include tones of pink or reddish brown. *Young:* Often greenish and with a fawn-colored band across middle of back.

A resident of limestone caves and ledges that rarely ventures out into the open, even during rains. When captured, as by snake or human being, it puffs itself up prodigiously. Sometimes called the "robber frog."

Voice: An explosive call, like the bark of a dog when heard at a distance, but more of a guttural *whurr* at close range. The single note may be repeated at regular intervals of 2 to 3 seconds. When females are grasped in the hand they may make a blaring screech. Breeds during rainy periods from late winter to May.

Range: Cent. Texas and se. New Mexico. Mexican subspecies. Map 204

Fig. 53   Ventral disc in the BARKING and MEXICAN WHITE-LIPPED FROGS

GREENHOUSE FROG
Eleutherodactylus ricordi planirostris   p. 271
    Identification: ⅝-1¼. A tiny immigrant, probably from Cuba.
Two pattern phases: (1) *striped*, with longitudinal light stripes;
and (2) *mottled*, with irregular dark and light markings. The
general coloration is brown, but usually with distinct reddish
tones. *Young:* With a tiny tail at hatching.
    These minute frogs are terrestrial, seeking shelter by day or
in dry weather beneath boards, leaves, trash, or other debris
where there is some moisture. They normally move about only
at night or in rainy weather. Usually to be found in gardens,
greenhouses, hardwood hammocks, and in small stream valleys.
    Voice: Short melodious birdlike chirps, usually 4 to 6 in a series.
Breeds during summer rainy season (May to September in
northern Florida). Only frog east of Texas that lays on land.
Eggs are deposited under damp vegetation or debris. Development takes place entirely in the egg; no free tadpole stage.
    Range: Cuba and several of the West Indies; introduced into
Florida; subspecies in Cuba and the Bahamas.   Map 206

CLIFF FROG *Syrrhophus marnocki*   p. 271
    Identification: ¾-1½. A Chirping Frog, greenish in coloration,
but mottled with brown and clad in a smooth skin.
    The flattened head and body facilitate rapid retreats into
cracks and crevices of cliffs that mark the eastern face and occur
in numerous other parts of the Edwards Plateau of central
Texas. This small amphibian normally is active only at night.
It leaps and hops as do other frogs, but it may also run when
seeking shelter.
    Similar species: Green Toad has a warty skin.
    Voice: A cricket-like chirp or trill that may be heard throughout
the year. The mating call, given only when a female is present,
is similar but clearer and sharper. Peak of breeding season is
in April or May, but egg deposition may occur at any time from
late February to early December.
    Range: Cent. Texas to Big Bend region.   Map 205

RIO GRANDE FROG *Syrrhophus campi*   p. 271
    Identification: ⅝-1. One of the Chirping Frogs. A nondescript
species, brown to grayish- or yellowish-olive and with no distinctive field marks. But since it barely enters the United
States from Mexico, it will cause little confusion except in extreme southern Texas. Dark line from nostril through eye usually not very prominent. Behavior will help. This little frog
not only leaps and hops but also runs, and is very quick and
adept at darting under cover.
    An abundant species in the lower Rio Grande Valley that
seems to thrive in the midst of civilization. At night it may

appear on lawns or in flower beds or gutters, especially if some sprinkling has been going on. By day it hides under boards, debris, flower boxes, or other objects that offer both moisture and shelter. More natural habitats include environs of palm groves, thickets, ditches, and resacas.

Voice: A cricket-like chirp, usually given erratically, not at regular intervals. Breeds in spring, but may be heard during any of the warm months when irrigation is in progress.

Range: Extr. s. Texas and ne. Mexico.   Map 205

TOADS: FAMILY BUFONIDAE

THE HOMELY "hoptoad" is readily recognized as such, but telling the different kinds apart is quite another matter. Recourse must be made to checking the shapes and sizes of the shoulder (parotoid) glands and cranial ridges, the relative number and prominence of the warts, and differences in coloration and pattern. To complicate matters, certain species are known to hybridize with others. This unfortunate state of affairs undoubtedly has been aggravated by mankind's propensity for altering habitats and thus bringing animals together that had remained isolated for one reason or another during prehistoric times.

Toads in general have dry, warty skins and they hop. Frogs have moist, relatively smooth skins and they leap. Only Spadefoot Toads (*Scaphiopus*) are likely to be confused with true Toads (*Bufo*). For ways of telling the two genera apart see p. 252.

One does not get warts from touching toads, but their skin-gland secretions are irritating to mucous membranes. Wash your hands after handling them, and keep your fingers away from your mouth and eyes until you do.

In the North, toads breed in the spring and, depending on weather conditions, at more or less the same time each year. In the South, they may mate more than once and, collectively, during almost any month. In the arid Southwest, where they occur in greatest variety, deposition of eggs usually depends upon the advent of rain. Breeding males have dark nuptial pads on their thumbs and inner fingers. Throats of males are dark or at least dusky. The vocal sac in most species is round when inflated; in others it is sausage-shaped (Fig. 54, p. 263). In most species the females grow larger than their mates. Individual toads may vary considerably in coloration, being dark at one time and light at another, depending upon conditions of temperature, animation, etc. Small toads, especially those which have recently transformed, are often virtually impossible to identify.

The family is nearly world-wide in distribution, except for Madagascar, Polynesia, and the Australian and polar regions.

Fig. 54. MALE TOADS WITH VOCAL SACS INFLATED (DIAGRAMMATIC)

Rounded in most species

Sausage-shaped in the GREAT PLAINS, TEXAS, and OAK TOADS

AMERICAN TOAD *Bufo americanus* p. 267

Identification: 2–3½; record 4¼. The widespread and abundant "hoptoad" of the Northeast. Throughout the great bulk of its range, only Fowler's Toad is likely to be confused with it, but, unfortunately, the two sometimes hybridize. Despite considerable individual and local variation, the following points normally hold for the American Toad: (1) only *1 or 2 large warts* in each of largest dark spots; (2) chest and forward part of abdomen *usually spotted* with dark pigment; (3) enlarged warts on thighs; and (4) parotoid gland either separated from the ridge behind the eye, or connected with it by a short spur (Fig. 55, p. 264). A light middorsal stripe may or may not be present. Many American Toads are almost plain brown, but others, females especially, are gaily patterned. The general ground color varies through numerous shades of brown from gray or olive to brick-red, but may be ornamented by patches of yellow or buff or other light colors. Dark spots are brown or black, and warts vary from yellow, orange, or red to dark brown.

Habitats are legion, spanning the gap from city back yards to mountain wildernesses. Requisites seem to be shallow bodies of water in which to breed (temporary pools or ditches or shallow portions of streams, for example), shelter in the form of hiding places where there is some moisture, and an abundant supply of insects and other invertebrates for food. Toads of this and several other species do well in captivity if they have loose soil in which to burrow, water to soak in occasionally, plenty of live insects, and a minimum of handling.

Similar species: See Fowler's Toad (p. 269) and Southern Toad (p. 264). Rocky Mountain Toad has a plain belly and its warts are more numerous and nearly all same size.

Voice: A rather long musical trill, one of the most pleasant sounds of early spring. Individual calls may last from 6 to 30 seconds; trill rate about 30 per second. Breeds from March to July; the later dates at high altitudes or latitudes.

Range: Maritime Provinces to se. Manitoba; south to Mississippi and ne. Kansas.

Subspecies: AMERICAN TOAD, *Bufo americanus americanus* (illustrated on Plate 36). As described and with range indicated above. HUDSON BAY TOAD, *Bufo americanus copei.* A far-northern race noted for vividness of colors and sharply defined markings, especially on the heavily spotted venter. Coast of Labrador to James Bay. DWARF AMERICAN TOAD, *Bufo americanus charlesmithi.* Size much smaller; max. about 2½". Very often reddish in coloration; venter only faintly spotted, or not at all. Call pitched about midway between calls of American and Southern Toads. S. Illinois to e. Oklahoma and extr. ne. Louisiana. Map 208

Fig. 55. CRANIAL CRESTS AND PAROTOID GLANDS OF VARIOUS TOADS

FOWLER'S
Parotoid touches
postorbital ridge

AMERICAN
Parotoid separated
from ridge or connected
to it by a spur

SOUTHERN
Pronounced knobs
at rear of inter-
orbital crests

HOUSTON
Postorbital ridges
thickened

DAKOTA
A boss
between eyes

GREAT PLAINS
Interorbital ridges
converge to meet a
boss on the snout

RED-SPOTTED
Parotoid round

GULF COAST
Deep "valley" on
center of head;
parotoid triangular

SOUTHERN TOAD *Bufo terrestris* p. 267

Identification: 1⅝–3; record 3⅞. Pronounced knobs and high cranial crests give the head a strongly "sculptured" appearance. Viewed in direct profile, large adults look almost "horned." The 2 crests that run forward from the knobs tend to approach each other toward the snout (Fig. 55, above). General coloration usually some shade of brown, but variable from red to black; with or without dark spots that contain 1 or 2 warts, or often more. There may be a light middorsal stripe, but this is often quite obscure, especially toward rear of back. *Young:* Knobs not well developed, but their future locations indicated by backward extensions from cranial crests.

The common toad of the South, and particularly abundant in sandy areas. Like other toads, it becomes active at twilight, foraging well into the night. Daylight hours are spent chiefly in hiding, often in burrows of the toad's own making.

Similar species: None of our other toads have such pronounced cranial knobs. Most trouble will come in trying to identify young specimens. Fowler's Toad has smaller, less elevated warts, and there are usually 3 or more in each large dark spot. In Oak Toad, cranial crests are inconspicuous, and the light middorsal stripe is prominent. In American Toad, even in young, there are no marked extensions backward from cranial crests (Fig. 55, p. 264).

Voice: A shrill musical trill almost an octave higher than that of American Toad. Duration of call varies from about 2 to 8 seconds. Trill rate rapid, about 75 per second. These toads breed in shallow water, and may be heard from March to October, depending upon locality and weather conditions.

Range: Coastal Plain from extr. se. Virginia to Mississippi River; south throughout Florida and on lower Keys. Map 210

HOUSTON TOAD *Bufo houstonensis*   p. 264

Identification: 2–2⅝. Here is an isolated relative of the American and Southern Toads which resembles them in most details of structure and voice. Cranial ridges quite thickened, especially those running across behind eyes. The dorsum bears a dark mottled pattern that may be arranged in a vague herringbone fashion. The mottling is brown to black on a ground color of cream to purplish gray and with or without patches of dark green. Usually a middorsal light stripe present. Venter with numerous small dark spots.

Similar species: In Rocky Mountain and Fowler's Toads the parotoid gland touches cranial ridge behind eye (Fig. 55, p. 264). In East Texas Toad the dorsum is usually brown or gray without much pattern (except for indications of striping), and the cranial crests are sharp and narrow. Gulf Coast Toad has a pronounced dark stripe along side of body and a deep valley between eyes (Fig. 55, p. 264). In Texas Toad both tubercles beneath hind foot have sharp cutting edges.

Voice: A piercing but rather musical trill, higher pitched than in American Toad, but with about same trill rate (32 per second) and of 4 to 11 seconds' duration.

Range: Se. Texas.   Map 208

DAKOTA TOAD *Bufo hemiophrys*   p. 267

Identification: 2–3; record 3¼. A far-northern toad with a pronounced boss between eyes (similar to boss of the Plains and

GIANT SALAMANDERS

WATERDOGS AND MUDPUPPY

(All have external gills and 4 well-developed legs.)

	Map	*Text*
GULF COAST WATERDOG Dark spots numerous and close together.	154	200
DWARF WATERDOG Almost uniformly dark above; paler below.	155	201
MUDPUPPY Dark spots few and well separated.	154	198

SIRENS AND AMPHIUMA

(Eel-like salamanders with 2 or 4 legs.)

LESSER SIREN Tiny front legs; external gills; small size (see text).	156	202
GREATER SIREN Small front legs; external gills; large size.	157	202
AMPHIUMA Tiny front *and* hind legs.	152	205

HELLBENDERS

(Broad, flat heads; folds of skin along sides.)

HELLBENDER Dark markings few and small.	153	197
OZARK HELLBENDER Dark markings large and blotchlike.	153	198

LARVAE OF WATERDOGS AND MUDPUPPY

MUDPUPPY GROUP   GULF COAST GROUP
(maculosus)   (beyeri)
Striped   Spotted

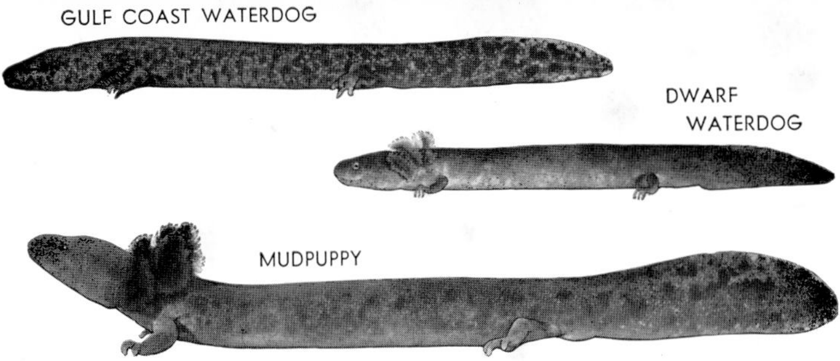

GULF COAST WATERDOG

DWARF WATERDOG

MUDPUPPY

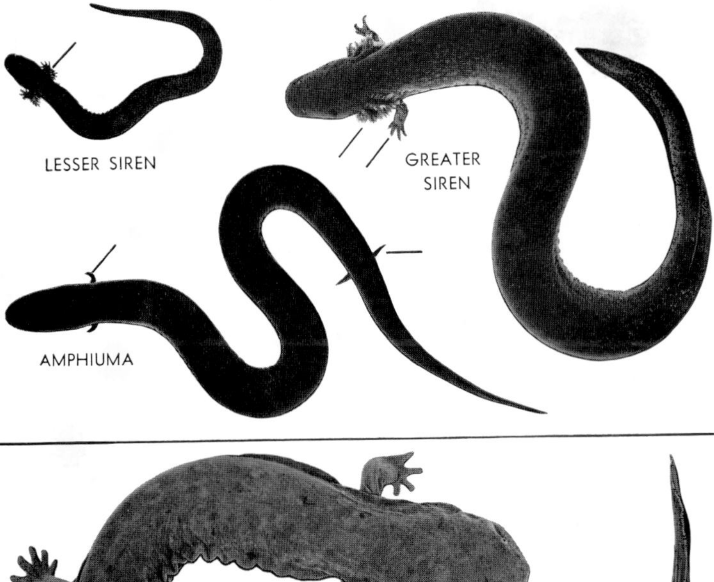

LESSER SIREN

GREATER SIREN

AMPHIUMA

HELLBENDER

OZARK HELLBENDER

SPADEFOOT TOADS

COUCH'S

HURTER'S

EASTERN

PLAINS

WESTERN

SOUTHERN

AMERICAN

DAKOTA

GULF COAST

FOWLER'S

ROCKY MOUNTAIN

RED-SPOTTED

TEXAS

GIANT

GREAT PLAINS

Plate 36   267

TOADS AND SPADEFOOT TOADS

SPADEFOOT TOADS

(A single sharp-edged "spade" under each hind foot.)

Map *Text*

COUCH'S SPADEFOOT TOAD   203 253
    Dark irregular pattern on yellowish or greenish ground
    color; variable (see text).

HURTER'S SPADEFOOT TOAD   200 253
    Light dorsal lines; boss* between eyes (Fig. 52, p. 257).

EASTERN SPADEFOOT TOAD   201 253
    Light lines in form of lyre.

PLAINS SPADEFOOT TOAD   199 256
    Faint longitudinal light stripes; boss* between eyes (Fig.
    52, p. 257).

WESTERN SPADEFOOT TOAD   202 257
    Gray or brown with small dark markings.

TRUE TOADS

(Two tubercles under hind foot — spadelike in some species.)

SOUTHERN TOAD   210 264
    Prominent cranial knobs (Fig. 55, p. 264).

AMERICAN TOAD   208 263
    1 or 2 large warts in each dark spot.

DAKOTA TOAD   207 265
    Boss* between eyes (Fig. 52, p. 257).

GULF COAST TOAD   216 272
    Broad dark lateral stripe bordered above by light stripe.

FOWLER'S TOAD   211 269
    3 or more warts in each dark spot.

ROCKY MOUNTAIN TOAD   211 268
    Warts in dark spots variable in number (see text).

RED-SPOTTED TOAD   215 274
    Parotoid† rounded in shape; no middorsal light stripe.

TEXAS TOAD   214 273
    Parotoid† oval; no middorsal light stripe.

GREAT PLAINS TOAD   212 272
    Large dark blotches with light borders.

GIANT TOAD   209 274
    Parotoid† enormously enlarged.

*A raised area.   †Shoulder gland.

Hurter's Spadefoot Toads — see Fig. 52, p. 257). The boss, which may be grooved on top, extends from snout as far backward as rear margin of eyelids. Ground color brownish or greenish. Warts brown or reddish and set in dark spots. A light middorsal stripe. *Young:* Cranial crests absent; these develop later, eventually uniting to form the boss.

Occurs in pools and puddles, roadside ditches, and in vicinity of lakes and streams.

Similar species: Rocky Mountain Toad has pronounced cranial crests, but normally lacks boss between eyes (at least in the eastern part of its range). Dark spots of Great Plains Toad are large, contain many warts, and are distinctly light-bordered.
Voice: A rather soft low-pitched trill lasting 2 to 5 seconds and repeated 2 or 3 times a minute. Trill rate very rapid, about 90 per second.
Range: Nw. Minnesota to most of Alberta; an isolated colony in s. Wyoming.   Map 207

ROCKY MOUNTAIN TOAD *Bufo woodhousei woodhousei* p. 267
Identification: 2½–4; record 5. Lacking any really distinctive markings, this large toad is best identified by a process of "boiling down" — by eliminating everything it couldn't be (see "similar species" below). There is a *light middorsal stripe*, cranial crests are *prominent*, and *parotoid glands* are *elongate*. The dark dorsal spots contain from 1 to several warts, and the spots themselves are irregular and not so prominent as in some other species. Belly whitish or yellowish, usually completely unmarked, but sometimes with a dark "breast spot" and dark flecks between forelegs. General coloration yellowish brown or gray, sometimes with an olive or greenish cast.

This amphibian, abundant in many localities, ranges from the grasslands of the Great Plains, through the Rocky Mountain region and beyond, and into the arid Southwest. Habitats include marshes and swales, river bottoms, mountain canyons, deserts, and irrigated areas, plus urban and suburban back yards. It usually appears at night and often near lights, where insects abound and may be had for the gulping.
Similar species: Texas Toad has *no light middorsal stripe* and no (or virtually no) cranial crests. Red-spotted Toad has *round* parotoids. Dakota Toad has raised *boss* between eyes. (Rocky Mountain Toads within our area normally lack such a boss.) In the American Toad and East Texas Toad there are numerous *dark markings on chest*. Fowler's Toad, related subspecifically to Rocky Mountain Toad, has large, dark, well-defined, dorsal spots, often 6 in number, and each containing 3 or more warts.
Voice: A nasal *w-a-a-a-h*, lasting 1 to 2½ seconds, and rather like a sheep bleating in the distance. Call very similar to that of Fowler's Toad, but somewhat lower in pitch. Breeds March to

July, usually after rains, and wherever there is shallow, standing or slightly moving water.

Range: The Dakotas and w. Missouri to se. Washington and south into Mexico. Map 211

FOWLER'S TOAD *Bufo woodhousei fowleri* p. 267
Identification: 2–3; record 3¼. A typical Fowler's Toad has: (1) *3 or more warts* in each of largest dark spots; (2) a virtually *unspotted* chest and belly; (3) no greatly enlarged warts on thighs; and (4) a parotoid gland that touches cranial ridge behind eye (Fig. 55, p. 264). There is some variation, but usually at least 3 of these characteristics are present. Many specimens have a single dark "breast spot" on an otherwise immaculate venter. The general dorsal coloration is brown or gray or, more rarely, greenish or brick-red. A light middorsal stripe.

An extremely abundant toad of the Atlantic Coastal Plain from Long Island to North Carolina. Farther inland its distribution is spotty, and it occurs chiefly in sandy areas, around shores of lakes, or in river valleys. In regions where their presence is not even suspected, these toads may appear suddenly in great numbers when warm heavy rains follow a long period of drought. Named for S. P. Fowler, an early Massachusetts naturalist.

Similar species: American Toad has: (1) only *1 or 2* large warts in each dark spot; (2) chest *spotted* with dark pigment; (3) enlarged warts on thighs; and (4) parotoid gland either separated from ridge behind eye or connected with it by short spur. Southern Toad has pronounced knobs at rear of cranial crests (see Fig. 55, p. 264). Gulf Coast Toad has broad dark stripe along the side. Fowler's Toad is known to hybridize with other species of toads; the offspring may show characteristics of both parents, and the calls of male hybrids may be intermediate and difficult or impossible to identify.

Voice: A short unmusical bleat—a nasal *w-a-a-a-a-h*—lasting 1 to 4 seconds. Breeds from spring to mid-August, and usually later than the American Toad in any given locality. Calls from ditches, temporary pools, or shallow margins of permanent bodies of water.

Range: Cent. New England to Gulf Coast and west to Michigan, ne. Oklahoma, and e. Louisiana; absent from southern part of the Atlantic Coastal Plain and most of Florida.

Subspecies: EAST TEXAS TOAD. *Bufo woodhousei velatus.* Similar in size and all characteristics except pattern. This is a "dark-breasted" toad, in contrast to its "light-breasted" subspecific relatives, the Rocky Mountain and Fowler's Toads. Chest is diffused with dark pigment, and is either uniformly dusky or marked in addition with numerous small black spots; the spots may continue onto abdomen. (In Fowler's Toad dark pigment on throat of male usually terminates abruptly about

NEWTS AND NEOTENIC SALAMANDERS

Map Text

RED-SPOTTED NEWT 159 214
Red spots in all phases. *Red Eft* (land form): Red or orange, transforming to dark olive (or other colors — see text). *Aquatic female:* Olive; belly yellow, spotted with black. *Aquatic male* (in breeding condition): High tail fin; black horny growths on hind legs and toes.

BLACK-SPOTTED NEWT 161 216
Large scattered black spots; irregular yellowish stripes; orange venter.

STRIPED NEWT 161 215
Red stripe.

BROKEN-STRIPED NEWT 159 215
Red stripe broken into dots and dashes.

CENTRAL NEWT 159 214
Dorsal and ventral coloration in sharp contrast; no red markings.

PENINSULA NEWT 159 215
Dorsum very dark; belly peppered with black.

TEXAS BLIND SALAMANDER 190 241
Toothpick legs; pale coloration; gills evident.

GROTTO SALAMANDER 190 240
Pale coloration; no gills. *Larva:* High tail fin; longitudinal streaks on sides; gills evident.

SAN MARCOS SALAMANDER 196 251
Brown; a row of small light spots; gills evident.

TEXAS SALAMANDER 196 250
Yellowish; rows of light spots; gills evident.

OKLAHOMA SALAMANDER 196 250
Gray above; lighter below; gills evident.

SLENDER DWARF SIREN 158 204
Tiny forelimbs; no hind limbs; gills evident; yellowish side stripes; darker stripes above.

NARROW-STRIPED DWARF SIREN 158 203
Tiny forelimbs; no hind limbs; gills evident; general coloration grayish with faint stripes.

TENNESSEE CAVE SALAMANDER 189 243
Pink or flesh-colored; gills evident; large tail fin.

♂ means male, ♀ female.

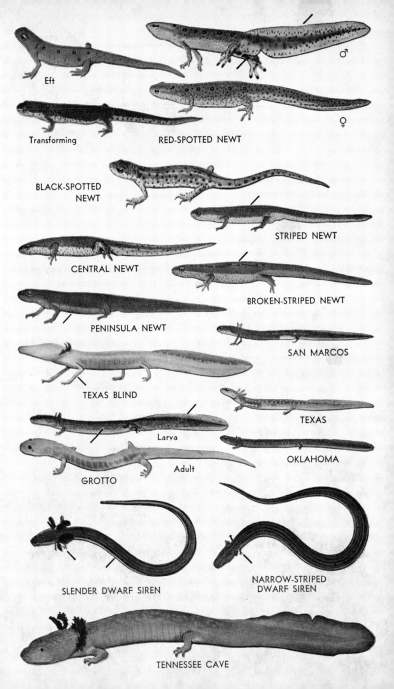

Eft

Transforming

RED-SPOTTED NEWT

♂

♀

BLACK-SPOTTED NEWT

STRIPED NEWT

CENTRAL NEWT

BROKEN-STRIPED NEWT

PENINSULA NEWT

SAN MARCOS

TEXAS BLIND

TEXAS

GROTTO

Larva

Adult

OKLAHOMA

SLENDER DWARF SIREN

NARROW-STRIPED DWARF SIREN

TENNESSEE CAVE

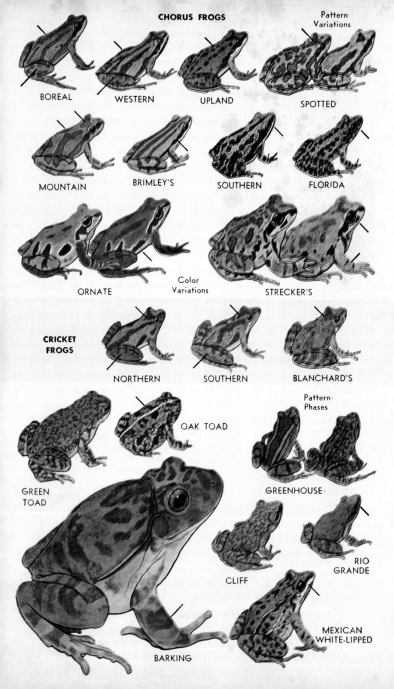

CHORUS FROGS

BOREAL   WESTERN   UPLAND   Pattern Variations   SPOTTED

MOUNTAIN   BRIMLEY'S   SOUTHERN   FLORIDA

ORNATE   Color Variations   STRECKER'S

CRICKET FROGS

NORTHERN   SOUTHERN   BLANCHARD'S

OAK TOAD

GREEN TOAD

Pattern Phases

GREENHOUSE

CLIFF

RIO GRANDE

BARKING

MEXICAN WHITE-LIPPED

Plate 38											271

CHORUS, CRICKET, AND TROPICAL FROGS

opposite angle of jaws.) Middorsal light stripe narrow, most prominent toward rear of body. In some specimens there is an additional but vague light stripe paralleling the middorsal stripe on each side. Dorsal pattern obscure, general effect usually being that of a rather uniformly dark toad, brown or reddish brown or gray. Voice about intermediate between that of Rocky Mountain and Fowler's Toads. Ne. Texas, but intergrading with Fowler's Toad through a wide area in Oklahoma, Arkansas, Louisiana, and Texas.   Map 211

GULF COAST TOAD *Bufo valliceps*   p. 267
Identification: 2–4; record 5. The broad dark lateral stripe is usually so prominent that it alone may assure identification. It is bordered above by a light stripe, and there is also a light middorsal stripe. General dorsal coloration variable from almost black, with touches of rich orange, to yellow-brown with whitish spots. Cranial crests strongly developed and bordering a broad, rather deep "valley" down center of head; parotoid glands often triangular (Fig. 55, p. 264). A rather flat toad; the normal resting posture tends to be more squat than in other species. *Male:* Throat clear yellowish green.

Roadside, railroad, or irrigation ditches are good sites in which to search for the Gulf Coast Toad, but it also occurs in a wide variety of other habitats, including coastal prairies, barrier beaches bordering Gulf of Mexico, and in all manner of places in cities and towns — even in dumps and storm sewers.

Voice: A short trill, lasting 2 to 6 seconds and repeated several times at intervals of about 1 to 4 seconds. Call similar to that of American and Houston Toads, but less musical. Might be likened to sound of a wooden rattle. Vocal sac a large globular pouch reaching from chin to abdomen when inflated. Breeds March to September.

Range: S. Louisiana, e.-cent. and s. Texas, and south to Costa Rica; an isolated record for s. Arkansas.   Map 216

GREAT PLAINS TOAD *Bufo cognatus*   p. 267
Identification: 1⅛–3½; record 4½. Our only toad with *large* dark blotches, each blotch containing several warts and being boldly bordered by light pigment. Ground color gray, brown, greenish, or yellowish. Blotches green, olive, or dark gray and bordered by light pigment. Some specimens have a narrow light middorsal stripe. Cranial crests well apart toward the rear, but extending diagonally forward to meet a boss on the snout (Fig. 55, p. 264). *Young:* Crest between eyes in form of a *V*; dorsum may be dotted with small red tubercles.

This is a common toad of the "great open spaces," of broad grasslands, and the arid Southwest. It is an accomplished burrower and normally moves about only at night. Often found

along irrigation ditches or in river bottoms or flood plains.
Voice: A shrill, piercing, metallic trill, suggestive of a riveting machine, sustained and often lasting 20 seconds or more. (Single calls of more than 50 seconds' duration are on record.) Trill rate 13 to 15 per second. The din of a large chorus is nerve-shattering. *Vocal sac sausage-shaped,* bulking ⅓ size of toad when fully inflated (Fig. 54, p. 263). Breeds April to September, usually May to July in northern part of range.
Range: Great Plains from Canada to Texas; Utah and extr. se. California and south into Mexico. **Map 212**

TEXAS TOAD *Bufo compactilis* p. 267

Identification: 2–3¼; record 3⅝. A chubby toad without distinctive features except on the underside of the foot, where the 2 tubercles are sharp-edged, often black, and the inner one is *sickle-shaped.* No light middorsal stripe. Cranial crests indistinct or absent. Parotoid gland oval. General coloration gray, but marked with yellowish-green spots and pink or greenish warts.

Habitats include grasslands, cultivated areas, and mesquite-savanna associations. All the obvious breeding sites are utilized — rain pools, cattle tanks, irrigation ditches, etc.
Similar species: Red-spotted Toad has small *round* parotoid glands, and its warts are buff or reddish. In Giant Toad, parotoid gland is *very* large and extends far down on side of body. In Rocky Mountain Toad, cranial crests are prominent.
Voice: A continuous series of loud, explosive trills, each ½ second or more in length. Like a high-pitched riveting machine. Trill rate 39 to 57 per second, hence much more rapid than in Great Plains Toad. *Vocal sac sausage-shaped* and ⅓ the bulk of the toad when fully inflated (Fig. 54, p. 263). Breeds April to September (with rains).
Range: Extr. sw. Kansas to n. Mexico. **Map 214**

OAK TOAD *Bufo quercicus* p. 271

Identification: ¾–1¼. An elfin toad clad in a tapestry of many colors. A conspicuous light middorsal stripe that may be white cream, yellow, or orange, and the 4 or 5 pairs of spots on the back are black or brown. Some warts are red, orange, or reddish brown. The ground color varies from pearl-gray to almost black, so that at times the Oak Toad is almost entirely black with very little pattern in evidence (except for light stripe).

An abundant amphibian of southern pine woods. Hides under all manner of objects, but is much more active by day than other toads.
Voice: Like *peeping* of newly hatched chicks, high-pitched and earsplitting in large choruses. Breeding occurs in shallow pools, ditches, cypress and flatwoods ponds, etc., from April to

October, depending on arrival of warm, heavy rains. *Vocal sac sausage-shaped* (Fig. 54, p. 263).
Range: Coastal Plain from North Carolina to e. Louisiana; south throughout Florida and on lower Keys.   Map 217

RED-SPOTTED TOAD   *Bufo punctatus*   p. 267
Identification: 1½–2½; record 3. Our only toad with *round* parotoid glands (Fig. 55, p. 264). Each gland is small, no larger than the eye. Cranial crests absent or only slightly developed. General coloration light brown or gray, warts buff or reddish and sometimes set in small dark blotches. No light stripe down back. A "flattish" toad, not so rotund as in most other species.

In rough, rocky regions and open grasslands. Also a resident of the desert, but most typically to be found near springs, seepages, persistent pools along streams, cattle tanks, etc., throughout the arid Southwest.
Similar species: Other toads have elongated parotoid glands, well-defined cranial crests, or both.
Voice: A clear, musical trill, high and essentially on one pitch. Duration about 4 to 10 seconds; interval variable, sometimes longer or sometimes shorter than call itself. Breeds April to September, coincident with rains.
Range: Sw. Kansas and cent. Texas to se. California; south into Mexico.   Map 215

GIANT TOAD   *Bufo marinus*   p. 267
Identification: 4–6; record 9¹⁄₁₆ (in So. Amer. — probably not over 7 in U. S.). A huge brown toad that barely enters the United States. It is characterized by immense, deeply pitted parotoid glands extending far down sides of body.

Pools and arroyos in Rio Grande Valley, but occupying a wide variety of habitats in the tropics. The skin-gland secretions are highly toxic to dogs and other animals.
Voice: A slow, low-pitched trill, suggestive of the exhaust noise of a distant tractor. Breeding depends upon advent of rains and may occur from early spring to autumn.
Range: Extr. s. Texas to Patagonia; introduced at Miami, Florida, and into many tropical parts of the world.   Map 209

(EASTERN) GREEN TOAD   *Bufo debilis debilis*   p. 271
Identification: 1¼–1⅞. The bright green coloration makes this the easiest of all toads to identify. Warts, including black ones, are numerous on the dorsal surfaces, although less conspicuous than in many other kinds of toads. Throat black or dusky in males, yellow in females.

A resident of rather arid regions; seldom seen abroad except during and after periods of heavy rain. Commonly found under rocks.

Similar species: Cliff Frog has smooth skin (no warts). The skins of Strecker's and Spotted Chorus Frogs also lack prominent warts.
Voice: A shrill trill, almost with the insistence of the whistle of an irate policeman, but not nearly so loud; of 5 to 6 seconds' duration at intervals of nearly same length. Louder and shriller than call of a Narrow-mouthed Toad. Breeds from March to September — if rains occur during that period.
Range: S. Kansas to ne. Mexico. Western subspecies. Map 213

TREEFROGS AND THEIR ALLIES: FAMILY HYLIDAE

A LARGE FAMILY with representatives in all the continents, including Australia. Within our area there are three genera: Treefrogs (*Hyla*), Chorus Frogs (*Pseudacris*), and Cricket Frogs (*Acris*). They are slim-waisted, usually long-legged frogs and most are small in size.

Cricket Frogs: Genus *Acris*

THESE ARE small, warty, nonclimbing members of the Treefrog Family. They are subject to extreme variation in coloration and details of pattern, and may exhibit a myriad of combinations of black, yellow, orange, or red on a base of brown or green. Fortunately there are two pattern details that remain virtually constant: (1) a dark triangle or *V*-shaped spot between the eyes; and (2) a longitudinal dark stripe (or stripes) on the rear surface of the thigh (Fig. 56, p. 276). Some of the Chorus Frogs (genus *Pseudacris*) may show dark triangles between the eyes, but their skins are less warty and their toes are only slightly webbed (Fig. 57, p. 285). The most positive check is the thigh stripe, which requires catching the frog and straightening out the leg to see it. Males have a single vocal pouch under the chin.

Behavior and habitat will help. These small, often very abundant frogs elude their enemies by a quick succession of erratic hops, usually coming to rest just tantalizingly out of reach. They are at home in or near permanent bodies of shallow water that provide cover in the form of vegetation, either emergent or along the shore, and which are exposed to the sun during the greater part of the day. They also are found on the sandy, gravelly, or muddy bars and banks of small sluggish or intermittent streams.

The genus ranges from southern Canada to northern Mexico.

Fig. 56. THIGH PATTERNS OF CRICKET FROGS AND A TREEFROG

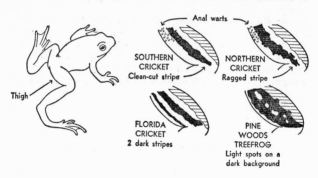

SOUTHERN
CRICKET
Clean-cut stripe

NORTHERN
CRICKET
Ragged stripe

FLORIDA
CRICKET
2 dark stripes

PINE
WOODS
TREEFROG
Light spots on a
dark background

SOUTHERN CRICKET FROG *Acris gryllus gryllus*   p. 271
   Identification: ⅝–1¼. A southern and lowland frog. Dark
   stripe on thigh usually clean-cut and between 2 well-defined light
   stripes; anal warts present (Fig. 56, above). Head pointed and
   legs proportionately longer than in the Northern Cricket Frog.
   Amount of webbing on toes less than in the northern species;
   the 1st toe is partly free of webbing and the 4th (longest) toe
   has the last 3 joints (phalanges) free (Fig. 57, p. 285).
      Chiefly a frog of the lowlands, of Coastal Plain bogs and ponds
   and river-bottom swamps. It follows river valleys northward
   into more upland regions, however.
   Voice: Like a rattle or metal "clicker" — *gick, gick, gick, gick,*
   etc., in rapid succession. Breeds February to October, the actual
   time depending largely upon rains.
   Range: Se. Virginia to Gulf Coast and Mississippi River.
   Subspecies: FLORIDA CRICKET FROG, *Acris gryllus dorsalis.* Similar but smaller; max. 1″ or less. There are *two* dark
   lines on rear of thigh, and no anal warts (Fig. 56, above). Breeds
   in any month of year. Se. Georgia to the tip of Florida. Map 231

NORTHERN CRICKET FROG *Acris crepitans crepitans* p. 271
   Identification: ⅝–1⅜. A northern and upland frog. Dark stripe
   on thigh often not clean-cut and it may have ragged edges (Fig.
   56, above). Head blunt. Leg short; when it is extended forward
   along side of body the heel usually fails to reach snout. In the
   Southern Cricket Frog, heel usually extends beyond snout, but
   this is an average character and should not be relied upon in
   itself for separating these two species. Consider geographic
   origin of the specimen and check amount of webbing on hind
   foot. In the northern species the 1st toe is completely webbed

and only 1½ to 2 joints (phalanges) of the 4th (longest) toe are free (Fig. 57, p. 285).

Voice: *Gick, gick, gick, gick,* etc. Like two pebbles being clicked together, slowly at first but picking up speed and continuing for 20 or 30 or more beats. Breeds April to July; in northern part of the range this is one of the last frogs to get into full chorus.

Range: Long Island to Louisiana and e. Texas. Map 232

BLANCHARD'S CRICKET FROG

Acris crepitans blanchardi p. 271

Identification: ⅝–1⅜. The western member of the group. Wartier, heavier, and bulkier than other Cricket Frogs. Dark stripe on thigh ragged (not clean-cut) and blending with the dark pigment above it and in the anal region. General coloration usually some shade of light brown or gray, with a tendency toward uniformity instead of the wide variety of strongly contrasting color patterns that are so prevalent in the other forms. Named for Frank Nelson Blanchard, a noted herpetologist of the University of Michigan.

Voice: Like the clicking of pebbles in rapid succession. Breeds from February in southern part of the range to late July farther north.

Range: Michigan and Ohio to e. Colorado and ne. Mexico.

Map 232

Treefrogs: Genus *Hyla*

As THEIR name implies, Treefrogs (or tree "toads") are well adapted for an arboreal existence. Their toes end in adhesive discs, and their long limbs and digits help them cling to twigs and bark. But only a few of them ascend high into trees. More common habitats include brushy thickets, swampland vegetation, moist woodlands, or even on the ground or burrowed in it.

Color changes are pronounced, and the same frog may be gray at one time and green or brown at another, or either patterned or plain-colored, depending upon conditions of light, moisture, temperature, or general activity. The young of several of the species may exhibit a plain bright green livery for long periods of time, rendering it difficult or even almost impossible to tell them apart. It is sometimes helpful to leave a Treefrog undisturbed in a collecting bottle or, preferably, a terrarium for a few days; it eventually may change its pattern and coloration to match one of the illustrations on Plate 39. Some species of Treefrogs have distinctive markings or colorations on the concealed surfaces of their hind legs, thus making capture imperative for close examination.

Chorus Frogs are often mistaken for Treefrogs, but their toe discs are smaller and the webbing between the toes is less well developed (Fig. 57, p. 285).

Many captive Treefrogs will survive for long periods of time if they are given a variety of live insects and other invertebrates to eat. Males have a throat pouch that looks like a round balloon under the chin when inflated; the only exceptions are the Mexican Treefrog, which has a *pair* of pouches, one at each side of the chin, and the Cuban Treefrog, whose single pouch inflates more to each side than in the middle, thus producing a suggestion of a double pouch. Members of the genus *Hyla* occur virtually throughout the range of the entire family Hylidae.

SPRING PEEPER *Hyla crucifer*   p. 286
Identification: ¾–1¼; record 1⅜. The dark cross on the back is usually an *X* and more often than not an imperfect one. This, the only small Treefrog in the North, varies through shades of brown, gray, or olive, but does not exhibit profound changes in pattern and coloration as do some of its relatives.

A frog of the woodlands, being especially abundant in areas of brushy second growth or cutover woodlots if these are near small, temporary or semipermanent ponds or swamps. In early spring virtually every small woodland pond has its quota of Peepers. In general these small singers tend to form their choral groups where trees or shrubs are standing in the water, or at least nearby. In contrast, the other small vernal choristers that sing with them throughout a large part of their range — the Chorus Frogs — usually choose open places for calling stations. There is actually much overlap, however, and the two types of frogs often call from virtually identical situations. Peepers are seldom seen except in the breeding season, but they do occasionally prowl through the woods by day in damp or rainy weather.

Similar species: Gray and Bird-voiced Treefrogs have a light spot beneath the eye. Pine Woods Treefrog has rounded light spots on rear of thigh (Fig. 56, p. 276). Most of the Chorus Frogs have a light line along upper lip; Mountain Chorus Frog also usually has a dark triangle between eyes.

Voice: A high, piping whistle, a single clear note repeated at intervals of about a second. There is a terminal upward slur, unlike the piping note of the Ornate Chorus Frog, which ends sharply. A large chorus of Peepers heard from a distance sounds like sleigh bells. A winter frog in the South, breeding from late November to March; a spring chorister in the North, beginning with first warm rains and sometimes continuing to call well into June.

Range: Maritime Provinces to n. Florida; west to e. Manitoba and e. Texas.

Subspecies: NORTHERN SPRING PEEPER, *Hyla crucifer*

crucifer (illustrated on Plate 39). This race, occurring throughout almost all of range of species, is characterized by a plain or virtually plain venter. SOUTHERN SPRING PEEPER, *Hyla crucifer bartramiana*. Similar, but with venter strongly marked with dark spots. S. Georgia and n. Florida. Map 219

GREEN TREEFROG *Hyla cinerea* p. 286
Identification: 1¼–2¼; record 2½. Usually bright green, but the coloration is variable; it may be nearly yellow, as it often is when the frog is calling, or a dull greenish- or slate-gray, as when it is hidden and inactive during periods of cool weather. Length of white or yellowish stripe along the side also variable; commonly it extends nearly to groin, but may terminate farther forward or be longer on one side of body than on other. Many individuals have tiny golden spots on their backs.

This is a "rain frog," a vernacular name shared by other members of the group, especially the Squirrel Treefrog. Some country people believe these amphibians are weather prophets, but although they tend to sing mostly in damp weather, they may call as lustily before fair weather as before foul. Habitats include swamps, borders of lakes and streams, floating vegetation, or in fact almost any place well supplied with water or dampness. Green Treefrogs are frequent visitors to windows at night, where they seek insects attracted by the lights.
Similar species: Pine Barrens Treefrog is ornamented with lavender stripes and much orange on concealed surfaces of legs. Many other Treefrogs, especially young ones, may turn bright green, but most of them lack light stripes. Squirrel Treefrog occasionally has a light lateral stripe, but it normally is a *brown* frog and will eventually return to that color from its temporary green livery.
Voice: Bell-like, and the origin of the local names of "bell-frog" and "cowbell frog." Call has a ringing quality, but is best expressed as *queenk-queenk-queenk* with a nasal inflection; may be repeated as many as 75 times a minute. Breeding calls may be heard from March to October in the Far South (in spring farther north); the congresses are sometimes enormous, with hundreds or even thousands of males participating.
Range: Delmarva Peninsula to Florida Keys; west in Gulf Coastal Plain to cent. and s. Texas and north to extr. s. Illinois.
Subspecies: GREEN TREEFROG, *Hyla cinerea cinerea* (illustrated on Plate 39). As described above and occupying all but a small part of range in the Northeast. NORTHERN GREEN TREEFROG, *Hyla cinerea evittata*. Similar but with light stripes on body and legs absent or greatly reduced in length; in more than 80 per cent of specimens the stripe either does not extend onto body at all or terminates forward of midbody. (Occasionally a Green Treefrog from the South may have the

body stripe very short or virtually absent.) Upper tidewater Potomac. The two races intergrade on the Delmarva Peninsula and in other portions of the Coastal Plain in Maryland and Virginia.   Map 224

PINE BARRENS TREEFROG *Hyla andersoni*   p. 286

Identification: 1⅛–1¾; record 1⅞. The lavender stripes, bordered by white, and set against green make this beautiful little frog easy to identify. Considerable orange on concealed surfaces of legs.

An abundant resident of the swamps, bogs, and brown, acid waters of the New Jersey pine barrens. Rarely seen, however, unless one follows the call of a singing male to its source.

Voice: A nasal *quŏnk-quŏnk-quŏnk* repeated at a rate of about 25 times in 20 seconds (on warm nights; more slowly on cooler ones). Call similar to that of Green Treefrog but lower in pitch. Breeds in late spring (in New Jersey).

Range: S. New Jersey; isolated colonies in North Carolina and Georgia.   Map 218

PINE WOODS TREEFROG *Hyla femoralis*   p. 286

Identification: 1–1½; record 1⅝. Here's a frog that simply must be caught to assure identification. There is a row of small orange, yellow, or whitish spots on the rear of the thigh (Fig. 56, p. 276), but these are completely concealed when the animal is at rest, and when it leaps you cannot see them either. The deep reddish-brown coloration is perhaps most common, but this frog may also be gray or greenish gray at times.

An arboreal acrobat that climbs high in the trees, but also frequents lower levels, even the ground. Commonly found in pine flatwoods and in or near cypress swamps.

Similar species: Several other Treefrogs strongly resemble this one, but they all lack light spots on concealed portion of thigh. Gray Treefrog and Bird-voiced Treefrog both have a light spot below eye.

Voice: The dot-and-dash frog. Morse code done with a snore — no messages, but with the abandon of an amateur playing with a telegraph key. Call much lower pitched than the dots and dashes we hear on our radio and TV sets with some of the news broadcasts. A large chorus sounds like a series of riveting machines all operating at once. Breeding calls may be heard from April to early September (March to October in Florida).

Range: Coastal Plain, Maryland to s. Florida and e. Louisiana.
                                                        Map 220

SQUIRREL TREEFROG *Hyla squirella*   p. 286

Identification: ⅞–1½. Like a "chameleon" in its myriad variations of coloration and pattern. The same frog may be brown at one time and green at another, plain or spotted. Often, but not always, there is a spot or dark bar between the eyes. Also, there may be a light stripe along the side of the body. Identify by a process of elimination, ruling out any species it couldn't be. You had better catch it first!

Called a "rain frog" in many parts of the South. A ubiquitous animal that may appear suddenly in and around houses, even literally "dropping from the sky" as it falls ˌfrom a tree during acrobatics in pursuit of insects. Found in gardens, weed or brush tangles, woods, trees — in fact, almost anywhere close to moisture, food, and a hiding place.

Similar species: Pine Woods Treefrog has light round spots on rear of thigh; Cricket Frogs have hidden stripes on theirs (Fig. 56, p. 276). Gray and Bird-voiced Treefrogs have a light spot beneath eye, the Spring Peeper an *X* on back. In addition to its large size, the Cuban Treefrog is warty and the toe discs are very large. Ornate Chorus Frog sports a black spot on its flanks, and additional ones rise from groin. Chorus Frogs, in general, have smaller toe discs and less webbing than Treefrogs (Fig. 57, p. 285).
Voice: Ducklike, but slightly more nasal. A harsh trill repeated at a rate of 15 to 20 times in 10 seconds (during height of breeding season). The so-called "rain call," usually voiced away from water, is a scolding rasp, quite squirrel-like. Breeds from March to October in Florida, April to August farther north.
Range: Se. Virginia to Florida Keys; west to Louisiana and along Texas coast to Corpus Christi Bay.   Map 223

GRAY TREEFROG *Hyla versicolor*   p. 286
Identification: 1¼–2; record 2⅜. The only large Treefrog in the North, but subject, like its southern relatives, to changes in color. Variations in the same frog may run the gamut from gray, brown, or green to pearl-gray, or even almost white. Light spot beneath eye almost invariably discernible, however. Concealed surfaces of hind legs *bright orange*. Skin of back quite warty for a Treefrog, the warts very numerous but not so prominent or protuberant as in the average Toad (*Bufo*).

Not often seen on ground, except in breeding season. Usually forages aloft, chiefly in relatively small trees or shrubs that are near or actually standing in shallow bodies of water. Extremely well camouflaged when clinging to brown or gray bark of a tree, and often its presence is known solely from its vibrant call.
Similar species: Likely to be confused only with Bird-voiced Treefrog of the South. Both have a light spot beneath eye, and both are extremely similar in general appearance — except on the hidden portions of hind legs. These are *pale yellowish green* in the Bird-voiced *Hyla*. In portions of southern states where the two occur together, they must be captured to make positive

identification, unless they are singing. Their voices are very different: the rapid piping notes of Bird-voiced Treefrog are easily distinguished from the trills of Gray Treefrog. Breeding congresses of Bird-voiced Treefrogs usually assemble where water is deep and tangles of brush make collecting difficult. Gray Treefrogs prefer more shallow, more open water, where they are easily approached and captured.

Voice: A short trill, loud and resonant, of from less than 1 to 3 seconds' duration, and suggestive of the call of a red-bellied woodpecker. The sound is flutelike to some ears. In some populations of this Treefrog the call is shorter, harsher, and more forceful. Breeds in quiet shallow water of many types, but avoids large permanent swamps; season extends from April to August, depending upon latitude and rainfall.

Range: New Brunswick (Canada) to n. Florida; west to extr. e. North Dakota and cent. Texas.

Subspecies: EASTERN GRAY TREEFROG, *Hyla versicolor versicolor* (illustrated on Plate 39). As described above and occupying most of the range. SOUTHERN GRAY TREE-FROG, *Hyla versicolor chrysoscelis*. Skin much smoother, not strongly warty; rear of thigh with extensive dark markings, leaving only isolated spots of orange that are about same size and circular shape as toe discs. E. Texas, sw. Arkansas, and adj. corners of Oklahoma and Louisiana. CENTRAL TEXAS TREEFROG, *Hyla versicolor sandersi*. Rear of thigh orange, with fine white flecks, and almost entirely lacking dark markings; song a longer, lower trill. Balcones Escarpment and adj. areas of cent. Texas.   Map 221

BIRD-VOICED TREEFROG *Hyla avivoca*   p. 286
Identification: 1⅛–1¾; record 2 1/16. A junior edition of the Gray Treefrog. Both species have a light spot under the eye, but in the Bird-voiced *Hyla* the *concealed* portions of the hind legs are washed with *green* instead of orange. General dorsal coloration gray, brown, or green.

A resident of permanent wooded swamps — of tupelo, cypress, birch, buttonbush, and vine tangles — along many of the creeks and larger waterways of the South.

Similar species: See Gray Treefrog.

Voice: A ringing, birdlike whistle, *wit-wit-wit-wit* rapidly repeated 20 or more times. A single frog calling reminds one of whistling for a dog. Breeds from spring to late summer.

Range: Mississippi Valley, chiefly east of the River, north to extr. s. Illinois; east to Savannah River drainage.

Subspecies: WESTERN BIRD-VOICED TREEFROG, *Hyla avivoca avivoca* (illustrated on Plate 39). Concealed surfaces of hind limbs washed with bright green or yellowish green. Swamps along streams of Gulf drainage. EASTERN BIRD-VOICED TREEFROG, *Hyla avivoca ogechiensis*. Concealed surfaces pale greenish white or yellowish white. Along streams of Atlantic drainage. Map 222

BARKING TREEFROG *Hyla gratiosa* p. 286
Identification: 2–2⅝; record 2¾. One of the larger, stouter Treefrogs — and the spottiest. The profuse round dark markings usually persist, at least in part, through the various color changes, but they may disappear when the frog turns dark brown or bright green or fades to tones of pale gray. At least some green pigment usually in evidence.

Both a high climber and a burrower, but also uses other habitats between these two extremes. In hot dry weather often takes shelter in sand or soil beneath roots or clumps of grass or other vegetation.
Similar species: Some Southern Leopard Frogs are profusely spotted, but they lack adhesive discs on toes.
Voice: This frog gets its name from its voice. A barking call of nine or ten raucous syllables is uttered from high in the treetops. The breeding call, given in or close to the water, is a single explosive *doonk* or *toonk* repeated at intervals of one or two seconds. Breeds March to August.
Range: Chiefly in the Coastal Plain from North Carolina to s. Florida and e. Louisiana; isolated records in Alabama and Georgia; introduced in s. New Jersey. Map 227

CUBAN TREEFROG *Hyla septentrionalis* p. 286
Identification: Males 1½–3½; females 2–5; record 5½. An immigrant from the West Indies and the largest of our Treefrogs. The out sized toe discs and warty skin suffice for distinguishing adults from other frogs, but smaller specimens may offer trouble. This species has no line or stripe, light or dark, running through or under eye. General coloration — variable, of course, in the same frog — runs mostly to greens and bronzes.

Largely nocturnal, sometimes appearing near lights in search of insects. By day this large amphibian hides where there is moisture — in cisterns, drains, cellars, the axils of palms or banana trees, even on porches of Key West houses in jardinieres or other containers holding potted plants that are watered daily. Don't put a Cuban Treefrog in a cage or terrarium with smaller frogs or toads. It may eat them.
Voice: Very suggestive of the snoring rasp of the Southern Leopard Frog, but less vigorous and usually higher pitched. Pitch may vary throughout an entire octave.
Range: Extr. se. Florida and the Keys; Cuba and n. Bahamas. Map 225

LITTLE GRASS FROG *Hyla ocularis* p. 286
Identification: ⅞₆–⅝; record ¹¹⁄₁₆. Tiniest North American frog. The dark line passing through the eye and onto side of

body is constant, and although this may be variable in length, it is the best characteristic to rely upon. Usually a narrow dark middorsal stripe starting as a triangle between eyes and extending to anal region. Another dark narrow stripe separates the middorsal color from the lighter ground color of the sides. General coloration extremely variable — tan, brown, greenish, pink, or reddish. Toes slightly webbed.

An elfin Treefrog whose climbing is restricted to low vegetation. Moist, grassy environs of ponds and cypress bays are favorite habitats.

Similar species: Most persons upon seeing or capturing this minute amphibian for the first time mistake it for the young of some other species. A dark lateral stripe passing through the eye also is often the most conspicuous pattern element in the larger Brimley's Chorus Frog, but that species usually has a *spotted chest*. Cricket Frogs have stripes on the rear of their thighs (Fig. 56, p. 276).

Voice: A tinkling, insect-like call — *set-see*, *set-see* — so high and shrill that some people have difficulty hearing it. May breed any month of year in Florida; from January to September farther north.

Range: Se. Virginia to s. tip of Florida; inland to edge of the Piedmont and to se. Alabama. Map 226

MEXICAN TREEFROG *Hyla baudini* p. 286
Identification: 2–2¾; record 3½. The most constant markings are the light spot beneath the eye, a light spot at the base of the arm, and a dark patch running backward from the eardrum onto the shoulder. The dark patch persists during even the most extreme color changes, changes that may produce a very dark gray or gray-green frog or, conversely, a pale yellow or pale gray one. In the very light coloration all traces of markings may disappear save for the ever present dark shoulder patch.

A tropical species entering the United States only in the lower Rio Grande Valley. Takes shelter in damp tree holes, beneath debris, or in the ground during dry weather.

Voice: Like the starting mechanism of a car: a series of blurred notes — *heck* or *keck* — sometimes interspersed with chuckles. Male has *two* vocal sacs, one at each side of chin.

Range: Extr. s. Texas to Honduras. Map 227

Chorus Frogs: Genus *Pseudacris*

VOICES IN the swamp. In the North these are vernal choristers that respond to the first warm rains as spring moves northward. In the South they are "winter frogs," their breeding season beginning at any time from November to late winter, but usually in correlation with *cool* rains. The call of many of them is a rasping

Fig. 57. WEBBING AND TOE DISCS OF VARIOUS HYLID FROGS

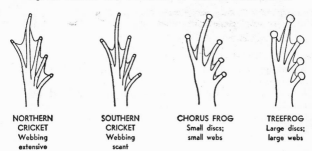

| NORTHERN CRICKET
Webbing extensive | SOUTHERN CRICKET
Webbing scant | CHORUS FROG
Small discs; small webs | TREEFROG
Large discs; large webs |

trill that can be imitated with fair success by running a finger along the teeth of a pocket comb. They sing in or near shallow, often temporary, bodies of water, sometimes in the open, but more often concealed in a clump of grass or other vegetation, where they are extremely difficult to find even when they advertise their presence by calling loudly. They are seldom encountered after the breeding season.

These are the "swamp treefrogs" or "swamp cricket frogs," small members of the Treefrog Family that climb very little and then only into weeds or low shrubs in pursuit of insects. Their toe discs are small, and the toes themselves are only slightly webbed (Fig. 57, above). A light line along the upper lip is common to most of them. Females average larger than their mates. Males have a single round vocal pouch, and when collapsed, this is gray or brown over a cream or yellowish ground color.

The genus is strictly North American, ranging from the Gulf to New York and southern Ontario in the East and from Arizona almost to the Arctic Circle in the West.

WESTERN CHORUS FROG
Pseudacris triseriata triseriata   p. 271

Identification: ¾–1½. Normally with 3 dark stripes down the back (Fig. 58, p. 289). These typically are as broad and strong as the dark lateral stripe that runs from snout to groin and passes through the eye, but they are subject to variation. They may be broken or reduced to rows of dark spots or be lacking altogether. Middle stripe often forks into 2 parts posteriorly. A dark triangle or other dark figure *may* be present between eyes. Always a *light line along upper lip*. Dorsal ground color varies from pale gray to dark brown but may also be dull green or olive. Markings are darker gray or brown. Under surfaces whitish, either plain or with a few dark spots on throat and chest.

NARROW-MOUTHED TOADS AND TREEFROGS

Map Text

GREAT PLAINS NARROW-MOUTHED TOAD   229 295
Plain gray, tan, or greenish and with or without small
black spots.

EASTERN NARROW-MOUTHED TOAD   230 294
Broad light dorsolateral stripe; center of back dark; variable (see text).
Key West phase: Center of back tan and bordered by
black.

SHEEP FROG   228 296
Yellow streak down back.

PINE WOODS TREEFROG   220 280
Dark dorsal blotches; light spots on concealed surface of
thigh (Fig. 56, p. 276).

SQUIRREL TREEFROG   223 280
Green or brown or combinations of both; highly variable
(see text).

SPRING PEEPER   219 278
Dark *X*-shaped mark on back.

BIRD-VOICED TREEFROG   222 282
Light spot below eye; concealed surfaces of hind legs
washed with green or yellowish white.

PINE BARRENS TREEFROG   218 280
Whitish and purplish stripes.

GREEN TREEFROG   224 279
Light stripe.

GRAY TREEFROG   221 281
Light spot below eye; concealed surfaces of hind legs
washed with orange.

BARKING TREEFROG   227 283
Profusion of dark rounded spots.

CUBAN TREEFROG   225 283
Large toe discs; warty skin.

MEXICAN TREEFROG   227 284
Light spot below eye; black patch on shoulder (back of
eardrum).

LITTLE GRASS FROG   226 283
Tiny size; dark line through eye; pattern and coloration
variable (see text).

NARROW-MOUTHED TOADS

GREAT PLAINS EASTERN Key West Phase

SHEEP FROG

TREEFROGS

PINE WOODS SQUIRREL Color Variations

SPRING PEEPER

BIRD-VOICED PINE BARRENS

GREEN

GRAY

BARKING

Color Variations.

CUBAN

MEXICAN

LITTLE GRASS FROG

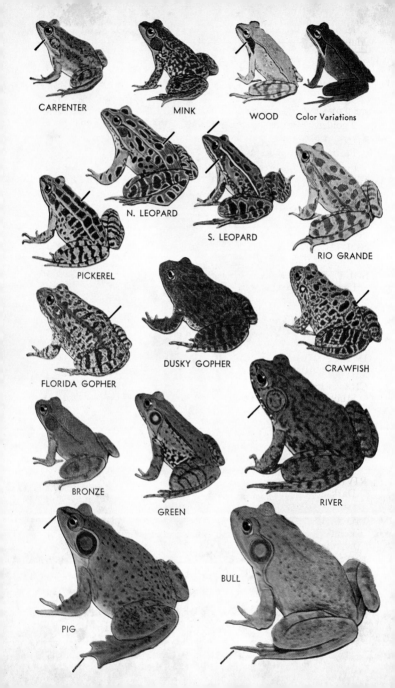

CARPENTER

MINK

WOOD Color Variations

N. LEOPARD

S. LEOPARD

RIO GRANDE

PICKEREL

DUSKY GOPHER

CRAWFISH

FLORIDA GOPHER

BRONZE

GREEN

RIVER

PIG

BULL

Plate 40   287

TRUE FROGS

(Most of these have dorsolateral ridges — see back endpaper.)

Map *Text*

CARPENTER FROG*   243 298
2 golden-brown lateral stripes.

MINK FROG*   240 299
Far-northern range; mottled or spotted pattern (Fig. 61,
p. 299); often no ridges; musky odor.

WOOD FROG   245 303
Dark mask through eye.

PICKEREL FROG   239 302
Squarish dark spots; bright yellow or orange on concealed surfaces of hind legs.

NORTHERN LEOPARD FROG   241 300
Rounded dark spots; highly variable (see text).

SOUTHERN LEOPARD FROG   241 301
Light spot on eardrum; pointed snout.

RIO GRANDE LEOPARD FROG   241 302
Pallid coloration.

FLORIDA GOPHER FROG   242 305
Stubby; irregular markings on light ground.

DUSKY GOPHER FROG   242 304
Stubby, dark; venter spotted (Fig. 62, p. 304).

CRAWFISH FROG   242 304
Stubby; dark spots rounded and with light borders; venter
mostly without markings (Fig. 62, p. 304).

BRONZE FROG*   244 299
General bronzy coloration.

GREEN FROG*   244 300
Bright green and brown; highly variable (see text).

RIVER FROG*   246 297
Dark appearance; white spots on lips; no ridges; river-
swamp habitat.

PIG FROG*   248 298
Pointed snout; 4th toe only slightly longer than others;
no ridges.

BULLFROG*   247 296
4th toe protruding well beyond others; no ridges; pattern
variable (see text).

*The tympanum (eardrum) is larger than the eye in males, and only the size of
the eye or smaller in females.

Shallow bodies of water are required during the breeding season and for the development of tadpoles, but otherwise this frog
survives in a wide variety of habitats, some of them surprisingly
dry and greatly altered by the activities of man. Originally this
was chiefly a frog of the prairies. Large populations exist nowadays both in agricultural areas and well within limits of large
cities, to judge by the sizes of choruses heard during the spring.
Similar species: Spring Peeper *lacks* light line on lip and usually
has a dark *X* on back. Mountain Chorus Frog has only 2 dark
dorsal stripes (Fig. 58, p. 289), and they curve inward and may
unite to form a crude *X*. Spotted Chorus Frog has bright
green spots or bars. Upland Chorus Frog, with which the
Western Chorus Frog intergrades along a broad line through
Mississippi Valley, will offer trouble. Both are variable, but the
Western *usually* is strongly striped, whereas the Upland *usually*
is spotted or weakly striped (Fig 58, p. 289). Striped specimens
of Upland Chorus Frog have stripes rather thin and frequently
broken, but the lateral stripe (one passing through eye) is broad
and strong and usually points up the weakness of the dorsal pattern. In the Western, length of tibia is considerably less than
½ length from snout to vent; in the Upland it is approximately
half. Geography (point of origin of specimen) may offer best
clue to identification (Map 235).
Voice: A vibrant, regularly repeated *crreek* or *prreep* (roll the *r*'s),
speeding up and rising in pitch toward the end. The sound may
be roughly imitated by running a finger over approximately the
last twenty of the *small* teeth of a good-quality pocket comb,
rubbing the shortest teeth last. Breeds from February to June,
the latest dates occurring in northernmost parts of range.
Range: W. New York and extr. s. Quebec to Kansas and Oklahoma; isolated colonies in New Mexico and Arizona.
Subspecies: NEW JERSEY CHORUS FROG, *Pseudacris
triseriata kalmi.* Very similar, but averaging more robust and
usually with broad, well-defined dorsal stripes. Coastal Plain
from Staten Island, New York, to s. tip of Delmarva Peninsula,
and intergrading with Upland Chorus Frog in n. New Jersey and
e. Pennsylvania.   Map 235

BOREAL CHORUS FROG *Pseudacris triseriata maculata* p. 271
Identification: ¾–1⅜. Northernmost of all the Chorus Frogs
and the one with the shortest legs. Length of tibia is noticeably
shorter than tibia of Western Chorus Frog, which in pattern and
gross appearance is very similar. General coloration brown or
greenish. The stripes may break up into rows of spots; the middorsal stripe is the one most commonly so affected.
Short legs in frogs seem to be adaptations for life in cold cli-
mates. Typical specimens have such abbreviated legs that they
hop instead of making long leaps like their more southern rela-

Fig. 58. DORSAL PATTERNS OF VARIOUS CHORUS FROGS

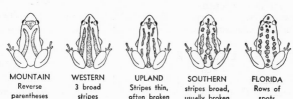

MOUNTAIN	WESTERN	UPLAND	SOUTHERN	FLORIDA
Reverse parentheses	3 broad stripes	Stripes thin, often broken	stripes broad, usually broken	Rows of spots

tives. This is a frog of marshy environs of far-northern ponds, lakes, meadows and of similar habitats in the Rocky Mountains.
Voice: A regularly repeated *prreep, prreep* (roll the *r*'s), much like call of Western Chorus Frog.
Range: N. Ontario to Great Bear Lake in nw. Canada; south through Utah and Colorado and intergrading with Western Chorus Frog through a broad area extending from n. peninsula of Michigan to Nebraska.   Map 235

UPLAND CHORUS FROG   *Pseudacris triseriata feriarum* p. 271
Identification: ¾–1⅜. A frog with an extremely variable pattern. The following are constant: (1) light line along the upper lip; (2) dark stripe from snout to groin and passing through eye. On the other hand, the middorsal pattern may be striped, partly striped, spotted — or even lacking. Basically there are 3 longitudinal dark stripes, but they are usually narrow and often broken up into streaks or rows of small spots (Fig. 58, above). Sometimes there are small scattered spots or virtually no dark markings at all. A dark triangle between eyes (or a suggestion of one) is usually present. General coloration brown or gray. Under surfaces cream-colored but often with dark stipplings on breast. Length of tibia about ½ length from snout to vent.

Grassy swales, moist woodlands, river-bottom swamps, and environs of ponds, bogs, and marshes are included among the habitats. This is an upland frog in the North, but it deeply invades the lowlands in the South.
Similar species: In Brimley's Chorus Frog the lateral stripe (one passing through eye) is *black* and often in strong contrast with other dark markings; also, chest is boldly spotted. In Southern Chorus Frog there are *black* stripes or rows of spots down back. Ornate Chorus Frog has a black stripe from *snout to shoulder* followed by black spots along the side of body. Also see "Similar species" under Western Chorus Frog (opposite page).
Voice: A regularly repeated *creek* or *prreep* similar to that of Western Chorus Frog. Usually calls from fairly open situations,

as is also the case among all the other races of *triseriata*. Breeds from February to May toward north; during winter or early spring in the South.

Range: N. New Jersey to Florida panhandle; west to e. Texas and se. Oklahoma; isolated localities in South Carolina. Map 235

SOUTHERN CHORUS FROG

Pseudacris nigrita nigrita   p. 271

Identification: ¾–1¼. Darkest of all the Chorus Frogs — the markings are usually black. The black stripe from snout to groin (and passing through eye) is prominent and continuous, but the 3 dorsal stripes have a strong tendency to break up into rows of large spots, especially the middle one, which usually forks into 2 rows posteriorly (Fig. 58, p. 289). Ground color light gray, tan, or silvery and often so pale as to appear almost white in contrast with black markings. *Prominent white line along lip.* The snout in this frog and Florida Chorus Frog tends to be more pointed than snouts of other Chorus Frogs.

Habitats include pine flatwoods, wet meadows, roadside ditches, moist woodlands, etc.

Similar species: Cricket Frogs have prominent stripes on rear of thigh (Fig. 56, p. 276).

Voice: A trill resembling sound of a rachet but with a musical quality. About 8 or 10 beats to each trill, and trills are repeated at regular intervals. Breeds November to April.

Range: E. North Carolina to n. Florida and s. Mississippi.
Map 238

FLORIDA CHORUS FROG

Pseudacris nigrita verrucosa   p. 271

Identification: ¾–1¼. The only Chorus Frog with the upper lip chiefly black instead of white. Normally there is a series of black spots on the lip, but these may join together so that the light pigment is much reduced. The dark dorsal spots seldom run together (Fig. 58, p. 289).

A resident of varied habitats — ditches, swales, flatwoods ponds, the prairie lands of south-central Florida, and pine forests and sinkholes on the eastern edge of the Everglades.

Similar species: Florida Cricket Frog has conspicuous stripes on rear of thigh (Fig. 56, p. 276). Young River Frogs have strongly webbed toes.

Voice: A regularly repeated rasping trill. Breeding is usually associated with fairly heavy rains and may occur during any month of year.

Range: Florida Peninsula.   Map 238

SPOTTED CHORUS FROG   *Pseudacris clarki*   p. 271

Identification: ¾–1¼. The only Chorus Frog garbed with

patches of bright green that are rimmed with black. Two extremes of pattern are illustrated. Spotted specimens are by far
the more common, and the spots are normally scattered, sometimes very numerous, and not arranged in rows. When stripes
are present, they tend to be longitudinal. Almost always a
green triangle between eyes. Belly plain white.

An amphibian gem of the grassland prairies. It is inactive
during dry weather, but even when conditions of moisture are
optimum it normally ventures abroad only at night or in the
early evening.

Similar species: Western Chorus Frog is normally brown or gray
— but sometimes dull green or olive — and is patterned with
stripes or with dark spots arranged in 3 longitudinal rows.
Strecker's Chorus Frog is larger, toadlike, and with a *black* stripe
from snout to shoulder; it also usually has a dark spot below eye.
In the very much larger Crawfish Frog the spots are dark with
light borders.

Voice: A rasping trill, *wrrank-wrrank-wrrank*, etc., rapidly
repeated 20 to 30 or more times. Interval between notes is
about equal to duration of notes themselves. Two males singing
together, but with their calls alternating, sound like rapid saw-
ing. Peak of season in April and May, but breeding may follow
rains in virtually any month in southern part of range.

Range: Cent. Kansas to s. Texas.   Map 237

BRIMLEY'S CHORUS FROG   *Pseudacris brimleyi*   p. 271
Identification: 1-1¼. A very changeable little frog that may
fade to virtually plain brownish yellow except for the bold dark
stripe down each side of the body. This stripe, extending without
interruption from snout to groin and passing through eye, is
always strongly evident. Under surfaces yellow and normally
there are *dark spots on chest*. Markings on legs tend strongly to
be longitudinal instead of forming crossbands. No dark triangle
between eyes.

An early singer in the marshes, swamps, ditches, and wet
open woods of the Coastal Plain. Named for Clement S. Brimley, North Carolina naturalist.

Similar species: In Ornate Chorus Frog, there are bold black
spots on sides and rising from groin. In both Southern and Upland Chorus Frogs, middorsal stripes or spots are same color as
lateral stripes.

Voice: A short rasping trill, lasting less than a second and repeated a dozen times or more. Similar to call of Squirrel Treefrog, but the individual notes are shorter and more strongly
accented at end. Breeds from February to April.

Range: Se. Virginia to e. Georgia.   Map 236

MOUNTAIN CHORUS FROG   *Pseudacris brachyphona*   p. 271
Identification: 1-1¼; record 1½. The frog with the reversed

parentheses (Fig. 58, p. 289). In some specimens the 2 curved stripes bend inward so far that they touch at center of back, producing a crude dark *X*. Occasionally, the stripes may be broken into spots. The dark triangle between the eyes is almost invariably present, and there is a white line on upper lip, as in most of the Chorus Frogs. Yellow pigment on concealed and lower surfaces of legs.

Like a miniature Wood Frog in habitat, leaping power, and gross appearance. A woodland species ranging upward to elevations of at least 3500 feet, occurring chiefly on forested slopes and hilltops and often at long distances from water. Breeds in small shallow bodies of water in woods or at its edge — in ditches, pools along streams or those that form below hillside springs.

Similar species: Spring Peeper, which normally has a fairly clear-cut dark *X* on back, lacks white line on lip. In both the Upland and Western Chorus Frogs the dorsal pattern consists basically of *three* longitudinal stripes; if stripes are broken into spots, as is often the case, then the spots are usually arranged in *three* rows. Wood Frog has dorsolateral ridges.

Voice: A rasp like that of Western Chorus Frog, but given more rapidly, higher in pitch, and more nasal in quality. Sounds like a wagon wheel turning without benefit of lubrication. Breeds February to April, depending upon latitude and altitude.

Range: Sw. Pennsylvania and se. Ohio to cent. Alabama.

Map 234

ORNATE CHORUS FROG *Pseudacris ornata* p. 271
Identification: 1–1¼; record 1⅞. More like the creation of an imaginative artist than a real live frog. A black masklike stripe running through the eye. *Dark spots on sides and near groin.* Yellow in groin and numerous small yellow spots on concealed portions of legs. Coloration highly variable — the individual frog may change from almost plain black to silvery white or to the brilliant colors shown on Plate 38. The reddish-brown coloration is the most common. *Young:* Pattern details not well developed.

Habitats include cypress ponds, pine barren ponds, flooded meadows, and flatwoods ditches — plus their environs.

Similar species: Strecker's Chorus Frog is larger and stouter, more toadlike, with a particularly stout foreleg and usually a dark spot below eye. Among all the other Chorus Frogs whose ranges overlap this species (Brimley's, Upland, Southern, and Florida), the pattern consists of longitudinal dark stripes or rows of spots and there are no conspicuous, light-bordered black spots along sides.

Voice: A series of shrill peeps, like the ring of a steel chisel struck by a hammer, 65 to 80 times a minute. Similar to Spring Peeper's call but quicker and lacking Peeper's terminal slur. Calls during late fall, winter, and early spring.

Range: Coastal Plain from North Carolina to e. Louisiana; south throughout most of Florida. Map 233

STRECKER'S CHORUS FROG *Pseudacris streckeri* p. 271

Identification: 1–1⅝; record 1⅞. Largest and chubbiest of the Chorus Frogs. The stout hand and forearm are quite toadlike. A dark masklike stripe, from snout to shoulder, and often continued as a series of dark spots along the side. General coloration highly variable — gray, hazel, brown, olive, or green, the dorsal markings sometimes even dark brown or black. The dark spot below the eye, present in most specimens, is variable in size; in some it may be little more than an upward bulge from the narrow dark line bordering lip.

This frog utilizes a wide variety of habitats, including moist, shady woods, rocky ravines, environs of streams and lagoons, sand prairies, and even cultivated fields. Named for John K. Strecker, a naturalist long associated with Baylor University.

Similar species: In all other Chorus Frogs occurring within the range of this species there is a *continuous* light line on upper lip.

Voice: Very similar to that of Ornate Chorus Frog. Clear and bell-like, a single and quickly repeated note. In strong chorus the effect is of a rapidly turning pulley wheel badly in need of greasing. Calls during and after rains from November to June, with peak of season in January and February in southern part of range.

Range: Cent. Oklahoma south through Texas to the Gulf; Arkansas, Missouri, and Illinois.

Subspecies: STRECKER'S CHORUS FROG, *Pseudacris streckeri streckeri* (illustrated on Plate 38). Dark stripe through eye and dark spots along side of body are in strong contrast with ground color; considerable yellow or orange-yellow pigment in groin. Most of range stated above. ILLINOIS CHORUS FROG, *Pseudacris streckeri illinoensis.* Dark lateral stripe is usually poorly developed in this pale-colored race; *no* yellow pigment in groin. Sand prairies of se. Missouri and w.-cent. Illinois. Map 233

NARROW-MOUTHED TOADS:
FAMILY MICROHYLIDAE

Two CLOSELY related genera, found only in North and Central America represent this family in our area. These are *Gastrophryne* (Narrow-mouthed Toads) and *Hypopachus* (Sheep Frogs). They are small, plump amphibians with short limbs, pointed heads, and a *fold of skin across the back of the head.* Males aln ost always have dark throats, females light ones. They are very secretive, hiding by day but venturing forth at night when the weather is warm and damp. In trying to escape they usually resort to running instead of leaping, but intersperse their gait with short hops of an inch or two or more. Once fully aroused they are difficult to catch, darting into the nearest crack or crevice and disappearing. Food consists very largely of insects, such as small beetles, termites, and especially ants. Other members of the family occur in Mexico, Central and South America, Africa, Asia, and the Indo-Australian archipelago.

EASTERN NARROW-MOUTHED TOAD
Gastrophryne carolinensis p. 286

Identification: ⅞–1¼; record 1 ⅞6. Shape and general appearance alone are usually enough to identify this small frog. (Confusion could only occur in the narrow strip where the range overlaps that of the Great Plains Narrow-mouthed Toad.) The general coloration varies through shades of gray, brown, or reddish, and the same frog may change from one shade to another, depending upon its environment and its activities. The pattern illustrated on Plate 39 — a broad dark middorsal area flanked by broad light stripes — is very frequently obscured (often completely) by patches, spots, and mottlings of dark or light pigment. Venter strongly mottled (Fig. 59, p. 295). *Key West phase:* Middorsal area only a little darker in coloration than the light dorsolateral stripes, and separated from them by an irregular dark line. About half the Narrow-mouthed Toads on Key West and adjacent Keys are marked in this fashion, about one-fourth are tan with virtually no pattern (like *olivacea*), and the rest are similar to mainland specimens.

A wide variety of habitats are used, but all have two things in common — shelter and moisture. Borders of swamps and small streams are good places in which to look for them. Actually, these toads are where you find them, and usually as a result of over-turning boards, logs, or other shelters, or raking through vegetable debris, abandoned sawdust piles, etc.

Similar species: Great Plains Narrow-mouthed Toad has only a few dark spots on its back or no pattern at all; its venter is unspotted.

Voice: Like the bleat of a lamb and occasionally with a very short preliminary *peep.* The call has a buzzing quality, something like an electric buzzer. It lasts for about 1 or 1½ seconds. Breeding sites are chiefly in shallow water, but deep-water situations also are used if covered by a dense floating mat of vegetation. Males usually conceal themselves when calling. Heavy rains initiate the breeding season, which may occur any time between early April and October.

Range: S. Maryland to Florida Keys; west to Missouri and e. Texas; an isolated colony in Iowa.   Map 230

Fig. 59. NARROW-MOUTHED TOADS (VENTERS)

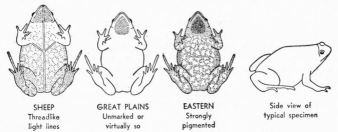

SHEEP	GREAT PLAINS	EASTERN	Side view of
Threadlike	Unmarked or	Strongly	typical specimen
light lines	virtually so	pigmented	

GREAT PLAINS NARROW-MOUTHED TOAD
Gastrophryne olivacea olivacea   p. 286

Identification: ⅞-1½; record 1⅝. The oddly shaped body and the near absence, or absence, of pattern make this an easy frog to identify. Adults vary from tan to gray or greenish, depending upon temperature and moisture. Venter light and unmarked or virtually so (Fig. 59, above). *Young:* Dark brown with a conspicuous dark leaflike pattern that may occupy half the width of the back. The dark pattern disappears and the general coloration becomes paler as frog grows in size.

A resident of grasslands, marshy sloughs, and rocky, open-wooded slopes. Occasionally may be discovered in hiding beneath rocks, boards, debris, etc., in damp places, but also takes shelter in rodent burrows and in cracks of drying mud. These Narrow-mouthed Toads sometimes are found in burrows of tarantulas, where they are apparently unmolested by and actually derive protection from some other predators by the presence of the big spiders. Their skin-gland secretions may be distasteful to potential enemies. Keep your fingers out of your mouth and away from your eyes after handling any Narrow-mouthed Toad, or you may have a sharp burning sensation that may last an hour.

Similar species: Eastern Narrow-mouthed Toad has strongly patterned dorsum, and its venter is mottled with dark pigment. Sheep Frog has a narrow yellow line down back.

Voice: A distinct but very short *peep* followed by a buzz like that of an angry bee. To some ears the buzz may sound like the bleat of a sheep but higher in pitch and with much less volume. Duration of call about 2 to 2½ seconds. Breeding begins upon arrival of heavy rains and it may take place at any time from March to September, with the earlier dates normally occurring toward the south.

Range: Se. Nebraska and w. Missouri to n. Mexico. Western subspecies. Map 229

SHEEP FROG *Hypopachus cuneus cuneus*   p. 286
Identification: 1–1½; record 1¾. The Narrow-mouthed Toad with the yellow streak down its back. There is a similar light threadlike line down the dark mottled belly with extensions outward across the chest toward the arms (Fig. 59, p. 295).

Remains secreted most of the year beneath partly buried objects (such as fallen palm trees), in burrows, or in the trash of packrat nests.
Voice: A sheeplike bleat lasting about 2 seconds and seldom repeated at less than 15-second intervals. Breeding is initiated by rains or flooding of the frogs' habitat by irrigation.
Range: S. Texas to Veracruz. Mexican subspecies.   Map 228

TRUE FROGS: FAMILY RANIDAE

THESE ARE the typical frogs. In general they are long-legged, narrow-waisted, and rather smooth-skinned, with fingers free and toes joined by webs. Check for the presence or absence of dorsolateral ridges (see back endpaper), which are raised longitudinal folds of glandular tissue. Males of some species have paired vocal pouches, situated at the sides of the throat; others have a single pouch, centered under the throat (Fig. 60, p. 297). Voice is not entirely restricted to males; females of several species scream loudly when captured, and other vocal sounds have been reported. Breeding males have the bases of their thumbs enlarged, and their forearms are swollen.

The family occurs in all continents. The big genus *Rana*, with about 250 species and most of them in the Old World, is the only North American representative. From this genus come the frogs' legs of commerce. The Gopher and Crawfish Frogs are discussed under a separate heading (p. 303).

BULLFROG *Rana catesbeiana*   p. 287
Identification: 3½–6; record 8. Our largest frog. Plain or nearly plain green above, or with gray or brown markings on a green background. Venter whitish, often mottled with gray, and with a yellowish wash, especially on throats of adult males. No dorsolateral folds on trunk; folds end near eardrum.

Aquatic and preferring larger bodies of water than most other frogs. A resident of lakes, ponds, bogs, sluggish portions of streams, cattle tanks, etc.; usually seen at water's edge or amidst vegetation or snags in or under which it can hide. Small streams are also utilized where better habitats are lacking.

Fig. 60. TWO TYPES OF VOCAL SACS IN TRUE FROGS

Paired pouches, swelling   Single pouch, largely internal
into spheres above arm

Similar species: Green Frog has dorsolateral ridges. In the Pig Frog the hind feet are webbed to tips of toes; the Bullfrog has them less fully webbed and the 4th toe protrudes *well beyond* other toes. In the southeastern part of its range the Bullfrog is usually very dark, being heavily patterned with dark gray or dark brown; some individuals are almost black above and heavily mottled below. These are easily mistaken for River Frogs, but the River Frog is rough-skinned and has light spots along the edges of the jaws.

Voice: A vibrant, sonorous series of bass notes best stated as *jug-o'-rum*. A single internal vocal sac, forming a flattened pouch under the chin when inflated. Breeds May to July; February to October in the South.

Range: Nova Scotia to cent. Florida; west to Wisconsin and Nebraska and south through the Great Plains. The natural western limits are now hopelessly confused because of the introduction of Bullfrogs into a vast number of localities as far west as British Columbia and California; also introduced in Mexico, Cuba, etc.   Map 247

RIVER FROG   *Rana heckscheri*   p. 287
Identification: 3¼–5; record 6. A large greenish-black, rough-skinned frog with the under surfaces heavily mottled with dark gray. Small but conspicuous light spots along edges of jaws. Rear of thigh mottled or with prominent light spots. Throat of male washed with yellow over a light gray background. No dorsolateral ridges. *Young:* With reddish eyes.

A frog of river swamps and swampy shores of ponds and bayous. Adults are not particularly wary, and are easily caught at night.

Similar species: The two other very large species, Bullfrog and

Pig Frog, have smoother skins and lack light spots on the jaws. Bronze Frog has dorsolateral ridges.

Voice: A deep, sonorous rolling snore; also a snarling, explosive grunt. Breeds June to August. A single internal vocal pouch.

Range: S. South Carolina to n.-cent. Florida; s. Mississippi.

Map 246

PIG FROG   *Rana grylio*   p. 287

Identification: 3¼–6; record 6⅜. A "bullfrog" with a rather narrow and pointed head, and with the hind feet fully webbed. The 4th toe *only a little longer* than adjacent toes. Pattern and coloration variable; olive to blackish brown and with prominent, scattered dark spots. Underparts often heavily mottled with black, brown, and yellow. No dorsolateral ridges. *Young:* Superficially like Carpenter Frog.

Very aquatic. Lakes, marshes, and cypress bays, water-lily prairies, or amid other floating or emergent vegetation. Shy and difficult to catch except at night with the aid of a flashlight.

Similar species: In both the Bullfrog and River Frog the webs are less extensive and the 4th toe protrudes *much farther* beyond other toes. All other southern frogs of the genus *Rana* have dorsolateral ridges except Carpenter Frog, but it has 2 light stripes down each side of body and a strongly protruding 4th toe.

Voice: Like the guttural grunt of a pig. Choruses sound like a herd of swine; very large groups produce a continuous roar. Males float high in the water when calling. There is only a single internal vocal pouch, but an extension at each side gives it a 3-sectional effect.

Range: S. South Carolina to extr. s. Florida and extr. se. Texas.

Map 248

CARPENTER FROG.   *Rana virgatipes*   p. 287

Identification: 1⅝–2⅝. The light stripes, 4 in all, the lack of dorsolateral ridges, and the Coastal Plain distribution are sufficient.

Sometimes called the "sphagnum frog," because of a close association with sphagnum bogs. It may be found in matted vegetation or dense stands of grass growing in water. In such habitats it is difficult to stalk, especially since its color blends so well with the acid, brown-stained waters of the bogs. In more open habitats it may be seen at the water's surface with only the head exposed. When approached, the head vanishes downward but reappears seconds later a few feet away.

Voice: *Pu-tunk,' pu-tunk,' pu-tunk.'* Like two carpenters hitting nails a fraction of a second apart. Several variations on this theme. Large choruses resemble a corps of workmen hammering away. Breeds April to August. Vocal pouches paired, spherical when inflated (Fig. 60, p. 297).

Range: Coastal Plain, s. New Jersey to e. Georgia.   Map 243

MINK FROG *Rana septentrionalis* p. 287
Identification: 1⅞–2¾; record 3. The skin produces an odor like the scent of a mink (or rotten onions) when the frog is rubbed or handled roughly. Webbing on toes of hind feet extends to last joint of 4th toe and to tip of 5th toe. The dorsolateral ridges may be absent, partially developed, or even prominent. The dorsal pattern may be mottled or spotted (Fig. 61, below). Dark spots often round and variable in size; in some frogs they dominate the pattern, in others the ground color is most conspicuous.

A frog of the North, found along watercourses, but especially partial to borders of ponds and lakes or the cold waters near the mouths of streams that empty into them. Look for it where water lilies are plentiful and where it can venture well out from shore by hopping from pad to pad.
Similar species: Likely to be confused only with Green Frog which often occurs abundantly with and strongly resembles Mink Frog. Green Frog lacks minklike odor, always has dorsolateral ridges, and webbing fails to reach tip of 5th toe and barely passes beyond second joint of the 4th.
Voice: A burred and rather deep *cut-cut-cut-cut-cut*, more rapid than but suggestive of the Carpenter Frog's "hammer blows." Breeds June to August. Vocal pouches paired.
Range: Labrador and Maritime Provinces to Minnesota and se. Manitoba; south to n. New York. Map 240

Fig. 61

MINK FROG

Spotted and
mottled types
of pattern
(Diagrammatic)

BRONZE FROG *Rana clamitans clamitans* p. 287
Identification: 2⅛–3; record 3⅜. A southern frog with a plain brown or bronzy back. The green of the upper lips is often lacking. Venter white, but with dark wormlike markings. In some males the throat is washed with light yellow. Dorsolateral ridges *ending on body*, not reaching groin. *Young:* Numerous dark dorsal spots; venter with heavy brown or black wormlike markings.

A secretive frog, taking shelter in logs and stumps, in crevices in limestone sinks, etc.; habitats include swamps, bayheads, wet hammocks, and environs of streams.
Similar species: The northern subspecies, the Green Frog, has markings in strong contrast with ground color. Bullfrog, Pig, River, and Carpenter Frogs lack dorsolateral ridges. In Pickerel

and Southern Leopard Frogs there is a light line on upper jaw, and dorsolateral ridges extend to groin.

Voice: A twanging, explosive bass note; usually a single *clung* or *c'tung*, but sometimes repeated rapidly 3 or 4 times. Two (internal) vocal pouches; the throat and sides expand when the frog is calling (Fig. 60, p. 297). Breeds April to August.

Range: Coastal Plain from s. North Carolina to n.-cent. Florida and west to e. Texas; north in Mississippi Valley to about mouth of Ohio River.　　　　　　　　　　　　　　　　　Map 244

GREEN FROG　*Rana clamitans melanota*　　　　　p. 287

Identification: 2¼–3½; record 4. Highly variable — may be more brown than green. Green to greenish brown above, dark brown or grayish dorsal spots or blotches usually present and often numerous. Venter white, but usually some dark spots or mottling under legs and head. Throat of adult male bright yellow. Dorsolateral ridges *ending on body*, not reaching groin.
Young: Numerous small dark dorsal spots; venter mottled.

An abundant frog that throughout a large part of its range may be found wherever there is shallow fresh water — in springs, rills, creeks, and ditches, and along edges of lakes and ponds. In many regions, however, it is characteristically a frog of brooks and small streams.

Similar species: The Bullfrog has no dorsolateral ridges. Leopard and Pickerel Frogs have a light line on upper jaw, and their dorsolateral ridges extend to groin. Green Frogs from Canada and northernmost parts of United States are likely to be very dark, with profusion of black or dark brown markings. Such frogs *strongly resemble* Mink Frog. (See p. 299 for ways to distinguish these two.)

Voice: Like a loose banjo string and rather explosive, either a single note or repeated 3 or 4 times, the notes progressively less loud. A pair of vocal pouches, but not evident externally. When the frog is croaking, the throat and sides of body expand considerably (Fig. 60, p. 297). Breeds April to August.

Range: Maritime Provinces to North Carolina; west to Minnesota and e. Oklahoma; introduced in Newfoundland.　Map 244

NORTHERN LEOPARD FROG　*Rana pipiens pipiens*　p. 287

Identification: 2–3½; record 4⅛. A brown or green frog with 2 or 3 rows of irregularly placed dark spots between conspicuous dorsolateral ridges. Spots *rounded and with light borders*; adjacent spots may run together. Numerous additional rounded dark spots on sides. A light line on upper jaw.

This is the "meadow frog," at least in summertime, a name earned by its wanderings well away from water. Leopard Frogs are widely used as laboratory animals.

Similar species: Pickerel Frog has squarish dark spots, **and**

concealed surfaces of its legs are bright yellow or orange. Craw-fish Frog is squat and stubby in appearance.

Voice: A deep rattling snore interspersed with clucking grunts, that may be single or of 2 or more syllables. Each frog *ad libs* its own solo, following a regular pattern or voicing numerous variations. Paired vocal pouches, swelling into spheres above the arms when inflated (Fig. 60, p. 297). Breeds March to May in the parts of the range that lie east of the 100th meridian.

Range: S. Labrador to extr. s. District of Mackenzie; south through uplands to n. Georgia; west to Pacific states, and south, in the West, into Mexico.

Subspecies: Herpetologists have long been wrangling about Leopard Frogs. Is there only one kind? Or are there subspecies, and, if so, how many? These frogs are highly variable in both coloration and pattern, and there is a tendency for local popula-tions to differ from one pond to the next. It is here assumed that there are three races east of the 100th meridian — the Northern, Southern, and Rio Grande Leopard Frogs. For many field naturalists it will be sufficient merely to identify a specimen as a "leopard frog" without considering subspecies.

In parts of Minnesota and adjacent states, a small percentage of the Leopard Frog population consists of two aberrant types of patterns: (1) black spots greatly reduced in number or even completely absent, except for a spot behind each elbow; or (2) ground color between spots strongly invaded by dark pigment. These have been named as subspecies (*burnsi* and *kandiyohi*), but they are merely mutations of the Northern Leopard Frog. The spotted one looks superficially like the Northern Crawfish Frog.   Map 241

SOUTHERN LEOPARD FROG
Rana pipiens sphenocephala   p. 287

Identification: 2–3½; record 5. The southern counterpart of the Northern Leopard Frog, but differing from the latter as follows: (1) light spot in center of tympanum; (2) longer, pointed head; and (3) only a few dark spots on sides of body. General colora-tion green or brown or a combination of both. Number of dark dorsal spots highly variable (occasionally completely absent); spots often longitudinally elongated.

In all types of shallow fresh-water habitats, and even entering slightly brackish marshes along coasts. Ventures well away from water in summer, when weeds and other vegetation provide shelter and shade.

Similar species: Pickerel Frog has squarish dark spots, and concealed surfaces of its hind legs are bright yellow or orange. Gopher and Crawfish Frogs have fat, chunky bodies and rounded, non-pointed snouts.

Voice: A deep rhythmic, rattling snore, often followed by 2 or 3 single clucks. Two vocal pouches, spherical when inflated (Fig. 60, p. 297). Breeds in early spring toward the north; in any month in the South.

Range: S. New Jersey to extr. s. Florida (and some of the *lower* Keys); west to extr. e. Texas and north in Mississippi Valley to Missouri, s. Illinois, and cent. Indiana.   Map 241

RIO GRANDE LEOPARD FROG

Rana pipiens berlandieri   p. 287

Identification: 2½–4. Like the other Leopard Frogs, but wartier, more pallid in coloration (especially toward the south), the toes more fully webbed, and the dorsal spots tending to be transverse. Also differs from the other subspecies in its behavior.

This frog is well adapted to arid conditions. It is an "explosive" breeder, ready to take advantage of the rains when they come, hence it may breed during almost any month of year. (Leopard Frogs of humid areas tend to have more definite breeding seasons.) Watercourses and cattle tanks are frequented, but this frog may appear suddenly, at the onset of rain, in regions where its presence is not suspected, specimens emerging from the shelter of underground retreats. Likely to be more agile and wary than other Leopard Frogs.

Similar species: See Southern Leopard Frog.

Range: S. Nebraska to Central America.   Map 241

PICKEREL FROG   *Rana palustris*   p. 287

Identification: 1¾–3; record 3⅛. A frog with "square" spots arranged in 2 parallel rows down the back. These dark markings and similar ones on the sides have the unevenness of squares drawn freehand; the edges are irregular and often curved, but the spots definitely are not circular. Adjacent "squares" may join to form "rectangles" or long, longitudinal "bars." *Bright yellow or orange on concealed surfaces of hind legs.* A light line along upper jaw. Dorsolateral ridges extending to groin. *Young:* With a metallic luster, but without bright colors under the legs; lower lip clouded with dark pigment.

Typically a species of cool water — sphagnum bogs, rocky ravines, and meadow streams, but also occupying a wide variety of other habitats. Wanders well out into grassy fields or weed-covered areas in summer. Often found in the twilight zones of caves. Few snakes will eat Pickerel Frogs, probably because the skin-gland secretions make them distasteful.

Similar species: In the Leopard Frogs the dark dorsal spots are circular or oval and surrounded by *light* borders, and there is no bright yellow or orange on the legs.

Voice: A steady low-pitched snore of 1 or 2 seconds' duration but with little carrying power. Males very often call while completely submerged in water. Two vocal pouches. Breeds March to May.

Range: Maritime Provinces to the Carolinas; west to Wisconsin and se. Texas; distribution spotty, especially toward the south and in prairie portions of Ohio, Indiana, and Illinois.   Map 239

WOOD FROG   *Rana sylvatica*   p. 287
  Identification: 1⅜–2¾; record 3¼. The frog with the robber's mask. A dark patch extending backward from the eye is always discernible despite pronounced variations in color. The two illustrations (Plate 40) show dark and light extremes of the same specimen; the gamut runs from pink through various shades of brown to almost black.

Usually encountered in or near moist wooded areas in United States and southern Canada; often wanders considerable distances from water. In the Far North it may occur wherever there is shallow water for breeding, even in tundra ponds.

Voice: A hoarse clacking sound suggesting the quack of a duck. Has little carrying power. Shorter, less loud and less deep, but otherwise resembling voice of Northern Leopard Frog. Appears very early, often heard calling before ice is completely off the ponds. An "explosive" breeder, the eggs being laid all in the course of a very few days and the adults then disappearing from the ponds instead of lingering sometimes for weeks, as do many other kinds of frogs. Two vocal sacs.

Range: Labrador to Alaska; south in the East to s. Appalachians. Isolated colonies in Ozarks, Kansas, Colorado, Wyoming, and Idaho. Ranges farther north than any other North American reptile or amphibian.

Subspecies: Toward the northern portions of the range, the hind legs of the Wood Frog become porportionately shorter, and specimens resemble toads in appearance and hopping abilities. The change is gradual (clinal), but at least two northern subspecies (*cantabrigensis* and *latiremis*) have been described. Since virtually no two authorities agree upon where the range of one race stops and the next begins, the Wood Frogs are here considered as constituting a single, geographically variable species.
                                                                      Map 245

Gopher and Crawfish Frogs:
Rana areolata and Its Races

FROGS OF stubby appearance — short, plump bodies, large heads, and relatively short legs. Nocturnal, normally spending the daylight hours underground in burrows or tunnels, in holes beneath stumps, etc. Both the Florida and Dusky Gopher Frogs utilize the burrows of the Gopher Tortoise; the Crawfish Frogs often use the abandoned burrows of the lobster-like crawfish (crayfish in the North). The breeding seasons occur in the spring, the dates often being correlated with the occurrence of heavy rains. Males have lateral vocal pouches which are enormous when inflated, each approaching the size of the frog's head.

(SOUTHERN) CRAWFISH FROG

Rana areolata areolata   p. 287

Identification: 2¼–3; record 3⅝. A stubby appearance plus rounded dark dorsal *spots encircled by light borders.* Coloration highly variable, depending on conditions of temperature, activity, etc. Chin and throat unspotted except at sides; belly immaculate whitish (Fig. 62, below). Dorsum often smooth or nearly so. Males may have yellow or greenish yellow on their dorsolateral ridges and on the concealed surfaces of the limbs.

Not restricted to crawfish holes, but often found in those which have lost their "chimneys" and contain water. Other habitats include mammal burrows, holes in roadside banks, and in sewers.

Similar species: Leopard Frogs have longer bodies, proportionately longer legs, and lack the stubby, squat appearance of the Crawfish Frogs. Pickerel Frog has squarish spots. Dusky and Florida Gopher Frogs have thickly spotted chins and throats, and lack light-bordered dorsal spots.

Voice: A loud (often chuckling) deep trill with considerable carrying power. Large choruses sound like a styful of hogs at feeding time. Breeds February to June.

Range: Gulf Coastal Plain of Texas and Louisiana and Red and Arkansas river valleys.

Subspecies: NORTHERN CRAWFISH FROG, *Rana areolata circulosa.* Somewhat larger; length to 4½″. Head shorter and broader, dorsolateral ridges more prominent, and dorsum rougher. Indiana to ne. Oklahoma and s.-cent. Mississippi.

                                                     Map 242

Fig. 62

VENTERS OF
GOPHER FROGS

CRAWFISH
Largely unmarked

DUSKY AND CAROLINA
GOPHER
Heavily pigmented

DUSKY GOPHER FROG   *Rana areolata sevosa*   p. 287

Identification: 2½–3½; record 3⅞. Warts always prominent, but variable in shape — circular, elongate-oval, or in long ridges. Dorsal coloration also variable, but always dark; the gamut runs from virtually uniform black to a pattern of reddish brown or dark brown spots on a ground of gray or brown. Venter spotted, at least from chin to midbody (Fig. 62, p. 304).

Similar species: River Frog has white spots on lips. In the two Crawfish Frogs dark dorsal spots are rounded and encircled by *light borders*.

Voice: A deep snore or like the roar of an outboard motor; more continuous and hoarser than the guttural notes of the Southern Leopard Frog.

Range: Gulf Coast, extr. w. Florida to extr. e. Louisiana.

Subspecies: CAROLINA GOPHER FROG, *Rana areolata capito*. Warts smaller, closer together, and almost pavement-like in arrangement (like cobblestones on an old-fashioned street, but very much in miniature). Venter heavily marked with dark flecks that produce a clouded or marbled pattern. Young with less ventral spotting, especially on abdomen, where it may be lacking entirely. Coastal Plain of the Carolinas and e.-cent. Georgia. Map 242

FLORIDA GOPHER FROG *Rana areolata aesopus* p. 287
Identification: 2¾–3¾; record 4¼. The light ground color has earned this species the name of "white frog." The coloration varies from creamy white to brown through various shades of yellow or purplish. The black or dark brown markings are irregular in shape and not encircled by light borders. Dorsum may be smooth or slightly warty. Chin and throat spotted; belly usually unmarked posteriorly. Males may have yellow on the dorsolateral ridges, on the warts, along upper jaw, and in armpits and groins.

This short, plump frog sometimes may be seen several feet back from the entrance of Gopher Tortoise burrows during daylight hours, but is best sought at night, when it ventures forth to feed.

Voice: A deep roaring snore. Large choruses produce an effect like that of pounding surf. Breeds in spring toward northern part of its range, but from February until autumn farther south.

Range: Coastal Plain, Georgia to s. Florida. Map 242

Glossary

For names of scales and other anatomical nomenclature see the end-papers.

Azygous. Odd, not paired.

Barbels. Small, fleshy downward projections from the chins and throats of turtles.

Boss. A raised rounded area; in toads, a rounded eminence on the midline of the head between the eyes or on or near the end of the snout.

Canthus rostralis. The ridge from the eye to the tip of the snout that separates the top of the muzzle from the side.

Cirri. Downward projections from the nostrils in males of certain Lungless Salamanders. The naso-labial groove extends downward to near the tip of each cirrus.

Cline. A gradual change in a variable characteristic (see p. 7).

Costal grooves. Vertical grooves on the flanks of salamanders.

Cranial crests. The raised ridges on the heads of toads — interorbital (between the eyes) or postorbital (behind the eyes).

Crepuscular. Active at twilight and/or dawn.

Cusp. A toothlike projection on the jaw of a turtle.

Dorsal. Of or pertaining to the upper surface.

Dorsolateral. Neither directly down the center of the back nor at the side of the body, but more or less intermediate between the two.

Dorsum. The entire upper surface of an animal.

Estivation. A state of inactivity during prolonged periods of drought or high temperatures, usually while the animal is in seclusion.

Form. A species or a subspecies; a distinct, identifiable population.

Gravid. Bearing eggs or young, ordinarily in the oviducts.

Growth rings. Concentric subcircular areas on the scutes of some turtles. Each "ring" represents a season's growth. Rings, if present, are most evident in young turtles; they are usually not countable in adults.

Hemipenis. The copulatory organs of males. There are two such organs in snakes and lizards, but only a single penis in turtles and crocodilians.

306

Keel. A ridge down the back (or along the plastron) of a turtle. Also, a longitudinal ridge on a dorsal scale in certain snakes.

Melanism. Abundance of black pigment, sometimes resulting in an all-black or nearly all-black animal; opposite of albinism.

Middorsal. Of or pertaining to the center of the back.

Midventral. Of or pertaining to the center of the abdomen.

Naso-labial groove. A groove extending downward from the nostril and across the lip in the Lungless Salamanders.

Neotenic. Mature and capable of reproduction but retaining the larval form, appearance, and habits.

Ocelli. Round, eyelike spots.

Papillae. Small nipple-like protuberances.

Parotoid. The external gland on the shoulder in toads, enlarged and prominent in many species.

Phalanges. The bones of the toes.

Postocular. Behind the eye.

Race. Subspecies.

Rugose. Wrinkled or warty.

Scale pits. Tiny depressions on the posterior portions of the dorsal scales in some kinds of snakes.

Scute. Any enlarged scale on a reptile; sometimes called "plate."

Spatulate. Flat and rounded at tip; shaped like the blade of a kitchen spatula.

Subcaudals. The scales beneath the tail; in a double row in most snakes, but in a single row in others. Sometimes shortened to "caudals."

Subocular. Beneath the eye.

Suture. A seam; the boundary between scales or scutes.

Tibia. The leg (of frogs and toads) from heel to knee.

Tubercles. Small knoblike projections.

Tuberculate. With raised projections.

Tympanum. The eardrum.

Venter. The entire under surface of an animal.

Ventral. Of or pertaining to the lower surface.

Vocal sac. An inflatable pouch on the throat or at the sides of the neck in male frogs and toads; single in most species, but paired in others.

Bibliography

In the strictest sense of the word a bibliography is an exhaustive compilation of all literature pertinent to a given subject. Such thoroughness is impossible within the limited pagination of a *Field Guide*, but all of the more recent state reports are listed below plus a number of general works and several important local or regional papers. Additional references will be found in the bibliographies of most of these publications. As this book goes to press a number of state herpetologies are in advanced stages of completion; some are actually in press. These are listed in their proper places even though it is impossible as yet to give full references to them.

GENERAL

Bishop, Sherman C. *Handbook of Salamanders*. Ithaca, N. Y.: Comstock Publishing Co., Inc., 1947.

Blair, Albert P., and Cagle, Fred R. (for sections on amphibians and reptiles). *Vertebrates of the United States*. New York: McGraw-Hill Book Co., 1957.

Carr, Archie. *Handbook of Turtles*. Ithaca, N. Y.: Comstock Publishing Associates, Cornell University Press, 1952.

Kauffeld, Carl. *Snakes and Snake Hunting*. Garden City, N. Y.: Hanover House, 1957.

Klauber, Laurence M. *Rattlesnakes: Their Habits, Life Histories, and Influence on Mankind*. Berkeley and Los Angeles: University of California Press, 1956. 2v.

Oliver, James A. *The Natural History of North American Amphibians and Reptiles*. Princeton: D. Van Nostrand Co., Inc., 1955.

Pope, Clifford H. *Snakes Alive and How They Live*. New York: Viking Press, 1937.

——. *Turtles of the United States & Canada*. New York: Alfred A. Knopf, 1939.

——. *The Reptile World*. New York: Alfred A. Knopf, 1955.

Schmidt, Karl P. *A Check List of North American Amphibians and Reptiles*, 6th ed. Chicago: American Society of Ichthyologists and Herpetologists, 1953. (Procurable from Professor N. Bayard Green, Dept. of Zoology, Marshall College, Huntington, W. Va.)

——, and Davis, D. Dwight. *Field Book of Snakes of the United States and Canada*. New York: G. P. Putnam's Sons, 1941.

——, and Inger, Robert F. *Living Reptiles of the World*. Garden City, N. Y.: Hanover House, 1957.

Smith, Hobart M. *Handbook of Lizards*. Ithaca, N. Y.: Comstock Publishing Co., Inc., 1946.

Wright, Albert Hazen, and Wright, Anna Allen. *Handbook of Frogs and Toads of the United States and Canada*, 3d ed. Ithaca, N. Y.: Comstock Publishing Co., Inc., 1949.
——. *Handbook of Snakes of the United States and Canada*. Ithaca, N. Y.: Comstock Publishing Associates, Cornell University Press, 1957. 2v.

REGIONAL

New England

Babcock, Harold L. *The Snakes of New England*. Boston: Natural History Guides, No. 1, Boston Society of Natural History, 1929.
——. *Field Guide to New England Turtles*. Boston: Natural History Guides, No. 2, New England Museum of Natural History, 1938.

Northeast

Conant, Roger. *Reptiles and Amphibians of the Northeastern States*, 3d ed. Philadelphia: Zoological Society of Philadelphia, 1957.
Pope, Clifford H. *Snakes of the Northeastern United States*. New York: New York Zoological Society, 1946.

West

Stebbins, Robert C. *Amphibians of Western North America*. Berkeley and Los Angeles: University of California Press, 1951.
——. *Amphibians and Reptiles of Western North America*. New York: McGraw-Hill Book Co., Inc., 1954.

Mexico

Smith, Hobart M., and Taylor, Edward H. *Annotated Checklists and Keys (to the Snakes of Mexico*, No. 187, 1945); (*the Amphibia of Mexico*, No. 194, 1948); and (*the Reptiles of Mexico Exclusive of the Snakes*, No. 199, 1950). Washington: Bulletins of the United States National Museum.

CANADA

Bleakney, Sherman. *A Zoogeographical Study of the Amphibians and Reptiles of Eastern Canada*. Ottawa: National Museum of Canada, Bulletin 155, Biological Series 54 (1958).
Logier, E. B. S. *The Frogs, Toads and Salamanders of Eastern Canada*. Toronto: Clarke, Irwin & Co. Limited, 1952.
——, and Toner, G. C. *Check-list of the Amphibians and Reptiles of Canada and Alaska*. Toronto: Contributions of the Royal Ontario Museum of Zoology and Palaeontology, No. 41 (1955).

Nova Scotia

Bleakney, Sherman. *The Amphibians and Reptiles of Nova Scotia*. Ottawa: Canadian Field-Naturalist, **66:** 125–29 (1952).

Ontario

Logier, E. B. S. *The Snakes of Ontario*. Toronto: University of Toronto Press, 1958.

UNITED STATES

Alabama

Chermock, Ralph L. *A Key to the Amphibians and Reptiles of Alabama.* University, Ala.: Geological Survey of Alabama, Museum Paper 33 (1952).

Arkansas

Dowling, Herndon G. *A Review of the Amphibians and Reptiles of Arkansas.* Fayetteville, Ark.: University of Arkansas Museum, Occasional Papers, No. 3 (1957).

Connecticut

Babbitt, Lewis Hall. *The Amphibia of Connecticut.* Hartford: State Geological and Natural History Survey, Bulletin No. 57 (1937).
Lamson, George Herbert. *The Reptiles of Connecticut.* Hartford: State Geological and Natural History Survey, Bulletin No. 54 (1935).

Delaware

Conant, Roger. *An Annotated Check List of the Amphibians and Reptiles of the Del-Mar-Va Peninsula.* Wilmington, Del.: Society of Natural History of Delaware, 1945.

Florida

Carr, Archie. *A Contribution to the Herpetology of Florida.* Gainesville, Fla.: University of Florida Publication, Vol. 3, No. 1 (1940).
——, and Goin, Coleman J. *Guide to the Reptiles, Amphibians and Fresh-water Fishes of Florida.* Gainesville, Fla.: University of Florida Press, 1955.

Georgia

Martof, Bernard S. *Amphibians and Reptiles of Georgia, A Guide.* Athens, Ga.: University of Georgia Press, 1956.

Illinois

Cahn, Alvin R. *The Turtles of Illinois.* Urbana, Ill.: University of Illinois Bulletin, Vol. 35, No. 1 (1937).
Pope, Clifford H. *Amphibians and Reptiles of the Chicago Area.* Chicago: Chicago Natural History Museum, 1944.
Smith, Philip W. *The Amphibians and Reptiles of Illinois.* Urbana, Ill.: Illinois Natural History Survey. (In press.)

Indiana

Minton, Sherman A., Jr. *Introduction to the Study of the Reptiles of Indiana.* Notre Dame, Ind.: American Midland Naturalist, **32**: 438-77 (1944).
——. *Herpetology of Indiana.* (In preparation.)

Iowa

Guthrie, J. E. *The Snakes of Iowa.* Ames, Iowa: Iowa State College of Agriculture and Mechanic Arts, Agriculture Experiment Station, Bulletin No. 239 (1926).

Kansas

Smith, Hobart M. *Handbook of Amphibians and Reptiles of Kansas,* 2d ed. Lawrence, Kan.: University of Kansas Museum of Natural History, Miscellaneous Publication No. 9 (1956).

Louisiana

Cagle, Fred R. *A Key to the Amphibians and Reptiles of Louisiana.* New Orleans: Tulane University, 1952.

Maryland

McCauley, Robert H., Jr. *The Reptiles of Maryland and the District of Columbia.* Hagerstown, Md.: Published by the Author, 1945.

Mansueti, Romeo. *A Descriptive Catalogue of the Amphibians and Reptiles Found in and around Baltimore City, Maryland.* Baltimore: Natural History Society of Maryland, Proceedings, No. 7 (1941).

Michigan

Ruthven, Alexander G., Thompson, Crystal, and Gaige, Helen T. *The Herpetology of Michigan.* Ann Arbor: University Museums, University of Michigan, Handbook Series, No. 3 (1928).

Minnesota

Breckenridge, W. J. *Reptiles and Amphibians of Minnesota.* Minneapolis: University of Minnesota Press, 1944.

Mississippi

Cook, Fannye A. *Snakes of Mississippi* (1954); *Alligator and Lizards of Mississippi* (1957); and *Salamanders of Mississippi* (1957). Jackson, Miss.: Mississippi Game and Fish Commission.

Missouri

Anderson, Paul. *The Amphibians and Reptiles of Missouri.* (In preparation.)

Hurter, Julius, Sr. *Herpetology of Missouri.* St. Louis: Transactions of the Academy of Science of St. Louis, **20:** 59–274 (1911).

Nebraska

Hudson, George E. *The Amphibians and Reptiles of Nebraska.* Lincoln, Nebr.: University of Nebraska, Nebraska Conservation Bulletin, No. 24 (1942).

New Hampshire

Oliver, James A., and Bailey, Joseph R. *Amphibians and Reptiles of New Hampshire.* Concord, N. H.: Biological Survey of the Connecticut Watershed: 195–217 (1939).

New Jersey

Trapido, Harold. *The Snakes of New Jersey: A Guide.* Newark: Newark Museum, 1937.

New York

Bishop, Sherman C. *The Salamanders of New York.* Albany: University of the State of New York, New York State Museum Bulletin, No. 324 (1941).

North Carolina

Brimley, C. S. *The Amphibians and Reptiles of North Carolina.* Raleigh, N. C.: Carolina Tips (printed by author in 32 installments, 1939 to 1943, inclusive).

North Dakota

Wheeler, George C. *The Amphibians and Reptiles of North Dakota.* Notre Dame, Ind.: American Midland Naturalist, **38**: 162–90 (1947).

Ohio

Conant, Roger. *The Reptiles of Ohio,* 2d ed. Notre Dame, Ind.: The American Midland Naturalist, 1951.

Walker, Charles F. *The Amphibians of Ohio: Part 1, The Frogs and Toads.* Columbus, Ohio: Ohio State Museum Science Bulletin, Vol. 1, No. 3 (1946).

Oklahoma

Webb, Robert G., and Ortenburger, A. I. *A Guide to the Reptiles of Oklahoma.* (In press.)

Pennsylvania

Harrison, Hal. H. *Pennsylvania Reptiles & Amphibians.* Harrisburg, Pa.: Reprinted from the Pennsylvania Angler, Pennsylvania Fish Commission, 1949–50.

South Dakota

Over, William H. *Amphibians and Reptiles of South Dakota.* Vermillion, S. D.: South Dakota Geological and Natural History Survey, Bulletin 12 (1923).

Tennessee

Gentry, Glenn. *An Annotated Check List of the Amphibians and Reptiles of Tennessee.* Knoxville, Tenn.: Journal of the Tennessee Academy of Science, **30**: 168–76 (1955) and **31**: 242–51 (1956).

Texas

Brown, Bryce C. *An Annotated Check List of the Reptiles and Amphibians of Texas.* Waco, Texas: Baylor University Press, 1950.

West Virginia

Green, N. Bayard. *The Amphibians and Reptiles of West Virginia, Their Identification, Habits and Distribution.* Huntington, W. Va.: Marshall College, 1954.

Wisconsin

Dickinson, W. E. *Field Guide to the Lizards and Snakes of Wisconsin.* Milwaukee: Milwaukee Public Museum, Popular Science Handbook Series, No. 2 (1949).

Pope, T. E. B., and Dickinson, W. E. *The Amphibians and Reptiles of Wisconsin.* Milwaukee: Bulletin of the Public Museum of the City of Milwaukee, Vol. 8, No. 1 (1928).

Sound Recordings of Frog and Toad Calls

Bogert, Charles M. *Sounds of North American Frogs: The Biological Significance of Voice in Frogs.* New York: Folkways Records & Service Corp., 117 West 46th Street, N.Y.C. 36. (12″ LP record; 92 calls of 50 species of frogs and toads; accompanied by a profusely illustrated essay on the subject.)

Kellogg, Peter Paul, and Allen, Arthur A. *Voices of the Night.* Ithaca N.Y.: Cornell University Records, Cornell University Press. (12″ LP record; calls of 34 kinds of frogs and toads of eastern North America.)

CROCODILIANS, SNAPPERS, AND POND TURTLES

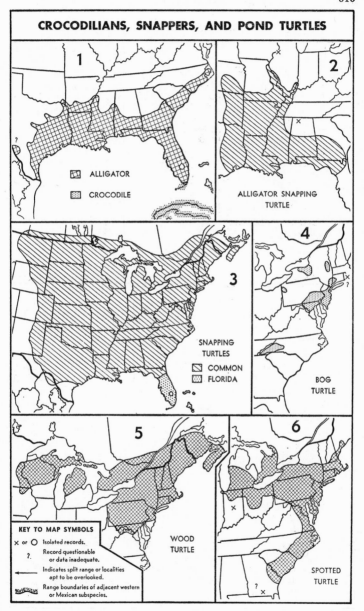

1

ALLIGATOR

CROCODILE

2

ALLIGATOR SNAPPING
TURTLE

3

SNAPPING
TURTLES

COMMON

FLORIDA

4

BOG
TURTLE

5

WOOD
TURTLE

6

SPOTTED
TURTLE

KEY TO MAP SYMBOLS

✗ or ◯ Isolated records.

?. Record questionable
    or data inadequate.

← Indicates split range or localities
   apt to be overlooked.

▨▨ Range boundaries of adjacent western
    or Mexican subspecies.

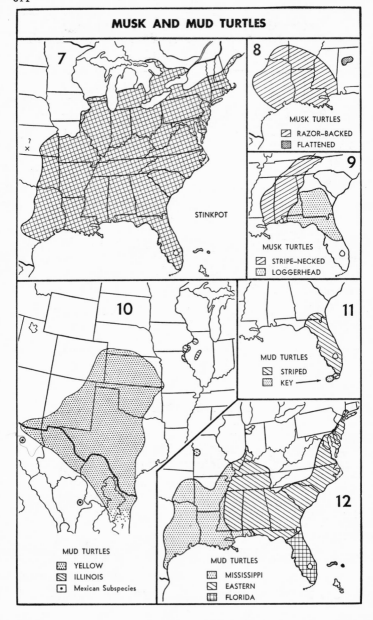

314

MUSK AND MUD TURTLES

7

STINKPOT

8

MUSK TURTLES
▨ RAZOR-BACKED
▧ FLATTENED

9

MUSK TURTLES
▨ STRIPE-NECKED
▨ LOGGERHEAD

10

MUD TURTLES
▨ YELLOW
▨ ILLINOIS
⊙ Mexican Subspecies

11

MUD TURTLES
◩ STRIPED
▦ KEY ⟶

12

MUD TURTLES
▨ MISSISSIPPI
◩ EASTERN
▦ FLORIDA

315

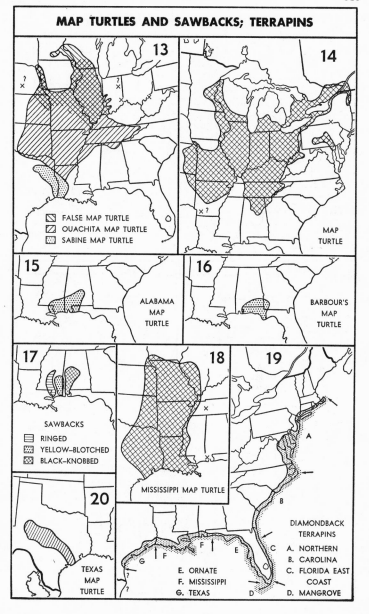

MAP TURTLES AND SAWBACKS; TERRAPINS

13

FALSE MAP TURTLE
OUACHITA MAP TURTLE
SABINE MAP TURTLE

14

MAP
TURTLE

15

ALABAMA
MAP
TURTLE

16

BARBOUR'S
MAP
TURTLE

17

SAWBACKS

RINGED
YELLOW–BLOTCHED
BLACK–KNOBBED

18

MISSISSIPPI MAP TURTLE

19

DIAMONDBACK
TERRAPINS

A. NORTHERN
B. CAROLINA
C. FLORIDA EAST
   COAST
D. MANGROVE

20

TEXAS
MAP
TURTLE

E. ORNATE
F. MISSISSIPPI
G. TEXAS

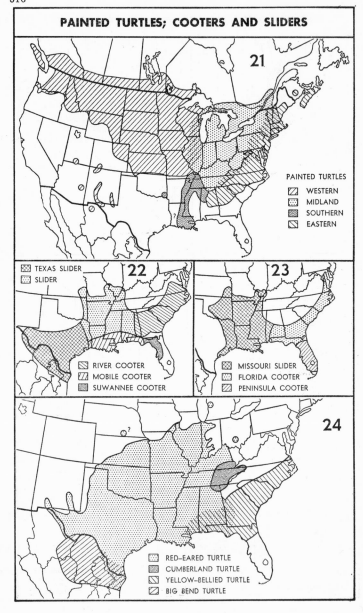

PAINTED TURTLES; COOTERS AND SLIDERS

21

PAINTED TURTLES

◪ WESTERN
▦ MIDLAND
▨ SOUTHERN
◩ EASTERN

22

▦ TEXAS SLIDER
⬚ SLIDER

◩ RIVER COOTER
▨ MOBILE COOTER
▤ SUWANNEE COOTER

23

▦ MISSOURI SLIDER
⬚ FLORIDA COOTER
▨ PENINSULA COOTER

24

⬚ RED-EARED TURTLE
▥ CUMBERLAND TURTLE
◩ YELLOW-BELLIED TURTLE
◪ BIG BEND TURTLE

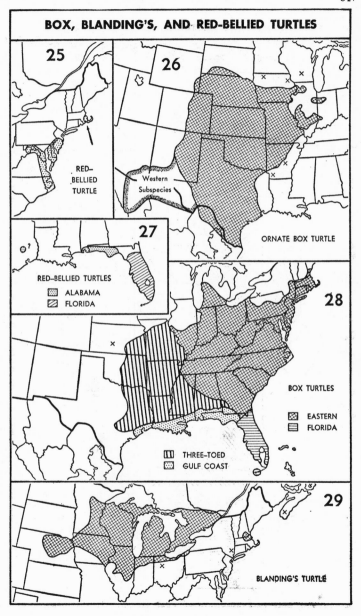

BOX, BLANDING'S, AND RED-BELLIED TURTLES

25

RED-
BELLIED
TURTLE

26

Western
Subspecies

ORNATE BOX TURTLE

27

RED-BELLIED TURTLES
- ALABAMA
- FLORIDA

28

BOX TURTLES
- EASTERN
- FLORIDA
- THREE-TOED
- GULF COAST

29

BLANDING'S TURTLE

318

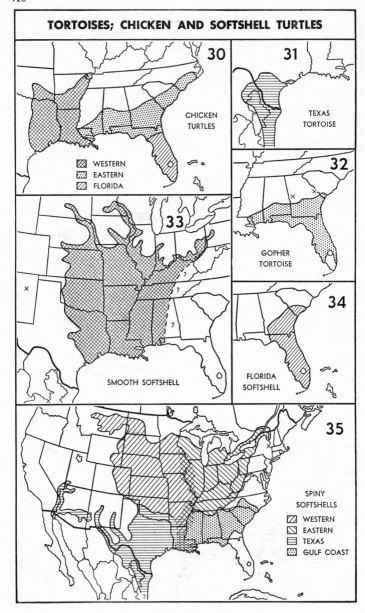

TORTOISES; CHICKEN AND SOFTSHELL TURTLES

30 CHICKEN TURTLES

WESTERN
EASTERN
FLORIDA

31 TEXAS TORTOISE

32 GOPHER TORTOISE

33 SMOOTH SOFTSHELL

34 FLORIDA SOFTSHELL

35 SPINY SOFTSHELLS

WESTERN
EASTERN
TEXAS
GULF COAST

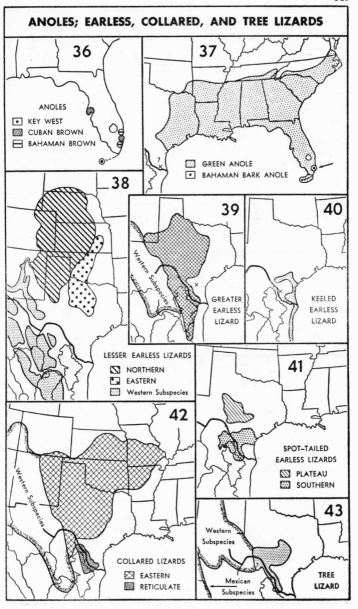

ANOLES; EARLESS, COLLARED, AND TREE LIZARDS

36

ANOLES
- ◉ KEY WEST
- ▨ CUBAN BROWN
- ▤ BAHAMAN BROWN

37

GREEN ANOLE
◉ BAHAMAN BARK ANOLE

38

LESSER EARLESS LIZARDS
- ▨ NORTHERN
- ▣ EASTERN
- ▦ Western Subspecies

39

Western Subspecies

GREATER EARLESS LIZARD

40

KEELED EARLESS LIZARD

41

SPOT-TAILED EARLESS LIZARDS
- ▨ PLATEAU
- ▦ SOUTHERN

42

Western Subspecies

COLLARED LIZARDS
- ▩ EASTERN
- ▨ RETICULATE

43

Western Subspecies

Mexican Subspecies

TREE LIZARD

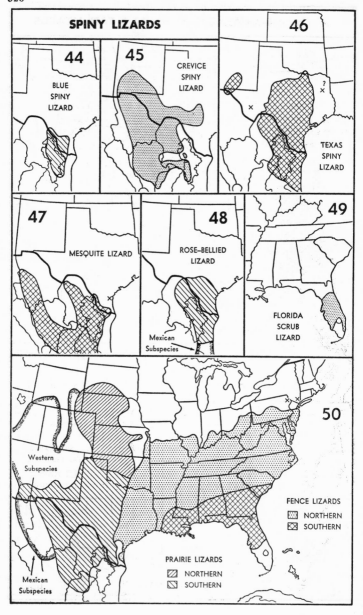

SPINY LIZARDS

44 BLUE SPINY LIZARD

45 CREVICE SPINY LIZARD

46 TEXAS SPINY LIZARD

47 MESQUITE LIZARD

48 ROSE–BELLIED LIZARD
Mexican Subspecies

49 FLORIDA SCRUB LIZARD

50
Western Subspecies
Mexican Subspecies

FENCE LIZARDS
▦ NORTHERN
▨ SOUTHERN

PRAIRIE LIZARDS
▨ NORTHERN
▨ SOUTHERN

HORNED LIZARDS AND GECKOS

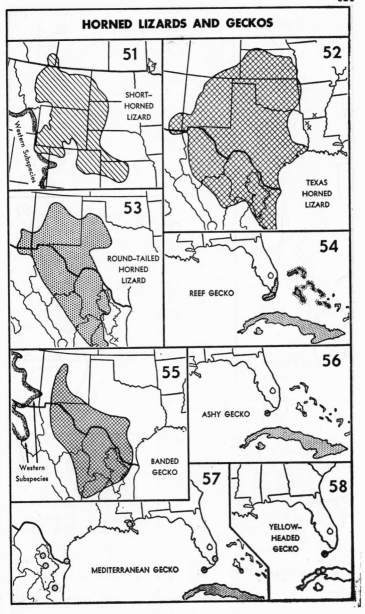

51 SHORT-HORNED LIZARD
Western Subspecies

52 TEXAS HORNED LIZARD

53 ROUND-TAILED HORNED LIZARD

54 REEF GECKO

55 BANDED GECKO
Western Subspecies

56 ASHY GECKO

57 MEDITERRANEAN GECKO

58 YELLOW-HEADED GECKO

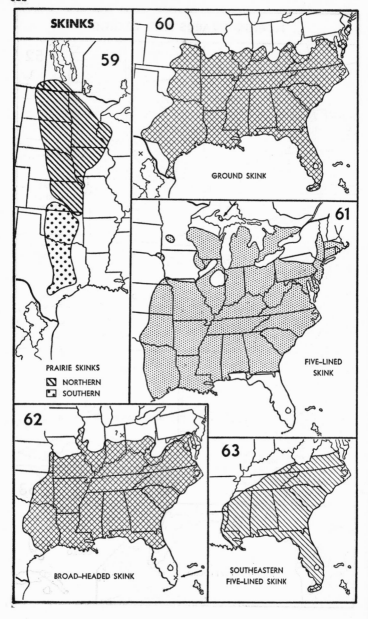

SKINKS

59

PRAIRIE SKINKS

⬛ NORTHERN
⬛ SOUTHERN

60

GROUND SKINK

61

FIVE–LINED
SKINK

62

BROAD–HEADED SKINK

63

SOUTHEASTERN
FIVE–LINED SKINK

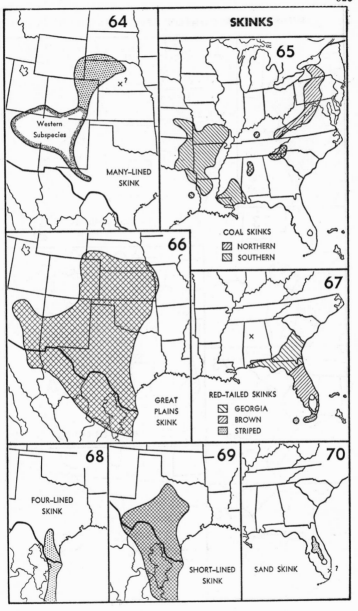

323

64 MANY-LINED SKINK

Western Subspecies

×?

SKINKS

65 COAL SKINKS

NORTHERN

SOUTHERN

66 GREAT PLAINS SKINK

67 RED-TAILED SKINKS

GEORGIA

BROWN

STRIPED

×

68 FOUR-LINED SKINK

69 SHORT-LINED SKINK

70 SAND SKINK

×?

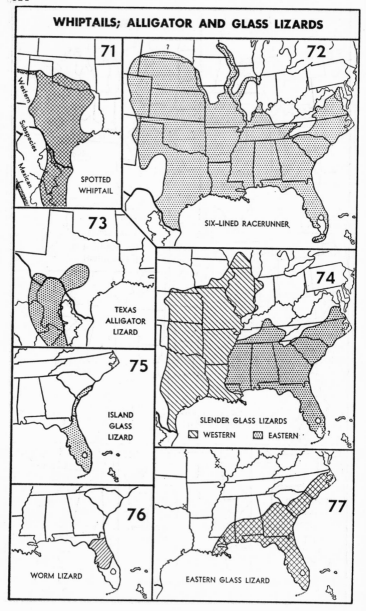

WHIPTAILS; ALLIGATOR AND GLASS LIZARDS

71 SPOTTED WHIPTAIL

Western Subspecies Mexican

72 SIX–LINED RACERUNNER

73 TEXAS ALLIGATOR LIZARD

74 SLENDER GLASS LIZARDS

◣ WESTERN   ▦ EASTERN

75 ISLAND GLASS LIZARD

76 WORM LIZARD

77 EASTERN GLASS LIZARD

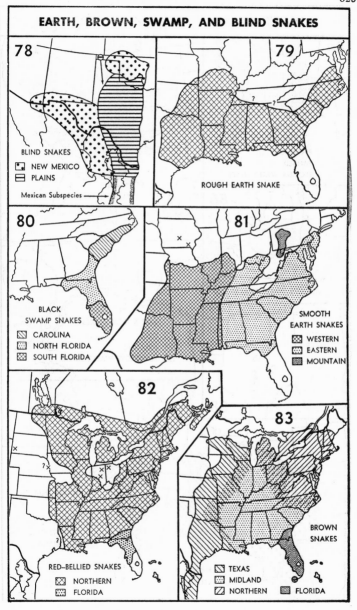

EARTH, BROWN, SWAMP, AND BLIND SNAKES

78

BLIND SNAKES
- ▪ NEW MEXICO
- ⊟ PLAINS

Mexican Subspecies ➤

79

ROUGH EARTH SNAKE

80

BLACK
SWAMP SNAKES
- ◨ CAROLINA
- ⬚ NORTH FLORIDA
- ⊠ SOUTH FLORIDA

81

SMOOTH
EARTH SNAKES
- ⊠ WESTERN
- ⬚ EASTERN
- ▨ MOUNTAIN

82

RED–BELLIED SNAKES
- ⊠ NORTHERN
- ⬚ FLORIDA

83

BROWN
SNAKES
- ◨ TEXAS
- ⬚ MIDLAND
- ▨ NORTHERN
- ◪ FLORIDA

326

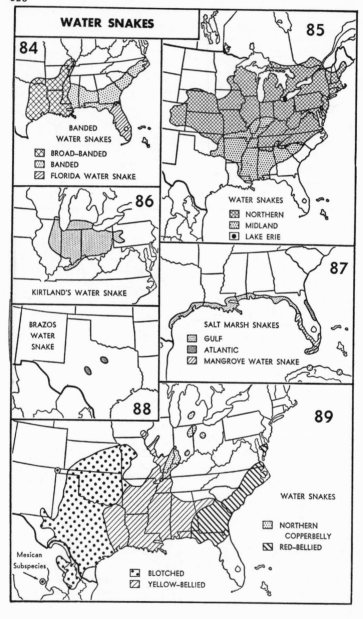

WATER SNAKES

84

BANDED
WATER SNAKES

⊠ BROAD-BANDED
▨ BANDED
▨ FLORIDA WATER SNAKE

85

WATER SNAKES

⊠ NORTHERN
▨ MIDLAND
⊙ LAKE ERIE

86

KIRTLAND'S WATER SNAKE

87

SALT MARSH SNAKES

▨ GULF
▨ ATLANTIC
▨ MANGROVE WATER SNAKE

BRAZOS
WATER
SNAKE

88

89

WATER SNAKES

▨ NORTHERN
COPPERBELLY
◤ RED-BELLIED

Mexican
Subspecies

▣ BLOTCHED
▨ YELLOW-BELLIED

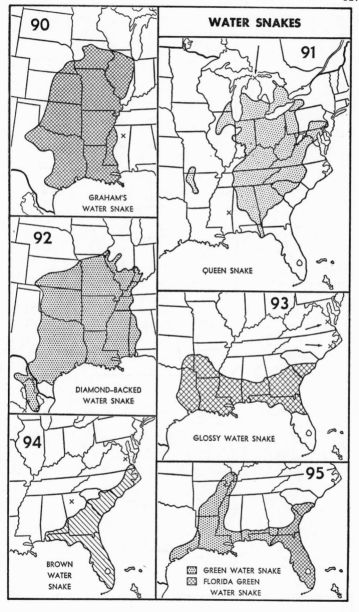

WATER SNAKES

90 GRAHAM'S WATER SNAKE

91 QUEEN SNAKE

92 DIAMOND-BACKED WATER SNAKE

93 GLOSSY WATER SNAKE

94 BROWN WATER SNAKE

95 GREEN WATER SNAKE
FLORIDA GREEN WATER SNAKE

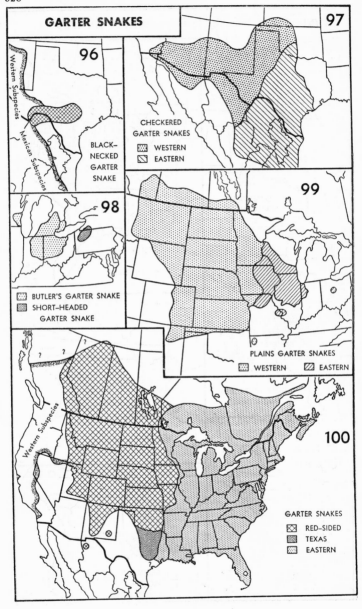

GARTER SNAKES

96

Western Subspecies
Mexican Subspecies

BLACK-NECKED GARTER SNAKE

97

CHECKERED GARTER SNAKES
WESTERN
EASTERN

98

BUTLER'S GARTER SNAKE
SHORT-HEADED GARTER SNAKE

99

PLAINS GARTER SNAKES
WESTERN   EASTERN

100

Western Subspecies

GARTER SNAKES
RED-SIDED
TEXAS
EASTERN

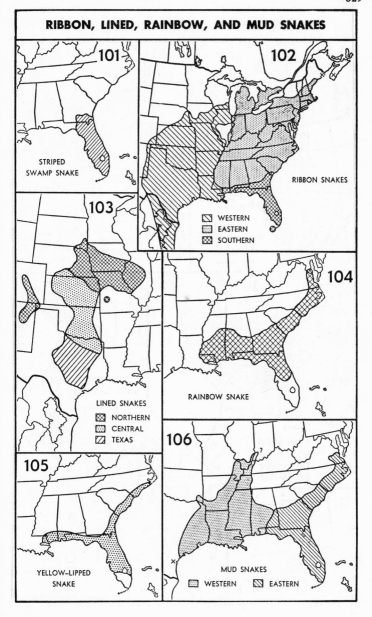

329

RIBBON, LINED, RAINBOW, AND MUD SNAKES

101 STRIPED SWAMP SNAKE

102 RIBBON SNAKES
- WESTERN
- EASTERN
- SOUTHERN

103 LINED SNAKES
- NORTHERN
- CENTRAL
- TEXAS

104 RAINBOW SNAKE

105 YELLOW-LIPPED SNAKE

106 MUD SNAKES
- WESTERN
- EASTERN

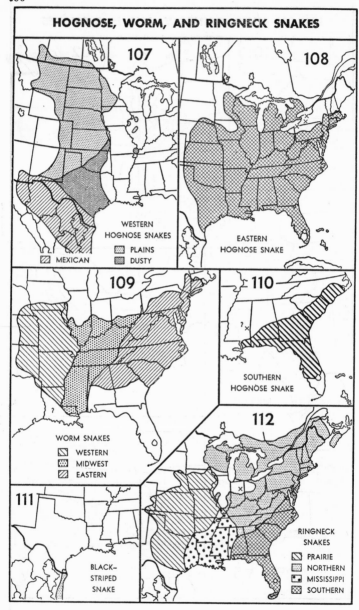

HOGNOSE, WORM, AND RINGNECK SNAKES

107

WESTERN
HOGNOSE SNAKES

MEXICAN PLAINS DUSTY

108

EASTERN
HOGNOSE SNAKE

109

WORM SNAKES

WESTERN
MIDWEST
EASTERN

110

SOUTHERN
HOGNOSE SNAKE

111

BLACK-
STRIPED
SNAKE

112

RINGNECK
SNAKES

PRAIRIE
NORTHERN
MISSISSIPPI
SOUTHERN

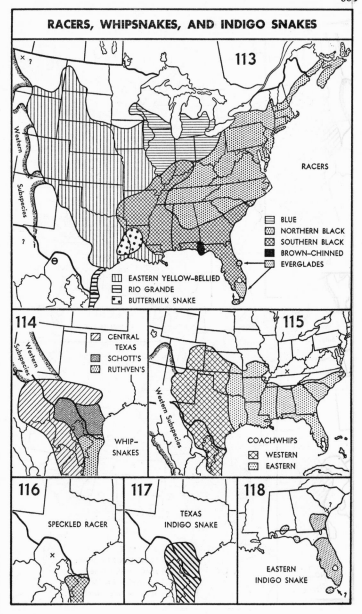

RACERS, WHIPSNAKES, AND INDIGO SNAKES

113

Western Subspecies

?

?

RACERS

⊟ BLUE
⊡ NORTHERN BLACK
⊠ SOUTHERN BLACK
■ BROWN-CHINNED
→ EVERGLADES

▥ EASTERN YELLOW-BELLIED
⊟ RIO GRANDE
• BUTTERMILK SNAKE

114

Western Subspecies

▨ CENTRAL TEXAS
▩ SCHOTT'S
⊞ RUTHVEN'S

WHIP-SNAKES

115

Western Subspecies

COACHWHIPS
⊠ WESTERN
⊡ EASTERN

116

SPECKLED RACER

117

TEXAS INDIGO SNAKE

118

EASTERN INDIGO SNAKE

332

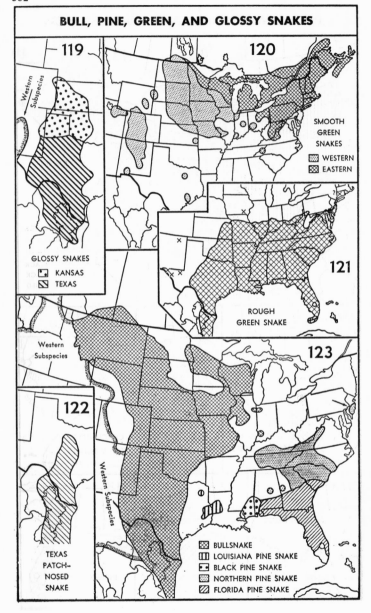

BULL, PINE, GREEN, AND GLOSSY SNAKES

119

Western Subspecies

GLOSSY SNAKES
- KANSAS
- TEXAS

120

SMOOTH GREEN SNAKES
- WESTERN
- EASTERN

121

ROUGH GREEN SNAKE

122

Western Subspecies

TEXAS PATCH-NOSED SNAKE

123

Western Subspecies

- BULLSNAKE
- LOUISIANA PINE SNAKE
- BLACK PINE SNAKE
- NORTHERN PINE SNAKE
- FLORIDA PINE SNAKE

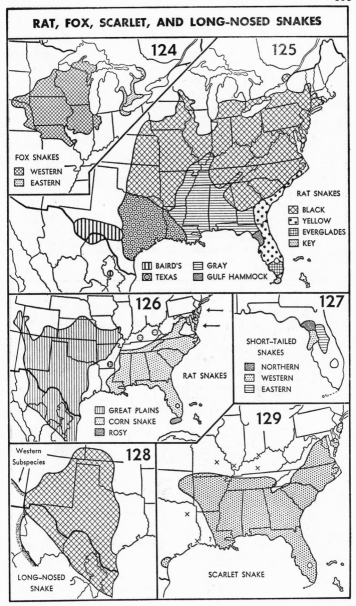

RAT, FOX, SCARLET, AND LONG-NOSED SNAKES

124 125

FOX SNAKES
⊠ WESTERN
▦ EASTERN

RAT SNAKES
⊠ BLACK
▦ YELLOW
▦ EVERGLADES
▦ KEY

▥ BAIRD'S   ▤ GRAY
▦ TEXAS   ▦ GULF HAMMOCK

126

RAT SNAKES

▥ GREAT PLAINS
▦ CORN SNAKE
▦ ROSY

127

SHORT-TAILED
SNAKES
▦ NORTHERN
▦ WESTERN
▤ EASTERN

128

Western
Subspecies

LONG-NOSED
SNAKE

129

SCARLET SNAKE

334

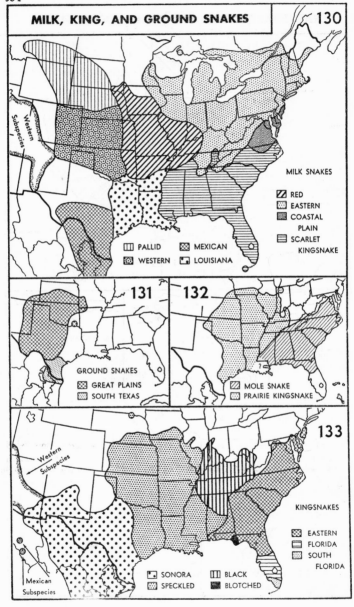

MILK, KING, AND GROUND SNAKES

130

Western Subspecies

MILK SNAKES

- ⧄ RED
- ▦ EASTERN
- ▨ COASTAL PLAIN
- ▤ SCARLET KINGSNAKE

- ⦀ PALLID
- ⊠ MEXICAN
- ⊙ WESTERN
- ▣ LOUISIANA

131

GROUND SNAKES

- ⊠ GREAT PLAINS
- ▦ SOUTH TEXAS

132

- ⧄ MOLE SNAKE
- ⦂ PRAIRIE KINGSNAKE

?

133

Western Subspecies

Mexican Subspecies

KINGSNAKES

- ⊠ EASTERN
- ▤ FLORIDA
- ▦ SOUTH FLORIDA

- ▣ SONORA
- ▦ SPECKLED
- ⦀ BLACK
- ▨ BLOTCHED

335

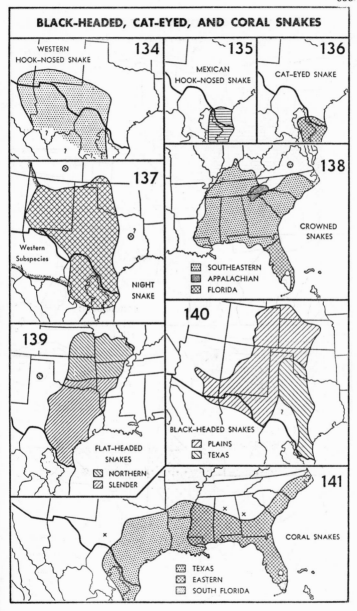

BLACK-HEADED, CAT-EYED, AND CORAL SNAKES

134 WESTERN HOOK-NOSED SNAKE

135 MEXICAN HOOK-NOSED SNAKE

136 CAT-EYED SNAKE

137 NIGHT SNAKE
Western Subspecies

138 CROWNED SNAKES
- SOUTHEASTERN
- APPALACHIAN
- FLORIDA

139 FLAT-HEADED SNAKES
- NORTHERN
- SLENDER

140 BLACK-HEADED SNAKES
- PLAINS
- TEXAS

141 CORAL SNAKES
- TEXAS
- EASTERN
- SOUTH FLORIDA

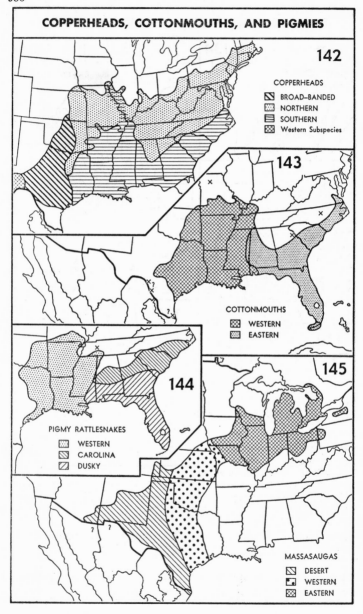

COPPERHEADS, COTTONMOUTHS, AND PIGMIES

142

COPPERHEADS
BROAD–BANDED
NORTHERN
SOUTHERN
Western Subspecies

143

COTTONMOUTHS
WESTERN
EASTERN

144

PIGMY RATTLESNAKES
WESTERN
CAROLINA
DUSKY

145

MASSASAUGAS
DESERT
WESTERN
EASTERN

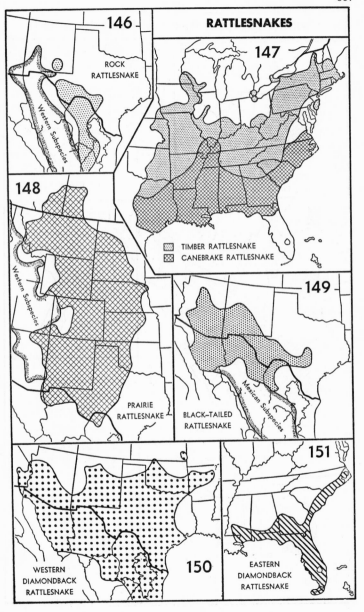

RATTLESNAKES

146 ROCK RATTLESNAKE — Western Subspecies

147 TIMBER RATTLESNAKE — CANEBRAKE RATTLESNAKE

148 PRAIRIE RATTLESNAKE — Western Subspecies

149 BLACK-TAILED RATTLESNAKE — Mexican Subspecies

150 WESTERN DIAMONDBACK RATTLESNAKE

151 EASTERN DIAMONDBACK RATTLESNAKE

338

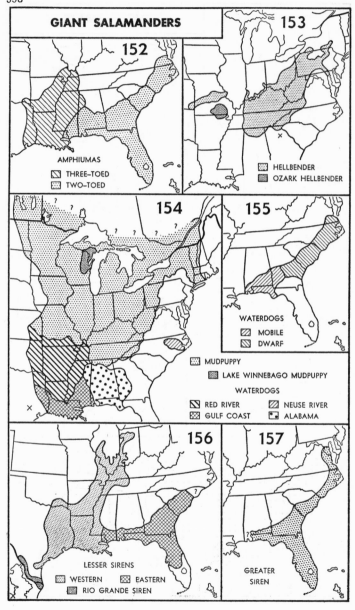

GIANT SALAMANDERS

152

AMPHIUMAS
▨ THREE-TOED
▦ TWO-TOED

153

▦ HELLBENDER
▨ OZARK HELLBENDER

154

155

WATERDOGS
▨ MOBILE
▨ DWARF

▦ MUDPUPPY
▨ LAKE WINNEBAGO MUDPUPPY

WATERDOGS
▨ RED RIVER   ▨ NEUSE RIVER
▨ GULF COAST   ▨ ALABAMA

156

LESSER SIRENS
▦ WESTERN   ▨ EASTERN
▦ RIO GRANDE SIREN

157

GREATER
SIREN

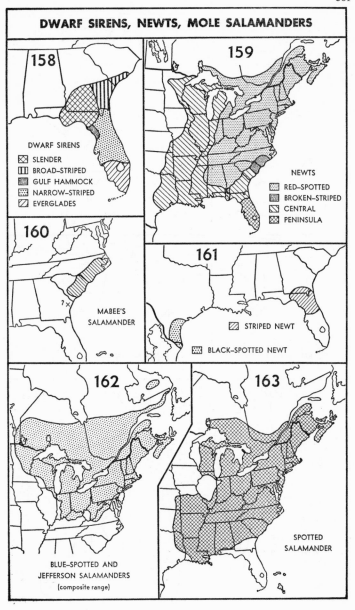

DWARF SIRENS, NEWTS, MOLE SALAMANDERS

158

DWARF SIRENS
- ⊠ SLENDER
- ⊞ BROAD–STRIPED
- ▦ GULF HAMMOCK
- ▤ NARROW–STRIPED
- ▨ EVERGLADES

159

NEWTS
- ▦ RED–SPOTTED
- ▦ BROKEN–STRIPED
- ⧄ CENTRAL
- ⊠ PENINSULA

160

MABEE'S
SALAMANDER

161

⧄ STRIPED NEWT

▦ BLACK–SPOTTED NEWT

162

BLUE–SPOTTED AND
JEFFERSON SALAMANDERS
(composite range)

163

SPOTTED
SALAMANDER

340

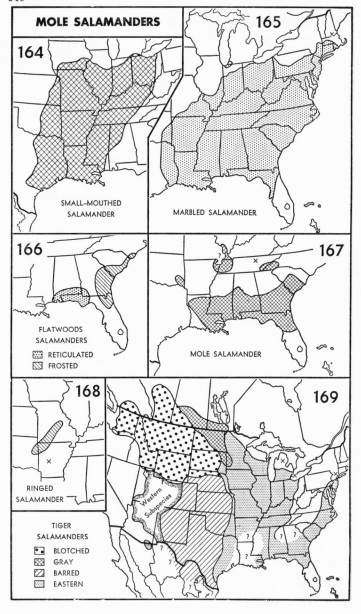

MOLE SALAMANDERS

164 SMALL-MOUTHED
SALAMANDER

165 MARBLED SALAMANDER

166 FLATWOODS
SALAMANDERS
⬚ RETICULATED
⬚ FROSTED

167 MOLE SALAMANDER

168 RINGED
SALAMANDER

169 TIGER
SALAMANDERS
⬚ BLOTCHED
⬚ GRAY
⬚ BARRED
⬚ EASTERN

Western
Subspecies

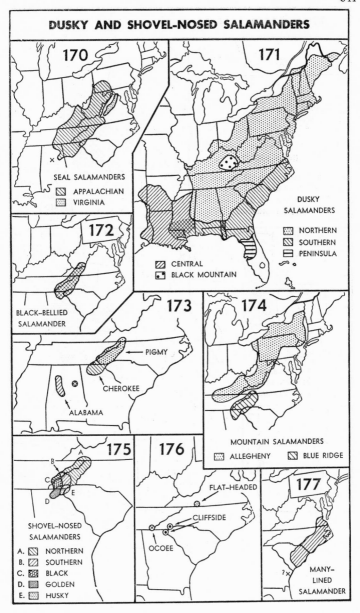

DUSKY AND SHOVEL-NOSED SALAMANDERS

170

SEAL SALAMANDERS
☒ APPALACHIAN
▨ VIRGINIA

171

DUSKY
SALAMANDERS

☷ NORTHERN
☒ SOUTHERN
☰ PENINSULA

▨ CENTRAL
⬛ BLACK MOUNTAIN

172

BLACK–BELLIED
SALAMANDER

173

PIGMY

CHEROKEE

ALABAMA

174

MOUNTAIN SALAMANDERS
☷ ALLEGHENY   ☒ BLUE RIDGE

175

A
B
C
E
D

SHOVEL–NOSED
SALAMANDERS
A. ☒ NORTHERN
B. ▨ SOUTHERN
C. ▦ BLACK
D. ▤ GOLDEN
E. ▦ HUSKY

176

FLAT–HEADED

CLIFFSIDE

OCOEE

177

MANY–
LINED
SALAMANDER

342

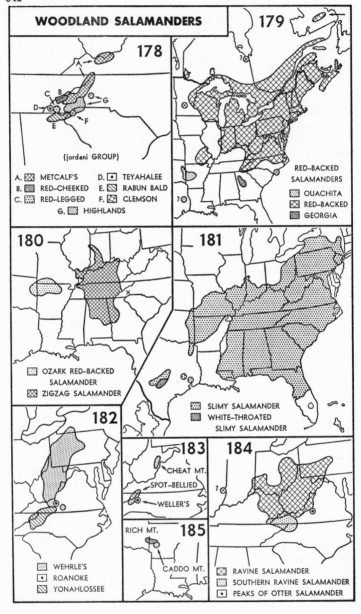

WOODLAND SALAMANDERS

178 (jordani GROUP)

A. METCALF'S   D. TEYAHALEE
B. RED–CHEEKED   E. RABUN BALD
C. RED–LEGGED   F. CLEMSON
G. HIGHLANDS

179

RED–BACKED SALAMANDERS

OUACHITA
RED–BACKED
GEORGIA

180

OZARK RED–BACKED SALAMANDER
ZIGZAG SALAMANDER

181

SLIMY SALAMANDER
WHITE–THROATED SLIMY SALAMANDER

182

WEHRLE'S
ROANOKE
YONAHLOSSEE

183

CHEAT MT.
SPOT–BELLIED
WELLER'S

185

RICH MT.
CADDO MT.

184

RAVINE SALAMANDER
SOUTHERN RAVINE SALAMANDER
PEAKS OF OTTER SALAMANDER

SPRING, RED, & OTHER LUNGLESS SALAMANDERS

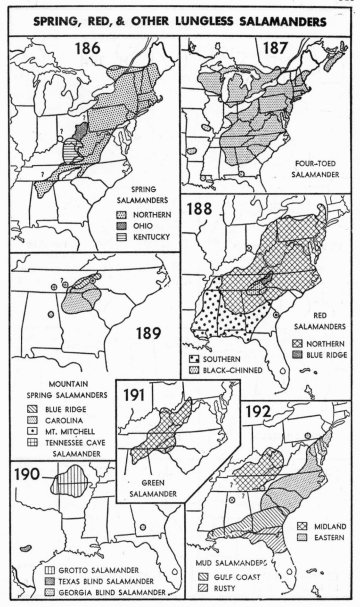

186

SPRING SALAMANDERS
- ▦ NORTHERN
- ▨ OHIO
- ▤ KENTUCKY

187

FOUR-TOED SALAMANDER

188

RED SALAMANDERS
- ⊠ NORTHERN
- ▦ BLUE RIDGE
- ⊡ SOUTHERN
- ▦ BLACK-CHINNED

189

MOUNTAIN SPRING SALAMANDERS
- ◪ BLUE RIDGE
- ▦ CAROLINA
- ⊡ MT. MITCHELL
- ⊞ TENNESSEE CAVE SALAMANDER

191

GREEN SALAMANDER

192

- ⊠ MIDLAND
- ▦ EASTERN

190

- ▥ GROTTO SALAMANDER
- ▨ TEXAS BLIND SALAMANDER
- ▦ GEORGIA BLIND SALAMANDER

MUD SALAMANDERS
- ◪ GULF COAST
- ▨ RUSTY

344

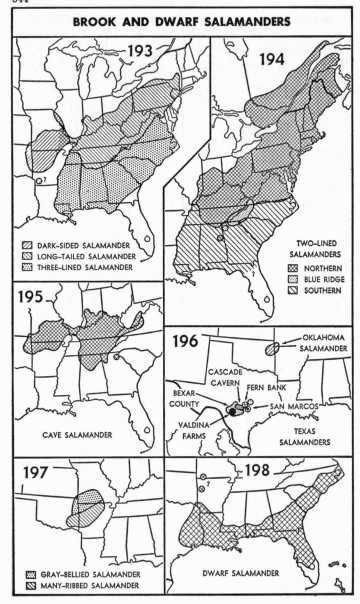

BROOK AND DWARF SALAMANDERS

193

DARK-SIDED SALAMANDER
LONG-TAILED SALAMANDER
THREE-LINED SALAMANDER

194

TWO-LINED
SALAMANDERS

NORTHERN
BLUE RIDGE
SOUTHERN

195

CAVE SALAMANDER

196

OKLAHOMA
SALAMANDER

CASCADE
CAVERN   FERN BANK

BEXAR
COUNTY   SAN MARCOS

VALDINA
FARMS   TEXAS
                              SALAMANDERS

197

GRAY-BELLIED SALAMANDER
MANY-RIBBED SALAMANDER

198

DWARF SALAMANDER

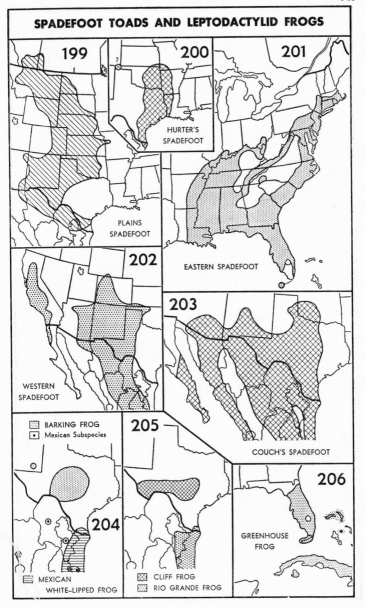

SPADEFOOT TOADS AND LEPTODACTYLID FROGS

199

200 HURTER'S SPADEFOOT

201

PLAINS SPADEFOOT

EASTERN SPADEFOOT

202

WESTERN SPADEFOOT

203

COUCH'S SPADEFOOT

▨ BARKING FROG
⊡ Mexican Subspecies

205

204

▤ MEXICAN WHITE-LIPPED FROG

▨ CLIFF FROG
▨ RIO GRANDE FROG

206

GREENHOUSE FROG

346

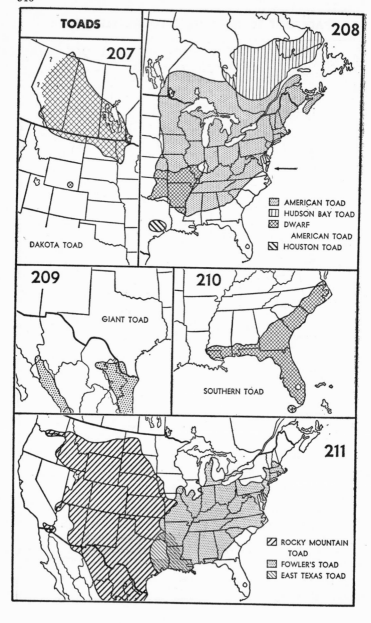

TOADS

207

DAKOTA TOAD

208

☷ AMERICAN TOAD
▥ HUDSON BAY TOAD
▩ DWARF
    AMERICAN TOAD
◨ HOUSTON TOAD

209

GIANT TOAD

210

SOUTHERN TOAD

211

▨ ROCKY MOUNTAIN
    TOAD
▦ FOWLER'S TOAD
◪ EAST TEXAS TOAD

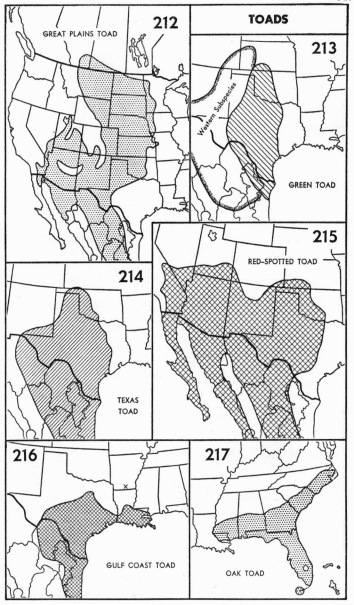

212 GREAT PLAINS TOAD

TOADS

213 GREEN TOAD

Western Subspecies

214 TEXAS TOAD

215 RED-SPOTTED TOAD

216 GULF COAST TOAD

217 OAK TOAD

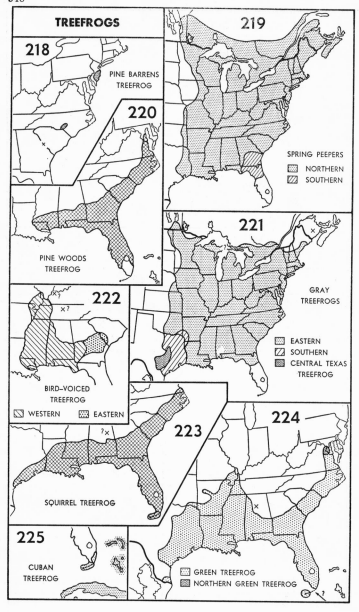

TREEFROGS

218 PINE BARRENS TREEFROG

219 SPRING PEEPERS
- NORTHERN
- SOUTHERN

220 PINE WOODS TREEFROG

221 GRAY TREEFROGS
- EASTERN
- SOUTHERN
- CENTRAL TEXAS TREEFROG

222 BIRD-VOICED TREEFROG
- WESTERN
- EASTERN

223 SQUIRREL TREEFROG

224 GREEN TREEFROG
- NORTHERN GREEN TREEFROG

225 CUBAN TREEFROG

349

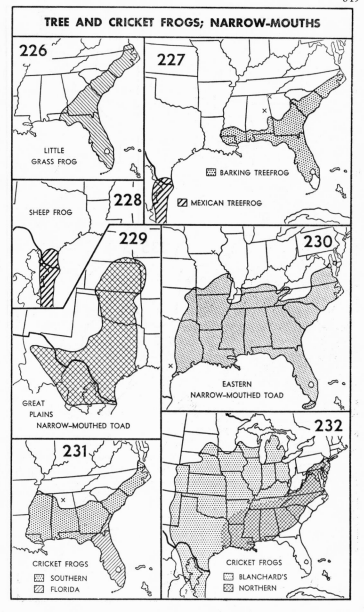

TREE AND CRICKET FROGS; NARROW-MOUTHS

226 LITTLE GRASS FROG

227
BARKING TREEFROG
MEXICAN TREEFROG

228 SHEEP FROG

229 GREAT PLAINS NARROW-MOUTHED TOAD

230 EASTERN NARROW-MOUTHED TOAD

231 CRICKET FROGS
SOUTHERN
FLORIDA

232 CRICKET FROGS
BLANCHARD'S
NORTHERN

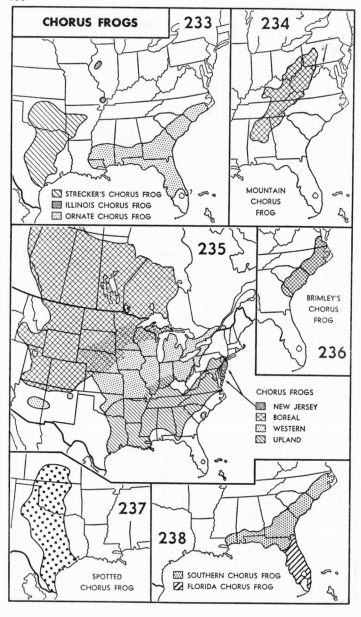

CHORUS FROGS 233

STRECKER'S CHORUS FROG
ILLINOIS CHORUS FROG
ORNATE CHORUS FROG

234

235

MOUNTAIN
CHORUS
FROG

BRIMLEY'S
CHORUS
FROG

236

CHORUS FROGS

NEW JERSEY
BOREAL
WESTERN
UPLAND

237

SPOTTED
CHORUS FROG

238

SOUTHERN CHORUS FROG
FLORIDA CHORUS FROG

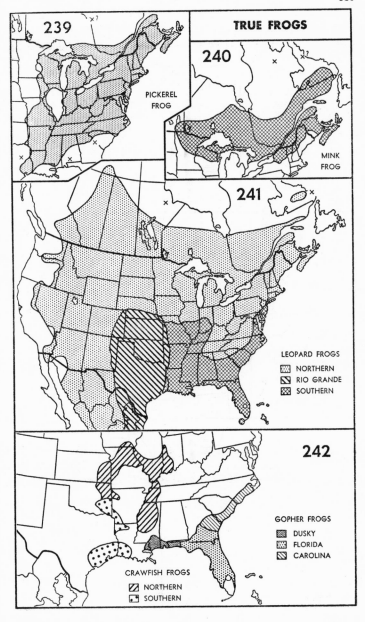

239 PICKEREL FROG

TRUE FROGS

240 MINK FROG

241 LEOPARD FROGS
- NORTHERN
- RIO GRANDE
- SOUTHERN

242 GOPHER FROGS
- DUSKY
- FLORIDA
- CAROLINA

CRAWFISH FROGS
- NORTHERN
- SOUTHERN

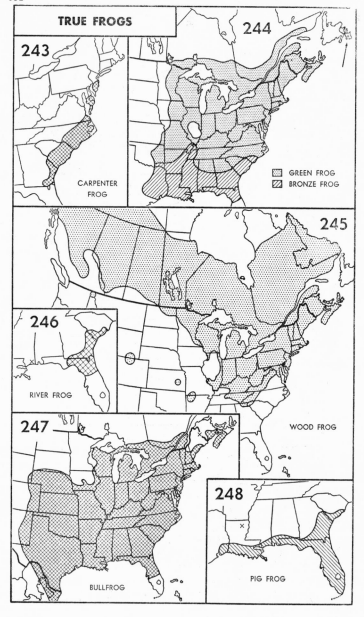

TRUE FROGS

243

244

CARPENTER
FROG

GREEN FROG
BRONZE FROG

245

246

RIVER FROG

WOOD FROG

247

BULLFROG

248

PIG FROG

Index

SALAMANDERS

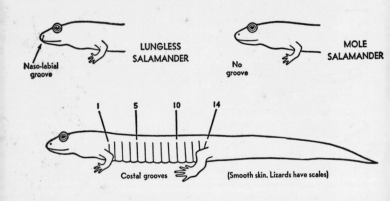

LUNGLESS SALAMANDER

Naso-labial groove

No groove

MOLE SALAMANDER

1 5 10 14

Costal grooves

(Smooth skin. Lizards have scales)

FROGS AND TOADS

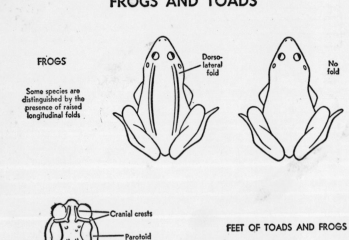

FROGS

Some species are distinguished by the presence of raised longitudinal folds

Dorso-lateral fold

No fold

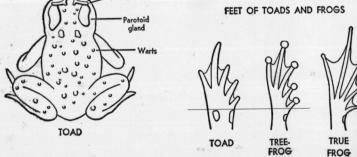

Cranial crests

Parotoid gland

Warts

TOAD

FEET OF TOADS AND FROGS

TOAD

TREE-FROG

TRUE FROG